# Company Law

KEITH ABBOTT, B.A.(Hons) M.B.A., Solicitor
Head of Business Studies
Hendon College

## 4th EDITION

DP PUBLICATIONS LTD.
Aldine House, Aldine Place,
142/144 Uxbridge Road,
Shepherds Bush Green,
London W12 8AW
1990

First Edition 1982
Reprinted 1983
Second Edition 1986
Reprinted with revisions 1987
Third Edition 1988
Fourth Edition 1990
Reprinted 1990

ISBN 1 870941 56 X



Typeset by DP Publications

Printed in Great Britain by
The Guernsey Press Co Ltd
Guernsey, Channel Islands

# Table of Contents

Preface....vii
Table of Cases....ix
Table of Statutes (with contents summary)....xiii

1. **Methods of Learning**....1
   Introduction....1
   Understanding....2
   Learning....3

2. **Examination Technique**....7
   General Points....7
   Style and Structure....8
   Content....10

## PART I INTRODUCTION

3. **The History of Company Law**....15
   Until 1825....15
   1825 Until Present Day....17

4. **The Modern Company and the European Community**....21
   Introduction....21
   Ownership and Control....24
   Company law harmonisation....28

## PART II INCORPORATION

5. **The Consequences of Incorporation**....37
   Legal Personality....37
   Lifting the Veil....41
   Public and Private Companies....44
   Registration Procedure....48

6. **Promotion**....55
   Promoters....55
   Pre-Incorporation Contracts....57

7. **The Memorandum of Association**....60
   Introduction....60
   The Name Clause....60
   Business Names....60
   The Registered Office....64
   The Objects Clause....66
   Alteration of Objects....73
   Limitation of Liability....73
   Other Clauses....75

8. **The Articles of Association**.....77
Form and Function.....77
Alteration of Articles.....77
The Effect of the Memorandum and Articles.....80
*Coursework Questions 1–5*.....83

## PART III THE RAISING AND MAINTENANCE OF CAPITAL

9. **Public Offers for Shares**.....89
Introduction.....89
Official Listing of Securities.....91
Offers of Unlisted Securities.....94
Misrepresentation and Omission.....97

10. **Capital**.....101
Types of Capital and Alteration of Capital.....101
Maintenance of Capital. Introduction.....103
Provisions Designed to Prevent Capital Being 'Watered Down'.....103
Provisions Designed to Prevent Capital Going Out of the Company.....107

11. **Dividends**.....124
*Coursework Questions 6–10*.....129

## PART IV COMPANY SECURITIES

12. **Shares**.....133
Types of Shares.....133
Variation of Class Rights.....135
Application and Allotment.....137
Share Certificates and Share Warrants.....140
Transfer of Shares.....141
Shares as Security for a Loan.....144
Calls.....145

13. **Membership**.....148
Methods of Becoming a Member.....148
Capacity.....148
The Register of Members.....151

14. **Debentures**.....154
*Coursework Questions 11–15*.....168

## PART V COMPANY OFFICERS

15. **Directors**.....173
Appointment and Removal.....173
Powers of Directors.....179
Enforcement of Fair Dealing by Directors.....183

Fiduciary Duties and Duties of Care and Skill ........ 193
Disqualification of Directors ........ 201

**16. The Secretary** ........ 205
Appointment and Qualifications ........ 205
Powers and Duties ........ 205
*Coursework Questions 16–20* ........ 207

## PART VI PROTECTION OF INVESTORS AND CREDITORS

**17. Publicity and Accounts** ........ 213
Official Notification in the Gazette ........ 213
Matters Requiring Registration at the Companies Registry ........ 215
Registers Which Must be Maintained by the Company ........ 216
The Annual Return ........ 219
The Accounting Records and the Accounts ........ 220
The Directors' Report ........ 244

**18. Auditors** ........ 247
Supervisory bodies and professional qualifications ........ 247
Appointment, Removal and Resignation ........ 251
Powers, Duties and Liabilities ........ 255

**19. Company Meetings** ........ 260
Types of Meeting ........ 260
Convening Meetings ........ 261
Conduct of Meetings ........ 263
Resolutions ........ 265

**20. Insider Dealing** ........ 270

**21. MinorityProtection** ........ 277
Majority Rule ........ 277
Minority Protection at Common Law ........ 278
S.459–461 Unfair Prejudice ........ 282
Department of Trade Investigations ........ 286
Summary ........ 293
*Coursework Questions 21–25* ........ 296

## PART VII RECONSTRUCTIONS, TAKEOVERS, LIQUIDATION, RECEIVERSHIP AND ADMINISTRATION

**22. Reconstructions, Mergers and Takeovers** ........ 301
Introduction ........ 301
Mergers and Reconstructions under S.110–111 IA 1986 ........ 302
Scheme of Arrangement under S.425–427 ........ 304
Voluntary Arrangements under S.1–7 IA 1986 ........ 306

Takeovers ........ 308
Conclusion ........ 312

23. **Liquidation** ........ 315
Introduction ........ 315
Insolvency Practitioners ........ 315
Compulsory Liquidation ........ 317
Provisions Applicable to Every Kind of Liquidation ........ 325
Voluntary Liquidation ........ 333

24. **Administration Orders** ........ 338

25. **Receiverships** ........ 344
*Coursework Questions 26–30* ........ 351

## PART VIII APPENDICES

Introduction to Appendices I and II ........ 355
Appendix 1 Suggested Answers to Coursework Questions ........ 357
Appendix 2 Revision Questions and Answers ........ 402
Appendix 3 Answers to Progress Tests ........ 444
Appendix 4 Questions Without Answers ........ 473
Index ........ 478

# Preface

This book is intended for anyone studying company law who needs to get a good grasp of the subject in a relatively short period of time. It has been specifically designed to cover the ACCA and CIMA company law syllabuses, consequently most of the past questions have been selected from their examination papers. Other professional courses where it would be useful include *Chartered Accountants, Chartered Secretaries*, the *Institute of Bankers* and the *Law Society*.

The basic requirement for passing a company law examination is a good factual knowledge of the relevant law. The bulk of the text is therefore devoted to the presentation of the rules of company law in a style and format which will help students to assimilate the necessary facts. The remainder of the text serves three purposes:

1. Chapters 1 and 2, the Progress Tests and the Coursework and Revision Questions recognise that examination success is not merely an indication of factual knowledge or even intelligence. Organisation in learning and examination technique are being tested and must be developed and practiced as much as possible.
2. Chapters 3 and 4 reflect the fact that company law cannot be fully understood if considered in isolation from the social institution which it aims to regulate. In this edition there is a new section describing the EEC institutions and summarising the current position on company law harmonisation.
3. Appendix 4 is designed as a teaching aid. Lecturers may obtain from the publishers, free of charge, provided the order is placed on college notepaper, summary answers to the questions.

This edition includes the Companies Act 1989 and a number of new past questions from recent ACCA, CIMA, and ICSA examination papers.

I would like to express my thanks to David Kobrin LLB (Hons) A.C.I.S. for carefully checking the original manuscript and making many helpful suggestions as to style and content. Many thanks also to the Association of Certified Accountants, the Chartered Institute of Cost and Management Accountants and the Institute of Chartered Secretaries and Administrators for permission to reproduce actual questions from recent examination papers.

*Keith Abbott*
*1st May 1990*

# Table of Cases


Aerators v Tollitt (1902) ....63
Alexander v Automatic Telephone Co (1900) ....145
Alexander Ward v Samyang Navigation (1975) ....389
Aluminium Industrie Vaassen v Romalpa (1976) ....158
AG v Lindi St Claire (1080) ....359
Attorney General's Reference, Re (No. 1 of 1988) ....273
Attorney General's Reference, Re (No. 2 of 1982) ....38
Automatic Bottle Makers, Re (1926) ....163

Bahia and San Francisco Railway, Re (1868) ....143
Baillie v Oriental Telephone Co (1915) ....278
Balkis Consolidated v Thompson (1893) ....143
Bamford v Bamford (1970) ....179
Barnett Hoares v South London Tramways (1887) ....206
Beattie v Beattie Ltd (1938) ....82
Belmont Finance v Williams Furniture (1980) ....113
Bird Precision Bellows, Re (1984) ....285
Bisgood v Henderson's Transvaal Estates (1908) ....438
Bleriot Aircraft Co, Re (1916) ....312
Borden v Scottish Timber Products (1981) ....158
Borland's Trustee v Steel (1901) ....133
Boston Deep Sea Fishing v Ansell (1888) ....198
Bradford Banking Co v Briggs (1886) ....455
Brady v Brady (1988) ....114
Briess v Woolley (1954) ....194
Brightlife, Re (1986) ....157
Brown v British Abrasive Wheel Co (1919) ....79
Brown, (Henry) v Smith (1964) ....38
Bugle Press, Re (1961) ....310
Bushell v Faith (1970) ....177

Caddies v Holdsworth (1955) ....180
Caparo Industries v Diskman (1990) ....258
Carlton Holdings, Re (1971) ....310
Castiglione's Will Trusts, Re (195 8) ....111
Charterbridge Corporation v Lloyds Bank (1969) ....71
City Equitable Fire Insurance Co, Re (1925) ....200
Claridge's Patent Asphalte Co, Re (1921) ....201
Cleadon Trust, Re (1939) ....458
Clemens v Clemens Ltd (1976) ....78
Clough Mill v Martin (1985) ....159
Company, Re A (1983) ....283
Company, Re A (No 00477 of 1986) ....283
Company, Re A (No 004377 of 1986) ....284
Cook v Deeks (1916) ....279

Copal Varnish, Re (1917) ........ 376
Cope, Re Benjamin (1914) ........ 163

D.H.N. Food Distributors v Tower Hamlets L.B.C. (1976) ........ 42
Dafen Tinplate v Llanelly Steel (1920) ........ 279
Daimler v Continental Tyre and Rubber Co (1916) ........ 42
Daniels v Daniels (1978) ........ 280
Dawson v African Consolidated Land Co (1898) ........ 176
Derry v Peek (1889) ........ 99
D.P.P. v Kent and Sussex Contractors (1944) ........ 421
Duomatic, Re (1969) ........ 201

El Sombrero, Re (1958) ........ 261
Eley v Positive Life Assurance Co (1876) ........ 81
Erlanger v New Sombrero Phosphate Co (1878) ........ 55
Estmanco (Kilner House) v Greater London Council (1981) ........ 280
Evans v Brunner Mond (1921) ........ 70
Ewing v Buttercup Margarine Co (1917) ........ 63

Five Minute Car Wash, Re (1966) ........ 381
Formento v Selsdon (1958) ........ 257
Foss v Harbottle (1843) ........ 277
Freeman and Lockyer v Buckhurst Park Properties (1964) ........ 182

Gerrard, Re Thomas (1968) ........ 257
Gilford Motor Co v Horne (1933) ........ 41
Gluckstein v Barnes (1900) ........ 56
Goodwin v Birmingham City Football Club (1980) ........ 43
Greenhalgh v Arderne Cinemas (1946) ........ 102
Greenhalgh v Arderne Cinemas (1951) ........ 78
Guinness v Saunders (1990) ........ 186

Hackney Pavilion, Re (1924) ........ 376
Hannibal v Frost (1987) ........ 72
Harmer, Re (1959) ........ 284
Harvela Investments v Royal Trust Co of Canada (1986) ........ 141
Head v Ropner Holdings (1952) ........ 366
Heald v O'Connor (1971) ........ 112
Hedley Byrne v Heller (1964) ........ 99
Hellenic and General Trust, Re (1976) ........ 305
Hendy Lennox v Grahame Puttick (1984) ........ 159
Hickman v Kent Sheep Breeders Association (1915) ........ 81
Hogg v Cramphorn (1967) ........ 196
Holders Investment Trust, Re (1971) ........ 279
Hong Kong and China Gas Co v Glen (1914) ........ 106
Horsley and Weight, Re (1982) ........ 71
Houldsworth v City of Glasgow Bank (1880) ........ 99
House of Fraser v A.C.G.E. Investments (1987) ........ 280
Howard Smith v Ampol (1974) ........ 196

Industrial Development Consultants v Cooley (1972) ....197
International Sales and Agencies v Marcus (1982) ....196
Islington Metal and Plating Works, Re (1984) ....329

Jones v Lipman (1962) ....362

Kelner v Baxter (1866) ....57
Kushler, Re (1943) ....166

Lee Behrens, Re (1932) ....71
Loch v John Blackwood (1924) ....319
London School of Electronics, Re (1985) ....282

Macaura v Northern Assurance (1925) ....37
Maidstone Building Provisions, Re (1971) ....444
Matthews, Re (1981) ....166
Menier v Hooper's Telegraph Works (1874) ....279
Moodie v Shepherd Bookbinders (1949) ....376
Moore v Bresler (1944) ....421
Moorgate Mercantile Holdings, Re (1980) ....262
Morris v Kanssen (1946) ....176
Mosely v Koffyfontein Mines (1904) ....155

N.F.U. Development Trust, Re (1972) ....304
New British Iron Co, Re (1898) ....81
Newboume v Sensolid (1954) ....58
Newdigate Colliery, Re (1912) ....348
Newhart Developments v Co-operative Commercial Bank (1978) ....346
Norwest Holst v Secretary of State for Trade (1978) ....287
Nottingham General Cemetery Co, Re (1955) ....327
Nurcombe v Nurcombe (1985) ....199

Ocean Coal Co v Powell Duffryn Steam Coal Co (1932) ....144
Ooregum Gold Mining Co v Roper (1892) ....19

Panorama Developments v Fidelis Furnishing Fabrics (1971) ....206
Parke v Daily News (1962) ....71
Pavlides v Jensen (1956) ....277
Peachdart, Re (1984) ....158
Pedley v Inland Waterways (1977) ....178
Pender v Lushington (1877) ....80
Penrose v Martyr (185 8) ....64
Percival v Wright (1902) ....194
Peso Silver Mines v Cropper (1966) ....199
Phonogram v Lane (1981) ....58
Produce Marketing Consortium, Re (1989) ....326
Prudential Assurance v Newman Industries (1980) ....281

Quin and Axtens v Salmon (1909) ....361

R v Kylsant (1932) ....99
R v McDonnell (1966) ....446

Rayfield v Hands (1960) ... 82
Read v Astoria Garage (1952) ... 181
Regal (Hastings) v Gulliver (1942) ... 198
Richmond Gate Property Co, Re (1965) ... 81
Roith, Re (1967) ... 196
Rolled Steel Products v British Steel Corporation (1986) ... 72
Rother Ironworks v Canterbury Precision Engineers (1973) ... 482
Royal British Bank v Turquand (1855) ... 182

St Piran, Re (1981) ... 290
Salmon v The Hamborough Co (1671) ... 16
Salomon v Salomon & Co (1897) ... 37
Savoy Hotel, Re (1981) ... 439
Scott v Scott (1943) ... 179
Scottish Co-operative Wholesale Society v Meyer (1959) ... 285
Shanley Contracting, Re (1980) ... 263
Shearer v Bercain (1980) ... 110
Sheffield Corporation v Barclay (1905) ... 373
Sidebottom v Kershaw Leese (1920) ... 79
Simmonds v Heffer (1983) ... 70
Simpson v Molson's Bank (1895) ... 150
Slavenberg's Bank v Intercontinental Natural Resources (1980) ... 50
Smith and Fawcett, Re (1942) ... 375
Southern Foundries v Shirlaw (1940) ... 79
Stanford Services, Re (1987) ... 202
Steinberg v Scala (1923) ... 149
Sussex Brick Co, Re (1904) ... 153

Taupo Totara Timber v Rowe (1978) ... 184
Teck v Miller (1972) ... 197
Tesco v Natrass (1972) ... 421
Trevor v Whitworth (1887) ... 111
Trix, Re (1970) ... 302
Twycross v Grant (1877) ... 55

Underwood v Bank of Liverpool (1924) ... 412

Wallersteiner v Moir (1974) ... 113
Westbourne Galleries, Re (1973) ... 318
Wilson v Kelland (1910) ... 376
Woodroffes (Musical Instruments), Re (1986) ... 157

Yenidje Tobacco Co, Re (1916) ... 318
Yorkshire Woolcombers Association, Re (1903) ... 431

Zinotty Properties, Re (1985) ... 319

# Table of Statutes


**Banking Act 1979** .......... 192

**Business Names Act 1985**

S.1 Persons subject to the Act .......... 64
S.2 Prohibition of use of certain names .......... 65
S.4 Disclosure requirements .......... 65
S.5 Civil remedies for breach of S.4 .......... 65

**Bubble Act 1720** .......... 16

**Chartered Companies Act 1837** .......... 17

**Companies Act 1862** .......... 18

**Companies Act 1985**

*Company Formation*

S.1 Mode of forming company .......... 44
S.2 Requirements with respect to memorandum .......... 68
S.3A Statement of objects .......... 69
S.4 Resolution to alter objects .......... 73
S.5 Objecting to alteration of objects .......... 73
S.7 Requirements for articles .......... 77
S.8 Table A .......... 77
S.9 Alteration of articles .......... 77
S.10 Documents to be sent to registrar .......... 49
S.11 Minimum authorised capital of public companies .......... 45
S.13 Effect of registration .......... 50
S.14 Effect of memorandum and articles .......... 80
S.16 Effect of alteration on company's members .......... 78
S.17 Conditions in memorandum which could have been in articles .......... 76
S.22 Definition of 'member' .......... 148
S.23 Membership of holding company .......... 150
S.24 Minimum membership for carrying on business .......... 42

*Company Names*

S.25 Name as stated in memorandum .......... 60
S.26 Prohibition on registration of certain names .......... 61
S.28 Change of name .......... 62
S.30 Exemption from requirement of 'limited' as part of name .......... 60
S.32 Misleading names .......... 63

*A Company's Capacity; Formalities of Carrying on Business*

S.35 Company's capacity not limited by memorandum .......... 69
S.35A Power of directors to bind company .......... 182
S.35B No duty to enquire as to capacity of company or authority of directors .......... 70

S.36A Company seal ....................59
S.36C Company contracts ....................58
S.42 Events affecting a company's status ....................214

*Re-Registration as a Means of Altering a Company's Status*

S.43 Re-registration of private company as public ....................51
S.44 Consideration for shares recently allotted to be valued ....................52
S.45 Additional requirements relating to share capital ....................51
S.49 Re-registration of limited company as unlimited ....................75
S.51 Re-registration, unlimited to limited ....................75
S.53 Re-registration of public company as private ....................52
S.54 Objection to resolution under S.53 ....................53

*Allotment of Shares and Debentures*

S.80 Company authority for allotment ....................138
S.84 Allotment were issue not fully subscribed ....................139
S.85 Effect of irregular allotment ....................139
S.88 Return as to allotments ....................140
S.89 Offers to be on pre-emptive basis ....................138
S.90 Communication of pre-emptive offers ....................139
S.91 Exclusion of S.89,90 by private companies ....................139
S.92 Consequences of contravention of S.89,90 ....................139
S.94 Definitions of S.89,90 ....................138
S.95 Disapplication of pre-emption rights ....................139
S.97 Underwriting commission ....................103
S.99 Payment for shares ....................104
S.100 Allotment of shares at a discount ....................105
S.101 Allotted shares to be at least one quarter paid-up ....................105
S.102 Restriction on payment by long term undertaking ....................105
S.103 Non-cash consideration to be valued ....................105
S.104 Transfer to public company of non-cash asset in initial period ....................107
S.106 Shares issued to subscribers ....................104
S.111 Matters to be communicated to registrar ....................214
S.111A Members' rights to damages ....................99
S.113 Relief from certain liabilities ....................107

*General Provisions about Share Capital*

S.117 Public company capital requirements ....................59
S.120 Reserve liability ....................102
S.121 Alteration of capital ....................102

*Class Rights*

S.125 Variation of class rights ....................135
S.127 Objection to variation ....................136

*Share Premiums*

S.130 Application of share premiums ....................109
S.131 Merger relief ....................110

*Reduction of Capital*


S.135 Special resolution for reduction ....108
S.139 Public company reducing below authorised minimum ....53


*Maintenance of Capital*


S.142 Serious loss of capital ....107
S.143 General rule against acquisition of own shares ....111
S.144 Acquisition of shares by company nominee ....150
S.146 Treatment of shares held by or for a public company ....146
S.150 Charges of public companies on own shares ....109


*Financial Assistance by a Company for Acquisition of its Own Shares*


S.151 Financial assistance generally prohibited ....112
S.152 Definitions ....112
S.153 Exceptions ....113
S.154 Special restriction for public companies ....114
S.155–158 Relaxation of S.151 for private companies ....115


*Redeemable Shares; Purchase by a Company of its Own Shares*


S.159 Power to issue redeemable shares ....116
S.160 Financing the redemption ....116
S.162 Power to purchase own shares ....117
S.163 Definitions 'off-market' and 'market' purchase ....117
S.164 Off-market purchase ....117
S.165 Contingent purchase contract ....118
S.166 Market purchase ....118
S.167 Assignment or release of right to purchase own shares ....118
S.168 Payment to be made out of distributable profits ....119
S.169 Disclosure requirements ....119
S.170 The capital redemption reserve ....117
S.171–177 Redemption or purchase out of capital by private company ....119
S.178 Effect of failure to redeem or purchase ....123


*Miscellaneous Provisions about Shares and Debentures*


S.183 Transfer and registration ....141
S.184 Certification of transfers ....142
S.185 Duty of company to issue certificates ....140
S.186 Certificate prima facie evidence of title ....140
S.188 Issue and effect of share warrant to bearer ....141


*Disclosure of Interests in Shares*


S.198–211 Substantial shareholdings ....217
S.212–216 Investigation by a public company of interests in its own shares ....218


*Accounts and Audit*


S.221 Accounting records ....220
S.222 Where and how long records kept ....220
S.223 Company's financial year ....225

| | | |
|---|---|---|
| S.224 | Accounting reference period and date | 221 |
| S.225 | Alteration of accounting reference period | 221 |
| S.226 | Duty to prepare individual company accounts | 221 |
| S.227 | Duty to prepare group accounts | 224 |
| S.233 | Approval and signing of accounts | 222 |
| S.235 | Auditors' report | 255 |
| S.236 | Signature of auditors' report | 222 |
| S.237 | Auditors' duties | 256 |
| S.238 | Persons entitled to copies of accounts | 244 |
| S.240 | Requirements in connection with publication of accounts | 242 |
| S.241 | Directors' duty to lay and deliver accounts | 221 |
| S.244 | Period for laying and delivering accounts | 222 |
| S.245 | Voluntary revision of accounts | 243 |
| S.246 | Exemptions for small and medium sized companies | 240 |
| S.247 | Qualification as small or medium sized company | 239 |
| S.250 | Dormant companies | 241 |
| S.251 | Summary financial statement | 243 |
| S.252 | Election to dispense with laying of accounts | 222 |
| S.254 | Publication of full accounts | 74 |
| S.258 | Parent and subsidiary undertakings | 222 |
| | *Distribution of Profits* | |
| S.263 | Dividends – basic rule | 124 |
| S.264 | Dividends – public company rule | 125 |
| S.265–268 | Dividends – investment companies | 128 |
| S.270 | Relevant accounts | 126 |
| S.272 | Interim accounts | 127 |
| S.277 | Consequences of unlawful distribution | 127 |
| S.281 | Rules subject to further restrictions in articles | 127 |
| | *Qualifications, Duties and Responsibilities of Directors and Secretaries* | |
| S.282 | Number of directors | 173 |
| S.283 | Secretary | 205 |
| S.285 | Validity of acts of directors | 176 |
| S.286 | Qualifications of secretaries | 205 |
| S.287 | Registered office | 67 |
| S.288 | Register of directors | 216 |
| S.291 | Share qualification | 174 |
| S.292 | Appointment of directors to be voted on individually | 174 |
| S.293 | Age limits | 176 |
| S.303 | Resolution to remove director | 177 |
| S.304 | Director's right to protest removal | 177 |
| S.305 | Directors' names on company stationery | 217 |
| S.308 | Assignment of office | 175 |
| S.309 | Directors' duty to employees | 194 |
| S.310 | Exemption of officers from liability | 201, 245 |

*Enforcement of Fair Dealing by Directors*


S.312 Compensation for loss of office .......... 184
S.313 Company approval for property transfer .......... 185
S.314 Director's duty of disclosure on takeover .......... 185
S.315 Consequence of non-compliance with S.314 .......... 185
S.317 Disclosure of interest in contracts .......... 185
S.319 Directors' service contracts .......... 186
S.320 Substantial property transactions .......... 187
S.321 Exceptions from S.320 .......... 187
S.322A Invalidity of certain transactions involving directors .......... 188
S.323 Share options .......... 189
S.324 Disclosure of shareholding in own company .......... 217
S.325 Register of interests notified under S.324 .......... 217
S.327 Extension of S.323 to spouses and children .......... 189
S.328 Extension of S.324 to spouses and children .......... 217
S.329 Duty to notify stock exchange .......... 217
S.330 Loans to directors – general rule .......... 189
S.331 Definitions .......... 184
S.332 Short term quasi-loans .......... 190
S.333 Inter-company loans in same group .......... 192
S.334 Loans not exceeding £5,000 .......... 191
S.335 Minor or business transactions .......... 191
S.336 Loans to holding company .......... 191
S.337 Funding of director's expenditure on duty to company .......... 191
S.338 Loans by money lending companies .......... 192
S.341 Civil remedies for breach of S.330 .......... 192
S.342 Criminal penalties for breach of S.330 .......... 193
S.346 Connected persons .......... 183


*Company Identification*


S.348 Company name outside place of business .......... 63
S.349 Company name in correspondence .......... 63
S.350 Company seal .......... 63
S.351 Particulars in correspondence .......... 64, 102


*Register of Members*


S.352 Obligation to keep register .......... 151
S.353 Location of register .......... 152
S.354 Index of members .......... 152
S.356 Inspection of register .......... 152
S.358 Power to close register .......... 152
S.359 Rectification of register .......... 152
S.360 Trusts not entered on register .......... 149
S.361 Register prima facie evidence .......... 151


*Annual Return*


S.363 Annual return .......... 219
S.365 Time for completion of return .......... 219

*Meetings and Resolutions*

| | | |
|---|---|---|
| S.366 | Annual general meeting | 260 |
| S.367 | Secretary of State's power to call meeting | 260 |
| S.368 | Extraordinary general meeting | 260 |
| S.369 | Length of notice for meetings | 261 |
| S.370 | Persons entitled to notice | 262 |
| S.371 | Power of court to order meetings | 261 |
| S.372 | Proxies | 264 |
| S.373 | Right to demand a poll | 264 |
| S.375 | Representation of corporations at meetings | 150 |
| S.376 | Members' resolutions | 263 |
| S.377 | Members' resolutions | 263 |
| S.378 | Extraordinary and special resolutions | 266 |
| S.379 | Special notice | 262 |
| S.379A | Elective resolution | 268 |
| S.381A –382A | Written resolutions | 267 |
| S.382 | Minutes | 180, 265 |
| S.383 | Inspection of minutes | 265 |

*Auditors*

| | | |
|---|---|---|
| S.385 | Appointment at general meeting | 251 |
| S.386 | Appointment by private company not obliged to lay accounts | 252 |
| S.387 | Appointment by Secretary of State | 252 |
| S.388 | Casual vacancies | 252 |
| S.388A | Dormant companies | 252 |
| S.389A | Auditors' rights | 256 |
| S.390A | Remuneration | 252 |
| S.390B | Remuneration for non-audit work | 252 |
| S.391 | Removal | 253 |
| S.391A | Rights of auditors who are removed | 253 |
| S.392 | Resignation | 254 |
| S.392A | Rights of resigning auditors | 254 |
| S.393 | Termination of appointment of auditors not appointed annually | 252 |
| S.394 | Statement by person ceasing to hold office as auditor | 255 |

*Registration of Charges*

| | | |
|---|---|---|
| S.395 | Introduction to S.396 | 160 |
| S.396 | Charges which have to be registered | 160 |
| S.398 | Delivery of particulars of charges for registration | 160 |
| S.400 | Late delivery of particulars | 161 |
| S.401 | Delivery of further particulars | 161 |
| S.402 | Errors and omissions in registered particulars | 162 |
| S.404 | Exclusion of voidness | 163 |
| S.405 | Restrictions on voidness | 164 |
| S.408–410 | Additional information to be registered | 162, 348 |

| | | |
|---|---|---|
| S.411 | Company's register of charges | 167 |
| S.416 | Constructive notice | 70 |
| | *Arrangements and Reconstructions* | |
| S.425 | Compromises with creditors and members | 304 |
| S.426 | Information to be circulated | 305 |
| S.427 | Provisions facilitating reconstructions | 306 |
| S.428–430 | Dissentients' rights | 309 |
| | *Investigations* | |
| S.431 | Investigation on application of members | 287 |
| S.432 | Other investigations | 287 |
| S.433–436 | Powers of inspectors | 288 |
| S.437 | Inspectors' report | 289 |
| S.438 | Power to bring civil proceedings on company's behalf | 290 |
| S.441 | Inspectors' reports as evidence | 290 |
| S.442 | Investigation of ownership | 290 |
| S.443 | Supplementary to S.442 | 290 |
| S.445 | Power to impose restrictions on shares and debentures | 291 |
| S.446 | Investigation of share dealings | 291 |
| S.447 | Secretary of State's power to require production of documents | 291 |
| S.448 | Entry and search of premises | 289 |
| S.449 | Security of information | 292 |
| S.450 | Punishment for destroying company documents | 292 |
| S.451 | Punishment for providing false information | 292 |
| S.451A | Disclosure of information by inspector | 291 |
| S.452 | Protection of information | 292 |
| | *Orders Imposing Restrictions on Shares* | |
| S.454–457 | Consequences and punishments | 291 |
| | *Fraudulent Trading* | |
| S.458 | Punishment for fraudulent trading | 325 |
| | *Unfair Prejudice* | |
| S.459 | Order on application of member | 282 |
| S.460 | Order on application of Secretary of State | 290 |
| S.461 | Provisions as to petitions and orders | 284 |
| | *Matters Arising Subsequent to Winding-Up* | |
| S.651 | Power of court to declare dissolution void | 331 |
| S.652 | Defunct companies | 331 |
| | *The Registrar of Companies* | |
| S.705 | Companies' registered numbers | 49 |
| S.707A | Delivery of documents to registrar | 49 |
| S.709 | Inspection of documents | 49 |
| S.711 | Official notification | 214, 332 |
| S.711A | Constructive notice | 70 |
| S.714 | Index of company names | 62 |

*Miscellaneous and Supplementary Provisions*

| | | |
|---|---|---|
| S.719 | Power to provide for employees on cessation of business | 72 |
| S.727 | Power to grant relief | 200 |

*Interpretation*

| | | |
|---|---|---|
| S.736 | Holding company etc | 222 |
| S.737 | Called-up share capital | 101 |
| S.738 | Allotment and paid-up | 104 |
| S.739 | Non-cash asset | 105 |
| S.741 | Director, shadow director | 173, 183 |
| S.742 | Expressions used in accounts | 173, 242 |
| S.744 | General expressions | 50 |
| Schedule 4 | | 226 |
| Schedule 4A | | 225 |
| Schedule 7 | | 244 |
| Schedule 8 | | 240 |

**Companies Act 1989**

*Company Accounts*

| | | |
|---|---|---|
| S.2 | Accounting records | 220 |
| S.3 | Financial year | 221 |
| S.4 | Individual company accounts | 221 |
| S.5 | Group accounts | 224 |
| S.7 | Approval and signing of accounts | 222 |
| S.9 | Auditors' report | 222, 225 |
| S.10 | Publication of accounts and reports | 242, 244 |
| S.11 | Laying and delivering of accounts | 221 |
| S.12 | Failure to comply with requirements | 243 |
| S.13 | Small and medium sized companies | 239 |
| S.14 | Dormant companies | 241 |
| S.15 | Summary financial statements | 243 |
| S.16 | Private companies election to dispense with laying of accounts before meeting | 222 |
| S.17 | Unlimited company exemptions | 74 |
| S.21–22 | Parent and subsidiary undertakings | 222 |

*Eligibility of Auditors*

| | | |
|---|---|---|
| S.25 | Eligibility for appointment | 250 |
| S.26 | Effect of appointment | 250 |
| S.27 | Ineligibility on ground of lack of independence | 251 |
| S.29 | Power of Secretary of State to require second audit | 251 |
| S.30 | Supervisory bodies | 247 |
| S.31 | 'Appropriate qualification' | 248 |
| S.32 | Qualifying bodies and recognised professional qualifications | 250 |
| S.33 | Overseas qualifications | 250 |
| S.36 | Information about firms to be available to public | 250, 288 |

*Investigations*

S.55 Investigations not leading to published report .....289
S.56 Production of documents .....288
S.57 Duty of inspectors to report .....289
S.58 Power to bring civil proceedings on company's behalf .....290
S.60 Power of Secretary of State to prevent winding-up petition .....290
S.61 Inspectors' reports as evidence .....290
S.62 Investigation of ownership .....290
S.63 Production of documents .....292
S.64 Entry and search of premises .....289
S.65 Security of information .....292
S.68 Disclosure of information .....291
S.69 Protection of information .....292
S.74 Investigations into insider dealing .....275
S.76 Entry and search of premises .....275
S.82–87 Power to assist overseas regulatory authorities .....292

*Registration of Company Charges*

S.93 Charges requiring registration .....160
S.95 Delivery of particulars .....160
S.96 Delivery of further particulars .....161
S.97 Effect of omissions and errors .....162
S.99 Provisions with respect to voidness .....163
S.100 Additional information to be registered .....162, 348
S.101 Register kept by company .....167
S.103 Supplementary provisions .....70

*Company's Capacity*

S.108 Company's capacity and power of directors to bind it .....69
S.109 Invalidity of certain transactions involving directors .....188
S.110 Company's objects .....69, 73

*De-Regulation of Private Companies*

S.113–114 Written resolutions .....77, 267
S.116 Elective resolutions .....268

*Appointment and Removal of Auditors*

S.119 Appointment .....251
S.120 Rights of auditors .....256
S.121 Remuneration .....252
S.122 Removal and resignation .....252, 253
S.123 Auditors' statements .....255

*Company Records*

S.125 Delivery of documents to registrar .....49
S.126 Keeping and inspection of company records .....49

*Miscellaneous*

S.129 Membership of holding company .....150
S.130 Company contracts and execution of documents .....58, 59

| | | |
|---|---|---|
| S.131 | Members' rights to damages | 99 |
| S.132 | Financial assistance | 113 |
| S.133 | Redeemable shares | 117 |
| S.136 | Registered office | 67 |
| S.137 | Insurance for officers and auditors | 245 |
| S.138 | Increase of limits on exemptions | 191 |
| S.139 | Annual returns | 219 |
| S.142 | Abolition of deemed notice | 70 |
| S.144 | 'Subsidiary' 'holding company' and 'wholly owned subsidiary' | 222 |
| Schedule 1 | | 226 |
| Schedule 2 | | 225 |
| Schedule 5 | | 244 |
| Schedule 6 | | 240 |
| Schedule 11 | | 247 |
| Schedule 12 | | 249 |
| Schedule 19 | | 283 |

**Companies Consolidation (Consequential Provisions) Act 1985** .......... 18, 47

**Company Directors Disqualification Act 1986**

| | | |
|---|---|---|
| S.2–4 | Disqualification criteria | 175 |
| S.6 | Disqualification of directors of insolvent companies | 202 |
| S.8 | Disqualification after investigation of company | 203 |
| S.10 | Disqualification of persons held liable to contribute to company's assets | 203 |
| S.11 | Bankrupts acting as directors | 175 |
| S.15 | Personal liability of persons acting while disqualified | 203 |

**Company Securities (Insider Dealing) Act 1985**

| | | |
|---|---|---|
| S.1 | Prohibition on stock exchange deals by insiders | 272 |
| S.2 | Public servants | 274 |
| S.3 | Exemptions | 274 |
| S.7 | Trustees and personal representatives | 275 |
| S.8 | Punishments | 275 |
| S.9 | Definition of 'connected with a company' | 271 |
| S.10 | Definition of 'unpublished price sensitive information' | 272 |

**Companies (Tables A to F) Regulations 1985** .......... 77

**County Court (Amendment) Rules 1989** .......... 66

**Financial Services Act 1986**

*Conduct of Investment Business*

| | | |
|---|---|---|
| S.48 | Conduct of business rules | 275 |

*Official Listing of Securities*

| | | |
|---|---|---|
| S.142 | Official listing | 91 |
| S.143 | Applications for listing | 89 |
| S.144 | Admission to list | 92 |
| S.145 | Discontinuance and suspension of listing | 94 |

S.146 General duty of disclosure in listing particulars ..... 92
S.147 Supplementary listing particulars ..... 93
S.148 Exemption from disclosure ..... 92
S.149 Registration of listing particulars ..... 93
S.150 Compensation for false or misleading particulars ..... 97
S.151 Exemption from liability to pay compensation ..... 97
S.152 Persons responsible for particulars ..... 98
S.154 Advertisements in connection with listing applications ..... 93
S.156 Listing rules; general provisions ..... 91
S.157 Alteration of competent authority ..... 91

*Offers of Unlisted Securities*

S.158 Definitions ..... 94
S.159 Offers of securities on admission to approved exchange ..... 95
S.160 Other offers of securities ..... 94
S.161 Exceptions ..... 95
S.162 Form and content of prospectus ..... 96
S.163 General duty of disclosure in prospectus ..... 96
S.164 Supplementary prospectus ..... 96
S.165 Exemptions from disclosure ..... 96
S.166 Compensation for false or misleading prospectus ..... 97
S.167 Exemption from liability to pay compensation ..... 97
S.168 Persons responsible for prospectus ..... 98
S.169 Terms and implementation of offer ..... 96
S.170 Advertisements by private companies ..... 89
S.171 Contravention ..... 96

*Takeover Offers*

S.172 Takeover offers ..... 309

*Insider Dealing*

S.173 Information obtained in official capacity ..... 274
S.174 Market makers, off market dealers ..... 274
S.177 Investigation into insider dealing ..... 275
S.178 Penalties for failure to co-operate with investigator ..... 276

*Miscellaneous*

S.199 Powers of entry ..... 275

**Insolvency Act 1986**

*Voluntary Arrangements*

S.1–7 Voluntary arrangements ..... 306

*Administration Orders*

S.8 Power to make administration order ..... 338
S.9 Application for order ..... 338
S.10 Effect of application ..... 339
S.12 Notification of order ..... 339
S.13 Appointment of administrator ..... 339
S.14–16 Powers of administrator ..... 339

| | | |
|---|---|---|
| S.17 | Duties of administrator | 340 |
| S.18 | Discharge or variation of administration order | 341 |
| S.19–20 | Vacation of office and release | 342 |
| S.21 | Information to be given by administrator | 340 |
| S.22 | Statement of affairs | 340 |
| S.23 | Statement of proposals | 341 |
| S.24 | Consideration of proposals by creditors meeting | 341 |
| S.25 | Approval of substantial revisions | 341 |
| S.26 | Committee of creditors | 341 |
| S.27 | Protection of creditors and members | 341 |
| S.30 | Corporate body not to act as receiver | 346 |
| S.31 | Bankrupt not to act as receiver | 346 |
| S.32 | Power for court to appoint official receiver | 346 |
| | *Receivers and Managers (General)* | |
| S.33 | Appointment of receiver or manager | 345 |
| S.34 | Liability for invalid appointment | 345 |
| | *Administrative Receivers* | |
| S.35 | Receivers appointed out of court | 346 |
| S.36 | Court's power to fix receiver's remuneration | 346 |
| S.37 | Receivers appointed out of court | 347 |
| S.39 | Notification that receiver or manager appointed | 348 |
| S.41 | Enforcement of duty of receiver to make returns | 351 |
| S.42 | Receiver's general powers | 347 |
| S.43 | Power to dispose of charge property | 347 |
| S.44 | Agency and liability for contracts | 347 |
| S.45 | Vacation of office | 350 |
| S.46–49 | Receiver's duties | 349 |
| | *Voluntary Winding-Up* | |
| S.74 | Contributories | 329 |
| S.84 | Circumstances for voluntary liquidation | 333 |
| S.86 | Commencement of voluntary liquidation | 333 |
| S.87–88 | Effect on business and status of company | 335 |
| S.89 | Declaration of solvency | 333 |
| S.94 | Final meeting and dissolution, members' voluntary liquidation | 337 |
| S.95 | Effect of insolvency on members' voluntary liquidation | 334 |
| S.96 | Effect of insolvency on members' voluntary liquidation | 334 |
| S.97–99 | Meeting of creditors in creditors' voluntary liquidation | 334 |
| S.100 | Appointment of liquidator | 334 |
| S.101 | Appointment of committee of inspection | 335 |
| S.102 | Effect of insolvency on members' voluntary liquidation | 334 |
| S.105 | Effect of insolvency on members' voluntary liquidation | 334 |
| S.106 | Final meeting and dissolution, creditors' voluntary liquidation | 337 |
| S.110–111 | Reconstructions | 302 |
| S.112 | Applications to court | 336 |

| | | |
|---|---|---|
| S.114 | No liquidator appointed in voluntary liquidation | 336 |
| S.116 | Saving for rights of creditors and contributories | 336 |
| | *Winding-Up by the Court* | |
| S.117 | Jurisdiction | 319 |
| S.122 | Circumstances for compulsory liquidation | 317 |
| S.123 | Inability to pay debts – definition | 317 |
| S.124 | Application for liquidation | 319 |
| S.127 | Avoidance of property dispositions | 320 |
| S.128 | Avoidance of attachments | 320 |
| S.129 | Commencement of compulsory liquidation | 320 |
| S.130 | Consequences of order | 320 |
| S.131 | Statement of affairs | 321 |
| S.132 | Investigation by official receiver | 321 |
| S.133–34 | Public examination | 321 |
| S.135 | Appointment and powers of provisional liquidator | 320 |
| S.136–37 | Functions of official receiver | 320 |
| S.139 | Choice of liquidator | 322 |
| S.141 | Committee of creditors | 322 |
| S.143 | General functions of liquidator | 322 |
| S.146 | Final meeting | 324 |
| | *Liquidators* | |
| S.165 | Powers of liquidator | 323 |
| S.166 | Powers of liquidator | 335 |
| S.167 | Powers of liquidator | 323 |
| S.169 | Powers of liquidator | 323 |
| S.171 | Removal of liquidator | 336 |
| S.172 | Vacation of office | 323 |
| S.173 | Release of liquidator | 336 |
| S.174 | Release of liquidator | 323 |
| | *General Provisions* | |
| S.175 | Preferential debts | 330 |
| S.176 | Preferential debts | 330 |
| S.177 | Special manager | 328 |
| S.178–82 | Disclaimer | 328 |
| S.183 | Effect of execution or attachment | 328 |
| S.187 | Power to provide for employees on cessation or transfer of business | 72 |
| S.201 | Final meeting and dissolution | 337 |
| S.202–3 | Early dissolution | 324 |
| S.205 | Dissolution | 324 |
| S.212 | Summary remedy against directors, liquidators | 326 |
| S.213 | Fraudulent trading | 325 |
| S.214 | Wrongful trading | 325 |
| S.216 | Restriction on use of company names | 326 |
| S.217 | Personal liability of persons acting while disqualified | 203 |
| S.233 | Supplies by utilities | 327 |

S.234 Delivery of property ....327
S.235 Duty to co-operate with office holder ....327
S.236–37 Inquiry into company's dealings ....327
S.238–41 Transactions at an undervalue and preferences ....165
S.244 Extortionate credit transactions ....327
S.245 Avoidance of floating charges ....164
S.246 Unenforceability of liens ....328
S.386 Preferential debts ....330

*Insolvency Practitioners*

S.388 Qualified insolvency practitioner ....316
S.390 Authorisation by members of professional bodies ....316
S.391 Authorisation by members of professional bodies ....316
S.392–97 Authorisation by relevant authority ....316
S.435 Meaning of 'associate' ....165
Sch 1 Powers of administrator or administrative receiver ....339
Sch 4 Powers of liquidator ....323

**Joint Stock Companies Act 1844** ....17

**Law of Property Act 1925** ....167

**Limited Liability Act 1855** ....17

**Misrepresentation Act 1967**
S.2(1) ....98
S.2(2) ....100

**Partnership Act 1890** ....39

**Sale of Goods Act 1979, S.17** ....158

**Single European Act 1986** ....29

**Stock Transfer Act 1963** ....142

# 1 Methods of Learning

## INTRODUCTION

1. The purpose of this chapter

The skills of learning are themselves learned, but seldom taught! In fact this chapter does not set out to teach a person how to learn. Learning is a very individual process and there is no set procedure which is best for everyone regardless of their personality. The contents of this chapter amount to a series of suggestions, some or all of which may be integrated into whatever method of learning a student has already developed. It therefore

a. Outlines the various resources available to a student;
b. Explains the essential requirements necessary to pass a law examination;
c. Gives some advice on the approach to learning; and
d. Suggests some methods of using the resources to achieve the requirements.

2. **Resources**

a. Lectures and the lecturer;
b. Lecture notes, both written and taped;
c. Text books;
d. Past questions;
e. Suggested answers to past questions;
f. Discussions with fellow students and arranged visits, for example, to the courts;
g. This book.

3. **Requirements**

Three qualities are necessary to pass company law examinations

a. Understanding the principles of law;
b. Learning the relevant legal facts; and
c. Skill in applying the principles and facts to examination questions.

This chapter suggests the best available resources for attaining the requirements of understanding and learning. Chapter 2 deals with the third requirement of application.

4. Approach

a. ***Mental approach***. It is vital to neither underestimate nor overestimate your own ability or the standard of the examination. Both undue pessimism and overconfidence can be the cause of failure. The methods described below should minimise the risk of failure because of an unrealistic assessment of either personal ability or of what is expected by the examiner. The best approach is summed up in a Chinese proverb:

> 'That the birds of worry and care fly above your head,
> This you cannot change,
> But that they build nests in your hair,
> This you can prevent.'

b. ***Physical approach***

i. ***Timetabling***. When the course is nearing its conclusion, ie 6–8 weeks before the examination, it is generally advisable to prepare a revision timetable which allows roughly equal time for each paper that it is to be taken. The timetable need not be complex, eg Mondays – Law; Tuesdays – Accounts; Wednesdays – Auditing. A target number of hours should be set for each day, and if time is lost one day, it should be made good as soon as possible. Timetabling avoids wasting time deciding what to study each day, and it ensures that no subjects are neglected. The timetable may be changed occasionally if the revision time considered necessary for a particular subject changes as the examination draws near.

ii. ***When to work***. This is mainly a matter of personal preference. It is however generally accepted that chances of success are not improved by working so late at night that you get less sleep than you need. A more contentious question is whether or not you should work up to the 'last minute' before an examination. The author believes that you should do so. The evening before the examination is most usefully spent on revision rather than trying to relax watching television.

## UNDERSTANDING

5. Law is easy to understand!

a. Such a statement by author or lecturer may appear to reveal a lack of sympathy with the problems faced by students. This is not the case. It is merely that experience has shown that most people who fail law examinations do not do so because they are unable to understand the subject. Law is after all a human creation. It is relevant to everyday life, and the medium of expression is words. Subjects such as mathematics, with abstract concepts and more indirect relevance, are arguably more difficult to understand. All students can therefore approach law with confidence that they will not encounter unsurmountable difficulties in understanding the subject.

b. If however you do encounter a principle, rule or case that you do not understand you must never accept defeat. Read about it in several textbooks if necessary, ask your lecturer for a second explanation or discuss it with fellow students. Even if they have the same problem a discussion will almost certainly help. If lack of understanding stems from not knowing the meaning of an individual word, then look it up in a dictionary. It seems an obvious solution, but is rarely done.

**6. The trap**

Since law is often not difficult to understand, by its nature it lays a trap. A comparison with mathematics is again useful. If a mathematical concept is understood the answer can usually be worked out. In contrast the understanding of a legal rule does not, by itself, mean that the rule can be recalled in an examination. The trap is that understanding can be mistaken for an ability to recall, ie understanding can be mistaken for learning. They are related, but they are not synonymous. Understanding by itself will not enable you to succeed in a law examination, but it is the vital first step. Clearly you will not be able to learn or apply what you do not understand.

## LEARNING

**7. Law is difficult to learn!**

Inadequate learning is the main reason why many students fail law examinations. It therefore follows that learning and memory are the main things which law examinations test. A good factual knowledge of the relevant law is therefore the basis for success. Acquiring this factual knowledge can at times be boring. It may involve repetition of well understood facts and it is usually a solitary and rather unsociable activity. Every effort must therefore be made to minimise boredom and maximise interest and enthusiasm, whilst using the limited time as effectively as possible. The best two ways to do this are:

a. Use as many different methods of study (ie resources) as possible; and

b. Constantly test yourself.

**8. The use of different resources**

If you have allocated a particular 2 hour period for the study of law, do not spend all of the time reading notes or a book, because your concentration will soon fade. It is much more productive to select a topic and then study it using 4 different methods. For example in 4 periods of half an hour each:

a. Read a textbook;

b. Read notes;

c. Test yourself on the notes; and

d. Write a timed answer (see below).

## 9. Self-testing

The main reason for self-testing is to avoid falling into the understanding/learning trap discussed above. If you test yourself you will find out whether or not you have learnt what you have understood. The actual method of self-testing will vary from person to person. For example:

Select 25 important cases and write out their names and brief details. Cover the details with a sheet of paper and attempt a brief summary of the details on a separate sheet of paper. Compare your summary with the details and award yourself a mark out of 4 for each case and write this mark down. Repeat this for all the cases to arrive at a mark out of 100. Record this mark. A few days later repeat the procedure and see if your mark improves. Keep repeating the exercise until you achieve 80–90 out of 100. Even if you find the actual mechanics of learning rather tedious you may enjoy the challenge of improving on your previous mark.

## 10. The usefulness of individual resources for learning

a. ***Textbooks***. It is not generally advisable to try to memorise facts from textbooks. Textbooks should only be referred to when a topic is not sufficiently understood or when a break is needed from the other study methods. Conventional textbooks should not be used as a basic learning method.

b. ***Lectures***. Lectures are primarily a time for the communication of the correct quantity of relevant information and for increasing understanding by discussion and asking questions. The actual learning of this information will take place after the lecture.

c. ***Lecture notes*** If lecture notes are 'good', ie adequate in detail (not excessive) and without 'gaps' they are probably the best resource for learning because they are personal to you. Read them regularly and if possible record them on cassette tape. These cassettes should not be used as your basic learning method, but they will be useful if you feel that you need a short break from more traditional methods of study. When taking notes in lectures it is important:

   i. To be as neat as possible. It is very difficult to earn from untidy notes;

   ii. To space the notes out (rather like this book). This assists the assimilation of facts;

   iii. To only write on one side of each sheet of paper. The other side can then be used at a later date to expand on a difficult topic, or to write down a question on which a lecturer's comment is required.

d. ***Past questions***. It is essential to obtain past questions as soon as possible after the start of the course, so that the standard of the examination can be assessed at an early date, and a good mental approach adopted. There are two main ways in which these past questions can be used.

i. Writing ***timed answers***, ie without the assistance of notes, books, or suggested answers, write an answer in the same amount of time as would be available in the examination. Clearly it is preferable for a lecturer to assess your answer, and even if he has not set the question he should be prepared to mark it if requested to do so. At the times when lecturer assessment is not possible (eg shortly before the examination) it is nevertheless useful to write timed answers. You will then have to critically assess your own answer, perhaps awarding yourself a mark, or even re-writing the answer if you consider your attempt very poor.

ii. Writing ***model answers***. If a topic appears with regularity in the examination it is often worth writing an exam-length model answer, ie using all the available resources spend 1–2 hours writing the best possible answer that you can achieve. Lecturer assessment of such an answer would again be helpful. It is not suggested that you attempt to memorise every word of such an answer. It would however be possible to remember the structure of your answer, ie remember the number of paragraphs and general point which each paragraph deals with.

e. ***Suggested answers***. These are helpful only if they are used responsibly. They will be of no help if you merely read the question, then glance at the answer and either:

i. Tell yourself (probably incorrectly) that you could write a similar answer in the examination; or,

ii. Get depressed because you think that you cannot produce such an answer. Remember that these answers are not an indication of the standard that the examiner expects. Although they are 'examination length' each answer takes the author several hours to plan and write, a much less competent answer would still achieve a good pass.

You must nevertheless aim high. Suggested answers help to achieve this aim by serving three purposes:

i. They illustrate the style, structure, and content necessary to answer the particular question. They should not however be regarded as the only possible correct answer. In most of the answers different cases will be just as acceptable as the cases quoted. Sometimes even a different conclusion is equally 'correct', for example if a question asks your views on the value of trial by jury. The most important advice in connection with style and content is ***write in your own words***. Never try to memorise word for word sentences or paragraphs from any suggested answer. Such attempts usually fail, even one wrong word can alter the meaning of a whole paragraph.

ii. They are a valuable means of self-testing.

iii. They provide an incentive to practice. ***Practice*** is just as important as self-assessment. No one would expect to pass his driving test if all he did was read about the brakes, steering wheel and clutch in a book and then step into a car for the first time on the day of the test. Sitting a written examination is the same, practice is essential, and because suggested answers are a help in self-assessment they provide an incentive to practice, particularly at those times, eg shortly before the examination, when lecturer assessment is not possible.

f. ***This book***. 'Company Law' may be used either as a study manual or as a textbook.

i. ***Use as a study manual***. If you do not have a good and adequate set of notes then use this book as a study manual, making it your basic method of study. Read it several times, as you would with notes, and use the coursework questions, revision questions and progress tests as part of your self-testing programme. Since the coursework questions are in groups of 5 they can either be attempted individually or as a 3 hour 'mock' examination.

ii. ***Use as a textbook***. If you do have good notes you may nevertheless choose to use this book as a study manual, or you may decide to use it as a textbook or a casebook referring to the text or cases when the need arises for a source of legal facts, a description of the facts of a case, or clarification of a particular point of law. To facilitate use as a textbook a table of cases and an index is provided.

**11. Mnemonics**

A mnemonic is an aid to memory. Some students find that a code sentence or code word is a useful memory aid. For example a code word could be made from the 6 clauses that appear in the memorandum of association of every company. The clauses are the Name; Registered office; Objects; Limitation of liability; Capital; and Association. The initial letters are NROLCA. These could be rearranged to form a 'word' that could more easily be remembered, for example CAROL.N. If this code 'word' could be remembered it should trigger-off recollection of the word which each letter represents, thus providing the basis for an answer.

**12. If study has gone badly!**

Finally some advice is offered to those persons for whom something goes wrong. It may be illness, or accommodation problems, or perhaps just wasted time. – So if you have about 4 weeks left to the examination and you seem to be heading towards certain failure, but have now decided to make a late attempt to pass, then your best chance of salvation is to predict from past questions which topics are most likely to be asked. These topics should then be learnt as thoroughly as possible. It is better to have a good knowledge of a few topics than a vague knowledge of everything. – You just have to hope that some of your predictions are correct.

# 2 Examination Technique

## General points

### 1. Introduction

This chapter contains both 'golden rules', breach of which could mean the difference between success and failure, and useful hints which are comparatively less important, but which could nevertheless save a few vital marks. The points are dealt with in order of importance. The chapter assumes a 3 hour examination, giving a choice of 5 out of 8 questions.

### 2. Answer all parts of all questions

Never leave a question unanswered. The first 5 marks out of 20 are the easiest to obtain, the second 5 moderately easy, the third 5 more difficult, and the final 5 almost impossible. Therefore if you find you have only 10 minutes remaining in which to answer 2 questions it is best to spend 5 minutes on each question, writing down in note form as much of the relevant law as you can remember. In such a situation it will be necessary to use the time that you would normally spend reading through your answers for this purpose.

### 3. Never leave the examination before the end

If you finish early check your answer paper carefully and re-read the question paper to make sure that you have not omitted part of any of the questions. Keep reading and re-reading the question paper and your answers until the last possible moment. You may find an error or remember a case or point of law which had previously eluded you. If you do, then include it at the end of the answer book and cross-reference it with the remainder of your answer.

### 4. Time allocation

The basic rule is that you should allocate equal time to each question, leaving 10–15 minutes at the end of the examination to read through your paper. If however you realise that you do not know enough to use all the time originally allocated to your fifth answer, whereas you could write in excess of your allocated time for your first answer, then deduct about 5 minutes from answer 5 and add it to answer 1.

### 5. The first 5 minutes

As you read the examination paper for the first time underline what appear to be the key words in each question. Also write down in the margin the names of any cases, statutes or mnemonics which may be relevant. This gives you two chances of recalling these details, once at the start and again as you write each answer.

**6. Choice of questions**

a. Read through the whole paper 'ticking' questions which you can definitely answer and 'crossing' those which you cannot answer. If this does not produce exactly the correct amount of ticks, do not spend any further time on question choice at present – start your answers. It will be easier later in the examination to delete excess ticks, or to choose your best question out of the remaining 4 than to choose your fifth best out of 8 at the start.

b. General essay questions, for example comparing preference shares and debentures, result in a narrower range of marks than problem questions, ie there will be less students falling in the 0–5 and 15–20 brackets. Therefore if you are aiming for a very high mark, it is advisable to choose problem questions, although if you miss the point of the problem many marks will be lost.

**7. Order of answering questions**

Start with the question which you are best able to answer. It is definitely very poor technique to save your best question to the end, because if you start with your 'worst' question and make an error in timing, you may find that you have inadequate time to answer the questions on which your knowledge is greatest.

## STYLE AND STRUCTURE

**8. Starting with a conclusion**

It is a bad and common error to start with a conclusion. Answers often commence, for example, 'John has broken his fiduciary duty as a director because...'. This is a conclusion and it should therefore come at the end. If it comes at the start, and is wrong, the rest of the answer will be spent in an attempt to justify an incorrect conclusion, which often produces an answer where only one side of the argument is presented. The answer should be structured as follows:

a. State the relevant principles of law illustrating them where applicable with decided cases. If there are two sides to a problem both of them must be discussed, and not merely the argument which supports the conclusion which will eventually be reached. The names of the characters of the problem need not necessarily be mentioned at this stage.

b. Apply the stated principles to the facts of the problem.

c. Give your conclusion. It does not have to be one hundred percent certain. It is acceptable to say '... therefore John will probably succeed' if there is some reasonable doubt as to his chance. You must however commit yourself one way or the other, do not finish by stating that 'John has a 50/50 chance of success'.

9. **Contradictory conclusions**

If you place your conclusion at the end this will help to avoid the danger of self-contradiction. If however on reading through your answer you find contradictory statements or conclusions, you must delete one of them. If you do not do this you will get the worst of both worlds rather than the best, ie even if one is correct it will not score any marks.

10. **Repeating the question**

This is a very common fault, it never scores any marks, it wastes time and it spoils the structure of the answer.

11. **The introduction**

It is not uncommon for an answer on removal of directors to commence 'Directors are the persons to whom management of the company is entrusted. A public company must have at least two directors whereas a private company needs only one. Directors are removed in accordance with the provisions of the Companies Act 1985. ***S.303 states that*** . . .' The whole of this quotation except the words in italics, although correct, is not sufficiently relevant to earn any marks. An introduction if any should be very brief, you should get to the point of the question as directly as possible. If you are stuck, then start with the phrase 'The relevant law is as follows . . .'

12. **Format**

Generally answers should be structured in un-numbered paragraphs. Occasionally it may be suitable to make several points under heading (a) (b) (c) etc in one particular paragraph. Even so this should not be the basic style of the answer. If you have very little time remaining for a question it is better to write as many relevant points as possible in note form, rather than one or two paragraphs in perfect English.

13. **Balance**

Answers often tend towards one of two extremes. An answer may contain a list of principles of law, without any mention of cases, or it may consist of a number of case descriptions apparently unconnected by legal principles. Both these extremes are very poor. An answer should be well-balanced, containing both statements of principles of law, and case law illustrations of those principles.

14. **Meaning**

Many students fail to express what they wish to say. An example from a recent paper stated 'A declaration of solvency must be made within 5 weeks of a resolution for a members' voluntary winding up'. It is not clear from this whether the student means 5 weeks before or after the resolution, so no marks would be awarded. In fact a declaration of solvency must be made within 5 weeks before (or on the day of) the resolution.

It is not possible to become an expert at expressing your desired meaning merely by effort or determination, it is a very slow process. All you can do is (i) be as careful as possible; (ii) do not try to write too fast; and (iii) read through what you have written.

## Content

### 15. Names, dates and facts of cases

Perhaps the most frequent question a law lecturer is asked is the importance of including names, dates and facts of cases in an answer.

a. ***Facts without names***. If you cannot remember the name of a case, but you can recall the facts, then include the facts in your answer, but introduce them in some other way, eg 'In a recent case . . .'. It is far better to do this than to omit the case.

b. ***Names without facts***. Where a principle of law is derived from a case it is acceptable for the case name alone to follow the principle. Some case names must however be supported by facts otherwise the answer will not be 'balanced'.

c. ***Dates***. Dates are comparatively less important than names. It is not worth specifically learning dates, but if you do remember the date then include it in the answer.

d. ***Choice of cases***. Sometimes a number of cases are equally good illustrations of a legal principle. In this situation choose the case which can be described most concisely.

### 16. 'Ltd' or 'Plc'

Prior to the ***COMPANIES ACT 1980*** examiners often stated whether a company referred to in the question was public or private. This is no longer necessary because, since 1980, a private company's name must end with the word 'Limited' or the abbreviation 'Ltd', and a public company's name must end with the words 'Public Limited Company' or the abbreviation 'Plc'. Thus if an exam question says 'X Ltd has four directors . . .' it is clear that the company is a private company and therefore any rules which apply only to public companies are not relevant. The opposite would be true if the question said 'Z Plc. . .'.

### 17. Jargon

Avoid the use of unnecessary 'jargon'. Do not for example start your final paragraph 'After taking all the relevant law into consideration it is submitted that . . .'. The simple 'In conclusion . . .' is far better.

### 18. Latin phrases

If you wish to say for example 'The contract is ultra vires X Ltd' you cannot assume that the examiner knows that you know what 'ultra vires' means. You should therefore add, perhaps in brackets – 'beyond the powers of'. The examiner then knows that you have remembered the meaning of the words as well as the words themselves.

**19. Miscellaneous points**

a. Never use slang, or attempt to introduce humour into your answer. For example 'X has not got a snowflake's chance in hell of success' would not impress the examiner.

b. Avoid the use of 'I', 'we', and 'us'. When asked in a question to 'Advise X' do not write 'You will fail in your claim', write 'X will fail in his claim'.

c. Never use red ink, even to underline cases. This causes confusion when two or more examiners read the script.

d. If you wish to cross-out anything that you have written use a single line drawn with a ruler. If you wish to reinstate words which you have previously crossed-out then draw a line of dots under the words deleted, and write 'stet' in the margin. This means 'let it stand'.

e. Finally there is no need to emphasise words by underlining them or writing them in capitals. It is acceptable to emphasise case names or statutes in this way but not general words.

**20. Conclusion**

The final advice regarding the examination is 'don't panic'. This is of course easy advice to give, but it can be very difficult to put into practice. Perhaps the best antidote to possible panic is to consider the consequences of failure. Failure of an examination does not necessarily mean that you follow an inferior path through life. It may mean that you follow a different path, but it is impossible to say, at the time of the examination, whether this different path will ultimately be for the better or the worse.

# PART I INTRODUCTION

# 3 The History of Company Law

## Until 1825

### 1. Introduction

At the present time there are two basic legal frameworks for private persons who wish to form an association with the object of carrying on business for profit, namely partnerships and companies. Partnership law is based on contract and partnerships are therefore only suitable for a relatively small number of persons who know and trust each other. Since such a basis would be impractical for larger more complicated organisations the law has, over many years, allowed the development of companies, ie associations with a legal personality distinct from that of their members. An association with such a separate personality is said to be incorporated. Today partnerships and companies are distinct in law, but the modern distinction between them took many years to achieve.

### 2. Early commercial associations

The earliest trade associations existed in medieval times. They were Guilds of Merchants. Some of them hoped to obtain a monopoly over local trade, or over a particular commodity. To do this it was necessary to be incorporated. At that time the only method of incorporation was to obtain a charter from the Crown. Although these Guilds had an existence separate from their members, they did not resemble a modern company, since the members traded on their own account (subject to the rules of the Guild) and were liable for their own debts. The Guilds became common by the end of the 16th century as overseas trade expanded. About this time they were first referred to as 'companies'

### 3. Joint stock companies

In the 17th century the Joint Stock Company emerged, ('stock' in this context means 'stock-in-trade', not 'stocks and shares'), ie in addition to trading on their own account the members would operate a joint account with joint stock. Many of the early joint stock companies were large and powerful monopolies, for example the East India Company, which was granted a charter in 1600, had a monopoly over all trade with the Indies. By this time there were two methods of incorporation, either by charter or by special Act of Parliament. The joint stock companies possessed some of the advantages of incorporation, for example they could sue outsiders in their own name and the property of the company was distinct from that of the members, but they did not possess the main advantage of modern companies, ie limitation of members' liability. The creditors of such companies had access to the members' private assets because the company's charter would give power to the company to raise levies from members to pay the company's debts. Alternatively the creditors would be allowed to take over the company's rights to recover sums due from members **(SALMON v THE HAMBOROUGH CO (1671))**.

4. **Domestic companies**

In the second half of the 17th century the large monopolistic companies began to decline and there was a boom in the formation of companies concerned with domestic trade. In many cases the procedure for obtaining a charter was far too slow and expensive. Companies were therefore formed based on contract. The contract would contain rules for the conduct of members and provide for the transfer of shares. In law such bodies were basically regarded as partnerships and the liability of members was unlimited. The domestic companies became unpopular with the legislature mainly because of the activities of fraudulent promoters and share dealers, for example promoters would acquire charters from obsolete companies. Thus a banking partnership acquired the charter of the Sword Blade Company and started to issue 'Sword Blade' notes and bonds, and acted as banker to the South Sea Company.

5. **The South Sea Company**

The South Sea Company was formed in 1711. A scheme was proposed whereby it would acquire the entire national debt (about £31,000,000). It was thought that possession of an interest bearing loan owed by the State would provide a sound basis on which it could raise large sums to extend its trade. It started to acquire the debt either by buying out the holders or by persuading them to exchange their holdings for the company's stock. The company however failed for 3 reasons:

a. It paid too much for the holdings it acquired;

b. It did not have adequate trade to expand;

c. Holders of company stock panicked when action was commenced against the company's bankers (the Sword Blade Company) on the ground that it was operating under an obsolete charter which ought to be forfeited.

In less than 6 months the value of the South Sea Company's stock fell to one eighth its previous value. The collapse of the South Sea Company was a serious blow to corporate enterprise because the Government had approved the scheme and subsequent investigation revealed fraud and corruption by members of the government and the royal family.

6. **The Bubble Act 1720**

a. In order to check the boom in speculative and fraudulent company promotion the ***BUBBLE ACT 1720*** was passed. Exactly what it intended is not clear. The main section ***(S.18)*** stated that all undertakings which were purporting to act as corporate bodies without legal authority 'tending to the common grievance, prejudice and inconvenience of His Majesty's subjects' should be illegal and void.

Examples were given including purporting to act under an obsolete charter or the transfer of shares without authority of Act of Parliament or charter. In addition brokers dealing in securities of illegal companies were liable to penalties.

b. The effect of the Bubble Act was to suppress business associations and make it difficult for them to obtain corporate form. In no way did it provide what was needed, ie an easy method for joint stock companies to adopt a corporate form, whilst safeguarding the public from fraudulent promotion and management.

c. It did however exempt partnerships carried on 'in such manner as has been hitherto usually and may be lawfully done'. Thus between the passing of the Bubble Act and its repeal in 1825 various types of 'partnerships' were formed, particularly common was the ***deed of settlement company***, which made use of trust law. The method was for several persons to agree by deed to be associated in an enterprise with joint stock. The deed could be varied with the consent of a specified percentage of the parties to it, and management of the enterprise would be delegated to a committee. The property would be vested in trustees who could sue or be sued on behalf of the 'company'. In law however these associations were still only partnerships and the members did not have limited liability.

## 1825 UNTIL PRESENT DAY

### 7. Repeal of the Bubble Act until 1844

a. In 1825 the Bubble Act was repealed and the Crown was given the power to grant charters which declared the extent of members' liability.

b. In 1837 the *CHARTERED COMPANIES ACT* empowered the Crown to grant letters patent, ie to grant the privileges of incorporation without actually granting a charter. However such associations were not regarded as corporate bodies and although members' liability was limited any judgement against the company could be enforced against every member until 3 years after his membership had ceased.

c. In 1844 the *JOINT STOCK COMPANIES ACT* provided for the registration of companies without the need to obtain a royal charter. However it retained members' liability as described above. In addition it drew a distinction between companies and partnerships by requiring registration as companies of all partnerships with more than 25 members (now 20).

### 8. The attainment of limited liability

Between 1844 and 1855 there was great pressure for limited liability and in 1855 the *LIMITED LIABILITY ACT* was passed. This introduced (subject to several conditions) liability limited by shares, ie a member's liability was limited to the amount (if any) unpaid on his shares. This Act was repealed by the ***JOINT STOCK COMPANIES ACT 1856*** which retained limited liability, but dispensed with many of the safeguards of the 1855 Act. It also introduced the modern constitution of the company, requiring a Memorandum of Association and a set of Articles of Association.

**9. 1862 until 1985**

The ***COMPANIES ACT 1862*** was the first modern Companies Act. It contained over 200 sections and repealed and consolidated all the previous Acts. It was followed by numerous amending Acts and further consolidating Acts in 1907 and 1929. The basis for the present legislation is the Companies Act 1948. It contained over 450 sections. This Act was amended and new provisions were introduced by Companies Acts in 1967, 1976, 1980 and 1981. In addition further rules relevant to companies appeared in other Acts of Parliament, for example the European Communities Act 1972.

**10. The present legislation**

a. The confusion caused by having five major Companies Acts led to pressure for consolidation of company legislation. The consolidating legislation received the Royal Assent on 11th March 1985 and came into force on 1st July 1985. It consists of one major Act and three satellite Acts:

   i. The ***COMPANIES ACT 1985***. This is the most substantial Act ever passed. It has 747 sections and 25 schedules, but it is arranged in a very logical manner and its provisions are expressed in as straightforward language as the subject allows.

   ii. The ***COMPANY SECURITIES (INSIDER DEALING) ACT 1985***. This consolidates provisions from the Companies Act 1980. It contains 19 sections. It was amended by the ***FINANCIAL SERVICES ACT 1986***.

   iii. The ***BUSINESS NAMES ACT 1985***. This short Act (11 sections) consolidates provisions from the Companies Act 1981

   iv. The ***COMPANIES CONSOLIDATION (CONSEQUENTIAL PROVISIONS) ACT 1985***. This Act makes provision for transactional matters, savings and repeals, and the consequential amendment of other Acts.

b. The consolidation of main company legislation is supported by the consolidation and amendment of subordinate legislation. This was necessary because references to the main enactments became out of date. Six new sets of regulations came into operation on 1st July 1985. The most important of these is the ***COMPANIES (TABLES A TO F) REGULATIONS 1985***. It contains model sets of articles for companies. These were previously appended to the Companies Act 1948. The new Table A (the model form for companies limited by shares) is based on recommendations of the Law Society, and it is quite different from the Table A in the 1948 Act.

c. The next major development was the ***INSOLVENCY ACT 1985***. This made important changes to the rules concerning company liquidation and receivership. It also introduced a completely new ***administration procedure*** as an alternative to liquidation or receivership. Although the Companies Act 1985 had only been in force for a few months a number of its provisions were repealed by the Insolvency Act 1985.

d. The Insolvency Act 1985 was rapidly followed by the ***INSOLVENCY ACT 1986***. This did not change the law, it merely consolidated most of the insolvency provisions in the Companies Act 1985 and the Insolvency Act 1985, and it repealed the Insolvency Act 1985. Provisions connected with the disqualification of directors of insolvent companies are contained in a short separate Act – The ***COMPANY DIRECTORS DISQUALIFICATION ACT 1986***.

e. 1986 also saw the arrival of the ***FINANCIAL SERVICES ACT 1986***. This major Act attempts to deal comprehensively with the regulation of the investment industry. Its main impact on Company Law is in the area of share issues. Insider dealing and takeovers are also affected.

f. The **COMPANIES ACT 1989** was passed to implement the EC Seventh Directive on consolidated accounts and the Eighth Directive on the regulation and qualification of auditors. However, the Government also took the opportunity to make a number of other important changes in the law, concerning for example ultra vires, company resolutions, investigations and registration of charges.

**11. Case law developments**

Throughout the latter half of the 19th century judicial decisions played a very important part in the development of many principles of company law, for example:

a. **FOSS v HARBOTTLE (1843)** (Chapter 21.1) – Where a wrong is done to a company, the company, rather than any individual member, is the proper plaintiff in the action.

b. **ROYAL BRITISH BANK v TURQUAND (1855)** (Chapter 15.15) – When a person deals with a company in a transaction which is not inconsistent with the registered documents he can enforce the transaction against the company despite any irregularity of internal management. This has now been superceded by ***S.108 CA 89 (S35.A)***.

c. **OOREGUM GOLD MINING CO v ROPER (1892)** (now ***S.100***) – A company cannot issue shares at a discount.

d. **SALOMON v SALOMON & CO (1897)** (Chapter 5.1) which established the legality of the incorporation of small businesses where one person holds the vast majority of the shares.

The role of modern judges in the field of company law also should not be underestimated. Although company law is mainly based on statute there will always be opportunity for judicial influence on the development of company law through the interpretation of statutes.

## 12. Types of modern company

There are now three basic types of company classified according to their means of formation:

a. *Chartered companies*. A chartered company is formed by the grant of a charter by the Crown under the Royal Prerogative or under special statutory powers. This method of incorporation is no longer used by trading companies since it is far quicker and cheaper to obtain incorporation by registration. It is only used by, for example, charitable organisations, learned and artistic societies and some schools and colleges. Chartered companies include the Institute of Chartered Accountants in England and Wales, the British Broadcasting Corporation and Oxford and Cambridge Universities. In many cases the only reason for obtaining the charter has been to confer prestige on the organisation. It is possible for organisations of this type to function without a charter by vesting their property in trustees, for example the Inns of Court and The Stock Exchange. Chartered companies are relatively unimportant. In 1979 there were only 7 trading companies still operating under a charter.

b. *Statutory companies*

   i. In the past companies were incorporated by special Act of Parliament when it was necessary for them to have special powers and monopolistic rights. This was the case when the supply of public services such as gas, water, electricity and railways was left to private enterprise. After the second world war most of these statutory companies were nationalised and their functions taken over by public corporations. Recently some public services have been 'privatised' ie returned to public company status.

   ii. There are also other types of organisation which owe their existence to statute. They include building societies, friendly societies and co-operative societies.

c. *Registered companies*. The Companies Act provides for the registration of

   i. Companies limited by shares;

   ii. Companies limited by guarantee; and

   iii. Unlimited companies.

These three types are described in Chapter 7 30–32. This book is almost completely concerned with registered companies, both public and private. The brief references to chartered and statutory companies above, and to guarantee and unlimited companies in Chapter 7 reflects their lack of importance.

# 4 The Modern Company and the European Community

## INTRODUCTION

### 1. The capitalist system

The basic purpose of company law is to provide a legal framework for the operation of the capitalist system. In this system the shareholders (who are regarded as the owners of the enterprise) supply the capital, run the risk of failure, and take the profit if the enterprise is successful. The entrepreneur provides the management skills and organisation, and the employees do the work. The finance of business in a capitalist system is aided by the Stock Market, through which companies may raise capital from the public. The Stock Market also enables the capitalist to withdraw finance from an enterprise at any time and (in theory) re-invest it in a more profitable enterprise.

### 2. The mixed economy

The British economy is regulated by a combination of free market forces and varying levels of government intervention. Inevitably companies have to operate within a model of great complexity. The participants may be represented as follows:

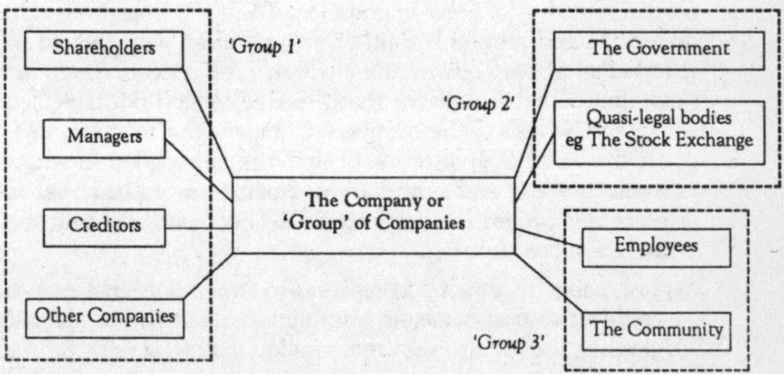


### 3. The purposes of company law

The basic purpose of all law is to classify the infinite variety of behaviour of which humans are capable into two categories – acceptable and unacceptable. (In criminal law a verdict of guilty or not guilty and in civil law a finding either for the plaintiff or for the defendant). Company law plays a part in classifying the behaviour of people when they form groups for the purpose of business. (Many other branches of law are also relevant to business activity, for example the law of partnership, taxation, advertising, cheques and employment). But the part company law plays is quite limited. Basically it is concerned with the participants in *'Group 1'*. This is evident from the following themes which dominate company law:

a. ***Majority rule and minority protection***. The basic rule of company law is majority rule. A simple majority of votes is sufficient to control the composition of the board of directors and to take most of the decisions at company meetings. A company is however a democracy, not a dictatorship and 51% do not have absolute power over 49%. Company law is constantly striving to strike a balance between the principle of majority rule and protection of the rest of the shareholders from abuse of power by the majority. Problems of this nature are most likely to occur in relatively small companies, especially family companies and quasi-partnerships.

b. ***Investor protection***. The majority of shareholders also need protecting, but not from other shareholders. Shareholders entrust the directors with responsibility for both policy decisions and day to day management of the company. In public companies directors have control over vast sums of other peoples' money. Yet it has become clear that they cannot be relied on not to abuse this trust. Thus there are many rules, statutory and otherwise, which attempt to ensure that directors do not abuse their position at the expense of shareholders in general and the creditors of the company. Problems of this kind are more likely to occur in large companies.

c. ***Creditor protection***. The position of creditors of companies has always been regarded as of great importance. The long struggle to achieve a reasonable and accessible form of incorporation with limited liability reflects Parliament's concern for creditors. The concern is well justified, since limited liability means that the creditors do not have access to the private wealth of the members. Company law therefore lays down detailed rules for the protection of creditors, although in some areas, for example holding and subsidiary companies it is clear that further protection is needed (see Chapter 5.5). There are three basic methods of creditor protection:

    i. The publicity which accompanies incorporation enables potential creditors to find out basic information about the company before granting credit, although most trade creditors do not take advantage of this opportunity.

    ii. There are many rules which protect the capital fund of the company. This is necessary because it is this fund on which the creditors rely for payment.

    iii. The rules on liquidations and receiverships allow the creditors to have a more active say in the company's affairs if their debts have not been paid, (or in some cases if they are threatened). However, unlike shareholders, creditors are not part of the company and until these times of difficulty they play no part in running the company.

d. Company law also provides the formal structure which enables a company to exist, trade, merge with, or acquire other companies and finally cease business. The government provides this structure via the Companies Act, and it is aided by bodies such as The Stock Exchange whose rules have to be observed if the company's activities come within its scope. Thus company law also strongly links the company to the participants in ***'Group 2'***.

4. Methods of achieving the purposes

The law uses two basic types of rule to achieve the above purposes.

a. ***Specific rules***. There are many rules which specify precisely what must be done in a particular situation. For example:

   i. A company must hold its first AGM within 18 months of incorporation;

   ii. The directors must call an EGM if requested to do so by holders of 10% of the paid-up voting shares;

   iii A private company's name must end with 'Limited'.

   Such rules are appropriate to define what must be done in a precise future situation. They clearly leave little scope for judicial discretion, ie Parliament basically makes the law.

b. ***General rules***. Since human behaviour is infinitely variable it is not possible to specify in advance for all situations exactly what is acceptable and unacceptable conduct. Thus many general rules exist. The best example is probably ***S.459*** (minority applications to the court in cases of ***unfair prejudice***). Such rules leave considerable scope for judicial discretion and when applying them it is generally accepted that judges make law. This shows that although company law is based on statute, judges nevertheless have considerable influence, both through the interpretation of statutes and in the traditional case law areas of company law, for example directors' fiduciary duties.

5. The position of employees

Until recently company law was almost exclusively concerned with relations between the company and its directors, shareholders and creditors. Company law was almost completely silent on the rights and interests of employees, preferring to leave 'Labour Law' as a topic quite separate from 'Company Law'. It was (and basically still is) considered that an employee's rights are governed by his contract of employment which he would either negotiate himself, or which would be determined by collective bargaining undertaken by a Trade Union. The legal position of employees has now changed in that there is some recognition of employees' interests both while the company is a going concern, and when it is in liquidation. The main provisions relating to employees are as follows:

a. **S.309** (Chapter 15.31), which requires directors to have regard to the interests of employees;

b. **S.175** (Chapter 7.26), which states that the powers of the company shall be deemed to include a power to make provision for the benefit of employees on the cessation of transfer of the whole or part of the undertaking of the company;

c. **S.175 INSOLVENCY ACT 1986** (Chapter 23.40), which states that the wages or salary of a clerk, servant, workman or labourer in respect of work done in the 4 months prior to winding-up, up to a prescribed maximum, rank as preferential debts;

d. **S.153** (Chapter 10.19), which allows for the provision by a company, in accordance with an employees' share scheme, of money for the acquisition of fully paid shares in the company;

e. The City Code on Takeovers and Mergers (which is not law, but which is complied with by companies) states as one of its general principles that directors must act on a takeover in the interest of the shareholders, employees and creditors. In addition the offer document must state the bidder's intention with regard to the continued employment of the employees of the offeree company;

f. Seventh Schedule, Paragraph 9. Where the company's average number of employees exceeds 250 the directors' report must state the company's policy as to:

   i. Employment of disabled persons,

   ii. Continued employment and training of persons who became disabled while in the company's employment and

   iii. Otherwise for the training, career development and promotion of disabled persons.

## OWNERSHIP AND CONTROL

### 6. Introduction

a. The shareholders in general meeting and the board of directors are sometimes referred to as the primary organs of the company. Company law envisages distinct roles for shareholders as owners, and for directors. The shareholders in general meeting have ultimate control through their power to appoint and remove the directors and alter the constitution and regulations of the company. The directors are entrusted with responsibility for the day-to-day management and general policy of the company and provided they do not act contrary to the law or the company's constitution their decisions cannot be set aside by the shareholders. For example:

   In SCOTT v SCOTT (1943) resolutions of the general meeting ordering the directors to pay an interim dividend were held to be void, since the power to declare dividends had been delegated to the directors by the articles and until amendment of the articles, the shareholders in general meeting could not interfere with the exercise of powers vested in the directors.

b. In small companies the major shareholders will usually be the company directors. A conflict of interest between directors and shareholders is therefore unlikely to arise. The 20th century has however been characterised by the growth of very large companies. Inevitably this has led to a separation between persons who own shares in these large companies and those who control their operations. The purpose of this section is to consider briefly whether this separation of ownership and control is important because it affects business ideology and behaviour, or whether it is unimportant because it is merely a functional division which does not have any real effect on the structure of business and society.

**7. Patterns of ownership**

a. The growth of large companies has been accompanied by wide dispersal of shareholdings. As long ago as 1932 a study showed that about half of the 200 largest companies in the USA had over 20,000 shareholders, and that as the size of company increased, the tendency to dispersal increased and the proportion of shares held by the management decreased. More recent studies have confirmed these findings.

b. In the 19th century the typical manager held a large proportion of the company's shares. Modern managers less often hold a substantial block of shares. Thus it is argued that they may have less sympathy for the shareholders' view of the company. They may be more concerned to maintain the company as a source of salary and prestige rather than as a source of dividend income, and in the event of a take-over bid they would no doubt think of their own future as well as the price offered to shareholders for their shares. Furthermore it has been argued that management is in a position to see that their view of the company prevails by ensuring that they are an independent and self-perpetuating group.

**8. Self-perpetuating management**

It has already been stated that the shareholders in general meeting have the formal power to appoint and remove the directors. A brief look at the law reveals that 50% plus 1 of the votes at a general meeting can control the composition of the entire board. However the practical reality is rather different.

The existing board will be in control of the general meeting and will almost always be able to secure a majority of votes for the following reasons:

a. The dispersal of share ownership means that a relatively small block of voting shares, if acting in a united manner, is sufficient for control. In a large quoted company as little as 5%–10% could well be adequate. The reason is that the majority of shareholders do not exercise their vote at all, and if they do they are unlikely to act in a concerted way. If they all came to the AGM they could not be accommodated. Thus as long as the controlling group acts in a concerted way an effective challenge is very unlikely.

b. Directors are able to utilise the proxy system. Until 1975 it was common practice for the directors to send to all shareholders cards offering themselves as proxies to vote in favour of the board's resolution.Now Stock Exchange regulations require the card to enable the shareholder to require the director to either vote for or against the resolution. Even so the directors can usually rely on a sufficient number of general proxies, ie authorising them to act at their discretion, to enable them to counteract any opposing group of shareholders.

c. Directors can usually ensure that there is no serious dispute over the election of new directors by arranging for outgoing directors to retire between general meetings and then using their power to co-opt new directors. In this way the members at the AGM are rarely given the opportunity to do anything except confirm a director's appointment.

**9. Motives of shareholders**

a. The shareholders are the persons who provide the capital for the enterprise. In theory the directors should conduct the company's affairs in the interest of the shareholders, ie they should attempt to maximise profit and ideally shareholders would wish the directors to maximise the company's profit. Shareholders however have no reliable measure of whether the business is maximising profit, they are not involved in making decisions and they only learn about the company's performance at a later date from the official reports of management. Shareholders are therefore generally satisfied with a steady rise in the value of their shares rather than maximum return and growth, since this will enable them to get back their investment plus a profit at any time. Provided the directors fulfil this 'satisfactory' criterion they are likely to gain the approval of most shareholders.

b. Institutional shareholders, for example pension funds, insurance companies and unit trusts hold about one half of all quoted company securities. However they see themselves primarily as investors rather than members. If they wished they could exercise considerable power at general meetings, but they do not generally choose to do so. They prefer to exercise influence by direct contact with senior management and in the event of disagreement they will generally prefer to sell rather than to fight.

**10. Motives of managers**

A main motive is likely to be the maximisation of income over their entire working life, ie not merely income from the present employer. In this context 'income' includes salary, bonus, expense account, share options and also non-monetary elements including leisure, power and status. The importance of these non-monetary elements is likely to rise as managers become more senior since they are likely to have 'enough' money. It is also relevant that a manager's income does not usually vary significantly with the firm's profits.

**11. The effect on the firm**

All large firms have a hierarchy of pyramid structure and each manager occupies a particular position in this hierarchy. Above are superiors who control salary and promotion. Below are subordinates upon whose efforts he relies to please his superiors. Beside him are peers with whom he competes for promotion. Thus managers at all levels will be very concerned to please their superiors in order to advance their own income. This may well have an effect on the performance of the firm. For example it has been argued that:

a. Some managers will tend to select policies and make decisions which will please their superiors rather than maximise ownership objectives.

b. Managers will screen information in their possession so that only data which is favourable to them is passed to their superiors. Thus at all levels of the enterprise vital information is not learned as managers are told only what it is thought they want to hear.

c. Managers at every level only carry out some of the orders given to them. They will try to avoid obeying orders which may reduce their income or status.

Of course a manager cannot go 'too far' – he would be sacked, and the senior managers can make checks, for example internal audits, independent organisation and methods studies and random inspections.

**12. The alternative view**

The discussion so far has presented some of the arguments which support the view that the separation of ownership from control is significant because it has had an effect on business ideology and behaviour. There are also strong arguments in favour of the view that the divorce of ownership from control is merely a functional division which has had no real effect on business. For example:

a. Although senior managers only hold a small proportion of the total shares in the company, their holding often comprises a large proportion of their personal wealth and may make a major contribution to their income. Thus they will not pursue policies detrimental to business ownership.

b. Even if senior managers do not possess significant shareholdings they will probably share similar aspirations and values with the large shareholders, because they are likely to have a similar social background and the same attitude to property and profit.

### 13. Counterveiling power

It is also clear that there are external restraints on business power. The term 'counterveiling powers' was first used to describe these restraints by J.K. Galbraith. They include:

a. Legal and quasi-legal restrictions, for example:
   i. Declaration of financial information;
   ii. Audit of company accounts;
   iii. Stipulation of shareholders' rights;
   iv. **S.309** which requires directors to have regard to the interests of employees;
   v. Rules imposed by The Stock Exchange;
   vi. The City Code on Take-Overs and Mergers;
   vii. Customary business rules.

b. The power of organised labour; and

c. The power of the government, working through such agencies as the Monopolies Commission and the Director General of Fair Trading.

### 14. Conclusion

It is difficult to reach a conclusion on the above discussion. In his book 'The Business Enterprise in Modern Society' John Child, after looking in detail at evidence for both sides, favours the view that the separation of ownership from control is primarily a functional division rather than a cause of changing business ideology and behaviour. Nevertheless the development of large companies has brought about a change in the traditional relationship between a person and his property. The modern shareholder has relinquished control over his property, he has ceased to bear any resemblance to the members of a partnership and has become a mere supplier of capital. Owners of other types of property retain a direct relationship with that property. In contrast owners of shares in large companies allow their property to be managed by other persons.

## COMPANY LAW HARMONISATION

### 15. The European Community and the Single Market

a. The European Economic Community was set up in 1957, the United Kingdom becoming a member on 1st January 1973. In all there are three European Communities to which all 12 member states belong.
   i. The European Coal and Steel Community (ECSC) set up in 1951.
   ii. The European Economic Community (EEC) set up in 1957.
   iii. The European Atomic Energy Community (EURATOM) also founded in 1957.

The term ***'Economic Community'*** (EC) is used to describe the three communities together.

b. The object of creating a common market goes back to the Treaty of Rome in 1957 which established the EEC. However, in 1985 EC Heads of Government committed themselves to establishing progressively a single market over a period expiring on 31st December 1992. This committment has been included in a package of treaty reforms known as the ***SINGLE EUROPEAN ACT 1986 (SEA)***. This Act, which came into operation on 1st July 1987 defines a single market as ***'an area without internal frontiers in which the free movement of goods, persons, services and capital is ensured in accordance with the provisions of this Treaty'***.

The Act will assist the free movement of goods by breaking down technical barriers (for example differing national product standards) national restrictions, subsidy policies and so on. The SEA also speeds up EC decision making by extending majority voting to most major areas of the single market programme. This replaces the unanimous voting requirements which applied before the Act came into force.

**16. Community institutions**

a. ***The Commission***

i. The Commission proposes EC policy and legislation. It executes decisions taken by the Council and supervises the day to day running of community policies.

ii. There are 17 Commissioners appointed by member state governments. Two each from France, Federal Republic of Germany, Italy, Spain and the UK, one each from Belgium, Denmark, Greece, Ireland, Luxemberg, the Netherlands and Portugal. Commissioners are not appointed as national delegates, but act in the interests of the Community as a whole. Each Commissioner is in charge of an area of Community policy and formulates proposals within that area aimed at implementing the treaties.

b. ***The Council***

i. The Council is the Community's decision making body. It agrees legislation on the basis of proposals put forward by the Commission.

ii. Each Council meeting will deal with a particular area of policy, for example agriculture, finance or industry and will be attended by the relevant Minister from each member state.

iii. There are three methods of decision making (a) unanimity (b) simple majority voting i.e. at least seven member states in favour, and (c) qualified majority (weighted) voting based on the relative population of member states. Most single market proposals are subject to qualified majority voting.

c. ***The European Parliament***

i. This directly elected body has 518 members, 81 from the UK. It has consultative and advisory functions.

ii. Most single market proposals are subject to the new co-operation procedure introduced by the SEA. This enables the Parliament to give an opinion when the Commission makes a proposal and again when the Council has reached agreement in principle,(known as a 'Common Position').

d. ***The Court of Justice***

This rules on the interpretation and applicability of Community Laws. It has 13 judges including one from each member state. Its judgments are binding in each member state.

**17. Types of community legislation**

In general legislative power rests with the Council, however, in many cases the Council delegates power to the Commission. Under the treaties the Council and Commission may make regulations, issue directives and take decisions.

a. ***Regulations***

These are binding in their entirety and will apply in all member states without the need for legislation by national parliaments. If there is a conflict between a regulation and national law, the regulation prevails.

b. ***Directives***

Unlike regulations, directives do not have immediate binding force in all member states. They are addressed to member states requiring the national parliament to make whatever changes are necessary to implement the directive within a specified time.

c. ***Decisions***

These may be addressed to either a member state or to an individual or institution. They are a formal method of communicating policy decisions and they are binding on those to whom they are addressed.

**18. The legislative process**

a. Community legislation is the result of lengthy and complex negotiations and consultations involving several Council and Commission working parties and other committees provided for by the treaties.

b. Briefly the procedure is for the Commission to discuss the proposal with officials from member states and other interested parties before adopting it as a formal proposal. It is then submitted to the Council and the European Parliament. Parliament may give an opinion and depending on the article of the treaty on which the proposal is based, the Council can either adopt the proposal or agree a common position by qualified majority voting. In the latter case the European Parliament may give a second opinion before the proposal is returned to the Council to be finally adopted. Most company law measures are adopted as directives.

**19. Company law directives which have been implemented**

a. The following directives, previously contained in earlier legislation, are now found in CA 1985.

i. ***First Directive*** (1968) on co-ordination of safeguards required by companies, including amendments to the ultra vires rule.

ii. ***Second Directive*** (1976) concerning the maintenance and alteration of public company capital.

iii. ***Fourth Directive*** (1978) dealing with company accounts.

b. Two directives have recently been implemented by the Companies Act 1989.

i. ***Seventh Directive*** (1983) on consolidated accounts.

ii. ***Eighth Directive*** (1984) laying down audit regulations and minimum qualifications for auditors.

c. Several other directives on mergers and divisions, prospectuses, admission of securities to listing and disclosure of information have been implemented through delegated legislation, principally the ***Companies (Mergers and Divisions) Regulations 1987*** and ***The Stock Exchange (Listing) Regulations 1984***.

**20. Directives adopted by the council**

There are five directives awaiting implementation. Two concern banks and credit institutions and one concerns recognition of professional qualifications. The other two are more relevant.

a. One requires persons who own shares in listed EC companies to disclose their holdings when they reach any of five thresholds (10%, 20%, 33⅓%, 50% and 66⅔%). This will require only minor amendments to UK law. The directive must be implemented by 1st January 1991.

b. The other will require a prospectus containing specified information to be published when securities are offered to the public for the first time. This is similar to existing UK law. Implementation is required by 17th April 1991.

**21. Directives on which a common position has been agreed**

a. The proposed ***Eleventh Directive*** deals with disclosures to be made in a member state by branches of companies registered in another member state or non-EC country.

b. The proposed ***Twelfth Directive*** would make a more fundamental change to UK Company Law. It requires member states to allow private limited companies to have a single member who could be either a natural or legal person. The purpose is to encourage the development of small enterprises by providing entrepreneurs with a business form that gives limited liability without the need to resort to the use of nominee shareholders.

c. Proposed Directive Co-ordinating Regulations on Insider Dealing. This requires member states to make insider dealing unlawful and to co-operate in obtaining and exchanging information about it for enforcement purposes. The directive will require UK legislation to cover gilts and local authority securities in addition to company securities.

**22. Formal draft proposals**

a. Proposed ***Fifth Directive*** on structure and management of public companies. This was originally drafted in 1972 and an amended proposal was issued in 1983. Discussion is expected to continue for several years. It applies to all public limited companies. The proposal offers member states two options for a board structure: a single board with a majority of non executive directors, or two separate boards, for management and for supervision. The directive also requires employee participation in company decision making where the company employs more than 1,000 people in the community, either directly or in subsidiaries. This participation would be achieved in one of the following ways

   i. Through board representation of employees at the supervisory level on a one or two tier board

   ii. By means of a Works Council

   iii. Through collective agreement giving at least the same rights to employees as (i) or (ii) above.

   The current Conservative Government is opposed to the introduction of compulsory measures of employee involvement, believing that voluntary involvement would be preferable. Many trade unions also do not welcome the proposals, preferring to trust the existing trade union machinery.

b. Proposed Directive on Procedures for Informing and Consulting Employees ('Vredeling' Directive). This provides for employees to be given substantial information on the business as a whole and specific information on their own subsidiary. It also requires management to consult employee representatives (with a view to reaching agreement) on decisions likely to have serious consequences for employees' interests.

c. Proposed ***Thirteenth Directive*** on Take-Over Bids. This requires any bid that would take the shareholding over 33⅓% to be for all the shares in the company. It also regulates the trading and other conduct of directors while the outcome of the bid is awaited.

d. Proposal for ***European Company Statute***. This measure will allow two or more companies based in at least two member states to merge to form a European company. A European company would operate under the provisions of the Statute which would cover most areas of company law. The proposal offers two options for board structure, as outlined in a. above. It also makes provision for compulsory employee participation.

e. There are several other draft directives covering for example insurance companies, company accounts and listing particulars.

# PART II INCORPORATION

# 5 The Consequences of Incorporation

## LEGAL PERSONALITY

### 1. A separate legal entity

a. The most important consequence of incorporation is that a company becomes a legal person distinct from its members.

In SALOMON v SALOMON & CO (1897) S formed a limited company with the other members of his family, and sold his business to the company for £39,000. He held 20,001 of the 20,007 shares which had been issued by the company, and £10,000 of debentures (documents acknowledging that S was a secured lender entitled to priority of repayment in a liquidation). The balance was payable in cash. About a year after its formation the company was wound-up. The assets at that time were just sufficient to discharge the debentures, but nothing was left for unsecured creditors with debts of about £7,500. The creditors claimed that they should have priority because S and the company were in effect the same person. The House of Lords however held that S and the company were separate legal entities, the company had been validly formed, and there was no fraud on the members or creditors. S was therefore entitled to the remaining assets.

b. Note that:

i. This case was very important because it finally established the legality of the 'one-man' company and showed that incorporation was available to small businesses as well as to large enterprises.

ii. It caused concern because it showed that it was possible to limit liability not merely to the money put into the company, but to avoid serious risk to some of that money by subscribing for debentures rather than shares. The decision has been criticised this reason, but it can be justified on the grounds that persons who deal with a limited company know the risks, although it is not usually practical to take all the available precautions, such as a search of the company's file at the Companies Registry.

c. The fact that a company is a separate legal entity from its members is not necessarily wholly beneficial to those members. For example if a trader sells his business to a company he will cease to have an insurable interest in its assets though he owns most of the shares.

In MACAURA v NORTHERN ASSURANCE (1925) M owned a timber estate. He formed a limited company and sold the timber estate to it. Like Salomon he was basically a 'one-man company'. Before he sold the estate to the company it had been insured in his own name.

After the sale to the company he neglected to transfer the insurance policy to the company. The estate was destroyed by fire. It was held that M could not claim under the policy because the assets that were damaged belonged to a different person, namely the company, and M, as a shareholder, had no insurable interest in the assets of the company.

d. The effects of separate corporate personality are further illustrated by the following cases.

In **ATTORNEY-GENERAL'S REFERENCE (No. 2 of 1982)** the respondents were accused of theft. They had appropriated for their own private purposes funds of various companies of which they were the sole shareholders and directors. Each acted with the consent of the other. Their defence was that they had appropriated their own property. The Court of Appeal held that even persons in total control of a company were capable of stealing its property. Furthermore it was not rational to treat the accused as having transmitted their knowledge to the company, so as to regard the company as having consented to the appropriation, in fact the company should be regarded as the victim of the crime.

In **HENRY BROWN v SMITH (1964)** a firm of yacht outfitters sold a steering system to Smith, however the written order for the goods was in the name of Smith's company, Ocean Charters Ltd. The company only had an issued capital of £2 and it failed to pay for the system. The plaintiff's action against Smith failed because they had clearly accepted that Ocean Charters Ltd was their customer and it was up to them to check the financial status of the company.

## 2. Other consequences of incorporation

The following consequences of incorporation all flow from the fundamental consequence of separate legal personality:

a. ***Limited liability***. The members are not liable for the company's debts. However complete absence of liability is not permitted. Each member is liable to contribute, if called upon to do so, the full nominal value of his shares so far as this has not already been paid. If he has agreed to pay more than the nominal value then his liability is limited to the amount he has agreed to pay.

b. ***Property***. An important advantage of incorporation is that the property of the company is distinguished from that of its members. In contrast the property of a partnership is jointly owned by the partners. This can cause problems when defining the true nature of the interests of the partners, which will be necessary when a partner retires. There is no similar problem when the membership of a company changes since the members do not have any direct rights to the property of the company, they only have a right to their shares. Thus when shares are transferred the company's property remains unaffected.

c. ***Contractual capacity***. The question of contractual capacity is closely related to that of property ownership. Companies have contractual capacity and can sue and be sued on their contracts.

d. ***Perpetual succession***. The continuity of the company is not affected by the death or incapacity of some or all of its members.

e. ***Transferable membership***. Incorporation greatly facilitates the transfer of members' interests. Shares are items of property which are freely transferable provided the constitution of the company does not contain an express provision to the contrary.

f. ***Increased borrowing powers***. It is logical to assume that sole traders or partnerships would find it easier to borrow money because of their personal liability. This is not the case since a company can give as security a floating charge. This is not available to a sole trader or partnership. A floating charge is a mortgage over the constantly fluctuating assets of a company. It does not prevent the company dealing with these assets in the ordinary course of business. Such a charge is very useful when a company has no fixed assets such as land which can be included in a normal mortgage, but nevertheless has a large and valuable stock-in-trade.

3. Companies and partnerships compared

a. ***Unincorporated associations and partnerships***

i. Unincorporated associations consist of a number of persons who have come together for a matter of common interest, for example a sports club, a trade union or a partnership.

ii. A partnership is defined by the **PARTNERSHIP ACT 1890** as 'relation which subsists between persons carrying on a business in common with a view to profit'. 'Business' includes any trade, occupation or profession.

b. ***The main differences between companies and partnerships***

i. A company is created by registration under the **COMPANIES ACT 1985**. A partnership is created by the express or implied agreement of the partners, no special form being required, although writing is usually used.

ii. A company incurs greater expenses at formation, throughout its life, and on dissolution, although the fees are not excessive.

iii. A company is an artificial legal person with perpetual succession. It may own property, make contracts, and sue and be sued. It has a legal personality distinct from its members. In contrast a partnership is not a separate legal person, although it may sue and be sued in the firm's name. The partners own the property of the firm and are liable on its contracts.

iv. Shares in a public company are freely transferable, whereas a partner cannot transfer his share without the consent of all of his partners. He may assign the right to his share of the profits, but the assignee does not become a partner

v. A company must have at least 2 members and there is no upper limit on membership. A partnership must not consist of more than 20 persons although there are some exceptions, for example solicitors, accountants, auctioneers and estate agents.

vi. Members of a company may not take part in its management unless they become directors, whereas all partners are entitled to share in management, unless the partnership agreement provides otherwise.

vii. A member of a company is not an agent of the company, and he therefore cannot bind the company by his acts. A partner is an agent of the firm, therefore it will be bound by his acts.

viii. The liability of a member of a company may be limited by shares or by guarantee. The liability of a general partner is unlimited, although it is possible for one or more partners to limit their liability provided there remains at least one general partner. The advantage of limited liability is unlikely to be real for many small companies since lenders will usually require a personal guarantee of their loan from the directors and/or majority shareholders.

ix. The powers and duties of a company are closely regulated by the Companies Acts, its constitution is specified in its Memorandum of Association, and its internal regulations are contained in its Articles of Association (although both can be freely altered by special resolution). In contrast, partners have more freedom to carry on any business they wish and to make their own arrangements with regard to the running of the firm.

x. A company must comply with more formalities, for example certain registers must be maintained and the accounts must (except for certain dormant companies) be audited annually.

xi. Greater publicity must be given to the affairs of a company, for example to its directorate, its financial position and to charges on its assets.

xii. Company law requires maintenance of issued capital through the rule that dividends may only be declared out of profits. Partners' drawings of profit and capital are a matter of agreement.

c. ***The similarity between companies and partnerships***. The main similarity is that both companies and partnerships are methods of carrying on business. Many companies are of course large and impersonal, having many institutional shareholders. Such companies bear little resemblance to partnerships. Small private companies are however often founded on the same basis as partnerships, ie a relationship of mutual trust and confidence.

d. **Conclusion**. Despite the greater degree of legal regulation affecting the registered company, it is undeniable that the advantages of incorporation – separate legal personality, limited liability, transferability of shares, and possible tax advantages have induced many partners and sole traders to convert their businesses into corporate form. However partnership remains important, and in many cases mutual trust and confidence are more highly regarded than the benefits of incorporation. Thus, subject to a few exceptions, partnership is the compulsory form of association for many professional persons, for example solicitors. This preserves the principle of individual professional accountability towards the client, a policy central to professional ethics.

e. ***Partnership companies***. As part of the Government's policy to encourage wider individual share ownership, it has introduced legislation making it easier to set up partnership companies. ***S.128* CA 89 *(S.8A)*** defines a partnership company as 'a company limited by shares whose shares are intended to be held to a substantial extent by or on behalf of its employees'. The Act allows the Secretary of State to prescribe, by regulations, a model set of articles appropriate for partnership companies, known as Table G.

## 'LIFTING THE VEIL'

### 4. The veil of incorporation

The fact that the separate corporate personality of a company prevents outsiders from taking action against its members, (even though the outsider can find out who they are and how many shares they hold), has led to comparison with a veil. The corporate personality is the veil, and the members are shielded behind this 'veil of incorporation'. However the internal affairs of the company are never completely concealed from view since publicity has always accompanied incorporation. In addition there are several situations when the law is prepared to lift the veil of incorporation either to go behind the corporate personality to the individual members, or to ignore the separate personality of several companies in a group in favour of the economic entity constituted by the group as a whole.

### 5. Examples of 'lifting the veil'

a. ***If the company is being used to enable a person to evade his legal obligations***

In GILFORD MOTOR CO v HORNE (1933) an employee covenanted that after the termination of his employment he would not solicit his former employer's customers. Soon after the termination of his employment he formed a company, which then sent out circulars to the customers of his former employer. The Court lifted the veil of incorporation, granting an injunction which prevented both the former employee and his company from distributing the circulars even though the company was not a party to the covenant.

b. ***If the controllers of the company are alien enemies***

In **DAIMLER v CONTINENTAL TYRE AND RUBBER CO (1916)** the respondent sued Daimler for money due in respect of goods supplied. Daimler's defence was that since Continental Tyre's members and officers were German, to pay the debt would be to trade with the enemy. Despite the fact that Continental Tyre was a company registered in England the defence succeeded.

c. ***Fraudulent or wrongful trading***

   i. By ***S.213 IA*** if in the course of winding-up it appears that business has been carried on with intent to defraud creditors, the persons responsible may be made personally liable to make such contribution to the company's assets as the court thinks proper.

   ii. A more useful provision is ***S.214 IA*** which enables the liquidator of an insolvent company to apply to the court to declare that a director be personally liable to contribute to the company's assets. Before making the order the court will have to be satisfied that the director knew or ought to have concluded that there was no reasonable prospect of avoiding insolvent liquidation and that he failed to take every step to minimise the creditors' loss.

d. ***Reduction in the number of members***

   i. By ***S.24*** if a company carries on business without having at least 2 members for more than 6 months, any person who is a member and knows of this irregularity shall be liable for the debts of the company contracted after the 6 months have expired.

   ii. This could arise where a company has 2 members and when one of them dies his executors fail to register themselves as members. Although this has happened on several occasions it seems that the section has never been invoked. It can in any case easily be avoided by the transfer of one share to a nominee during the 6 month period. ***S.24*** therefore is of little practical importance.

e. ***Holding and subsidiary companies***

   i. The most significant inroads to the concept of separate corporate personality have concerned holding and subsidiary companies. For certain purposes, in particular the presentation of financial statements, the companies in a group must be treated as one.

   ii. In several cases the courts have recognised the fact that a holding company and its subsidiaries are often a single commercial enterprise. For example

In **DHN FOOD DISTRIBUTORS v TOWER HAMLETS LBC (1976)** DHN ran its business through two wholly owned subsidiaries.

One of the subsidiaries owned the premises from which business was conducted, and the other dealt with distribution of the group's goods. The council then compulsorily purchased the premises. This caused all three companies to go into liquidation because they could not find suitable alternative premises. It was held that for the purpose of the acquisition the three companies should be treated as one, the 'one' being the holding company. This decision meant that the group as a whole was entitled to an award of compensation for disturbance to business in addition to compensation for the value of the land. It also established that a holding company is entitled to compensation on the acquisition of land held by its wholly owned subsidiary.

iii. It may be argued that further protection is necessary for the creditors of companies comprised in a group. In particular should a holding company be liable for the debts of its wholly-owned subsidiary. The Cork Committee on Insolvency Law and Practice in its report, published in June 1982, concluded that the matter was 'of such importance and of such gravity that there should be the widest possible review of the different considerations, with a view to the introduction of reforming legislation within the foreseeable future'.

The Cork Committee unfortunately did not propose a solution to the problem, although other countries have been able to find one. For example in New Zealand the court may hold a 'related company' liable for the debts of a failed company if it is just and equitable to do so.

iv. It must be emphasised that there is nothing improper in the separation of a group into distinct companies. It may be the best arrangement when the enterprise carries on a number of different businesses, or if it wishes to distinguish between the manufacturing and selling parts of the same business.

f. There are many more examples of lifting the veil, both case law and statutory. The tendency to lift the veil has increased in recent years. For example.

In GOODWIN v BIRMINGHAM CITY FOOTBALL CLUB (1980) a football club manager formed a company (Freddie Goodwin Ltd) and supplied his services to it. The company made a five year contract with the club to supply Mr Goodwin' s services to it. After three years the club broke the contract, but Mr Goodwin soon found another job at a higher salary. His company then sued the club for breach of contract. The action was successful, but the court only awarded nominal damages of £10. The reason was that because Mr Goodwin had mitigated his loss, and the company's only asset was its contract with Mr Goodwin, then the company must be regarded as having mitigated its loss, ie the company and Mr Goodwin were treated as being one person.

# PUBLIC AND PRIVATE COMPANIES

## 6. Public companies

a. ***Definition***. By ***S.1*** a public company must:

   i. Be registered as a public company;

   ii. Have at least two members; and

   iii. State in its memorandum that it is a public company.

b. Public companies are subject to many provisions which do not apply to private companies, in particular with respect to capital, payment for shares and dividends. These provisions are outlined in 8. below and are dealt with in detail at appropriate points in the text.

c. The number of differences now means that it is generally advantageous to register as a private company. The only advantage of a public company is the ability to issue shares and debentures to the public. This is of course a very significant advantage..

## 7. Private companies

a. ***Definition***. By ***S.1*** a private company is any company which is not a public company. Such companies may have any number of members as long as there are at least two members.

b. In order that a private company remains under the control of the 'family' or 'partners' concerned, the articles will contain a clause restricting the right to transfer shares, even though such a restriction is no longer required by statute. Such a restriction is generally regarded as an advantage of a private company. However it would be a disadvantage to an individual member who wished to sell his shares, but was unable to find an acceptable buyer.

c. The restriction is likely to be either:

   i. A power vested in the directors to refuse to register a transfer; or

   ii. A right of pre-emption (first refusal) granted to existing members when another member wishes to transfer his shares (Chapter 12.25).

d. It is important to distinguish pre-emption rights granted by the articles on the transfer of existing shares from the pre-emption rights granted by ***S.89–96*** on the issue of new shares.

## 8. Differences between public and private companies

***THE COMPANIES ACT 1980*** removed most of the small insignificant differences between public and private companies, for example as to the minimum number of members, and the number of members necessary for a quorum at meetings. It also widened the substantive differences between them. There follows a list of the main differences. This is included at this point for the sake of completeness. It will however be much easier to understand if it is referred to again at the end of your course. In each case where a fact is stated in respect of one type of company, by implication the reverse is true of the other type of company.

a. ***Memorandum and articles***
   i. The memorandum of a public company must state that the company is a public company. ***(S.1)***.
   ii. The name of a public company (clause one of the memorandum) must end with the words 'public limited company'. A private company's name must end with the word 'limited'. ***(S.25)***.
   iii. Only private companies limited by guarantee and private companies allowed to dispense with the word 'limited' by virtue of a licence granted under **S.19. CA 1948** qualify to apply for exemption from the requirement that 'limited' shall be the last word of their name. ***(S.30)***.
   iv. Only a private company can convert to an unlimited company. ***(S.49)***.
   v. The statutory pre-emption rights (ie new shares must first be offered to existing members) can be excluded by the memorandum or articles of a private company. ***(S.91)***.
   vi. To retain the private nature of a private company its articles will restrict the right to transfer its shares.

b. ***Share capital***
   i. A private company must not apply for its shares to be listed on The Stock Exchange ***(S.143 FINANCIAL SERVICES ACT 1986)***.
   ii. A private company must not issue any advertisement offering its shares for sale ***(S.170 FINANCIAL SERVICES ACT 1986)***.
   iii. A public company must have an allotted capital with a nominal value of at least £50,000 ***(S.11)***. There is no minimum capital requirement for a private company.
   iv. The directors of a public company must convene an extraordinary general meeting if the company's net assets fall to half or less of its called-up share capital. ***(S.142)***.
   v. A public company is subject to restrictions in respect of a lien or charge on its own shares. ***(S.150)***.
   vi. The restrictions in **S.151** relating to a company giving financial assistance for the purchase of its own shares are relaxed in respect of private companies. ***(S.155)***.
   vii. The resolution authorising a public company to purchase its own shares must specify a date (not later than 18 months after passing the resolution) on which the authority is to expire. ***(S.164)***.
   viii. The disclosure requirements connected with a purchase by a company of its own shares are more stringent in the case of public companies. ***(S.169)***.

ix. Subject to conditions, a private company may redeem or purchase its own shares out of capital. ***(S.171–177)***.

c. ***Payment for shares***

i. A public company must not accept as payment for its shares an undertaking to do work or perform services for the company. ***(S.99)***.

ii. A public company's shares must be paid up to the extent of 25% of the nominal value plus the whole of any premium. ***(S.101)***.

There is no minimum payment requirement for a private company.

iii. Where the shares of a public company are to be paid for by the transfer to the company of a non-cash asset, the asset must be transferred to the company within 5 years of the allotment. ***(S.102)***.

iv. In the case of a public company such an asset must be independently valued by an expert and a report made to the company. ***(S.103)***.

v. A public company cannot acquire non-cash assets from subscribers to the memorandum in the two years following registration unless such assets are independently valued by an expert and a report made to the company. ***(S.104)***.

vi. The subscribers to the memorandum of a public company must pay cash for shares taken in pursurance of an undertaking in the memorandum. ***(S.106)***.

d. ***Disclosure of interests in shares***. The rules in **PART VI** only apply to public companies. The main provisions relate to:

i. Disclosure of interests in voting shares. ***(S.198–210*** and ***S.134 CA 89))***.

ii. The register of interests in shares. ***(S.211)***.

iii. The investigation by a company of interests in its shares. ***(S.212-218)***.

e. ***Dividends***

i. A public company must file with the registrar interim accounts to support any proposed interim dividend. ***(S.272)***.

ii. A public company must not declare a dividend if its net assets are less than the aggregate of its called-up share capital and undistributable reserves. ***(S.264)***.

f. ***Directors and the secretary***

i. A public company must have at least two directors. A private company need only have one director. (S.282).

ii. In a public company two or more directors cannot be appointed by a single resolution. ***(S.292)***.

iii. There is no statutory age limit on directors of a private company, unless the company is a subsidiary of a public company. A director of a public company must (subject to exceptions) retire at 70. ***(S.293)***.

iv. A life director of a private company holding office on 18th July 1945 cannot be removed by an ordinary resolution. ***(S.14 COMPANIES CONSOLIDATION (CONSEQUENTIAL PROVISIONS) ACT 1985)***.

v. A private company which is not in the same group as a public company may make quasi-loans to its directors. Such a company may also enter into credit transactions with its directors, and may make loans to persons connected with its directors. ***(S.330)***.

vi. The secretary of a public company must have the requisite knowledge and experience or certain specified qualifications. ***(S.286)***.

g. ***Trading***. A public company must obtain a certificate of compliance with the capital requirements of the Act before it can commence trading. ***(S.117)***.

h. ***Meetings***. A proxy may speak at a meeting of a private company. ***(S.372)***.

i. ***Accounts***

i. The period for laying and delivering the annual accounts of a public company is seven months after the end of the accounting reference period. In the case of a private company the period is ten months. ***(S.11 CA 89 (S.244))***.

ii. The accounting records of a public company must be preserved for six years, whereas the accounting records of a private company need only be preserved for three years. ***(S.2 CA 89 (S.222))***.

iii. A private company which is not in the same group as a public company may be entitled to the accounting exemptions relating to small and medium-sized companies. ***(S.13 CA 89 (S.247))***.

iv. A private company which qualifies as a 'small' company and which is dormant is relieved from the requirement to have its accounts audited if a special resolution of the shareholders so resolves. ***(S.14 CA 89 (S.250))***.

j. ***Written resolutions***. Anything which may be done by resolution of a private company in general meeting may be done by a written resolution signed by or on behalf of all members ***(S.113 CA 89 (S.381A))***.

k. ***Elective resolutions***. A private company may pass an elective resolution (this must be agreed by all members entitled to attend and vote at the meeting) if it wishes:

i. To extend the duration of directors' authority to allot shares

ii. To dispense with the requirement to lay accounts and reports before the company in general meeting.

iii. To dispense with the requirement to hold an AGM.

iv. To dispense with the requirement to appoint auditors annually.

v. To reduce the majority required to consent to the holding of a general meeting at short notice. ***(S.115–119 CA 89)***.

**9. Listed companies**

A public company may obtain a Stock Exchange listing by complying with the listing rules issued by The Stock Exchange under powers given in ***PART IV FINANCIAL SERVICES ACT 1986*** (Chapter 9). The rules also impose continuing obligations for listed companies. For example a listed company must notify The Stock Exchange of substantial realisations or acquisitions of assets, changes in its directors and changes in the general character of its business. The Stock Exchange requirements are not 'law', but a company in breach may be removed from the Official List.

**10. The Unlisted Securities Market and the Third Market**

a. Since 1980 it has been possible for a public company to obtain a different type of quotation. In 1980 The Stock Exchange established the ***Unlisted Securities Market*** (USM) to accommodate smaller companies and companies with a shorter trading period. The rules for admission are not as strict as for an official listing, for example the proportion of shares released to the market need only be 10% as opposed to 25%.

b. In 1987 The Stock Exchange opened the ***Third Market*** for dealings in company securities. However, as part of the European harmonisation programme, the International Stock Exchange decided that, from 31st December 1989, there would be no further entries to the Third Market. It is expected that those companies quoted there will move up to the USM. Entry onto the USM will in future be based on two year accounts instead of three, but no arrangements have been made for companies with only a one year record. Previously the Third Market had catered for such companies.

## REGISTRATION PROCEDURE

**11. The functions of the registrar of companies**

a. The registrar is an official of the Department of Trade. His basic functions are:

i. To issue certificates of incorporation and change of name;

ii. To be responsible for the registration and safe custody of documents required by statute to be filed with him and to pursue companies which fail to comply with such requirements;

iii. To issue certificates of registration of mortgages and charges;

iv. To provide facilities for the examination of filed documents by members of the public (the current search fee is £1) and to give copies of documents or certificates on payment of a fee;

v. At the conclusion of the winding-up of a company the registrar will complete final dissolution by striking the company off the register.

b. In addition

i. By **S.705** the registrar must allocate a number (which may include a letter) to all companies and corporate bodies within the meaning of the 1985 Act.

ii. By **S.709** a member of the public is only allowed to inspect a copy of the documents kept by the registrar, not the originals.

iii. By ***S.125 CA 89 (S.706)*** all documents delivered to the registrar must meet any requirements specified by the registrar in order to allow them to be read and copied. They must also show prominently the registered number of the company.

iv. By ***S.126 CA 89 (S.707A)*** the registrar may keep the information in whatever form he thinks fit, as long as it is possible to inspect the information and produce copies. The original documents must be kept for at least ten years, after which they are destroyed.

**12. Registration of new companies**

a. By **S.10**, to obtain registration the promoters must deliver to the registrar:

i. Memorandum of Association;

ii. Articles of Association;

iii. A statement containing the name, address, nationality, business occupation, other directorships and age of each person who is to be a first director or the secretary of the company. The statement must contain the signed consent of each person named to act. When the company is incorporated they are deemed to be appointed ***(S.13)***;

iv. Address of the registered office;

v. A Statement of Capital, the purpose of which is to bear the stamp which evidences payment of the required capital duty;

vi. A Declaration of Compliance, made by the solicitor engaged in the formation, or a person named as director or secretary, stating that the requirements of the Act have been complied with.

vii. Registration fee.

b. The registrar could rely on the declaration of compliance, but in practice his staff check that the documents are formally in order and that the name and objects are legal. If satisfied the registrar will issue a certificate of incorporation and publish a notice in the London Gazette that it has been issued.

## 13. Certificate of incorporation

a. The certificate of incorporation refers to the company by name. It is often described as the 'birth certificate' of the company, although in the case of a public company the ***S.117*** certificate is more accurately its birth certificate. The certificate of incorporation of a public company must state that it is a public company.

b. By ***S.13*** the certificate of incorporation is conclusive evidence that the formalities of registration have been complied with. This means that even if it is subsequently discovered that the formalities of registration were not in fact complied with, the registration will not be invalidated. The reason for this is that once a company has commenced business and entered into contracts it would be unreasonable for either side to be able to avoid the contract because of a procedural defect in the registration of the company.

## 14. Oversea companies

a. An oversea company is one incorporated outside Great Britain which establishes a place of business in Great Britain ***(S.744)***.

b. Various provisions of the Companies Act apply to oversea companies. The most important are:

i. ***Registration***. Within one month of establishing a place of business in Britain the company must deliver to the registrar a copy of its constitutional documents, particulars of its directors and secretary, and the name and address of at least one person resident in Great Britain authorised to accept service of formal documents. These details must be kept up to date.

ii. ***Accounts***. A balance sheet, profit and loss account and, if it is a holding company, group accounts, must be filed each year.

iii. ***Name***. The name must be exhibited at every place of business and on all its letters, invoices etc. The company cannot use a name which would be precluded from being registered in Great Britain.

iv. ***Prospectus***. Any prospectus issued must comply with special rules.

v. ***Charges***. In **SLAVENBERG'S BANK v INTERCONTINENTAL NATURAL RESOURCES (1980)** it was held that the registration of charges provisions applied to foreign companies with an established place of business in Great Britain, whether or not they had registered as an oversea company. The 1989 Act has now made it clear that charges are only registerable under the 1985 Act. Thus an unregistered oversea company which has created a charge over assets in Great Britain will be unable to register particulars and persons dealing with such companies will not be able to ascertain whether assets situated in Great Britain are charged. Previously, as a result of the above case, the registrar maintained the 'Slavenberg Index' containing such information. This is now abolished.

**15. Re-registration of a private company as public**

a. ***The contents of the resolution***. By ***S.43*** the company must pass a ***special resolution*** that it should be re-registered as public. The special resolution must:

   i. Alter the company's memorandum so that it states that the company is to be a public company;

   ii. Make any other necessary changes to the memorandum, for example changing the name of the company so that it ends with 'Public Limited Company'; and

   iii. Make the necessary changes to the articles, for example by removing any restriction on the right to transfer shares.

b. ***Documents to accompany the application***. An application to re-register must then be sent to the registrar. This must be signed by a director or the secretary and must be accompanied by:

   i. A printed copy of the new memorandum and articles;

   ii. A written statement by the auditors that in their opinion the relevant balance sheet shows that, at the balance sheet date, the net assets were not less than the aggregate of called-up capital plus undistributable reserves. For this purpose ***'relevant balance sheet'*** means a balance sheet prepared as at a date not more than 7 months before the application to re-register;

   iii. A copy of the relevant balance sheet, plus a copy of an unqualified auditors' report on the balance sheet;

   iv. A copy of any report made in respect of valuation of non-cash consideration for the allotment of shares, (see d. below);

   v. A statutory declaration, signed by a director or secretary stating that the required special resolution has been passed and stating that the requirements as to share capital, (see c. below) and as to the valuation of non-cash consideration, have been complied with. The statutory declaration must also state that between the balance sheet date and the application date the net assets have not fallen to less than the aggregate of called-up share capital and undistributable reserves.

c. ***Compliance with capital requirements***. The new public company must comply with the appropriate requirements as to share capital. In addition by ***S.45***.

   i. Where any of the shares or any premium payable on them have been treated as either fully or partly paid up by an undertaking of a person to do work or perform services for the company the undertaking must have been performed;

ii. Where any of the shares were allotted as fully or partly paid up for a consideration consisting of an undertaking to transfer an asset, that undertaking must have been performed. Alternatively there must be a contract requiring performance within 5 years.

These conditions are necessary because of the rules in **S.99** (Chapter 10.7)and **S.102** (Chapter 10.10)which only apply to public companies.

d. ***Compliance with asset valuation requirements***. By **S.44** where, between the balance sheet date and the date of the special resolution, shares are allotted for a consideration other than cash, the company may not apply to re-register as public unless:

i. The consideration has been independently valued in accordance with **S.103** (Chapter 10.10); and

ii. A report has been made as to its value in accordance with those provisions in the 6 months prior to allotment. (This is to prevent a private company evading rules which apply to a public company by carrying out the relevant transaction immediately before re-registration).

e. ***The certificate of incorporation***. When the registrar is satisfied that all the conditions have been complied with he will issue a certificate of incorporation stating that the company is to be a public company. This gives immediate effect to the alterations made to the memorandum and articles by the special resolution and it is conclusive evidence that the requirements of the Act have been complied with and that the company is a public company.

## 16. Public company to re-register as private

a. ***The contents of the resolution***. By **S.53** the company must pass a ***special resolution*** that it should be re-registered as private.

The special resolution must:

i. Alter the company's memorandum, in particular it must no longer state that the company is to be a public company. The name clause must also be changed;

ii. Alter the company's articles, probably to include a restriction on the right to transfer shares.

b. ***The application***. This must be signed by a director or the secretary and sent to the registrar with a printed copy of the new memorandum and articles.

c. ***Cancellation period***. The period for making an application to the court to cancel the resolution must have expired without any application having been made, (see 17 below). Alternatively if an application was made it must have been withdrawn or the court must have made an order confirming the resolution and a copy of the order must have been delivered to the registrar.

d. ***The certificate of incorporation***. When the registrar is satisfied that all the conditions have been complied with he will issue a new certificate of incorporation appropriate for a private company. This gives immediate effect to the alterations to the memorandum and articles and is conclusive evidence that the company is private and that the requirements of the Act have been complied with.

**17. Rights of a minority when a company resolves to become private**

a. By **S.54** within 28 days of the resolution an application to court to cancel the resolution may be made by either:

   i. Holders of not less than 5% in nominal value of the company's issued shares or any class thereof; or

   ii. Not less than 50 of the company's members.

b. When an application has been made the company must give notice to the registrar. The company must also deliver to him, within 15 days, a copy of any order made by the court.

c. Where an application has been made the court must make an order confirming or cancelling the resolution. It may however impose such terms or conditions as it thinks fit; for example:

   i. It may adjourn proceedings to allow time for dissentient members' interests to be purchased, if necessary, by the company itself; or

   ii. It may make an order requiring the company not to alter its memorandum or articles, or requiring that a specific alteration be made. The company then could not make any alterations unless it had the permission of the court.

**18. Provisions relating to a reduction of capital**

a. By **S.139** if the court makes an order under **S.135** (Chapter 10.14) that confirms the reduction of capital of a public company and the reduction brings the nominal value of the issued share capital below the authorised minimum, the registrar may register the order only after the company has been re-registered as private.

b. The court may dispense with the need for a special resolution to re-register. Consequently the court (rather than the resolution) must specify the changes to be made to the company's memorandum and articles.

## PROGRESS TEST 1

1. What is the effect of the certificate of incorporation?
2. Name two methods by which a private company may restrict the right to transfer its shares.
3. What is the minimum allotted capital of a public company?
4. A director must also be a shareholder. True or False?
5. ABC Ltd has 3 members – X, Y and Z. They are also its directors. A few months ago X and Y were killed in a car accident. Z has continued to run the company but, lacking financial expertise, he has incurred losses and fears the company must be wound up. He has heard that he may be in danger of becoming personally liable for the company's debts. Advise Z.

# 6 Promotion

## PROMOTERS

### 1. Definition

a. Although the Companies Acts contain many references to promoters they do not provide a statutory definition. The best known definition was given by Cockburn C.J. in **TWYCROSS v GRANT (1877)**. He defined a promoter as

> 'one who undertakes to form a company with reference to a given project, and to set it going, and who takes the necessary steps to accomplish that purpose'.

b. A person who assists a promoter in a paid professional capacity, for example a solicitor or accountant, is not deemed to be a promoter.

c. A promoter is therefore any person involved in the planning, incorporation, or initial running of a company, other than persons involved in a purely professional capacity. A promoter need not necessarily be the main person behind the incorporation, but he must have some executive function. The stereotype of a promoter may well be a city businessman, but any small trader who forms a company and sells his business to it is also a promoter.

### 2. Duties of promoters

a. In the 19th century there existed a few disreputable professional promoters who would form bogus companies, and sell the shares in them to the public, for their own profit and to the public detriment. Such figures are now extinct because the law is more rigorous and because public issues are conducted through the large issuing houses and are closely scrutinised by The Stock Exchange.

b. The duties of promoters are contained in case law rather than statute. This probably reflects the lack of serious problems compared with, for example, directors. The courts have however been conscious of the possibility of abuse of trust by promoters and have therefore established the principle that a promoter stands in a ***fiduciary relationship*** with the company which he is forming. This does not mean that he is barred from making a profit out of the promotion. It means that any profit he does make must be ***disclosed*** to the company.

c. The difficulty was to decide how disclosure should be made to an artificial entity.

   i. In **ERLANGER v NEW SOMBRERO PHOSPHATE CO (1878)** it was suggested that disclosure must be made to an independent board of directors who would assess whether or not the profit was reasonable.

ii. This rule was obviously impractical since in most cases the promoters would also be the first directors, and therefore the board would not be independent.

iii. Thus since **SALOMON v SALOMON & CO (1897)** it has been clear that disclosure to the members is adequate. 'Members' however includes potential members, ie the promoter cannot form a company and sell his own land to it at a vast profit, disclosing this only to a few of his associates who constitute the initial members, and then float off the company to the public. If the company is to be sold to the public the promoter's profit must be disclosed to potential members in the prospectus. Thus, knowing what proportion of the price of their shares will go to the promoters, the public are adequately informed when making the decision of whether or not to purchase the shares.

**3. Remedies for breach of duty**

In the event of non-disclosure of profits the company may commence proceedings for rescission or for recovery of the undisclosed profits.

a. The right to rescind is exercised on the usual contractual principles. Therefore:

i. The company must have done nothing to ratify the agreement after finding out about the non-disclosure or misrepresentation; and

ii. Restitution must be possible. – In fact the court can order financial adjustments to be made when ordering rescission, so the restitution rule rarely operates as any real restraint. This is particularly useful if it is the fraudulent promoter, in his capacity as director, who has been responsible for the transactions which have made restitution impossible.

b. If the contract is rescinded the promoter's secret profit will normally disappear as a result. If however he has made a profit on some ancilliary transaction this may also be claimed by the company.

c. A secret profit may be recovered even if the company elects not to rescind.

In **GLUCKSTEIN v BARNES (1900)** G and 3 others formed a syndicate. Their purpose was to buy Olympia, (which was owned by a company which was in liquidation), and sell it to a company which they were about to promote. They first purchased at a discount charges (mortgages) on Olympia, and then purchased the freehold for £140,000. Next they promoted and registered their company, becoming its first directors. This company then purchased Olympia from them for £180,000, the money being raised by a public issue of shares. In the meantime they had had the charges on the property repaid out of the £140,000 sale proceeds, making a further profit of £20,000. In the prospectus for the public issue the £40,000 profit on the sale of Olympia was disclosed, but the £20,000 profit on the other transaction was not mentioned. This was discovered four years later when the company went into liquidation, and the liquidator (Barnes) was successful in his attempt to recover the £20,000 from G and other members of the syndicate.

d. The company may sue the promoter for damages under the **MIS-REPRESENTATION ACT 1967**, or for negligence, or for fraud. This will be useful if rescission is barred.

e. In addition to the remedies of the company the promoter may be liable to a subscriber if he was party to a false statement in listing particulars or in a prospectus.

**4. Criminal liability**

A promoter commits a criminal offence if he is party to an untrue statement in listing particulars or in a prospectus.

**5. Payment for promotion**

a. Promoters are not entitled to payment because
   i. Before incorporation the company cannot contract to pay them since it does not exist; and
   ii. After incorporation any such contract would be void since the consideration would be past.

b. However the articles will provide that 'the business of the company shall be managed by the directors who may exercise all the powers of the company' (Table A Article 70). The directors may therefore pay the promoters their expenses. In practice there will be few problems since the promoters will normally be the first directors.

c. Another method of payment would be for the promoter to sell property to the company at an over-valuation (the difference being his ('payment'). This would be acceptable provided all the disclosure requirements are satisfied.

## PRE-INCORPORATION CONTRACTS

**6. The effect on the company**

a. A contract made on behalf of a company before its incorporation does not bind the company, nor can it be enforced or ratified by the company after incorporation.

In KELNER v BAXTER (1866) a company was about to be formed to buy an hotel. Before the company was formed the promoters signed a contract 'on behalf of' the proposed company for the purchase of a quantity of wine. The company was formed, the hotel purchased, and the wine was delivered and consumed, but before payment was made the company went into liquidation. It was held that the promoters were personally liable to pay for the wine, any purported ratification by the company being ineffective.

b. Therefore any pre-incorporation agreements will either have to be binding in honour only, or the promoter will have to undertake personal liability.

   i. Where a small trader sells his business to a company of which he is promoter, director and majority shareholder clearly no binding agreements are necessary.

   ii. If however the promoters are arranging for the company to acquire someone else's business, or if the promoters are purchasing goods for the new company, the seller will require a binding contract.

**7. The effect on the person who purports to contract on behalf of the company**

a. By **S.130 CA 89 (S.36C)** where a contract purports to be made by a company, or by a person as agent for a company, at a time when the company has not been formed, then subject to any agreement to the contrary the contract has effect as one entered into by the person purporting to act for the company or as agent for it, and he is personally liable on the contract accordingly.

b. In the past there has been some doubt as to the position of a person who signs not as an agent, but merely as purporting to authenticate the signature of the company. At common law this is most unlikely to place personal liability on the signer **(NEWBORNE v SENSOLID (1954))**. However it is now clear that **S.36C** abolishes the distinction between signature as an agent and a signature authenticating the signature of the company. In Lord Denning's words the distinction has been 'obliterated'.

   In **PHONOGRAM v LANE (1981)** Lane intended to form a company 'Fragile Management Ltd' to manage a new pop group. Before the company was formed he signed a contract 'for and on behalf of Fragile Management Ltd'. Under the contract Lane received an advance payment of £6,000 which was re-payable if a recording contract was not entered into within one month. In fact Fragile Management was never formed and no recording contract was made. Phonogram sued for the return of the £6,000. Lane's main defences were:

   i. The words 'subject to any agreement to the contrary' exempt a person who by signing as an agent expresses an agreement that he will not be personally liable.

   ii. The word 'purports' implies that the company already exists, so the sub-section does not apply where the parties know that the company has not yet been formed.

   The Court of Appeal rejected these arguments and held Lane liable despite the fact that at common law his signature could be regarded as mere authentication of a corporate signature.

c. It has already been noted that **S.36C** provides for an express agreement to the contrary. The Act does not however envisage an agreement whereby the promoter incurs no liability and cannot enforce the contract since such an agreement would be invalid for lack of consideration. The Act envisages that the promoter protects himself by:

i. Agreeing that the promoters' liability shall cease when the company, after incorporation, enters into a similar agreement; or

ii. Agreeing that if the company does not enter into such an agreement within a fixed period either party may rescind.

**8. Contracts made by a public company before the issue of a certificate under *S.117***

a. It has already been stated that a public company may not commence business until it has obtained a certificate of compliance with the capital requirements of public companies.

b. If a public company does business in contravention of this section the transaction will be valid, but if the company fails to comply with its obligations within 21 days of being called upon to do so, the directors are liable to indemnify the other party if he suffers loss due to the company's failure to comply. This is an example of 'lifting the veil' of incorporation. In addition the company and its officers may be fined.

**9. Execution of documents by companies**

a. Prior to 1989 a document was executed by affixing the company seal and adding the signature of two directors or one director and the secretary.

b. By *S.130 CA 89 (S.36A)* there is now no requirement for a company to have a seal. A document will be executed if signed by two directors or a director and the secretary, provided it is expressed to be executed by the company. This new provision relieves companies of the obligation to use seals, it does not prohibit them from continuing as before.

## *PROGRESS TEST 2*

1. What are the main charges which must be made in the memorandum and articles of a company that changes from private to public?
2. What is the maximum number of partners in a trading partnership?
3. What type of resolution is needed to:

   (a) Remove a director;

   (b) Ratify a pre-incorporation contract;

   (c) Re-register a private company as public?
4. What are the consequences of a public company commencing trading before the issue of a certificate under *S.117* CA?
5. How may a promoter protect himself from the personal liability imposed by *S.36C* CA?

# 7 The Memorandum of Association

## INTRODUCTION

**1. Memorandum and articles**

The regulations of every company will be contained in two separate documents:

a. The ***memorandum*** sets out its basic constitution and presents the company to the outside world.

b. The ***articles*** deal with matters of internal administration.

**2. Contents of the memorandum**

a. ***Every company*** memorandum must contain the following six clauses:

i. Name;

ii. Registered Office;

iii. Objects;

iv. Limitation of Liability;

v. Capital; and

vi. Association.

b. In addition the memorandum of every ***public company*** must state that 'The company is to be a public company'.

## THE NAME CLAUSE

**3. Basic rules**

a. By ***S.25(2)*** the last word of a private company's name must be 'Limited'. This warns persons who deal with companies that they will not have access to the private funds of the members to satisfy their debts. 'Limited' may be abbreviated to 'Ltd'. A partnership name must not end with the word 'Limited'.

b. By ***S.25(1)*** a public company's name must end with the words 'Public Limited Company' or the abbreviation 'P.L.C.'

**4. Power to dispense with the word 'Limited' *(S.30)***

a. ***Companies entitled to apply for exemption***. Only the following types of company may apply to be registered with a name which does not include the word 'limited':

i. Private companies limited by guarantee; and

ii. Companies which on 25th February 1982 were private companies whose names did not, by virtue of a licence granted under **S.19. CA 1948** (which contained similar provisions but is now repealed) include the word 'limited'

Thus entirely new applications will only be considered for private companies limited by guarantee.

b. ***Requirements for exemption***. A company is only entitled to the exemption if its objects are the promotion of commerce, art, science, education, religion, charity or any profession or anything incidental or conducive to any of those objects, ***and*** its memorandum or articles:

i. Require its profits or other income to be applied in promoting its objects; and

ii. Prohibit the payment of dividends; and

iii. Require all the assets which would otherwise be available to its members to be transferred on winding up either to another body with objects similar to its own, or to another body whose objects are the promotion of charity or anything incidental or conducive thereto.

c. The registrar may refuse to grant exemption unless a ***statutory declaration*** is delivered to him stating that the company is one to which **S.30** applies. The declaration must be made by a director or secretary or a solicitor engaged in the formation of the company.

d. If **S.30** is contravened by an exempt company the Secretary of State may direct the company to change its name, by resolution of the board of directors, to one ending with 'limited'. A copy of the resolution must be delivered to the registrar and the company may not, in future, be registered with a name which does not include 'limited' without the approval of the Secretary of State.

e. A company granted exemption under **S.30** is also exempt from the requirements of **S.348** and **S.349** (see 8. below) which relate to the publication of names. However by **S.351** exempt companies must still state the fact that they are limited on all business letters and order forms.

**5. Prohibition on registration of certain names (*S.26*)**

a. A company may not be registered with a name:

i. Which includes any of the following (or abbreviations thereof) ***other than*** at the end of the name: 'limited', 'unlimited' or 'public limited company';

ii. Which is the same (disregarding minor differences, see b. below) as a name already appearing in the index kept by the registrar (see 6. below);

   iii. The use of which would, in the opinion of the Secretary of State, constitute a criminal offence; ***or***

   iv. Which in the opinion of the Secretary of State is offensive.

b. When determining, for the purpose of a.ii. above whether one name is ***'the same'*** as another 'and' and '&' shall be taken to be the same and the following minor differences shall be disregarded:

   i. The word ***'The'*** where it is the first word in the name. For example 'The Bagshot Buckshot Company Limited' is ***the same*** as 'Bagshot Buckshot Company Limited';

   ii. The following words and expressions (and abbreviations thereof) appearing at the end of the name: 'company', 'and company', 'company limited', 'and company limited', 'limited', 'unlimited', 'public limited company'. For example 'Bagshot Buckshot Company Limited' is ***the same*** as 'Bagshot Buckshot Limited' or 'Bagshot Buckshot and Company Limited';

   iii. Type and case of letters, spaces between letters, accents and punctuation marks.

c. In addition to the above restrictions a company may not, without the approval of the Secretary of State, be registered with a name which:

   i. Would be likely to give the impression that the company is in any way connected with the Government or with a local authority; or

   ii. Includes any word or expression specified in any statutory instrument which may be issued under the provisions of the Act.

**6. Index of company names**

By ***S.714*** the registrar must keep an index of the names of the following bodies:

a. Limited and unlimited companies registered under the Companies Act;

b. Overseas companies, ie companies incorporated outside Great Britain, but which have established a place of business in Great Britain;

c. Limited partnerships; and

d. Certain other types of corporation, for example industrial and provident societies.

**7. Change of name *(S.28)***

a. Subject to the restrictions in ***S.26*** a company may change its name by ***special resolution***. A new certificate of incorporation will be issued and the change is effective from the date of that certificate.

b. If a company is registered after the Act comes into force with a name which:

   i. Is the same as or, in the opinion of the Secretary of State, is too like a name which was already in the index; or

ii. Is the same as or, in the opinion of the Secretary of State, is too like a name which should have appeared in the index at the time of registration;

then the Secretary of State may, within 12 months, direct the company to change its name within such period as he may specify.

c. The Secretary of State may, within 5 years of registration, direct a company to change its name within such a period as he may specify if the company has provided misleading information for the purposes of registration or has given undertakings which have not been fulfilled.

d. By **S.32** a company must change its name if at any time the Secretary of State orders it to do so because it is so misleading as to be likely to cause harm to the public.

e. The court may also order a change of name following a successful 'passing off' action.

In **EWING v BUTTERCUP MARGARINE CO (1917)** E, whose business was called 'The Buttercup Dairy Company' was successful in his attempt to prevent a newly registered company from using the name 'Buttercup Margarine Company' because it was considered that the public might think that the two businesses were connected.

In the above case the key word was 'buttercup', a word which had been used outside its usual context. Where a company uses a word in its correct context as part of its name it cannot usually prevent another company from using that word.

In **AERATORS LTD v TOLLITT (1902)** the plaintiffs were unable to prevent the registration of a company called Automatic Aerators Patents Ltd because the word 'aerator' was a word in common use and had not been taken out of context.

**8. Publication of name and address**

a. Every company (except those exempted under **S.30**) must publish its name:

i. Outside all its places of business ***(S.348)***;

ii. On all letters, orders, invoices, notices, cheques and receipts ***(S.349)***; and

iii. On its seal, if it has a seal (**S.350** as amended).

b. If a company does not comply with the above requirements, the company and every officer in default are liable to a fine. In addition if an officer or other person issues or signs any company letters, orders, cheques, etc which do not bear the full name of the company he may be fined and he will be liable to any creditor who has relied on the document if the company fails to pay him.

In **PENROSE v MARTYR (1858)** a bill was drawn on a limited company which was described on the bill as 'The Saltash Waterman's Steam Packet Company, Saltash'. The bill was accepted by the company secretary who used the words 'Accepted, John Martyr, Secy to the sd Coy'. The bill was dishonoured and it was held that the secretary was personally liable since the company's correct name had not been mentioned on the bill in that there was no indication that it was a limited liability company.

c. By ***S.351*** a company must, on its business letters and order forms, state:

   i. The company's place of registration, ie whether its registered office is situated in England or Scotland. Thus a person who receives a letter from the company will know whether, if he wishes to make a search, the file is in Cardiff (if the company is registered in England (which includes Wales)) or Scotland. Microfiche copies of files held in Cardiff are available for inspection in London.

   ii. The address of the registered office; and

   iii. The number under which the company is filed at the registry.

## BUSINESS NAMES

### 9. Introduction

Most companies, partnerships and sole traders trade under their own names, but sometimes they prefer to use another name. This is known as a business name. Until 1981 business names were registered at a Registry of Business Names, established by an Act in 1916. The Companies Act 1981 abolished the Registry of Business Names and introduced a new framework based on self regulation. The current rules on business names are not in the Companies Act 1985, but in a separate ***BUSINESS NAMES ACT 1985 (BNA)***.

### 10. Persons to whom the rules apply

a. By ***S.1 BNA 1985*** the rules described below apply to persons carrying on a business in Great Britain under a name which does not consist of:

   i. In the case of an individual, his surname;

   ii. In the case of a partnership, the surnames of all partners who are individuals and the corporate names of all partners who are corporate bodies;

   iii. In the case of a company, its corporate name.

b. Certain additions are permitted:

   i. In the case of an individual his forename or initial;

   ii. Where two or more partners have the same surname, the addition of 's' at the end of that surname;

iii. In any case an addition merely indicating that the business is carried on in succession to a former owner.

c. Certain names require the approval of the Secretary of State, ie any name which:

i. Would be likely to give the impression that the business is connected with the Government or a local authority, or

ii. Includes any word or expression specified in any statutory instrument which may be issued under the provisions of the Act. **(S.2)**.

**11. Disclosure requirements**

By ***S.4(1) BNA*** a person to whom the rules apply must:

a. State legibly on all business letters, order forms, invoices, demands for payment and receipts:

i. In the case of a partnership, the name of each partner. Note the exemption for partnerships of more than 20 persons (see 12. below);

ii. In the case of an individual, his name;

iii. In the case of a company, its corporate name; ***and***

iv. For each person named, an address in Great Britain at which service of documents relating to the business will be effective;

b. In any premises to which suppliers or customers have access, display prominently a notice containing the names and addresses referred to in a. in a place where it may easily be read; ***and***

c. Supply in writing the names and addresses referred to in a. to any person with whom anything is done or discussed in the course of business and who asks for such details.

**12. Partnerships of more than 20 persons**

By ***S.4(3) BNA*** such partnerships need not list the names and addresses of all the partners on the business stationery provided a list of their names is kept at the principal place of business. However:

a. The list of names and addresses may not be omitted from any business document which contains the name of any partner otherwise than in the text or as a signatory; ***and***

b. The stationery must state legibly the address of the partnership's principal place of business and that the list of partners' names is open to inspection there. Any person may inspect the list during office hours.

**13. Non-compliance**

Failure to comply with the above requirements is a criminal offence for which the guilty parties may be fined. In addition by **S.5 BNA** legal proceedings brought to enforce a business contract may be dismissed if:

a. The plaintiff was in breach of the disclosure requirements with respect to that business at the time the contract was made; ***and***

b. The defendant shows that:

   i. He has been unable to pursue a claim against the plaintiff arising out of the contract because of that breach; or

   ii. He has suffered financial loss in connection with the contract because of that breach;

unless the court is satisfied that it would be just and equitable to enforce the contract.

## THE REGISTERED OFFICE

### 14. The registered office clause

This clause does not state the address of the registered office, it merely states that the registered office will be situated in England and Wales (or Wales alone if it is to be a Welsh company) or Scotland, thus fixing the nationality and domicile of the company.

### 15. The purpose of the registered office

a. The registered office is the official address of the company. It is also the place where writs, notices and other communications can be served, and where certain registers and documents are usually kept. It need not be a place of business of the company, in fact many companies arrange for the premises of their solicitors or accountants to be their registered office.

b. The ***COUNTY COURT (AMENDMENT) RULES 1989*** now enable a person who wishes to commence proceedings against a company in a County Court to serve a summons at a local place of business of a company. It is no longer necessary for the plaintiff to ascertain the address of the registered office.

### 16. Documents and registers kept at the registered office

The following documents and registers are usually kept at the registered office, and must be kept there unless otherwise stated:

a. The register of members, unless it is made up elsewhere in which case it can be kept where it is made up.

b. The register of directors and secretaries.

c. The register of directors' interests in shares and debentures. If the register of members is not kept at the registered office, the register of directors' interests may be kept with the register of members.

d. The register of debenture holders. If the register is made up elsewhere it may be kept where it is made up.

e. The register of charges.

f. Copies of instruments creating the charges.

g. The minute book of general meetings.

h. Directors' service contracts. These may instead be kept at the principal place of business.

i. The minute book of directors' meetings. This may be kept at any convenient place.

j. The accounting records. These may also be kept at any convenient place.

k. A copy of any contract for an off-market purchase, market purchase or contingent purchase by a company of its own shares (or if the contract is not in writing, a written memorandum of its terms) must be kept for 10 years from the date of completion of the purchase.

l. A ***public company*** must keep a register of interests in shares. The level at which a holding becomes notifiable is 3%. This register must be kept with the register of directors' interests.

**17. Rights of inspection of documents and registers**

The above registers and documents with the exception of d. and f. are the statutory books, ie the registers and documents which every company is required to keep by law. They are subject to the following rights of inspection:

a. Members may inspect all except i. and j. free of charge.

b. Creditors may inspect e. and f. free of charge.

c. Debenture holders may inspect d. free of charge.

d. Directors may inspect all of the documents and registers.

e. The public may inspect a., b., c., d., e., and l. on payment of a small fee. They may inspect k. only if the company is a public company.

**18. Change of address *S.136 CA 89 (S.287)***

a. The company cannot change the clause in the memorandum which states the country in which the registered office will be situated. It may however move the registered office within that country. This change of address is effected by ordinary resolution, or if there is authority in the articles, by a resolution of the board of directors.

b. The change in the registered office will take effect from the time that notice of the fact has been delivered to the registrar and entered on the register. Thus a person can at all times determine the whereabouts of the company's registered office. However, for 14 days following the date of registration a person may validly serve any document on the company at its previous registered office.

c. The company is also allowed 14 days from the date of the change (ie the date of registration of the change) to move its registers to the new registered office. Similarly if it is necessary to move registers quickly and it has not been practicable to give prior notice, no offence will be committed as long as notice of the change is given to the registrar within 14 days.

## THE OBJECTS CLAUSE

### 19. The purposes of the objects clause

*S.2* requires every company to state its objects. This defines and limits its permissible activities. Originally the objects clause served two purposes:

a. Prospective members were told what kind of business they were investing in; and

b. Creditors were able to ensure that the funds from which they could expect payment were not used for unauthorised activities.

### 20. Introduction to the 1989 Act

a. Prior to 1989 the basic rule was that an act outside the objects clause was ***ultra vires*** and void and therefore could not be enforced by the company or by an outsider. This was unpopular with companies (for whom it could be inconvenient to have restricted powers) and outsiders (who might find that their contract could not be enforced). This was generally the case even if the outsider did not actually know of the restriction on the company's power, because of the doctrine of ***constructive notice***, by which everyone was deemed to know of the contents of the company's registered documents.

b. Companies therefore sought to avoid the ultra vires rule by drafting lengthy objects clauses (30–40 paragraphs) allowing them to do almost anything they could ever wish to do. They also usually included general powers allowing anything incidental to any of their other objects and powers. The effect of the ultra vires rule was further restricted by **S.35 CA 85** (now repealed) which stated that if an outsider dealt with the company in good faith, any transaction decided on by the directors would be deemed to be within the company's capacity, regardless of any limitations in the memorandum or articles.

c. In 1985 the DTI commissioned a report from Dr Dan Prentice of Oxford University to advise on the implications of abolishing the ultra vires rule. His report recommended complete abolition. The Government has taken the view that total abolition would be undesirable. The 1989 Act has therefore abolished the application of ultra vires in respect of outsiders, but retained the power of members to bring proceedings to restrain ultra vires acts. This ensures that commercial transactions cannot be set aside once they have been entered into, but retains some members' rights.

d. The 1989 Act basically deals with 4 issues.

   i. Drafting the company's memorandum so as to widen its capacity

   ii. The protection of outsiders entering into contracts with the company

   iii. The ability of members to restrain ultra vires acts

   iv. The powers of directors to bind the company and restrictions on their powers (see chapter 15.14)

**21. Statement of objects in memorandum**

a. By ***S.110 CA 89 (S.3A)*** it will be sufficient for the memorandum to state that the object of the company is to carry on business as a general commercial company. This will allow the company

   i. To carry on any trade or business whatsoever and

   ii. To do all such things as are incidental or conducive to the carrying on of any trade or business by it.

b. This new provision should relieve companies of the need to draft long objects clauses. However it is not clear that such a short statement will be sufficient for all purposes, for example it is not clear whether it will cover all types of gifts by companies, or the disposal of a business by general commercial company.

c. Where a company does adopt such a clause the effect will be to virtually abolish the ultra vires rule for internal purposes (see 23 below), the Act having already abolished it so far as outsiders are concerned.

**22. Validity of acts done by companies**

a. By ***S.108 CA 89 (S.35(1))*** the validity of an act done by a company shall not be called into question on the ground of lack of capacity by reason of anything in the company's memorandum.

b. Consequently a ***completed act*** will have ***total protection*** from the ultra vires rule and will be ***enforceable*** by both the company and an outsider.

**23. Members' right to restrain ultra vires acts**

a. By ***S.108 CA 89 (S.35(2))*** any member may bring proceedings to restrain an intended act which would be beyond the capacity of the company. However this right is restricted in that if a company is required to carry out an ultra vires act in pursuance of a legal obligation arising from a previous act of the company, the company may proceed and members cannot bring proceedings to restrain that act.

b. The right of members to restrain ultra vires acts is restricted by a new rule in ***S.108 CA 89 (S35(3))*** which allows the company to ratify an ultra vires act by ***special resolution***.

c. If the company fails to ratify, a completed act will still be valid. However the Act preserves the right of members to sue directors in respect of liability incurred in relation to that act, but the company may pass a further ***special resolution*** for the purpose of relieving the directors of such liability.

**24. Constructive notice**

a. ***S.108 CA 89 (S.35B)*** makes it clear that an outsider is not bound to enquire as to whether an act is permitted by the memorandum or subject to any limitations on the authority of the directors.

b. This reform has clear implications for the doctrine of constructive notice by which persons were deemed to have knowledge of the details of registered documents.

c. Thus to ensure that the reforms are co-ordinated ***S.142 CA 89 (S.711A)*** has abolished the doctrine of constructive notice for almost all purposes. The exception is ***S.103 CA 89 (S.416)*** under which a person taking a charge over a company's property is deemed to have notice of any matter requiring registration and disclosed on the register of charges at the time the charge was created.

d. ***S.142 CA 89*** also provides that a person cannot rely on the fact that he did not have notice of certain matters if he failed to make such enquiries as should reasonably have been made in the circumstances. However, the circumstances when it would be reasonable for a person not to inspect documents are not clear.

**25. The power to make gifts**

Despite the new legislation the question of gifts by companies may still give rise to problems. Gifts fall into several different categories.

a. ***Political and charitable donations***

Provided the company is a going concern and provided the directors make the donation in what they consider to be the best interests of the company the court is unlikely to regard the gift as ultra vires.

In **EVANS v BRUNNER MOND (1921)** a chemical manufacturing company made gifts of £100,000 to universities and research institutions for the furtherance of scientific education and research'. The company had no express power to make gifts, but its objects clause did authorise anything' incidental or conducive to the attainment of the above objects'. It was held that since the company would benefit generally from scientific progress the gift was intra vires.

Contrast **SIMMONDS v HEFFER (1983)** where The League Against Cruel Sports (a company limited by guarantee) made a donation, of £50,000 to the Labour Party. The League's main object was to prevent cruelty to animals, it also had a general clause similar to the clause in Evans' case. It was held that the payment was ultra vires because it was not restricted by reference to the League's aims, and the aims of the Labour Party extended far beyond the aims of the League. The general clause did not remove the restriction implicit in the main object that money could not be spent for a purpose not mentioned therein.

***Note:*** Another payment of £30,000 was held to be intra vires because it was made on condition that it was applied to publicise the Labour Party manifesto commitment to animal welfare.

b. ***Gifts to former directors or their dependents***
   i. In **RE LEE BEHRANS (1932)** it was held that even an express power to grant pensions to dependents of former directors was ineffective since it was not for the benefit of the company.
   ii. Although there is some slight doubt, it now seems that such payments will be ultra vires.

   In **RE HORSLEY and WEIGHT (1982)** a company granted a pension to a retiring director. The director had no contractual right to a pension but the objects empowered the company to grant pensions to employees and directors. It also stated that every clause was an independent main object. The pension was upheld, the court taking the view that the paragraph relating to pensions was not a mere power, but it stated a main object of the company. As such it did not have to be exercised for the benefit of the company.

c. ***Provision for employees on the cessation or transfer of the business***
   i. In **PARKE v DAILY NEWS (1962)** it was held that such payments (basically redundancy payments) were ultra vires since they were not for the benefit of the company.
   ii. PARKE's case was overruled by **S.719**, which provides that the powers of a company are deemed to include the power to make provision for employees on the cessation or transfer of the whole or part of the business of the company. It is considered in paragraph 26 below.

d. ***Commercial guarantees***. The 'benefit of the company' test has also been criticised in cases concerning guarantees.

   In **CHARTERBRIDGE CORPORATION v LLOYDS BANK (1970)** a company which was a member of a group of associated companies had an express power to enter into guarantees. It guaranteed a loan made by Lloyds to the main company in the group. The guarantee was supported by a charge on its property. Charterbridge had agreed to buy this property, but did not want to take it subject to the charge. They therefore disputed its validity. It was held that the charge was valid. One of the reasons for the decision was that the charge was for the benefit of the company since it helped the group as a whole. It was therefore not necessary to comment on the Re Lee Behrans decision. The judge nevertheless made an obiter dicta statement that when considering whether the exercise of an express power is ultra vires it is irrelevant to enquire whether it is for the benefit of and to promote the prosperity of the company.

In ROLLED STEEL PRODUCTS v BRITISH STEEL CORPORATION (1986), the facts were very complex. Basically RSP guaranteed a debt due from a company controlled by one of RSP's directors to BSC. The guarantee was not for the purposes of, nor for the benefit of RSP, the main purpose being to assist the financial position of the director in question. The objects clause of RSP contained a power (not an object) to give guarantees, furthermore BSC knew of the improper purpose. Nevertheless it was held that since the guarantee could have been within the objects clause it was not ultra vires.

e. *Bribes*

In **HANNIBAL v FROST (1987)** a company claimed £34,000 from its managing director, claiming that he had wrongfully converted it to his own use. The director's defence was that the money had been used to pay bribes to obtain work for the company. The Court of Appeal accepted that the money had been used in this way, but held that it was certainly beyond a director's authority and probably ultra vires. Judgement was given for the company.

f. *Conclusion*

i. If the gift is complete it cannot be set aside **S.108 CA 89** (22 above).

ii. If a member challenges an incomplete gift and the company has adopted the objects of a general commercial company, it is not clear whether all types of gift will be covered or whether the 'benefit of the company' test will be applied in any situations.

iii. If a member challenges an incomplete gift and the company has a long and detailed objects clause, it is not clear how the rules of construction will be applied. The courts may make a distinction between substantive objects and powers (as in some previous cases) and hold that objects need not be exercised for the benefit of the company, whereas powers must be. Alternatively the courts may adopt the method used in **ROLLED STEEL PRODUCTS v BRITISH STEEL CORPORATION (1986)** and regard the matter as a question of the authority of the directors, rather than the capacity of the company.

## 26. Power to provide for employees on cessation or transfer of a business (*S.187 IA* and *S.719*)

a. *Basic rule*

i. By **S.719** the powers of the company shall be deemed to include a power to provide for the present or former employees of the company, or those of any of its subsidiaries, on the cessation or transfer of the whole or any part of its undertaking or that of any subsidiary.

ii. **S.719** therefore overrules **PARKE v DAILY NEWS (1962)** but neither it nor **S.309** (Chapter 15.31) force the directors or members to do any particular beneficial act in favour of the employees.

**S.719** merely gives the company the right to take action which may well be regarded as good business practice, but which would have been ultra vires prior to 1980.

b. ***Other rules***

i. The company may exercise the power conferred by **S.719** even though its exercise is not in the best interests of the company.

ii. The power may be exercised by passing an ordinary resolution or if the memorandum or articles so require, a directors' resolution or a special resolution.

iii. Any payment made prior to the start of liquidation may only be made out of profits available for distribution.

iv. If, after deciding to make a provision for employees, the company goes into liquidation the position will not be affected since the liquidator may make the payment. In the case of a compulsory winding-up the exercise of the power is subject to the control of the court ***(S.187 IA)***.

v. If winding-up has already started a provision for employees may still be made, (but not on the authority of a directors' resolution since their powers have ceased).

vi. The liquidator can only make the payment out of the assets which are available for members ***(S.187 IA)***.

## ALTERATION OF OBJECTS

### 27. Basic rule

By ***S.110 CA 89 (S.4)*** a company may freely amend its objects clause by ***special resolution***. Previously the objects clause could only be altered for specified purposes.

### 28. Minority protection

a. By **S.5** holders of 15% of the issued capital may apply to the court within 21 days of the resolution to have it set aside. The court may confirm or refuse the resolution, or it may arrange for the purchase of the dissentient members' interests, if necessary by the company itself.

b. If no application is made the company must, within 15 days after the end of the 21 day period, deliver to the registrar a printed copy of the memorandum as altered.

## LIMITATION OF LIABILITY

### 29. Contents of the clause

Where a company is limited by shares or by guarantee this clause will merely state: 'The liability of the members is limited'.

**30. Companies limited by shares**

The vast majority of companies, both public and private are companies limited by shares. In such a company the capital is divided into shares, for example capital of £5,000 divided into 10,000 shares of 50 pence each. The members of the company are liable to pay for their shares, either in money or money's worth (ie non-cash assets, goodwill or know-how). Once they have paid for their shares they are under no further liability. The company is therefore said to be 'limited by shares'. It is however important to note that it is not the company's liability which is limited, it must discharge its debts as long as it has assets to do so. It is the members' liability to the company which is limited.

**31. Companies limited by guarantee**

a. Such companies are usually formed for educational or charitable purposes. They usually raise their funds by subscription. Limitation of liability by guarantee is not appropriate for trading companies.

b. The liability of each member is limited to the amount he has agreed to contribute in the event of winding-up. The amount (usually £1 or £5) will be specified in the memorandum. Moreover a member's liability is contingent, his money is only called-up in the event of liquidation.

c. A company limited by guarantee may also have a share capital, in which case the members have dual liability, ie to pay the amount of the guarantee and the amount unpaid on their shares. However by ***S.1(4)*** a company limited by guarantee ***with*** a share capital may not now be registered, although existing companies limited by guarantee with a share capital remain in existence.

d. A company limited by guarantee without a share capital must set out its memorandum and articles in the form prescribed by ***TABLE C THE COMPANIES( TABLE A TO F) REGULATIONS 1985***. If it has a share capital the form of memorandum and articles prescribed by ***TABLE D*** of the above regulations must be used.

e. A company limited by guarantee may apply for exemption from the requirement that the word 'limited' be part of its name ***(S.30)***.

**32. Unlimited companies.**

a. There is no limit to the liability of the members of such companies. Thus although the company is a separate legal entity, the members' liability resembles that of partners, except that technically their liability is to the company itself and not to the creditors.

b. Unlimited companies are not popular because of this personal liability. However unlimited companies do have the advantage of greater privacy since by ***S.17 CA 89 (S.254)*** such companies are not required to deliver to the registrar copies of their accounts (unless the company is a subsidiary of, or the holding company of, a limited company).

c. Since the re-definition of public companies by the Companies Act 1980 it has not been possible for a public company to be unlimited.

**33. Re-registration of limited companies as unlimited**

a. An unlimited company may come into existence by being registered as such or by being re-registered under ***S.49***.

b. An application is made to the registrar setting out the appropriate changes to the memorandum and articles. The application is accompanied by:

   i. The prescribed form of assent signed by or on behalf of ***all the members***;

   ii. A statutory declaration by the directors that the signatories constitute all the members;

   iii. A printed copy of the new memorandum and articles.

c. These safeguards are necessary since the members are giving up the limitation to their liability.

**34. Re-registration of unlimited companies as limited**

By ***S.51*** if an unlimited company wishes to re-register as limited it must:

a. Pass a ***special resolution*** to that effect stating the manner in which liability is to be limited and, if it is to be limited by shares, what the capital will be;

b. Make appropriate changes to its memorandum and articles;

c. Apply to the registrar, sending with the application a printed copy of the new memorandum and articles; and

d. In order to protect creditors, if the company goes into liquidation within three years of re-registration every person who was a member at the date of re-registration is liable without limit in respect of any outstanding debts and liabilities which were incurred before the date of re-registration.

## OTHER CLAUSES

**35. The capital clause**

a. This states amount of capital and its division into shares of a fixed amount. For example Table B of The Companies (Table A to F) Regulations 1985 (the specimen form of memorandum for a company limited by shares), states that 'The share capital of the company is £50,000 divided into 50,000 shares of £1 each'.

b. The capital of a public company must be not less than the authorised minimum, at present £50,000.

c. When shares are first issued they may be issued at a premium, (ie for more than the nominal value), at par (ie at the nominal value), but not at a discount, (ie less than the nominal value).

d. Once the shares have been allotted they will change hands at market value which may be above or below the nominal value. The two figures are not related. The nominal value is fixed by the promoters or directors of the company. The market value reflects the prosperity of the company and the extent of speculative dealing in the shares.

## 36. The association clause

In this clause the subscribers to the memorandum, (minimum two) declare that they desire to be formed into a company, and agree to take the number of shares set opposite their names. Each subscriber signs the memorandum.

## 37. Class rights

These are the rights attached to different classes of shares, for example preference shares and ordinary shares. Usually they are placed in the articles, but if a company wishes to protect its shareholders by making it more difficult to change class rights they may be placed in the memorandum. Variation of class rights is discussed in Chapter 12.

## 38. Alteration of the memorandum generally

Every clause of the memorandum may be altered except the registered office clause, ie the country of incorporation cannot be altered. In addition to the methods of alteration of the clauses required by statute, **S.17** allows the company to alter clauses that it has chosen to include in the memorandum instead of the articles. Such clauses can be altered by ***special resolution*** unless the memorandum provides for another method. Holders of 15% of the issued shares have 21 days to apply to court to challenge that alteration.

### *PROGRESS TEST 3*

1. A business name must be registered. True or False?
2. State ***S.35(1) CA 85*** (inserted by ***S.108 CA 89***) concerning a company's capacity.
3. What type of resolution is needed to:
   (a) Change the company name
   (b) Appoint a director
   (c) Re-register a limited company as unlimited?
4. What is a company limited by guarantee?
5. What information is included in the registered office clause of the memorandum?
6. The director and controlling shareholder of a 'one man' company fraudulently represented the company as a genuine and honest concern. He is charged with conspiring with his company to defraud investors. Advise the prosecutor.

# 8 The Articles of Association

## FORM AND FUNCTION

### 1. The nature of the articles

The articles are the internal regulations of the company. They deal with, for example, the issue and transfer of shares, directors' powers, procedure at meetings, the payment of dividends and the secretary.

### 2. Table A

Every company must have articles. 'Table A' is the model form for a company limited by shares. Table A is now contained in ***THE COMPANIES (TABLES A TO F) REGULATIONS 1985***. These regulations amend rather than consolidate the law. Although the new Table A basically deals with the same subject matter it is substantially different from the old Table A. It has also been reduced in length from 136 to 118 paragraphs. By ***S.8*** if a company does not register articles Table A will apply to that company. In practice companies will modify Table A to suit their own requirements.

### 3. Statutory requirements

By ***S.7*** articles must be

a. Printed (typing is not acceptable);

b. Divided into numbered paragraphs; and

c. Signed by each subscriber to the memorandum in the presence of a witness who must also sign.

## ALTERATION OF ARTICLES

### 4. Basic rule

a. By ***S.9*** the articles may be altered by ***special resolution***. Any provision which attempts to deprive the company of this power is void, for example a power given to a particular member to veto an alteration. However it was stated in **BUSHELL v FAITH (1970)** (Chapter 15.9) that there is nothing in the Act that prevents weighted voting rights (for example three votes per share instead of one vote) being attached to particular shares on a resolution to alter the articles or remove a director.

b. The articles of a ***private company*** may also be altered by ***written resolution***. ***S.113–114*** **CA 89** have introduced new rules allowing private companies to substitute the unanimous written agreement of all shareholders for any resolution passed at a general meeting. Clearly such a procedure can also be used, for example to change the company name or to alter the objects clause in the memorandum.

## 5. Limitations on the freedom to alter the articles

No alteration of the articles can constitute a fraud on the minority (see below), nor overrule the general law, the memorandum, or the provisions of the Acts. For example

a. By **S.16** no increase of a member's liability is possible without his written consent, ie a member cannot be compelled to purchase more shares.

b. Minority protection provisions, for example the right of a dissentient 15% to object to a change of objects, cannot be excluded. (Note that there is no corresponding right given by **S.9** for any dissentient minority to object to a change of articles).

## 6. Fraud on the minority

An alteration of the articles must not amount to a 'fraud on the minority'. The meaning of this term is not absolutely clear, however Professor Gower suggests that the test is to ask whether the majority have exercised their powers for a ***proper corporate purpose***. The purpose would be proper if it is to benefit the company or the generality of the members of the class concerned. It would be improper if it is primarily to injure other members.

a. Professor Gower's view is supported by **CLEMENS v CLEMENS (1976)** which, although it is a case concerning the issue of shares rather than a change of articles, is nevertheless appropriate.

   In **CLEMENS v CLEMENS LTD (1976)** the plaintiff held 45% of the issued shares and her aunt, who was one of the directors of the company held 55%. The aunt's shares were used at a general meeting o secure the passing of resolutions to issue further shares to directors and to trustees of an employees' share ownership scheme. The resolutions were carefully designed to reduce the plaintiffs holding from 45% to about 24.5% of the issued shares. This deprived her of her power to block a special or extraordinary resolution. It also reduced the value of her rights under a pre-emption clause in the articles (a clause entitling her to first refusal if another member wished to sell shares). The court set aside the resolutions on the ground that they were oppressive to the plaintiff, since they were specifically designed (i) to ensure that she could never get control of the company and (ii) to remove her negative control.

   Contrast **GREENHALGH v ARDERNE CINEMAS (1951)** where the articles contained a similar pre-emption clause. The majority shareholder wished to transfer his shares to an outsider, so the articles were altered to permit a transfer to any person with the sanction of an ordinary resolution. This meant that the majority shareholder could transfer his shares to non-members, whereas the minority shareholder had to offer them to the majority shareholder first. The purpose of the change of articles was the same as the purpose of the share issue in

Clemen's case, ie to ensure that the plaintiff could never get control of the company. It was held that the change of articles was not a fraud on the minority. The court considered whether the alteration would benefit an 'individual hypothetical member' regardless of whether he held the majority or a minority of the shares. It was decided that such a member would benefit since there would be less restriction on the right to sell his shares. The result of the case was clearly not satisfactory and was not followed in **CLEMENS v CLEMENS** where the judge considered the position of the actual minority member rather than that of an individual hypothetical member.

b. Several cases have concerned an alteration of the articles to expropriate a member's interest.

   In **BROWN v BRITISH ABRASIVE WHEEL CO (1919)** a resolution was passed adding to the articles a clause compelling a member to transfer his shares upon a request in writing by the holders of 90% of the issued shares. Although the majority were acting in good faith, and despite the fact that the clause could have been inserted in the original articles the alteration was successfully challenged. The court held that since the minority had bought their shares when there was no such power, the change could not be for the benefit of the company as a whole, but solely for the benefit or the majority.

   Contrast **SIDEBOTTOM v KERSHAW LEESE (1920)** where a private company altered its articles to give the directors power to require any shareholder ***who competed with the company*** to transfer his shares to nominees of the directors at a fair price. The alteration was held to be valid since it was for the benefit for the company as a whole to be able to expel a competitor from its membership.

c. It is probable that in future the case law concept of 'fraud on the minority' will become much less significant. **S.459–461** enable the court to restrain any actual or proposed act which is ***unfairly prejudicial*** to the interests of the members. These sections improve the position of the minority and would certainly be available if the alleged unfairly prejudicial act was an alteration of the articles.

**7. The effect of an alteration on outsiders**

An alteration of the articles which causes a breach of contract with an outsider is valid, and cannot be restrained by an injunction. The outsider's remedy is to claim damages for breach of contract.

In **SOUTHERN FOUNDRIES v SHIRLAW (1940)**, Shirlaw had been appointed the managing director of Southern Foundries for 10 years. The articles contained a clause, similar to Table A Article 107, that the managing director's appointment shall automatically cease if he should cease to be a director. Southern Foundries was then merged into a group called Federated Industries. All group members agreed to make certain alterations to their articles, one such change being that FI would have power to remove any director of a member company. FI then used this power to remove Shirlaw. As a result he automatically ceased to be managing director of SF, even though his contract had several years left to run. Shirlaw's claim for damages for wrongful dismissal succeeded because his contract as managing director was held to contain an implied term that the company would not do anything to make it impossible for him to continue as managing director.

## THE EFFECT OF THE MEMORANDUM AND ARTICLES

### 8. Basic rule

a. By ***S.14*** the memorandum and articles when registered bind the company and the members as if they had been signed and sealed by each member and contained covenants on the part of each member to observe their provisions.

b. A provision similar to the present ***S.14*** first appeared in the **JOINT STOCK COMPANIES ACT 1844**. It concerned the method of forming a joint stock company by deed of settlement (which did in fact constitute a contract between the members who sealed it). When the first 'modern' Companies Act was passed in 1856 the provisions of the 1844 Act was adopted in a modified form. The 1856 Act did not however take account of the fact that a company is a separate legal entity. Thus after the words 'each member' the words 'and the company' were surprisingly omitted. Although this irregularity has survived until the present day the results of ***S.14*** are nevertheless clear.

### 9. The results of *S.14*

a. ***The company is bound to each individual member in his capacity as member***

   i. Thus for example it must record a properly given vote.

   In **PENDER v LUSHINGTON (1877)** the articles provided that each member should be entitled to one vote for every 10 shares, but that no member would be entitled to more than 100 votes. One member had more than 1,000 shares, but because of the above provision was prevented from using his full potential vote. Some of the shares were therefore transferred to the plaintiff. At a meeting the chairman, Lushington, refused to accept Pender's votes on the ground that the transfer to him was merely a device to avoid the provisions of the articles. It was held that Pender's votes must be counted, failure to do so would amount to a breach of his personal rights as a member.

   ii. The company is not bound by a right given by the articles to a member acting in another capacity, for example as company solicitor.

In **ELEY v POSITIVE LIFE ASSURANCE CO (1876)** the articles contained a clause appointing the plaintiff as company solicitor, and he acted as such for some time. The company then ceased to employ him and he brought an action for breach of contract. It was held that the articles did not constitute a contract between the company and Eley because even though he was a member they could not confer rights on him in any other capacity, including that of company solicitor.

iii. It has however been held that if a person, for example a director, takes office on the basis of an article providing for his remuneration, although the article itself is not a contract between him and the company, its terms may be part of such a contract:

In **RE NEW BRITISH IRON CO (1898)** the articles provided for directors' remuneration of £1,000. The directors accepted office on this basis. The company went into liquidation before payment of any remuneration to the directors. It was held that the terms of the article were also the terms of a contract between the directors and the company. They were therefore entitled to recover the arrears of remuneration.

iv. It therefore follows that if a managing director is appointed by a company whose articles incorporate Table A, Article 84 and no remuneration is in fact determined, then the managing director will not be entitled to remuneration:

In **RE RICHMOND GATE PROPERTY CO (1965)** a managing director was appointed under Table A Article 108 which stated that 'A managing director shall receive such remuneration. . . as the directors may determine'. (This is similar to the current Article 84). The company went into liquidation before any remuneration had been determined. The managing director made a claim in contract, but this failed because no remuneration had been determined. He also made a quantum meruit claim (a claim for as much as he deserves) but this failed because it was held that the existence of an express contract excluded a quantum meruit claim.

b. ***Each member is bound to the company***. Therefore a provision in the articles referring disputes between a member and the company to arbitration will be enforceable against the member provided the dispute concerns membership rights.

In **HICKMAN v KENT SHEEP BREEDERS ASSOCIATION (1915)** the articles provided for disputes between members and the company to be referred to arbitration. The Association wished to expel the plaintiff from membership of the Association and the plaintiff applied for an injunction to prevent this. It was held that the Association was entitled to have the action stayed since the dispute concerned membership rights and the articles provided for such disputes to initially be settled by arbitration rather than legal action.

In **BEATTIE v BEATTIE LTD (1938)** the articles contained a similar arbitration clause. In this case the dispute concerned a director's right to inspect the company's books and accounts and his remuneration. When legal action was taken against the director his request for a stay was refused because, even though he was a member, the dispute concerned his capacity as director.

c. ***The members are contractually bound to each other***

i. The main occasions when this question is likely to arise are when the articles give members pre-emption rights when another member wishes to sell his shares, or more rarely, when the articles place on members a duty to buy the shares of a retiring member. In such cases a direct action between the shareholders concerned is possible. It is not necessary to bring the action through the company since this would involve the company in unnecessary litigation.

In **RAYFIELD v HANDS (1960)** the articles stated that 'Every member who intends to transfer his shares shall inform the directors, who ***will*** take the said shares equally between them at a fair price'. The plaintiff informed the directors that he wanted to transfer his shares, but the directors denied that they were compelled to purchase them. It was held that the directors must take the shares. The word 'will' did not give them an option to purchase, it imposed on them an obligation to purchase. It was also clear that the court regarded the clause as creating a contractual relationship between the plaintiff as a member and the defendants as members. This is rather surprising and arguably inconsistent with **ELEY v POSITIVE LIFE ASSURANCE CO**, since the clause imposes the obligation to buy the shares on ***'the directors'***.

ii. A situation where members are able to sue other members may well give rise to practical difficulties. To avoid this (and the uncertainty that still exists following the decision in Rayfield v Hands) modern articles will make the transaction a two stage process, each stage being a dealing with the company to which ***S.14*** clearly applies. The articles first require any member who intends to transfer his shares to inform the company. They then require the company to give notice to other members that they have an option to purchase the shares. If the first stage is not complied with the company can sue the transferor. If the second stage is broken a shareholder may sue the company.

**10. Differences between the contract in *S.14* and other contracts**

a. The normal remedy of damages for breach of contract is not available because of the court's desire to maintain the capital of the company. A member may however obtain an injunction to prevent a breach by the company of any provision in the memorandum or articles and he may sue for a liquidated sum due to him as a member, for example unpaid dividends.

b. The contract does not guarantee the future rights and duties of members, since both the memorandum and articles may be altered. Thus when becoming a member a person agrees to a contract which is alterable by the other party (the company) at a future date.

### *PROGRESS TEST 4*

1. What type of resolution is needed to:
   (a) Alter the articles
   (b) Alter the objects
   (c) Re-register an unlimited company as limited?
2. Where must a company publish its name?
3. What is the minimum number of members for
   (a) A public company
   (b) A private company
   (c) A partnership?
4. To what extent are the articles a contract between the company and its members?
5. You are consulted by John, a shareholder in Suds Ltd, a company which manufactures soap powder. John explains that he has just received a notice convening the AGM of the company which includes a proposal that an ordinary resolution be passed requiring John to sell his shares to nominees of the directors on the grounds that he is an employee of NBG, a company which also manufactures soap powder. Advise John.

## COURSEWORK QUESTIONS 1–5 INCORPORATION

1. *James is engaged in the promotion of a company and he seeks your advice on several points relating to promotion activities.*

   *You are required to write a report dealing with the following matters:*

   *(a) the restrictions upon the choice of corporate name with which a promoter must comply;*

*(b) the legal duties of a promoter and in particular his responsibility where he sells property of his own to the company he is promoting;*

*(c) the problem of a promoter obtaining payment for his services from the company once the company has been incorporated.*

*(15 marks)*

CIMA *November* 1983 *Question* 52

2. *Give an account of the legal procedure which must be followed in order to effect the registration of a new public company which is entitled to do business.*

*(15 marks)*

ACCA *December* 1986 *Question* 1

3. **S.20 Companies Act 1948** *(now* **S.14 CA 1985***) states that the memorandum and articles of association of a company shall, when registered, bind the company and the members to the same extent as if they respectively had been signed and sealed by each member, and contained covenants on the part of each member to observe all the provisions of the memorandum and of the articles.*

   *Explain the effect of this section on the relationship between shareholders and their company and between the shareholders themselves. Illustrate your answer with decided cases.* *(20 marks)*

ACCA *June* 1985 *Question* 2

4. *(a) The general legal principle is that a company has a separate legal existence from that of its members. In what circumstances does that general principle not apply? Give examples of such situations.*

*(10 marks)*

*(b) Walter is employed as managing director by Clipse Ltd whose main object is to retail office equipment. His contract of employment contains a clause which states that in the event of his leaving the employment of Clipse Ltd he will not solicit their customers for a period of two years. He resigns his employment and together with is wife Jean forms a new company, Desks Ltd, whose main object is also retailing office equipment. Bill is a salesman employed by Desks Ltd. He is given customer lists by Walter and immediately begins soliciting Clipse Ltd's customers.*

*In order to raise cash for his new business, Walter enters into a contract to sell his house to Wilf for £50,000. Bill who has always admired the house approaches Walter and makes him an offer of £60,000. Walter transfers ownership of the house to Desks Ltd, and on behalf of the company enters into negotiations to sell the house to Bill.*

*Advise Clipse Ltd and Wilf on any action they can take.*

*(10 marks)*

*(20 marks)*

ACCA *June* 1987 Question 8

5. (a) *Compare and contrast the legal nature of a private and public company.* *(5 marks)*

   (b) *What are 'companies limited by guarantee' and what special legal provisions apply to them?* *(5 marks)*

   (c) *Explain the object and procedure of re-registration of a private limited company as unlimited.* *(5 marks)*

*(15 marks)*

ACCA December 1981 Question 1

# PART III THE RAISING AND MAINTENANCE OF CAPITAL

# 9 Public Offers for Shares

## INTRODUCTION

1. **Raising funds**

   Private companies will usually raise their funds from their own membership or from a bank. Public companies are formed when it is necessary to obtain funds from an issue of shares or debentures to the public. This has led to many provisions to protect the investing public. These are now contained in ***PARTS IV*** **and** ***V FINANCIAL SERVICES ACT 1986***. This Act repeals ***PART III COMPANIES ACT 1985***. All sections referred to in this chapter are sections of the ***FINANCIAL SERVICES ACT 1986***.

2. **Listed and unlisted securities**

   a. ***Listed securities. PART IV FSA 1986*** deals with the official listing of securities, ie the Official List of The Stock Exchange. It provides for an application to be made to the ***'competent authority'*** (the Council of the Stock Exchange) by the method specified in the ***'listing rules'***. These rules contain details of the information to be included in 'listing particulars'. The term ***'prospectus'*** no longer applies where there is a public share issue of listed securities. The prospectus is replaced by the ***listing particulars***.

   b. ***Unlisted securities. PART V FSA 1986*** deals with offers of unlisted securities which are to be admitted for dealing on an ***'approved exchange'*** for example the Unlisted Securities Market. In such cases no advertisement offering securities may be issued unless a ***'prospectus'*** has been approved by the exchange and delivered to the registrar of companies.

3. **Private companies**

   a. Two provisions in the Act make it clear that (except as described in b. below) the Act does not apply to private companies:

      i. By ***S.143(3)*** a private company must not apply for its shares to be listed on the Stock Exchange.

      ii. By ***S.170*** a private company must not issue any advertisement offering its shares for sale.

   b. A private company may issue an advertisement offering securities if the advertisement falls inside a category exempted by the Secretary of State, ie it is of a private character, an incidental nature, or aimed at a specialist market. Permission given to any company, by order of the Secretary of State, may specify additional requirements.

## 4. Methods of public issue

a. ***The role of the issuing house***. When a company wishes to raise money from the public it will usually enlist the aid of an issuing house (usually a merchant bank). These enterprises will be associated with the company either as principals or as its agents. If the issue is unsuccessful their funds and/or their reputation may suffer. They will therefore closely examine all public issues with which they are involved. Their scrutiny provides an effective additional check on uneconomic or misleading share issues. The nature of the role which they play depends on the type of share issue.

b. ***Direct offer***. The company itself makes a direct offer to the public by publishing listing particulars inviting applications. The company will have to bear the risk of the issue being unsuccessful, and will therefore have to arrange to have it underwritten. The issuing house assisting the company will probably only appear in the prospectus as an underwriter. This method of issue is rarely used today.

c. ***Offer for sale***

   i. Here the company transfers all of the securities to an issuing house which in turn publishes listing particulars inviting the public to purchase from it at a slightly higher price. This method is more common than direct offers and there is no risk for the company, although the issuing house will underwrite. The issuing house will not be registered as holder except in respect of shares which the public do not take. The practice is to issue renounceable letters of allotment to the issuing house. This enables the issuing house to assign its right to membership by signing forms of renunciation in favour of purchasers.

   ii. Recently there have been a number of ***offers for sale by tender***. The offer will state ***a minimum tender price*** which is potentially the minimum purchase price. The ***striking price*** is the price at which the shares are eventually sold and is determined by the tender process. If there are less applications than shares on offer the minimum tender price will be the striking price. If applications exceed shares the striking price will be the highest price at which sufficient applications are received ( at that price or at a higher price) for all the shares being offered. Each share is sold at the striking price even though some applicants will have tendered more. The advantage of an offer for sale by tender is that it prevents ***'stagging'*** ie the speculative purchase of new shares in the hope that the issue will be oversubscribed and any shares acquired can be sold immediately for a profit. The disadvantages are that procedure is more complex and investors are less enthusiastic about such issues.

d. ***Placing***. An issuing house will ***either*** subscribe for shares and invite its clients to purchase from it at a slightly higher price, ***or*** it will place the shares as agent for the company, in which case it will be paid commission known as *'brokerage'* (see Chapter 10.6).

5. **Rights issues**

a. The modern practice when a public company wants to raise capital is to make a rights issue, ie new shares are created and offered to existing shareholders in proportion to their existing shareholding. Since 1980 it has been a legal requirement that existing shareholders be given a right of first refusal when new shares are issued ***(S.89 CA 1985)***.

b. To make a rights issue attractive the shares will usually be offered at 10%–20% less than the current market value. This can give added worth to the existing shares until they go 'ex rights' when buying them will no longer entitle the holder to participate in the rights issue. After the issue the market may mark down the price of the shares since they will have lost some scarcity value.

## OFFICIAL LISTING OF SECURITIES

6. **Application and admission to the official list**

a. ***Basic rule***. No securities may be admitted to listing ie quoted, unless an application has been made, by or with the consent of the issuer, to the competent authority in the way required by the ***listing rules***.

b. ***The competent authority*** is the Council of the Stock Exchange ***(S.142(6))***, although the Secretary of State for Trade may order a transfer of the Council's powers if the Council exercises them improperly ***(S.157)***.

c. The ***listing rules*** are made by the Council. By ***S.156*** they must be available to the public and it will be a defence in any action for breach of the rules to show that, at the time of the breach, the particular rule had not been made available to the public.

The Act specifies some matters which may be included in the listing rules, but the Council has a general power, not restricted in any way by the matters specified. It may include for example:

i. A requirement that 'listing particulars' (or some other document) be submitted, approved and published as a condition of admission.

ii. The information to be specified in the listing particulars.

iii. Provisions as to the action which the Council may take if the listing rules are not complied with.

iv. The fees payable to the Stock Exchange.

d. The Council must inform the applicant of its decision within 6 months. If it does not do so, it is taken to have refused the application.

e. ***Refusal to list***. By ***S.144(3)*** an application may be refused if:

i. The Council considers that because of any matter relating to the issuer, the admission would be detrimental to investors.

ii. In the case of shares already officially listed in another EEC state, the issuer has failed to comply with his obligations in connection with that listing.

f. Once an application has been approved and the securities admitted to the Official List, neither the grant of listing, nor subsequent transactions can be challenged on the ground that the admission requirements were not met. However this does not prevent investors from suing if they have suffered loss due to false or misleading statements in, or omissions from, the listing particulars.

**7. Listing particulars**

a. ***Content***. The listing rules specify the content of the listing particulars. The information required are very detailed, but will include basic essential information, for example:

i. The names, addresses and descriptions of the directors.

ii. The capital to be subscribed, the amount to be paid in cash, and the nature of the consideration for the remainder.

iii. Voting and dividend rights for each class of share.

The Act also allows the Council to impose further requirements in relation to any particular application.

b. ***The general duty of disclosure***. In addition to any matters required by the listing rules the Act imposes a general duty of disclosure. By ***S.146*** the listing particulars must give the information that investors and their advisors would reasonably require to make an informed decision on whether to buy the securities. It must enable them to ascertain the assets and liabilities, financial position, results and prospects of the issuer, and the rights attaching to those securities. The general duty is however limited to information which the person responsible for the listing particulars knew or could reasonably have discovered by making enquiries. The Act lays down the following criteria to assist in determining what information should be given:

i. The nature of the securities and the issuer.

ii. The nature of prospective buyers. (Thus less information need be given to experienced or professional investors).

iii. That certain matters are known by the professional advisors likely to be consulted by prospective investors.

iv. That other information may be available to investors under this, or any other Act.

c. ***Exemption***. By ***S.148*** the Council may grant exemption from the general duty of disclosure if disclosure of the information would be:

i. Contrary to the public interest (following the issue of a certificate to that effect by the Secretary of State or the Treasury); or

ii. Seriously detrimental to the issuer (unless investors could be misled about essential facts, in which case the information must be published).

**8. Supplementary listing particulars *(S.147)***

a. These will need to be submitted to the Council for approval and publication if between the submission of listing particulars and start of dealings:

i. There is a significant ***change*** affecting any matter included in the original particulars, ***or***

ii. A significant ***new matter*** arises that would have had to be included had it arisen when the particulars were being prepared.

b. ***'Significant'*** means anything which affects the making of an informed assessment of the issuer's assets and liabilities, financial position, results and prospects.

c. The issuer is under a duty to make known changes or new matters only to the extent that he is aware of them. If any other person responsible with the issuer for the listing particulars becomes aware of such matters, he must notify the issuer.

**9. Registration of listing particulars *(S.149)***

On or before the date when listing particulars or supplementary listing particulars are published a copy must be delivered to the registrar of companies. A statement that a copy has been delivered to him must appear in the particulars. Default is a criminal offence.

**10. Advertisements in connection with listing applications *(S.154)***

a. Before an advertisement of the kind specified in the listing rules can be issued, the Council must have approved its contents or, in the case of innocuous advertisements, authorised publication without approval.

b. Publication of an advertisement by an authorised person, but without approval, is a civil wrong. Publication by an unauthorised person without approval is a criminal offence.

c. A person will not be liable for issuing an advertisement on behalf of someone else if he believed on reasonable grounds that approval had been obtained.

d. Where an advertisement has been approved the issuer will not be liable in contract or tort for any mis-statement or omission if the advertisement and listing particulars, taken together, would not be likely to mislead the kind of person likely to buy the securities.

**11. Discontinuance and suspension of listings *(S.145)***

a. The Council may, in accordance with the listing rules, discontinue the listing of any securities satisfied that there are special circumstances which prevent normal regular dealings.

b. The Council may also, in accordance with the listing rules, temporarily suspend listing. This sometimes occurs at the issuer's request, for example when rumours of a takeover bid distort the normal market for the securities.

## OFFERS OF UNLISTED SECURITIES

**12. Introduction**

***PART V FINANCIAL SERVICES ACT 1986*** controls advertisements for securities for which an official Stock Exchange listing is not being sought. Parts IV and V are therefore mutually exclusive. ***PART V*** applies to:

a. Advertisements offering securities which are to be admitted to dealing on an approved exchange; and

b. Other offers (primary and secondary offers).

**13. Definitions**

For the purposes of ***PART V*** note the following:

a. ***Advertisement offering securities***. By ***S.158(4)*** an advertisement offers securities if:

   i. It invites a person to enter into an agreement for subscribing for or otherwise acquiring or underwriting any securities; ***or***

   ii. It contains information calculated to lead directly or indirectly to a person entering into such an agreement.

b. ***Approved exchange***. – A recognised investment exchange (ie designated as such by the Secretary of State) which has been approved by the Secretary of State for the purposes of ***PART V (S.158(6))***.

c. ***Prospectus***. – A document containing information about securities to be offered which is submitted for approval to an approved exchange ***(S.159(1))***.

d. ***Primary offer***. – An advertisement (not connected with an approved exchange) directly or indirectly inviting persons to subscribe for or underwrite the securities ***(S.160(2))***.

e. ***Secondary offer***. – An advertisement (not connected with an approved exchange) by someone who has acquired the securities for the purpose of selling them on, or who is (or was within the previous 12 months) controller of the issuer and is acting with the issuer's consent ***(S.160(3))***. A person will be presumed to have acquired the securities with a view to making a secondary offer if he advertises them for sale within 6 months of acquisition or before he pays for them ***(S.160(4))***. Secondary offers are 'offers for sale' and are more common than primary (direct) offers.

**14. Offers of securities on admission to an approved exchange**

a. By ***S.159*** no person may issue an advertisement offering securities which are to be admitted to dealing on an approved exchange unless:

i. A prospectus has been submitted to and approved by the exchange and delivered to the registrar of companies; ***or***

ii. The advertisement is worded so that no agreement can be made as a result of it until a prospectus has been submitted, approved and delivered as above.

b. In the following ***exceptional cases*** a prospectus will not be required:

i. Where a prospectus has been issued in the previous 12 months and the approved exchange certifies that potential investors will have sufficient information from that earlier prospectus ***(S.159(2))***.

ii. Where the offer is conditional on Stock Exchange listing, or the securities have been listed in the previous 12 months, and the approved exchange certifies that potential investors will have sufficient information ***(S.161(1))***.

iii. Where the issuer invites subscriptions for cash and the advertisement consists of a registered prospectus or contains only the following matters:

- Name and address of issuer;
- Nature, number, nominal value and price of the securities;
- A statement that a prospectus is available; and
- Instructions for obtaining a copy. ***(S.161(2))***.

iv. Where the issuer has other securities already being dealt with on the exchange and the exchange certifies that potential investors will have sufficient information.

v. Where the Secretary of State grants exemption to securities subject to equivalent controls under an overseas exchange.

**15. Other offers of securities**

a. By ***S.160(1)*** no person may issue an advertisement offering securities which is a primary or secondary offer unless:

i. He has delivered a prospectus to the registrar; ***or***

ii. The advertisement is worded so that no agreement can be made as a result of it until delivery of a prospectus to the registrar.

b. The ***exceptions*** applicable to ***S.160*** are:

i. Where a prospectus relating to the same securities has been delivered to the registrar within the previous 6 months ***(S.160(5))***.

ii. Where in the following cases the Secretary of State has granted exemption:
   - Advertisements of a private character (ie because of a connection between the issuer and the potential investor);
   - Advertisements dealing with investments only incidentally;
   - Advertisements issued only to experienced investors who can understand the risks;
   - Any other class of advertisement as he thinks fit ***(S.160(6))***.

iii. Offer conditional on Stock Exchange listing etc ... as 14.b.ii. above.

iv. Advertisements consisting of a registered prospectus etc ... as 14.b.iii. above.

v. Securities already being dealt with etc ... as 14.b.iv. above.

vi. Overseas securities etc ... as 14.b.v. above.

**16. Contents of prospectus**

Detailed requirements are set out in rules issued by the Secretary of State under ***S.162***. They are similar to the listing particulars required from applicants seeking official listing. ***S.163*** imposes a general duty of disclosure similar to that imposed by ***S.146*** (see 7.b. above) and ***S.165*** includes exemption criteria similar to ***S.148*** (see 7.c. above).

**17. Supplementary prospectus**

***S.164*** requires the registration of a supplementary prospectus in exactly the same circumstances as ***S.147*** requires the registration of supplementary listing particulars (see 8. above).

**18. Contravention of Part V *(S.171)***

a. An authorised person who commits a breach of ***S.159*** or ***S.160*** commits a civil wrong and may be liable to compensate anyone who suffers loss. If the breach relates to the offer of securities of a private company a criminal offence is committed. Also any agreement will be voidable unless the advertisement was irrelevant in terms of the agreement or fair in all the circumstances.

b. An unauthorised person in breach of any of the rules commits a criminal offence.

**19. Rules made by Secretary of State *(S.169)***

The Secretary of State is authorised to make rules governing the terms upon which unlisted securities are offered so that potential investors are treated equally and fairly.

## MISREPRESENTATION AND OMISSION

### 20. Summary of available remedies

a. Compensation under *S.150–152* or *S.166–168 FINANCIAL SERVICES ACT 1986*.

b. *Damages*, either

   i. Under *S.2(1) MISREPRESENTATION ACT 1967*;

   ii. In tort for deceit;

   iii. In tort for negligent misrepresentation under the principle of HEDLEY BYRNE v HELLER (1964).

c. *Rescission*.

### 21. Compensation

a. *S.150–152* apply to misrepresentations in or omissions from listing particulars or supplementary listing particulars. *S.166–168* contain almost identical provisions in respect of the prospectus. These statutory remedies are in addition to the other remedies set out below.

b. *Heads of liability (S.150, S.166)*

   i. A *'person responsible'* for listing particulars (references to listing particulars can be taken to apply equally to the prospectus) shall be liable to compensate any person who acquires the securities in question and suffers loss as a result of any untrue or misleading statement or the omission of any of the required particulars.

   ii. Any person who fails to issue supplementary listing particulars (or a supplementary prospectus) when required to do so shall be liable to compensate any person who acquired those securities and suffered loss as a result of the failure.

c. *Defences (S.151, S.167)*

   i. Reasonable belief that the statement was true and not misleading, or that the matter was properly omitted, ***and***

      (a) He held that belief until the securities were acquired; ***or***

      (b) They were acquired before he could make potential investors aware of the correction; ***or***

      (c) Before they were acquired he had taken all reasonable steps to bring the correction to the attention of the persons concerned; ***or***

      (d) He held that belief until dealing commenced (listed securities) and the acquisition occurred after a reasonable lapse of time.

   ii. If the person responsible relied on statements made by or on behalf of an expert, the person responsible has a defence if he can prove the expert consented to the inclusion of the statement and if he can show reasonable belief in the expert's competence. He must also show i.(a)–(d) above.

iii. That the person responsible took reasonable steps to bring a correction or a defect in an expert's consent or competence to the attention of potential investors before the securities were acquired.

iv. That the loss resulted from the fair and accurate reproduction of a statement by an official person or contained in an official document.

v. The plaintiff acquired the securities with the knowledge that the listing particulars were false or misleading.

vi. In the case of supplementary listing particulars that the change or new matter was too trivial to warrant them.

d. ***Persons responsible (S.152, S.168)***

i. The issuer.

ii. The directors of the issuer, unless the particulars were published without their knowledge or consent and on becoming aware of publication they gave reasonable public notice of that fact.

iii. Persons named as having agreed to become directors.

iv. Persons stated to have accepted responsibility for any part of the particulars.

v. Any other person who authorised the contents of any part of the particulars.

Persons responsible under iv. and v. are only liable for the parts for which they have accepted responsibility or authorised.

e. ***Conclusion***. The sections on compensation are far more useful than their predecessor ***(S.67 CA 1985)*** In particular:

i. They are not limited to 'subscribers' (ie persons who purchase direct from the company). Subsequent purchasers will therefore be able to claim provided they acquire the securities within a reasonable time.

ii. The range of persons responsible is much wider, and now includes the company.

As a result there will be less need to resort to the other remedies described below.

22. Damages

There are three avenues leading to an award of damages. The action chosen will depend on several factors, including the type of misrepresentation.

a. By ***S.2(1) MISREPRESENTATION ACT 1967*** the innocent party has a right to damages for misrepresentation if he has suffered loss. However if the maker of the statement proves that he had reasonable grounds for believing, and in fact did believe, up to the time the contract was made, that the facts represented were true, then he has a defence.

The problem with ***S.2(1)*** is that the range of persons who can be sued is rather narrow. Only the other party to the contract can be sued. Thus directors and experts are excluded, as is the company, unless the securities were acquired directly from it.

b. If the misrepresentation is fraudulent, damages may be recovered in tort for deceit. A fraudulent misrepresentation is a statement which is known to be false, or made without belief in its truth, or made recklessly, not caring whether it is true or false. **(DERRY v PEEK (1889))**.

   The action will lie against all those who made the false statement. By ***S.131 CA 89 (S.111A)*** a person is not prevented from bringing an action against a company in which he holds shares. This abolishes the rule in **HOULDSWORTH V CITY OR GLASGOW BANK (1880)** which prevented a person from claiming damages for misrepresentation or breach of the contract of allotment unless that person first rescinded the contract.

c. The third possibility is that damages for negligent misrepresentation may be claimed under the rule in **HEDLEY BYRNE v HELLER (1964)**. The duty not to make negligent statements will be owed if the plaintiff can show that he relied on the special skill and judgement of the defendant, and the defendant knew, or ought to have known, of the reliance, thus accepting responsibility for making the statement carefully.

   The persons liable will be those who both owed and broke the duty of care. This would include directors and experts, but it probably does not include the company.

**23. Rescission**

a. Rescission is an equitable remedy available for misrepresentation.

b. A misrepresentation is an untrue statement of fact which is one of the causes which induces the contract.

c. A half-truth, ie where silence distorts a true statement is a misrepresentation.

   In R v KYLSANT (1932) the prospectus stated that the company had paid a regular dividend throughout the years of the depression. This clearly implied that the company had made a profit during those years. This was not in fact the case since the dividends had been paid out of profits accumulated in the pre-depression years. The company's silence as to the source of the dividends was held to be a misrepresentation since it distorted the true statement that dividends had been paid.

d. Since rescission is an equitable remedy its award is at the discretion of the court. In general the plaintiff will not be granted rescission in the following circumstances:

   i. If he delays in seeking his remedy;

ii . If he affirms the contract, ie with knowledge of his right to rescind he acts in a way which is consistent with ownership of the shares, for example by voting at meetings or attempting to sell the shares; or

iii. If the company goes into liquidation, since the rights of third parties, such as creditors and debenture holders, will then intervene.

e. The remedy of rescission is affected by ***S.2(2) MISREPRESENTATION ACT 1967*** which gives the court a discretion to award damages in lieu of rescission if it thinks it equitable to do so.

### *PROGRESS TEST 5*

1. What is the difference between a direct offer and an offer for sale?
2. What is the difference between a rights issue and a bonus issue?
3. When are supplementary listing particulars required?
4. Who are the 'persons responsible' for listing particulars?
5. What must be proved by a person wishing to rescind an allotment of securities?
6. In what circumstances would the right to rescind be lost?
7. What is the 'general duty of disclosure' imposed by the **FINANCIAL SERVICES ACT**?
8. What is the difference between subscribing for and purchasing shares?

# 10 Capital

## TYPES OF CAPITAL AND ALTERATION OF CAPITAL

### 1. Capital, share capital, and loan capital

a. The word capital is generally used to describe the amount by which the assets of a business exceed its liabilities. This implies a fluctuating measure of the net worth of the business.

b. The share capital of a limited company is not a constantly fluctuating figure. It is the minimum value of net assets which must be raised initially, and so far as possible retained in the business, ie it is the amount that purchasers of shares have agreed to contribute to the company in return for their shares.

c. Share capital, which is subject to many rules of preservation and disclosure, must be distinguished from loan capital. When money is lent to a company the lender does not become a member of the company and the money raised is not subject to the same rules of preservation.

### 2. Different meanings of 'share capital'

a. *Nominal or authorised capital*. Every company must state in its memorandum the amount of its nominal capital. This figure shows the maximum number of shares the company is authorised to issue and the nominal value of each share. It does not indicate that any shares have been issued and paid for.

b. *Issued capital*. Some or all of the nominal capital must be issued in return for cash or the transfer of non-cash assets. Issued capital is of far more importance than nominal capital since each shareholder is liable to pay the price of shares issued to him. It is the issued capital which therefore comprises the creditors' guarantee fund. Subsequent references to 'capital' are references to issued capital.

c. *Called-up capital*

   i. ***S.1*** provides that the liability of shareholders shall be limited to the amount, if any, unpaid on their shares. The Act therefore allows the issued shares to be partly called-up.

   ii. By ***S.737*** called-up capital equals the aggregate of the calls made on shares, whether or not the calls have been paid, together with any share capital paid-up without being called and any share capital to be paid on a specified future date under the articles.

iii. In practice companies usually require fairly prompt payment of the full amount of issued capital by instalments, so that issued capital and called-up capital are generally the same.

d. ***Paid-up capital***. This is the sum of the payments received by the company. Unless some shareholders refuse to pay calls the paid-up capital will equal the called-up capital. Paid-up capital is important because if a company makes a reference on its stationery to the amount of its capital, the reference must be paid-up capital ***(S.351)***.

e. ***Uncalled capital***. This is the difference between the amount already paid-up and the total nominal value of the issued shares. Uncalled capital is rare because it is unpopular with both companies and investors, companies because of the possibility that calls will not be met, and investors because of uncertainty as to when calls will be made. Where it exists, uncalled capital is a type of guarantee fund for creditors. It is an asset equivalent to debtors, the debtors in this case being the members. The creditors can however only gain access to this fund in the event of a liquidation since they cannot compel the directors to make calls, nor can they levy execution on uncalled capital.

f. ***Reserve capital***. In order that the guarantee fund referred to above can be removed from the directors' control and made more permanent, **S.120** provides that a company may, by ***special resolution***, determine that it shall only be called up in the event of winding-up. The special resolution creating reserve capital is irrevocable. Reserve capital, which is also known as 'reserve liability' must not be confused with 'General Reserve' or ' Reserve Fund' . These terms refer to undistributed profits.

3. Alteration of capital

By **S.121** provided a company has authority in its articles (eg Table A Article 32), it may pass an ***ordinary resolution*** to alter the capital clause of its memorandum in any of the following ways:

a. ***Increase***, ie an increase of nominal capital. This will only be necessary when all of the nominal capital has been issued.

b. ***Consolidation***, ie the merging of a number of shares into one share of the nominal value of the aggregate, for example ten 5 pence shares are consolidated into one 50 pence share.

c. ***Subdivision***. This is the reverse of consolidation. It has been held that a subdivision of shares does not vary the class rights of other shares even if voting equilibrium is altered.

In GREENHALGH v ARDERNE CINEMAS (1946) 10 pence ordinary shares ranked equally as regards voting with 50 pence ordinary shares. Each 50 pence share was then sub-divided into five 10 pence ordinary shares with one vote each. It was held that the voting rights of the original 10 pence shares had not been varied even though the holder of these shares had now lost his power to block a special resolution.

d. ***Conversion.*** Fully paid shares may be converted into stock and vice versa.

e. ***Cancellation.*** This refers to a decrease in the nominal capital of the company, ie un-issued shares are cancelled. Cancellation, which is also known as diminution, must be distinguished from reduction of capital, which is a decrease in the amount of issued share capital.

The registrar must be notified of an increase within 15 days. In other cases the registrar must be notified within one month.

## MAINTENANCE OF CAPITAL INTRODUCTION

### 4. The need to maintain capital

The acceptance of limited liability has led to a need to protect the capital contributed by the members since the members cannot be required to contribute funds to enable the company to pay its debts once they have paid for their shares in full. The capital therefore represents a guarantee fund for creditors. It is protected in two basic ways:

a. Provisions designed to prevent the capital being 'watered down' as it comes into the company; and

b. Provisions designed to prevent capital going out of the company once it has been received. The dividend rules (Chapter 11) fall within this category.

### 5. Other methods of creditor protection

Creditors are also protected by many other rules not connected with maintenance of capital, for example concerning publicity and liquidations.

## PROVISIONS DESIGNED TO PREVENT CAPITAL BEING 'WATERED DOWN'

### 6. Underwriting commission

a. An underwriter is a person (or finance house) which, on a public issue of shares, agrees to purchase those shares which are not taken up by the public.

b. By *S.97* (as amended by the *FINANCIAL SERVICES ACT 1986*) underwriters may be paid a commission not exceeding 10% of the issue price provided there is authority in the articles (for example Table A Article 4) and compliance with any rules made by the Secretary of State under powers given in the *FINANCIAL SERVICES ACT 1986*. These rules include the requirement of disclosure in the listing particulars. The commission is charged on the number of shares underwritten and must be paid even if the issue is a success and the public take all the shares. The usual rate is 1¼%.

c. When a company has been in existence for some years it will probably be able to pay underwriting commission from its accumulated profits or its Share Premium Account. In contrast when a company makes its first issue of shares these funds will not exist. Underwriting commission must therefore be paid out of the proceeds of the issue, ie out of capital. Thus, whether or not the issue is successful, the shares will have been issued at a discount. This is why underwriting commission is subject to statutory control.

d. The underwriting agreement will usually cover the whole issue, although it may cover merely the minimum subscription. The consequences of not achieving the minimum subscription are so serious that underwriting is virtually compulsory.

e. ***S.97*** does not apply to debentures, nor does it apply to private companies, since it is only necessary to underwrite a public issue.

f. Distinguish underwriting commission from brokerage. Brokerage is a payment made to a bank, issuing house, or broker for placing shares without buying. Brokerage is not controlled by the Act. However payment of brokerage will only be lawful if

   i. There is authority in the articles;

   ii. The amount is reasonable, ie ¼–½%;

   iii. The amount is disclosed in the prospectus;

   iv. It is paid to a person carrying on the business of broker, and not to a private person.

**7. Payment for share capital**

a. It is not possible for a company to make a gift of its shares to an allottee, the shares must always be paid for.

b. ***S.99(1)*** states that they may be paid for in money or in money's worth, including goodwill or know-how.

c. However by ***S.99(2)*** a ***public company*** may not accept as payment an undertaking to do work or perform services for the company. This means that the shares of a public company must be paid up in ***cash*** or non-cash assets.

d. Also by ***S.106*** shares issued by a ***public company*** to a subscriber to the memorandum, in pursuance of an undertaking in the memorandum, must be paid up in cash.

e. By ***S.738*** 'cash' includes

   i. A cheque;

   ii. The release of a liability of the company for a liquidated sum; and

   iii. An undertaking to pay cash to the company at a future date.

f. By **S.739** a 'non-cash asset' is any property or interest in property other than cash.

g. If **S.99(2)** is contravened the person to whom the shares were allotted becomes liable to pay the nominal value, plus the premium (if any) plus interest, to the company. In addition any subsequent purchaser who is aware of the contravention is also liable.

h. **S.99** does not apply to private companies, which may therefore accept work or services as payment for their shares.

**8. The issue of shares at a discount**

a. By **S.100** the issue of shares at a discount is prohibited. This section applies to all companies.

b. If shares are allotted in contravention of **S.100** the allottee shall be liable to pay the company the amount of the discount plus interest at the appropriate rate. A subsequent purchaser who is aware that the shares were issued at a discount is also liable.

c. There are two situations when shares may lawfully be issued at a discount:

   i. When underwriting commission is paid; and

   ii. When the shares of a private company are issued in exchange for an over-valued consideration, (see 10 below).

**9. Minimum payment for allotted shares**

a. By **S.101** a public company may not allot shares unless they are paid-up to the extent of one quarter the nominal value plus the whole of the premium.

b. This provision does not apply to shares allotted under an employees' share scheme.

c. If **S.101** is contravened the allottee, or any subsequent purchaser who is aware of the contravention, must pay the additional amount required plus interest.

**10. Allotment for non-cash consideration**

a. By **S.102** where a ***public company*** allots shares which are fully or partly paid for by an undertaking to transfer to the company a non-cash asset at a future date, that asset must be transferred with in five years of the date of allotment.

b. In the event of contravention of **S.102** the allottee becomes liable to pay for his shares in cash, with interest. Liability extends to subsequent holders who were aware of the contravention.

c *Valuation of non-cash consideration, public companies*

   i. By **S.103** a ***public company*** may not allot shares for a consideration other than cash unless the non-cash asset has been independently valued and a report on the valuation has been made to the company within the six months prior to the allotment. The report must also be sent to the proposed allottee.

ii. The independent person must be qualified to be the auditor of the company. The valuation may be his own, or that of some other person, provided the other person appears to him to have the requisite knowledge and experience.

iii. The contents of the report are very detailed. However the most important item is the statement that the value of the consideration (including and cash payable) is not less than the nominal value of the shares plus any premium, ie that the shareholders are getting value for money.

iv. If ***S.103*** is contravened the allottee is liable to pay to the company the nominal value of his shares in cash, with interest. As with previous sections subsequent holders who were aware of the contravention are also liable.

v. ***S.103*** does not apply when shares are allotted in the course of a takeover bid, ie X Ltd offers to acquire Y Ltd shares in exchange its own shares. In such a case X Ltd need not obtain a valuation of Y Ltd's shares.

d. ***Valuation of non-cash consideration, private companies***. When a private company issues shares ii return for a non-cash consideration the court will not usually enquire into the adequacy of consideration. For example although the valuation of Salomon's business at £39,000 was described by the House of Lords as 'a sum which represented the sanguine expectations of a fond owner rather than anything that can be called a businesslike or reasonable estimate of value' they were not prepared to set aside the transaction even though the correct valuation of the business was about £10,000. (See Chapter 5.1)

There are three exceptional situations when the court is concerned with the adequacy of consideration

i. Where the contract is fraudulent;

ii. Where the consideration is past; and

iii. Where the inadequacy appears on the face of the contract.

In **HONG KONG AND CHINA GAS CO v GLEN (1914)** the company agreed to allot to the vendor of a concession to supply gas to the city of Victoria in Hong Kong, 400 fully paid shares, plus one fifth of any future increase in capital, allotted as fully paid. It was held that the part of the agreement relating to future increases in capital was invalid because it meant that the company had agreed an unlimited value for the purchase of the concession.

**11. Valuation of non-cash assets acquired by public companies from subscribers to the memorandum**

a. The following provisions are designed to ensure that when a subscriber to the memorandum of a public company transfers non-cash assets to the company in return for shares (except subscribers' shares, which must be paid up in cash, **S.106**) those assets are valued in the same way as prescribed by **S.103**.

b. By **S.104** for the two years following the issue of its trading certificate a ***public company*** may not acquire non-cash assets from a subscriber to the memorandum where those assets have an aggregate value equal to 10% or more of the nominal value of the issued share capital unless:

   i. The assets have been valued in accordance with **S.103** and a report made to the company; and

   ii. The terms of the acquisition have been approved by an ordinary resolution, a copy of the ordinary resolution and the report having been circulated to the members not later than the time of giving notice of the meeting at which the resolution is to be proposed.

c. A copy of the resolution and report must be delivered to the registrar within 15 days of the resolution having been passed.

d. Similar rules apply to assets acquired within two years of re-registration, from a member of a company which re-registered as public.

e. These rules do not apply to assets acquired in the ordinary course of business.

f. If **S.104** is contravened the allottee and any successor in title who knew of the contravention is liable to repay to the company the consideration received plus interest.

**12. Relief from liability**

By **S.113** any person who becomes liable to the company under the sections dealing with payment for allotted shares (Sections 99,102,103 and 104) may apply to the court for exemption from liability. The court may grant exemption if it appears just and equitable to do so.

## PROVISIONS DESIGNED TO PREVENT CAPITAL GOING OUT OF THE COMPANY

**13. Serious loss of capital**

a. By **S.142** the directors of a ***public company*** must call an extraordinary general meeting when it becomes known to a director that the net assets have fallen to ***half or less*** of the company's called-up share capital.

b. The meeting must be called within 28 days from the date when the above fact became known and must be convened within 56 days from that date.

c. The purpose of the meeting is to decide what action, if any, should be taken. In some cases the meeting will decide on a reduction of capital.

**14. Reduction of capital**

a. By ***S.135*** a company may, ***if authorised by its articles***, pass a ***special resolution*** and obtain the ***consent of the court*** to reduce its capital and alter its memorandum accordingly.

b. ***S.135*** enables a company to reduce its capital in any case but in particular it specifies:

   i. To extinguish liability on share capital not paid up.

   For example Company A is doing well. Its shares have a nominal value of £1 and 75 pence is paid-up. It does not anticipate ever calling-up the other 25 pence, but it cannot merely pass a resolution that they will be regarded as £1 shares, fully paid. It must convert them to shares with a nominal value of 75 pence.

   ii. To cancel paid up capital which is lost and no longer represented by assets.

   For example Company B is doing badly. It has a share capital of £100,000 divided into 100,000 fully paid shares of £1 each. Its net assets are worth only £60,000. Provided this is a permanent loss and not merely a short term fluctuation it may reduce its capital to 100,000 shares of 60 pence each, fully paid.

   iii. To repay share capital in excess of the company's needs.

   For example Company C may be doing well, or it may have sold part of its undertaking. If it has 50,000 £1 shares, fully paid, but does not require this amount of capital it may reduce its capital to 50,000 fully paid shares of 50 pence each and return 50 pence per share to the members.

c. If the reduction affects creditors (ie i. or iii. above) the court will not confirm the reduction unless the creditors

   i. Agree to it; or

   ii. Are paid off; or

   iii. Are given security.

d. In addition to the interests of the creditors the court will also ensure that the reduction is equitable between the various classes of shareholders involved. Note **RE HOLDERS INVESTMENT TRUST (1971)** and **HOUSE OF FRASER v A.C.G.E. INVESTMENTS (1987)** (Chapter 21.3).

e. If the nominal value of a public company's allotted shares is reduced below the authorised minimum it will have to be re-registered as private. However by **S.139** the court may dispense with the need for a special resolution of the company and may itself specify the changes to be made to the company's memorandum and articles.

f. Capital may be lawfully reduced without court consent:

   i. When a private company purchases any of its own shares (including redeemable shares) out of capital under **S.171** (see 27 below);

   ii. When shares are forfeited for non-payment of a call; or

   iii. When shares are surrendered to avoid a forfeiture.

g. A reduction of capital must be distinguished from a cancellation of unissued shares under **S.121**.

**15. Charges of public companies on own shares *(S.150)***

A public company cannot have a lien or other charge on its own shares except:

a. For unpaid capital.

b. Where lending is ordinary business and the charge is offered by a borrower in the ordinary course of business.

c. Private companies which had a charge in existence before becoming re-registered as public.

All charges other than those listed above are void.

**16. The issue of shares at a premium – basic rule**

a. It is usual to issue shares at a price above their nominal value, ie at a premium. This may be because the net assets of the company exceed the nominal value of the shares, or because previously issued shares of the same class have a market value in excess of their nominal value.

b. By **S.130** when shares are issued at a premium ( whether for cash or in exchange for property, goods or services) the premium must be paid into a ***share premium account*** which can only be used

   i. To finance an issue of fully paid bonus shares to members;

   ii. To write off preliminary expenses;

   iii. To write off commissions paid, or discounts allowed, or the expenses of an issue of shares or debentures.

   iv. To provide the premium payable on the redemption of any debentures of the company;

   v. Where redeemable shares are issued at a premium, to provide the premium payable on redemption. This is subject to conditions (see 22.f. below).

c. **S.130** therefore requires that, except for the above purposes, share premiums are treated as capital, for example they cannot be distributed as dividends. In doing so it recognises that what is important is not the arbitrarily fixed nominal value, but the actual value received for the shares when issued.

d. There are however situations involving mergers where a non-distributable share premium account need not be established. This is considered below.

**17. The issue of shares at a premium – merger relief**

a. The requirement to create a share premium account can give rise to difficulties in the type of merger where shares in 'Company A' are issued to shareholders of 'Company B' in return for a transfer to Company A of Company B's shares. Company B would then be dissolved and Company A (as its majority shareholder) would acquire its assets. This is basically a takeover by agreement.

b. Prior to 1980 there was uncertainty as to whether a share premium account need be established by Company A when the assets of Company B exceed the nominal value of Company B's shares. If a share premium account had to be opened the pre-acquisition profits of Company B could not be distributed by Company A. It was therefore preferred not to open a share premium account. This method is known as ***'merger accounting'***. The alternative method (ie opening a share premium account) is known as ***'acquisition accounting'*** and has the result that the pre-acquisition profits of Company B cannot be distributed by Company A.

   In **SHEARER v BERCAIN (1980)** it was confirmed that merger accounting was illegal and that a true value must be attributed to non-cash assets (such as shares in another company) acquired in consideration for an issue of shares and that the excess of the 'true value' over the nominal value of the shares issued must be transferred to a share premium account.

c. As a result of pressure from the business community the 1981 Act allowed the use of merger accounting in specified circumstances. The basic provision is now in ***S.131***.

d. By ***S.131*** merger relief is available when the issuing company has acquired at least 90% of the equity share capital of another company in consequence of the allotment of its own equity shares. In such cases ***S.130*** does not apply to the premium on the shares allotted by the acquiring company. Note that:

   i. It is not necessary that all of the 90% holding be acquired as a consequence of the allotment;

   ii. Shares held by another company in the same group as the issuing company are regarded as being held by the issuing company;

   iii. Merger relief is retrospective, ie it legalises merger accounting carried out before the Act was passed. In such cases the 90% threshold is not necessary. All that is required is acquisition of a subsidiary. *S.131* does not however allow cancellation of a share premium account already established by an acquiring company which used the 'acquisition accounting' method.

**18. The acquisition by a company of its own shares – background and general rule**

a. For many years it has been a basic principle of company law that a company may not purchase its own shares. This was established in TREVOR v WHITWORTH (1887).

b. The basic rule is now contained in *S.143(1)* which states that(subject to the following provisions) a company shall not acquire its own shares. Any purported acquisition in contravention of this section is void.

c. There are a number of exceptions to the basic rule:

i. Where it acquires its own fully paid shares otherwise than for valuable consideration *(S.143(3))*.

In RE CASTIGLIONE'S WILL TRUSTS (1958), a testator by his will directed that 1,000 shares in a private company be held in trust for his son for life, and if his son should die without children, should be transferred to the company. The son died without children and validity of the bequest was questioned. It was held that the company itself could not hold the shares but they could be held by nominees in trust for the company.

ii. A purchase of redeemable shares *(S.159–160)*.

iii. A purchase of own shares under *S.162–178*.

iv. An acquisition as part of a capital reduction scheme.

v. An acquisition in pursuance of a court order under *S.5* (alteration of objects); *S.54* (re-registration of a public company as private); or *S.461* (unfair prejudice).

vi. Where shares are forfeited for non-payment of a call, or where shares are surrendered in lieu of forfeiture.

d. There are a number of reasons why it is undesirable for a company to be able to purchase its own shares:

i. It is a reduction of capital, ie if it pays shareholder A cash for his shares, less cash is available to satisfy the claims of creditors X, Y and Z;

ii. If it paid shareholder A too much for his shares this would dilute the value of the remaining assets, ie on winding-up there would be less cash available for shareholders B, C and D;

iii. If it paid shareholder A too little for his shares this would enhance the value of the remainder and could be used by the directors to increase the value of their own holdings;

iv. A method of frustrating a takeover bid is to buy shares on the open market. If the directors could use the company money to do this, no doubt they would do so, thus entrenching themselves in control of the company.

e. In recent years there has been increasing interest in relaxing the prohibition for the benefit of the company and its shareholders provided the position of creditors and other interested parties could be protected. The advantages of allowing a company to purchase its own shares are:

i. It facilitates the retention of 'family' control of a private company;

ii. It increases the marketability of a company's shares, since the company itself is a potential buyer. This in turn would increase interest in employee share schemes, and may therefore help the company to raise further capital;

iii. It enables both public and private companies to use surplus cash to the company's advantage. For example if redeemable shares have a market value of less than their redemption price, they could be redeemed immediately rather than waiting to pay the higher price on the redemption date;

iv. It may make it easier for companies to raise venture capital from merchant banks since the banks have the possibility of 'getting out' by selling their shares back to the company.

**19. Financial assistance for acquisition of shares. General prohibition**

a. By **S.151** it is illegal for a company directly or indirectly to give any financial assistance for the acquisition of any of its shares or shares in its holding company. It is irrelevant whether the financial assistance is given before, at the same time as, or after, the acquisition. The purpose of **S.151** is to extend the rule in **S.143** in an attempt to prevent evasions of it.

b. ***'Financial assistance'*** is defined by **S.152** to include:

i. A gift;

ii. Provision of a guarantee, security, indemnity, release or waiver;

iii. A loan and related arrangements; and

iv. Any other financial assistance by a company whose net assets are as a result reduced to a material extent or which has no net assets.

c. **S.151** can be illustrated by the following cases:

In HEALD v O'CONNOR (1971) the seller of the controlling shareholding in a company lent part of the price to the buyer. The loan was secured by a floating charge on the company's assets. In addition this debenture was guaranteed by the purchaser. It was held that the debenture amounted to financial assistance. Also the seller could not enforce the guarantee since it was not possible to guarantee an illegal transaction.

In **BELMONT FINANCE v WILLIAMS FURNITURE (1980)** Group 'A' wanted to buy Belmont from Group 'B' without paying for the shares with their own money. It was arranged that the purchase would be financed from Belmont's own assets, which were extracted by Group 'A' first selling to Belmont for £500,000 shares in another company which were worth only £60,000. The £500,000 was then used by Group 'A' to pay Group 'B' for Belmont's shares. It was held that the arrangement was illegal.

d. The effects of contravention of **S.151** are:

   i. The financial assistance, for example the guarantee or security, is void;

   ii. The company and any officer in default is liable to a fine and/or up to two years imprisonment;

   iii. Every director who is party to a contravention of **S.151** is guilty of a breach of duty and is liable to recoup any losses which the company suffers as a result. **(WALLERSTEINER v MOIR (1974))**.

**20. Financial assistance. Exceptions applying to all companies**

By **S.153** a company may give financial assistance:

a. If is principal purpose is not to give assistance for the acquisition of any of its own or its holding company's shares.

   *For example* a company might purchase goods and pay the supplier in advance. If the supplier then uses the payment to purchase the company's shares the company will have provided financial assistance. However the action would be lawful since the company's purpose was to make a normal business contract, not the provision of financial assistance.

b. If the purpose of the assistance is the acquisition of own shares, but this is an incidental part of a larger purpose of the company.

   *For example* a group may need to increase its general borrowing for commercial reasons after the acquisition of a new subsidiary. If the new subsidiary assists in providing security for the increase in indebtedness, it would be acting with the purpose of providing financial assistance in connection with the acquisition of its shares, but this would be an incidental part of a larger purpose.

c. Where the lending of money is part of the ordinary business of the company, and the loan is in the ordinary course of its business.

   *For example* a bank may lend to its customer so that he can buy shares in the bank.

d. Where the loan is provided in good faith in the interests of the company, for the purposes of an employees' share scheme. **S.153** was amended by **S.132 CA 89**. Prior to the 1989 Act the only form of financial assistance was the provision of money for the acquisition of fully paid shares to be held under an employee share scheme. Any form of financial assistance is now permitted as long as it is provided in good faith.

*For example* a company may give a guarantee or some other form of security to a bank that lends money to an employees' share scheme.

e. Where the loan is to employees (other than directors) to enable them to purchase fully paid shares to be held by them as beneficial owners.

f. The payment of dividends; any distribution made in the course of a winding-up; the allotment of any bonus shares; a reduction of capital; any compromise under ***S.425*** and any redemption or purchase of its own shares.

In the case of a public company, exceptions c, d, and e only apply if the company's net assets are not thereby reduced, or to the extent that they are reduced, the financial assistance is provided out of distributable profits. ***(S.154)***.

In situations a. and b. the financial assistance must be given in good faith and in the interests of the company.

Recently ***S.153*** (and the question of gratuitous dispositions of company assets) was considered by the House of Lords.

In **BRADY v BRADY (1988)** B Ltd, a family company carried on a haulage business and a drinks business. Its only directors were brothers Jack and Bob Brady. They also owned the majority of the shares, a minority being held equally by Bob's two sons Robert and John. B Ltd had been very successful, although recently it had run into difficulties because of the 'animosity and mutual intransigence' of Jack and Bob. In the dispute John sided with his father and Robert with his uncle Jack. This resulted in a management deadlock that was beginning to damage the business.

A complex scheme was therefore devised to split the business, Jack taking the haulage side and Bob the drinks side. This however required a substantial movement of assets from the haulage to the drinks side. New companies were formed, M Ltd to run the haulage business and A Ltd to run the drinks business. Put simply a situation was arrived at whereby A Ltd held loan stock issued by M Ltd. This indebtedness of M to A would be discharged by a transfer of B Ltd's assets to A. M Ltd (whose only asset was shares in B) would then acknowledge its debt to B Ltd. After this position had been agreed by letter, Bob formed the view that the adjustments in his favour were insufficient. Not accepting his contentions, Jack started proceedings for specific performance of the contract contained in the letter.

Bob resisted the claim on the grounds of ultra vires and unlawful financial assistance. In the High Court the Judge awarded Jack an order for specific performance. This was reversed by a majority of the Court of Appeal. On further appeal to the House of Lords the order for specific performance was reinstated. Briefly summarised the main points were:

a. ***Ultra vires***. That the disposition of assets by B Ltd to A was not gratuitous since the debt by M was not valueless, since M's shares in Brady represented underlying net assets at least sufficient to cover the debt.

b. ***Financial assistance***. It was held that although all concerned had acted in good faith and in the interests of B Ltd (certainly the position of creditors was strengthened) B Ltd's financial assistance (ie the discharge of M's loan stock) was not 'an incidental part of some larger purpose of the company'. The House of Lords considered that the words 'larger purpose' must be given a narrow meaning and do not provide a blank cheque for avoiding the effective application of **S.151**. They did not accept that a larger purpose could be found in the reorganisation as a whole nor in the breaking of the management deadlock.

c. As a result of (b) above it might appear that specific performance should be refused since the overall scheme has failed. However the House of Lords accepted a new argument, not put forward at the trial or in the Court of Appeal, namely that the terms of the contract contained in the letter obliged B Ltd to give financial assistance with the aid of **S.155–158**. Since the conditions imposed by these sections could be satisfied without requiring Bob to do anything he had not agreed to do, the House of Lords awarded Jack the order for specific performance.

21. Financial assistance. Relaxation of **S.151** for private companies ***(S.155–158)***

a. ***Basic provision***. Subject to the conditions specified below, a private company may give financial assistance for the acquisition of its shares or the shares of its holding company (if also a private company) provided the company's net assets are not thereby reduced, or to the extent that they are reduced the financial assistance is provided out of distributable profits. This would allow a private company to arrange a ***'management buyout'***, ie the disposal of a company to its management. The management could either buy shares in the company with a loan from company funds, or more usually, the management would buy the shares with a bank loan which would be secured by company assets.

b. ***Conditions which must be complied with***:

i. A ***special resolution*** must be passed;

ii. The directors must make a statutory declaration in the prescribed form. It must give particulars of the assistance to be given and of the business of the company and it must identify the person to whom assistance is given. It must state that in the directors' opinion the company will be able to pay its debts immediately after, and during the 12 months following, the date on which the assistance is given;

iii. A report by the company's auditors must be attached to the statutory declaration. It must state that they have enquired into the company's state of affairs and are not aware of anything to indicate that the opinion expressed by the directors is unreasonable;

iv. The financial assistance must not be given earlier than four weeks after the resolution is passed;

v. The financial assistance must not be given more than eight weeks after the statutory declaration;

vi. The resolution must be passed on the date of, or within the week following the statutory declaration;

Points iv.–vi. may be clarified as follows:

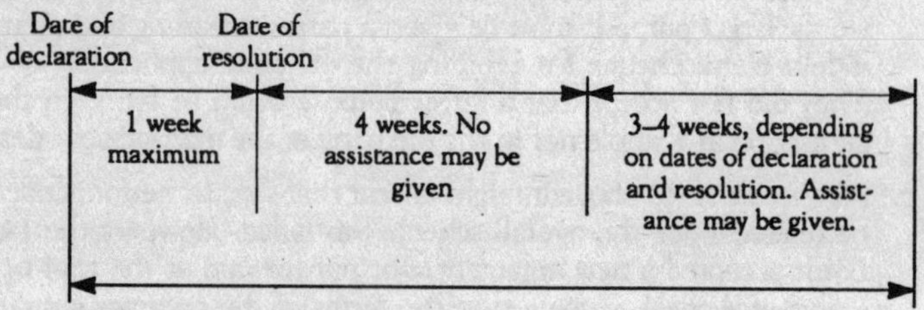


vii. The statutory declaration and auditors' report must be available for inspection by members at the meeting where the resolution is passed;

viii. The statutory declaration, auditors' report and resolution must be delivered to the registrar within 15 days of making the declaration.

c. ***The right of members to object***. Holders of 10% of the nominal value of any class of issued shares may apply to the court within 28 days of the resolution to cancel the resolution. The applicants must not have voted in favour of the resolution.

**22. The power to issue redeemable shares**

a. By ***S.159*** a company may, if authorised by its articles, issue shares which are to be redeemed, or may be redeemed at the option of the company or the shareholder.

b. The following conditions must be fulfilled:

i. No redeemable shares may be issued unless there are shares in issue which are not redeemable;

ii. Shares may not be redeemed unless they are fully paid;

iii. The terms of the redemption must provide for payment on redemption;

iv. Except for private companies which take advantage of the power to redeem shares out of capital (see 27 below) the shares may only be redeemed out of the company's distributable profits or out of the proceeds of a fresh issue of shares made for the purpose of the redemption ***(S.160)***.

v. The terms and manner of redemption must be specified at or before the time of issue, including the date on or by which (or dates between which) the shares will be (or may be) redeemed. The amount payable on redemption must be specified in, or determined in accordance with, the articles and in the later case the articles cannot provide the amount to be determined by reference to any person's discretion or option. **S.133 CA 89 (S.159A).**

c. By **S.170** where shares are redeemed out of profits a sum equal to their nominal value must be transferred from profits to a capital redemption reserve. This reserve, like the share premium account, is a statutory capital reserve. Except for a reduction of capital under **S.135**, or a redemption or purchase of shares out of capital under **S.171**, the capital redemption reserve can only be applied in the allotment of fully paid bonus shares.

d. If the shares are redeemed out of the proceeds of a fresh issue, capital is automatically replaced and no capital redemption reserve is needed.

e. If the shares are redeemed at a premium the basic rule is that the premium must be paid out of distributable profits. There is an exception where the shares were originally issued at a premium. In such cases the premium on redemption may be provided out of the share premium account to the extent that it does not exceed the lesser of:

   i. The premiums received on the issue of the shares being redeemed; and

   ii. The balance on the share premium account.

f. Shares redeemed are treated as cancelled on redemption and the amount of the company's issued capital is reduced accordingly, but the company's authorised capital is not affected.

**23. The purchase by a company of its own shares – general rule**

a. By **S.162** a company (public or private) may, if authorised by its articles, purchase its own shares (including redeemable shares).

b. The conditions that apply to the redemption of redeemable shares also apply to the purchase of own shares, for example the need for a capital redemption reserve.

c. A company may not purchase its own shares if, as a result, there would no longer be any member of the company holding shares other than redeemable shares.

d. The requirements for the authorisation of purchase of own shares depend on whether the transaction is an off-market purchase or a market purchase.

**24. Off-market purchase of own shares *(S.163–164)***

a. A purchase is an off-market purchase if either:

   i. The shares are purchased otherwise than on a recognised stock exchange; or

   ii. They are purchased on a recognised stock exchange but are not publicly traded on that stock exchange.

b. Before a company may make an off-market purchase, a ***special resolution*** must be passed authorising the purchase and its terms. The shares that are to be purchased ***may not vote*** on the resolution. Despite anything in the articles ***any member*** may demand a poll on such a resolution.

c. A note of the terms of the proposed purchase contract must be available for inspection at the company's registered office for at least 15 days before the meeting at which the special resolution is to be voted and at the meeting itself. The names of members holding shares to which the contract relates must be made clear.

d. In the case of a ***public company*** the authority for an off-market purchase must specify a date, not later than 18 months after passing the resolution, on which the authority is to expire.

e. By ***S.165*** a company may enter into a ***contingent purchase contract***. For example a small family-owned company may arrange with an outsider employed as managing director, that the latter should hold shares for as long as his connection with the company continues, but that the shares should be offered back to the company when his connection with the company ceases. Such contracts are treated by the Act as off-market purchases of the company's own shares (ie basically an option contract, under which the company may become entitled or obliged to purchase shares). A contingent purchase contract must be authorised in advance by ***special resolution***.

**25. Market purchase of own shares *S.166***

a. A market purchase is one made on a stock exchange, including the Unlisted Securities Market.

b. Before a company may make a market purchase an ***ordinary resolution*** must be passed. The resolution must:

   i. Specify the maximum number of shares to be purchased;

   ii. Specify the maximum and minimum prices which may be paid for those shares; and

   iii. Specify a date, not later than 18 months after the resolution, on which the authority is to expire.

c. A copy of the resolution must be delivered to the registrar within 15 days of it being passed.

d. The shares to be purchased may vote on the ordinary resolution. Contrast a special resolution for the off-market purchase of own shares.

**26. Purchase of own shares – additional matters**

a. ***Assignment and release***. By ***S.167*** the rights of a company acquired under a contract to purchase its own shares cannot be assigned. This prevents a company from speculating in its own shares. A company may however release its rights under a contract for an off-market purchase provided the release is authorised in advance by a special resolution.

b. ***Payments to be made out of distributable profits***. By ***S.168*** the following payments (ie payments apart from the purchase price) must be made out of distributable profits. Any payment made in consideration:

   i. Of acquiring a right to purchase its own shares, ie a payment under a contingent purchase contract;

   ii. For a variation of a contract for an off-market purchase or a contingent purchase contract;

   iii. For a release of any obligations under any contract for the purchase of its own shares.

c. ***Disclosure requirements***. By ***S.169***

   i. ***All companies*** must, within 28 days of a purchase of their own shares, deliver a return to the registrar stating the number and nominal value of the shares purchased and the date (or dates) of purchase.

   ii. In addition a ***public company*** must state the aggregate amount paid by the company for the shares, and for each class of shares purchased, the maximum and minimum price paid.

   iii. A copy of every contract or contingent purchase contract must be retained by the company at its registered office from the time the contract is concluded until 10 years after the purchase takes place. This may be inspected by any member and, in the case of a public company, by any person.

**27. The redemption or purchase of its own shares out of capital by a private company (*S.171–177*)**

a. ***Introduction***. The permission for a private company to purchase its own shares out of capital was first granted in 1981. It represented a significant change in company law philosophy. It potentially strikes at one of the basic functions of company law, ie to protect the creditors by maintaining the capital fund. The power to purchase is therefore subject to the full battery of protective measures available to modern company law.

b. ***The power to purchase***. By ***S.171*** a private company may, if authorised by its articles make a payment out of capital for the redemption or purchase of its own shares under ***S.159*** or ***S.162***.

c. ***The permissible capital payment***. The amount which may be paid out of capital is the amount by which the price of the redemption or purchase exceeds the sum of distributable profits ***plus*** the proceeds of any fresh issue shares made for the purpose of the redemption or purchase. Thus a payment out of capital can only be made after distributable profits have been exhausted.

d. ***The capital redemption reserve***

i. The provisions in **S.171** are similar to earlier provisions in the 1948 Act. Their object is to ensure that the capital of the company is maintained when a company purchases its own shares. The position is much more complicated when a private company redeems or purchases its own shares out of capital. Clearly capital cannot be maintained, even so a capital redemption reserve may be needed. The following rules are rather difficult to grasp. Reference will probably be needed to the examples set out in 28. below.

ii. Where the aggregate of the permissible capital payment plus the proceeds of any fresh issue of shares is ***less than*** the nominal amount of the shares redeemed or purchased, the difference must be transferred to a capital redemption reserve.

iii. Where the aggregate of the permissible capital payment plus the proceeds of any fresh issue of shares ***exceeds*** the nominal amount of the shares redeemed or purchased, any capital redemption reserve, share premium account, revaluation reserve, or fully paid share capital may be reduced by the excess.

e. ***Accounts***. The amount of the company's distributable profits must be determined by accounts prepared not more than three months before the date of the statutory declaration (see h. below).

f. ***The resolution to approve payment***. The provisions are similar to those which apply when a company makes an off-market purchase of its own shares, ie:

i. A special resolution must be passed;

ii. The shares which are to be purchased out of capital may not vote on the resolution;

iii. Any member may demand a poll;

iv. In addition the resolution must be passed on the date of the statutory declaration or the following week.

g. ***The date of payment***. The payment out of capital must take place between five and seven weeks after the resolution.

h. ***The statutory declaration***. The directors must make a statutory declaration specifying the amount of the permissible capital payment and stating that, having made full enquiries into the affairs and prospects of the company, they are of the opinion that:

i. There will be no ground on which the company could be found unable to pay its debts immediately after the payment out of capital is to take place; ***and***

ii. That the company will be able to carry on business as a going concern throughout the following year, ie it will be able to pay its debts as they fall due.

j. ***Auditors' report***. This must be attached to the statutory declaration. The auditors must state that:

   i. They have enquired into the company's state of affairs;

   ii. The permissible capital payment specified in the declaration has been properly determined; ***and***

   iii. They are not aware of anything to indicate that the opinion expressed by the directors in the declaration is unreasonable.

k. ***Publicity***

   i. Within one week after passing the resolution a notice containing specified details (for example the amount of the permissible capital payment) must be published in the Gazette;

   ii. The company must also publish the notice in a national newspaper, or send a copy of it to each of its creditors;

   iii. The company must deliver a copy of the statutory declaration and the auditors' report to the registrar not later than the date of first publication of the notice;

   iv. The statutory declaration and auditors' report must be available at the registered office during business hours for inspection by members and creditors. They must be available from the date of publication of the notice until five weeks after the date of the resolution. They must also be available for inspection by members and creditors at the meeting at which the resolution is passed.

l. ***The right of members and creditors to object***

   i. Within five weeks after the resolution:

      (a) any member who did not consent to, or vote in favour of, the resolution; or

      (b) any creditor; may apply to the court to cancel the resolution.

   ii. The court may cancel or confirm the resolution subject to such terms and conditions it thinks fit;

   iii. When an application for cancellation is made to the court the company must notify the registrar and, within 15 days of the court order, deliver a copy of the order to the registrar.

m. ***Liability of past shareholders and directors***. If winding-up commences within one year after payment out of capital, the following persons may be liable to contribute to the assets of the company:

   i. The persons whose shares were redeemed or purchased; ***and***

   ii. The directors who signed the statutory declaration (unless a director shows that he had reasonable grounds for forming the opinion expressed in the declaration).

   Such person need only contribute if the assets and all other contributions are not sufficient to meet the liabilities of the company. The extent of a person's liability is the extent that the payment out of capital relates to his shares. The directors are jointly and severally liable with each such person.

**28. Examples of transfers to the capital redemption reserve**

a. ***Example 1***

Company A redeems or purchases its shares at par out of distributable profits:

| | £ |
|---|---|
| Nominal value of shares redeemed or purchased | 10,000 |
| Redemption or purchase price | 10,000 |
| Funded from: | |
| Distributable profits | 10,000 |
| Proceeds of a fresh issue | – |
| ***Transfer to Capital Redemption Reserve*** | 10,000 |

b. ***Example 2***

Company B redeems or purchases its own shares at a discount of 10% partly out of profits and partly out of the proceeds of a fresh issue.

| | £ |
|---|---|
| Nominal value of shares redeemed or purchased | 10,000 |
| Redemption or purchase price | 9,000 |
| Funded from:- | |
| Distributable profits | 6,000 |
| Proceeds of a fresh issue | 3,000 |
| ***Transfer to Capital Redemption Reserve*** | 7,000 |

**Note:** £7,000 is the amount by which the company's issued share capital is diminished.

c. ***Example 3***

Company C, a private company, redeems shares at par, partly out of the proceeds of a fresh issue, partly out of distributable profits and partly out of capital.

| | £ |
|---|---|
| (a) Nominal value of shares redeemed | 10,000 |
| (b) Redemption price | 10,000 |
| Funded from: | |
| (c) Distributable profits (which must be fully utilised) | 2,000 |
| (d) Proceeds of issue | 7,000 |
| (e) Permissible capital payment ((b) – [(c) + (d)]) | 1,000 |
| ***Transfer to Capital Redemption Reserve*** ((b) – [(d) + (e)]) | 2,000 |

**Note:** The effect of the above is that capital has been reduced by £3,000 and that a capital redemption reserve of £2,000 has been created. The difference of £1,000 represents the amount of the payment out of capital.

d. ***Example 4***

Company D, a private company, redeems shares at a premium of 50%, partly out of the proceeds of a fresh issue, partly out of distributable profits and partly out of capital. Company D has a share premium account of £5,000 and no other reserves.

| | £ |
|---|---|
| (a) Nominal value of shares redeemed | 10,000 |
| (b) Redemption price | 15,000 |
| Funded from: | |
| (c) Distributable profits (which must be fully utilised) | 2,000 |
| (d) Proceeds of issue | 7,000 |
| (e) Permissible capital payment ((b) – [(c) + (d)]) | 6,000 |
| ***Amount which may be charged against the Share Premium Account*** ([(d) + (e)] – (a)) | 3,000 |

***Note:*** The effect of the above is that share capital has been reduced by £3,000 and the Share Premium Account has been reduced by £3,000 accounting for the payment out of capital of £6,000.

**29. Failure by a company to redeem or purchase its own shares**

A company will not have to pay damages for breach of a contract to redeem or purchase its own shares, but an order for specific performance may be granted unless the company is unable to meet the cost of the redemption or purchase out of distributable profits ***(S.178)***.

*PROGRESS TEST 6*

1. What conditions must be complied with if a company wishes to issue redeemable shares?
2. What conditions must be complied with if a company wishes to reduce it capital?
3. What types of resolution are needed to:
   (a) Confer authority on the directors to allot shares.
   (b) Increase authorised capital.
   (c) Authorise a market purchase of own shares?
4. In what circumstances must a share premium account be created?
5. You are the financial advisor to X Ltd and Y Plc. Your clients require advice on the following matters:
   (a) X Ltd propose to issue 10,000 fully paid £1 pence shares and 5,000 fully paid debentures to Harry in return for a release by Harry of X Ltd's liability to pay him a contract debt of £13,500.
   (b) Y Plc propose to issue 200,000 fully paid 50 pence shares to Dick in return for an assignment to Y Plc of Dick's 99 year exclusive right to shoot game birds on Lady Peacock's 2,000 acre estate in Scotland.

# 11 Dividends

## 1. Definition

a. Dividends are payments made out of profits to the members of a company. Dividends paid to preference shareholders will be at a fixed rate, whereas dividends paid to ordinary shareholders will vary with the prosperity of the company. Shareholders do not have an automatic right to dividends even if profits are available. They may consider it more prudent to retain profits within the company. A dividend is therefore not a debt of the company until it is declared. Even then, on liquidation, it is not payable until after the outside creditors have been paid.

b. Dividends must be distinguished from interest. Interest is paid to debenture holders. It is a debt and must be paid out of capital if no profits are available.

## 2. The requirement of solvency

Dividends cannot be paid if this would result in the company being unable to pay its debts as they fall due. All the rules are subject to this overriding condition of solvency. Clearly if a company did pay a dividend in this situation it would have to pay its debts out of capital.

## 3. The basic rule

By ***S.263*** no company, whether public or private, may make a distribution (ie pay dividends) except out of its accumulated realised profits less its accumulated realised losses. In addition unrealised profits may not be used in paying up debentures or amounts unpaid on issued shares. Note that:

a. A ***'distribution'*** is defined as any distribution of a company's assets to its members (including preference shareholders) whether in cash or otherwise except:

   i. The issue of fully or partly paid bonus shares;

   ii. The redemption or purchase of any of the company's own shares out of capital (including the proceeds of any fresh issue of shares) or out of unrealised profits;

   iii. A reduction of capital;

   iv. A distribution in a winding-up.

b. ***'Profits'*** includes both capital and revenue profits and ***'losses'*** includes both capital and revenue losses.

c. A provision (other than one arising as a result of a revaluation of all the fixed assets) must be treated as a realised loss. A provision is an amount set aside to meet a known liability the exact amount of which cannot be determined with accuracy.

d. To avoid a company having to translate an unrealised surplus on the revaluation of a fixed asset into a realised loss as a result of depreciating the higher value of the fixed asset, it is provided that the part of the revaluation surplus that equals the excess depreciation which has been charged as a result of the revaluation may be treated as realised profit.

For example a company pays £10,000 for an asset and decides to write it off over 10 years (straight line method). The depreciation charge is therefore £1,000. After 5 years the asset is revalued at £15,000, but its useful life does not change. In future the depreciation charge will be £3,000 per year, ie £2,000 more than if the revaluation had not been made. Thus £2,000 would have to be retained from realized profits but for **S.275** which allows this £2,000 to be distributed rather than retained.

e. The Act is not precise about what is to be regarded as realised profit. However the courts will be guided by modern accounting practice. For example a profit will be regarded as realised when a sale is completed, even if the debtor has not paid.

4. Public companies

a. By ***S.264*** a public company may not make a distribution if its net assets are less than the aggregate of its called-up capital plus undistributable reserves, or if the result of the distribution would be to reduce its net assets below the aggregate of called-up capital plus undistributable reserves.

b. ***'Undistributable reserves'*** means

i. The share premium account and the capital redemption reserve;

ii. Any other reserve which the company is prevented from distributing by law or by its memorandum or articles; and

iii. The excess of accumulated unrealised profits over accumulated unrealised losses.

c. The practical effect of ***S.264*** is that a public company must take into account an unrealised loss, whereas a private company need not do so. Such unrealised losses will usually arise from the writing down (other than by way of depreciation) of capital assets, since other unrealised losses will usually be charged to the profit and loss account.

**5. Example of the calculation of the distributable profits of private and public companies**

| | | X Ltd/Plc | | Y Ltd/Plc | |
|---|---|---|---|---|---|
| Share capital | A | | 100,000 | | 100,000 |
| Unrealised surplus/ (deficit) on revaluation | B | | 80,000 | | (80,000) |
| Realised profit | | 140,000 | | 140,000 | |
| Realised loss | | (40,000) | | (40,000) | |
| | C | | 100,000 | | 100,000 |
| Total share capital and reserves/net assets | D | | £280,000 | | £120,000 |

Calculation of distributable profit

| | X Ltd/Plc | Y Ltd/Plc |
|---|---|---|
| If the company is private | £100,000 (C) | £100,000 (C) |
| If the company is public | £100,000 [D – (A + B)] | £100,000 (D – A) |

Thus the distribution of a public company is restricted by the rule that its net assets must not be reduced below the aggregate of its called up share capital plus undistributable reserves as a result of a distribution, ie the unrealised deficit has been deducted from the realised profits in arriving at the distributable amount.

**6. Relevant accounts**

a. **S.270** specifies the accounts which must be referred to when determining the legality and amount of any distribution.

b. The relevant accounts are the last annual accounts. The following requirements must be complied with:

   i. They must have been properly prepared under **S.4 CA 89 *(S.226)***.

   ii. The auditors must have made a report in respect of them under **S.235**.

   iii. If, by virtue of anything referred to in the auditors report, the report is not unqualified, the auditors must have stated in writing whether that thing is material for the purpose of determining the legality of the distribution;

   iv. A copy of any such statement must have been laid before the company in general meeting or delivered to the registrar.

**7. Interim dividends**

a. Interim dividends are dividends which are paid between annual general meetings. Usually companies will try to make the interim dividend about the same amount as the final dividend and make the payment mid-way through the year.

b. Where a ***public company*** proposes to pay an interim dividend which would be unlawful if reference were made only to the last annual accounts then interim accounts will be necessary to justify the distribution. These must be properly prepared and a copy must be delivered to the registrar, but they do not have to be audited. ***(S.272)***.

**8. Consequences of unlawful distribution**

a. By ***S.277*** every shareholder who has received an unlawful distribution and who knew or ought to have known that it was paid out of undistributable funds is liable to repay it to the company.

b. Where dividends cannot be recovered from shareholders, every director who was knowingly a party to the unlawful distribution must pay to the company the amount lost plus interest.

**9. The Articles**

a. By ***S.281*** the above rules must be read subject to any provision in the articles which places further restrictions on the amount available for distribution. For example if the articles state that dividends may only be paid out of 'the profits of the business' then capital profits, ie realised profits on the sale of fixed assets, are not available for distribution.

b. The main provisions of Table A in relation to dividends are as follows:

i. The company declares the dividend by ***ordinary resolution***, but the declaration cannot exceed the amount recommended by the directors (Art 102), ie the shareholders can reduce the amount of the recommended dividend but they cannot increase it;

ii. The directors may pay interim dividends if this is justified by the profits (Art 103);

iii. Dividends shall be paid proportionate to the amounts paid-up on shares (Art 104);

iv. Instead of payment in cash the directors may direct payment of a dividend by the distribution of specific assets or paid up shares or debentures of any other company (Arts 105 and 110).

v. Any dividends payable in cash may be paid by cheque sent by post to the registered address of the holder (Art 106).

vi. Dividends do not bear interest (Art 107).

vii. Dividends unclaimed after 12 years shall, if the directors resolve, be forfeited and cease to be owed by the company.

**10. Capitalisation issues**

a. A capitalisation issue is an allotment of fully or partly paid shares in the company to members in proportion to their existing shareholding. The money used to pay up the shares may have come from:

i. The distributable profits of the company.

ii. The share premium account or the capital redemption reserve; or

   iii. Any other reserve which is not available for distribution.

b. A capitalisation issue is sometimes referred to as a 'bonus' or 'scrip' issue. The term 'bonus issue' is rather misleading since it implies that the shares are free. This is not the case since if the funds had not been used to pay up the bonus shares they could (if of type i. above) have been distributed as dividends.

c. If the shares are paid up from the funds referred to in ii. or iii. above this is not a true capitalisation issue since these funds must already be treated as capital. No profits have been capitalised.

d. In order to make a capitalisation issue:

   i. A company must have authority in its articles. Table A Article 110 authorises such an issue provided an ***ordinary resolution*** is first passed;

   ii. The nominal capital must be sufficient. If it is not it will have to be increased under ***S.121***.

e. Following an issue of bonus shares a company must make a return of allotments under *S.88*.

**11. Investment companies *(S.265-268)***

a. It would be inappropriate to apply the above rules to investment companies since their assets may well consist of a portfolio of investments with a value that has fallen to less than the aggregate of called up capital plus undistributable reserves, yet their assets could still be well in excess of their liabilities to third parties. The Act therefore provides different rules for the calculation of their distributable profits.

b. An ***investment company*** is a ***public company*** which has given notice to the registrar of its intention to carry on business as an investment company ***and***:

   i. Its business consists of investing its funds in securities with the aim of benefiting shareholders and spreading their risk;

   ii. None of its individual investments exceeds 15% in value of its total investments;

   iii. Its memorandum and articles prohibit distribution of its capital profits; ***and***

   iv. It does not retain more than 15% of its income from securities.

c. The concession for investment companies is that they may make a distribution out of accumulated realised ***revenue*** profits less accumulated ***revenue*** losses (both realised and unrealised) ***provided*** the distribution does not reduce the company's assets below one and a half times its liabilities. The advantage is that capital losses can be ignored and dividends or other income received can be passed on, even when the market value of the investments has fallen.

**PROGRESS TEST 7**

1. Debenture interest may be paid out of capital. True or false?
2. Explain the term 'interim dividends'.
3. What conditions must be complied with if a company wishes to make a bonus issue?
4. What is the Table A procedure for declaration of a final dividend?
5. What is the position of the directors if, after payment, it is discovered that there were insufficient distributable reserves?
6. Can the company recover from its members a dividend that has been unlawfully paid to them?

## COURSEWORK QUESTIONS 6–10 THE RAISING AND MAINTENANCE OF CAPITAL

6. *A Limited has an issued capital of £325,000 comprising 200,000 ordinary shares of £1 each, 50 pence paid; £100,000 share premium account; and 125,000 6% cumulative preference shares £1 each, fully paid. The accounts show a debit balance on profit and loss account of £150,000 and there are five years' arrears of preference dividends undeclared*

   *Indicate the steps available for restoring this capital structure to a healthy condition and state what considerations need to be borne in mind.*

   *(15 marks)*

   CIMA *May* 1978 *Question* 1

7. *A Limited and B Limited each has an issued share capital of £200,000 in shares of £1 each fully paid.*

   *In July this year all members involved accepted an arrangement whereby each company transferred its assets to AB Limited, a new company, which in return made a one-for-one issue of £1 shares fully paid to all existing shareholders in A Limited and B Limited. The actual value of the assets transferred to the new company was £500,000 in all and the assets were entered in AB Limited's books at that figure.*

   *Indicate the statutory requirements which must be complied with in relation to these transactions.* *(15 marks)*

   CIMA *November* 1980 *Question* 3

8. *A and B, the two directors of Dog Ltd, each hold 40% of the ordinary shares. The remainder is held by C. A also holds debentures issued by Dog Ltd, redeemable on 1 January 1984. A wishes to dispose of his shares and debentures; and B and C do not wish A's substantial interest in the company to pass into other hands. The following alternative schemes are proposed:*

   *(a) Dog Ltd will raise the necessary funds and purchase the shares and debentures.* *(3 marks)*

   *(b) Dog Ltd will raise funds and lend them to C so that he may purchase A's debentures. C will further arrange a private loan, guaranteed by Dog Ltd, so that he may purchase A's shares.* *(4 marks)*

   *(c) B will arrange a private loan so that he may purchase A's shares and debentures. Dog Ltd will guarantee the loan to B.* *(4 marks)*

   *(d) A new company, Fox Ltd, will be formed. 80% of its ordinary shares will be held by Dog Ltd and 10% each by B and C. Fox Ltd will borrow money and with it buy A's shares and debentures.* *(4 marks)*

   *ADVISE Dog Ltd on the legality of each of these FOUR schemes and on the enforceability of the proposed guarantees.* *(15 marks)*

   ACCA December 1978 Question 3

9. *In what circumstances and subject to what safeguards can public companies purchase their own shares?*

   ACCA December 1984 Question 2

10. *(a) When does a dividend become payable and enforceable as a debt against the company?* *(3 marks)*

    *(b) WHY and HOW does the law seek to control the fund from which dividends are paid?* *(12 marks)*

    *(15 marks)*

    ACCA December 1981 Question 4

# PART IV COMPANY SECURITIES

# 12 Shares

## TYPES OF SHARES

**1. The main distinction between shares and debentures**

There are two basic types of company security, shares and debentures. The distinction is that a shareholder is a member of the company, whereas a debenture holder is a creditor of the company.

**2. The definition of a share**

a. A share was defined by Farwell J. in **BORLAND'S TRUSTEE v STEEL (1901)** as

> 'The interest of the shareholder in the company ***measured by a sum of money***, for the purpose of ***liability*** in the first place and of ***interest*** in the second, but also consisting of a series of ***mutual covenants*** entered into by all the shareholders'.

b. Note that:

i. ***'Measured by a sum of money'*** is a reference to the nominal value;

ii. ***'Liability'*** indicates that the member has a duty to pay for his shares;

iii. ***'Interest'*** shows that the shareholder has rights, for example to attend and vote at meetings;

iv. ***'Mutual covenants'*** stresses the contractual nature of a shareholder's rights and is a reference to what is now **S.14.** (Chapter 8.8).

**3. Points to note**

a. Ownership of shares does not constitute part ownership of the assets of the company. Since the company is a separate legal entity it owns its own assets.

b. Shares are personal property. They can be bought, sold, mortgaged or bequeathed. A fraction of a share cannot exist, but one share may be held by two or more people.

c. A share must be distinguished from the share certificate, which is merely evidence of title to the shares.

d. Both preference shares and ordinary shares may be issued as redeemable or irredeemable.

**4. Preference shares**

a. Preference shares are designed to appeal to investors who want a steady return on their capital combined with a high level of safety. As their name implies they confer on holders preference over other classes of shareholder in respect of either dividends, repayment of capital or both.

b. ***Dividends***

i. Preference shares have a fixed rate of dividend, for example 8%. This dividend must be paid before the ordinary shareholders receive anything.

ii. Preference shares are ***cumulative*** unless the articles or terms of issue state otherwise. This means that if the company cannot pay a dividend in one year the arrears must be carried forward to future years and all the outstanding preference dividends must be paid before the ordinary shareholders receive anything. If preference shares are ***non-cumulative*** and the company cannot pay a dividend the arrears are not carried forward, so the preference shareholder will not receive a dividend for that year.

iii. Preference shares are normally ***non-participating***, ie they are not entitled to share in the surplus profits of the company after payment of a specified dividend on the ordinary shares.

c. ***Voting***

i. Unless the articles otherwise provide, preference shares carry the same voting rights as other shares.

ii. However it is usual to restrict the preference shareholders' rights to vote to specified circumstances which directly affect them, for example when the rights of preference shareholders are being varied.

d. ***Rights on liquidation***

i. Preference shareholders do not automatically have a right to prior return of their capital. If the articles are silent preference shareholders and ordinary shareholders rank equally.

ii. In most cases the articles will give preference shareholders priority of return of capital. In such cases this right is deemed to be ***exhaustive***, ie it is presumed that the total rights of the preference shareholders have been specified. They will therefore have ***no right*** to share in the distribution of any assets that remain after all the capital has been returned.

iii. If a dividend has been declared it must be paid. If a dividend has not been declared then arrears of dividend may only be paid if there is a provision in the articles. The articles must provide for the payment of ***arrears*** rather than ***arrears due***, because arrears are not due until declared. The words 'arrears due' would therefore exclude undeclared arrears. Where arrears of dividend are paid on liquidation they are paid out of the assets remaining after payment of the other debts. It does not matter that the dividends are not being paid out of distributable profits.

**5. Ordinary shares**

Ordinary shares are sometimes described as a residuary class, ie their rights are the rights that remain after the rights of the other classes of shareholders (if any) have been satisfied. Thus in good years ordinary shareholders take the major share of the profits. Also since the preference shareholders' right to vote is usually restricted, the ordinary shareholders control resolutions at general meetings. The other advantages are that they have a statutory right of pre-emption on the issue of new shares *(S.89)* and they usually take the surplus assets if a profitable company is wound up. The disadvantage is that they take the major share of the risk of failure.

## VARIATION OF CLASS RIGHTS

**6. The definition of 'class rights'**

a. Class rights are the rights attached by the memorandum, articles or terms of issue to any class of shares. They are concerned mainly with voting and dividend rights.

b. If a company has only ***one class of shares***, the rights are usually contained in the articles and may be altered by special resolution. If the rights are in the memorandum, they may be changed using the procedure and safeguards of ***S.17*** (Chapter 7.38). ***S.125*** does not apply to companies with only one class of shares *(S.125(1))*.

c. If a company has ***different classes of shares***, it can only vary class rights by following the rules and safeguards contained in ***S.125*** and set out below.

**7. Basic rules**

a. ***If there is no variation clause***:

   i. If the class rights are in the memorandum the variation requires the agreement of ***all the members of the company***;

   ii. If the class rights are in the articles or terms of issue then the variation requires the written consent of the holders of three-quarters of the shares of that class or the passing of an extraordinary resolution at a class meeting.

b. ***If there is a valuation clause***:

   i. If the variation is connected with the authority granted to the directors to allot shares *(S.80)* or with the reduction of the company's share capital *(S.135)*, the variation requires the written consent of the holders of three-quarters of the shares of that class or the passing of extraordinary resolution at a class meeting, in addition to compliance with the variation clause;

   ii. If the class rights are in the memorandum and the variation clause is in the articles the class rights may only be varied in accordance with that clause if it was inserted ***at the time of the company's incorporation***;

iii. If the class rights are in the articles or terms of issue and the variation clause is in the articles, class rights may only be varied in accordance with that clause. It does not matter when the clause was inserted.

c. ***S.125*** also provides that:

i. An alteration of a provision in the articles for the variation of rights or the insertion of such a provision shall itself be treated as a variation of class rights and the provisions of ***S.125*** will therefore apply to it;

ii. The term 'variation' is extended to include abrogation. Therefore attempts to remove or cancel class rights must be dealt with under ***S.125***;

iii. The quorum at a 'class meeting' is at least two persons, holding or representing by proxy one-third of the issued shares of the class. At a class meeting any holder of the shares of the class in question or his proxy may demand a poll.

8. Minority protection

By ***S.127*** holders of at least 15% of the issued shares of the class concerned, provided they did not vote in favour of the variation, may apply to the court within 21 days to have it cancelled. The court may cancel or confirm the variation.

9. Table A

The variation clause in the old Table A was similar to ***S.125***. It provided that class rights could be varied with the consent in writing of holders of three quarters of the issued shares of the class or the passing of an extraordinary resolution at a class meeting. The new Table A does not contain a provision for the variation of class rights.

10. The meaning of variation

a. It was held in GREENHALGH v ARDERNE CINEMAS (1946), (for facts see Chapter 10.3) that class rights are not varied by the subdivision of other shares.

b. It is also clear that the issue of new shares which rank equally with existing shares does not vary the class rights of the existing shares. In practice this is the most common and important way in which rights are changed since the new issue reduces a person's share in the wealth of the company and reduces his voting rights. This is why it is important that:

i. The company's authority is required for a new issue of shares ***(S.80)***. See 13. below.

ii. Members have a right of first refusal when there is a new issue of equity shares *(S.89)*. See 15. below.

c. Thus 'variation' means the direct alteration of the rights of a class, for example dividend or voting rights, rather than a consequential alteration resulting from the variation of the rights of other classes or from the issue of new shares. This is logical in that it would not be practical to allow a minority to claim their rights have been varied every time new shares are issued. On the other hand where the subdivision or share issue is not for a proper corporate purpose, for example **CLEMENS v CLEMENS (1976)** (Chapter 8.6), it would probably be set aside.

## APPLICATION AND ALLOTMENT

### 11. Application

a. When a person applies for shares he is offering to purchase new shares from the company. He is not purchasing existing shares from a previous holder.

b. The general law of contract applies to an application for shares:

  i. The prospectus is an invitation to treat;

  ii. The subscriber makes the offer when he sends in the application form;

  iii. The company accepts the offer by resolution of the board of directors. The acceptance becomes binding when a letter of allotment is posted to the allottee.

c. The rules of contract are however modified in three ways:-

  i. By **S.89** existing shareholders usually have a statutory right to be offered new shares before they are offered to outsiders;

  ii. The acceptance need not coincide precisely with the offer. Many issues are over-subscribed. In such cases the company will either ballot to decide to whom to allot the shares or it will allot only a proportionate part of those applied for. The company is able to do this because, on the application form, the subscriber agrees to take either the shares applied for or such lesser number as are allotted to him.

  iii. Further modifications may result from rules issued by the Stock Exchange or the Secretary of State under powers given in the ***FINANCIAL SERVICES ACT 1986. S.169 FSA 1986*** authorises the Secretary of State to make rules regulating the terms on which unlisted securities are offered so that potential investors are treated equally and fairly. It is therefore likely that (as under previous legislation) an offer will be irrevocable until several days after the closing date for applications. The reason for this is to inhibit *'stagging'*, ie the revocation of an offer if it appears that the shares or debentures cannot quickly be re-sold at a profit.

**12. Statutory restrictions on allotment**

There are now numerous statutory provisions relating to the allotment of shares. The following were dealt with in Chapter 10 since they are concerned with maintenance of capital:

a. Minimum payment for allotted shares – ***S.101***.

b. Allotment for a non-cash consideration – ***S.102***.

c. Valuation of non-cash consideration – ***S.103***.

The remaining restrictions on allotment are dealt with below. (**13.–17.**).

**13. Company authority required for the allotment of shares**

a. By *S.80* directors may not allot shares, except subscribers' shares or shares allotted under an employees' share scheme, without the authority of the company in general meeting or in the articles.

   (Subscribers' shares are shares shown in the memorandum to be taken by the subscribers to the memorandum).

b. The authority may be general or specific, and it must state the maximum amount of shares which may be allowed, and must limit the time during which the authority may be exercised. This time limit must not exceed five years.

c. An ***ordinary resolution*** is necessary to grant authority to the directors, and since this may have the effect of altering the articles a copy of the resolution must be delivered to the registrar within 15 days. Registration of an ordinary resolution is not normally required.

d. If the rules imposed by *S.80* are broken the validity of the allotment is not affected, although any director who was knowingly a party to the contravention is guilty of an offence.

**14. Private companies**

By *S.170 FINANCIAL SERVICES ACT 1986* a private company must not issue any advertisement offering its shares for sale.

**15. Pre-emption rights *S.89–96***

a. A company may not allot ***equity shares*** unless it has made an offer to the existing shareholders to subscribe on the same or more favourable terms for such shares in proportion to their present holding (*S.89*).

b. By *S.94* 'Equity shares' means shares other than:

   i. Shares which as respects dividends and/or capital distribution have restricted rights, ie preference shares; and

   ii. Shares held, or to be held, under an employees' scheme.

The definition of equity shares basically means ordinary shares, however it also includes the ***right*** to subscribe for, or convert to, shares.

c. Shareholders must be notified in writing and the offer must be open for at least 21 days. No allotment may be made until either 21 days has expired or every offer has been accepted or refused ***(S.90)***.

d. By ***S.95*** these provisions do not apply:

   i. Where the shares are to be wholly or partly paid-up other than in cash;

   ii. To ***private companies*** who exclude the provisions in their memorandum or articles; ***(S.91)***

   iii. Where the directors of ***any company*** have authorisation to allot shares under ***S.80*** they may be given authority, either by the articles or by special resolution, to exercise the power without complying with the pre-emption right provisions;

   iv. Where ***any company*** by special resolution resolves that the provisions shall not apply to a specific allotment, or shall only apply in a modified form. In such cases the directors must recommend the resolution, and circulate a written statement setting out the reasons for their recommendation.

e. If ***S.89*** or ***90*** is contravened every officer who knew of the contravention is liable to compensate any person entitled to receive the offer for any damage suffered or expenses incurred due to the contravention ***(S.92)***.

**16. Disclosure in prospectus where issue not fully subscribed**

a. By ***S.84(1)*** a public company may not allot shares unless:

   i. The shares are subscribed for in full; or

   ii. The prospectus states that, even if the shares are not fully subscribed, those subscribed for will be allotted in any event.

b. If shares are prohibited from being allotted under sub-section (1) and 40 days have elapsed the money received must be repaid to the applicants within a further 8 days, otherwise the directors become liable to repay it themselves, with interest from the end of the 48th day, unless they can prove that the default was not due to their misconduct or negligence.

**17. Effect of an irregular allotment**

An allotment in contravention of ***S.84*** is voidable by the applicant within one month after the date of allotment. In addition any director who knowingly contravenes ***S.84*** is liable to compensate the company and the allottee for any loss suffered ***(S.85)***.

**18. The return of allotments *(S.88)***

a. When ***any company*** allots shares (including bonus shares) it must, within one month of the allotment, deliver to the registrar a return of allotments. This document must state:

   i. The number or nominal value of the shares allotted;

   ii. The names, addresses and descriptions of the allottees;

   iii. The amount paid and payable on each share; and

   iv. Details of any non-cash consideration.

b. The return must be accompanied by a payment of capital duty at the rate of 1% of the actual value of the consideration for the shares.

c. In the case of a public company the registrar must publish notice of receipt of the return of allotments in the Gazette ***(S.711)***.

d. If ***S.88*** is contravened the allotment remains valid, but every officer in default is liable to be fined.

# SHARE CERTIFICATES AND SHARE WARRANTS

**19. The share certificate**

a. By ***S.185*** a share certificate must be made out by the company and delivered to the member within two months of allotment or the date when a transfer was lodged for registration. If the shares are quoted on The Stock Exchange the rules of the Exchange substitute a period of 14 days.

b. The certificate states that the person named is the holder of the shares and specifies the amount paid-up on them. It is not a negotiable instrument since an entry in the company's register of members is necessary to transfer ownership. However by ***S.186*** it is ***prima facie evidence of title***.

c. Since a share certificate is prima facie evidence of title it gives rise to ***estoppels*** (both as to title and as to the amount paid on the shares), as against the company in favour of a person who has relied on the certificate. Estoppel is a rule of evidence. It arises when a person has conducted himself in such a way that reasonable inferences as to his legal position may be drawn from his conduct. He cannot then give evidence to show that his legal position is not what it appeared to be, he is estopped (ie barred by his own conduct) from doing so.

d. Estoppel does not operate:

   i. Where the share certificate is a forgery; or

   ii. In favour of a person who lodged a forged transfer.

### 20. Share warrants

a. By *S.188* a company may issue share warrants if there is authority in the articles and the shares are fully paid.

b. In contrast to a share certificate a share warrant is a negotiable instrument. It will state that the ***bearer*** is entitled to the number of shares specified. Title to the shares can therefore be transferred by delivery of the warrant. In practice share warrants will only be issued by public companies since private companies will restrict the right to transfer their shares.

c. When a share warrant is issued the fact is entered on the register of members and the name of the member who held the shares is removed, although the bearer of a warrant may at any time surrender it and have his name entered on the register. Since the name of the bearer of a share warrant does not appear on the register of members he is not a member of the company, however the articles may provide that the bearer may be deemed to be a member.

d. If the articles require directors to hold qualification shares, the shares comprised in a warrant do not count towards the qualification *(S.291(2))*.

## TRANSFER OF SHARES

### 21. Validity of agreement to transfer

There must be a valid agreement to transfer, either by contract or by gift.

In HARVELA INVESTMENTS v ROYAL TRUST COMPANY OF CANADA (1986) the House of Lords held that if the vendor of shares in a private company invited purchasers to submit sealed bids for shares the vendor could not accept a referential bid, ie one expressed as the amount above that submitted by another bidder. In this case the bid was as follows:

> '2,100,000 Canadian dollars or 101,000 Canadian dollars in excess of any other offer which you may receive, whichever is higher'.

It was held that such bids were unacceptable since one party cannot win and the other party cannot lose. Also if more than one referential bid were to be submitted the process would be frustrated.

### 22. Transfer of all of the shares comprised in one certificate

a. By *S.183* whenever shares are transferred a ***proper instrument of transfer*** must be delivered to the company, ie the transfer must be in writing. Thus an attempt to provide for the automatic transfer of a member's shares, for example to his wife on his death, is void.

b. A transfer form signed by the transferor is sent by the transferee, with the share certificate and the registration fee, to the company. If the articles restrict the right to transfer shares the transfer must be submitted to the board to ensure that the restrictions are compiled with. After approval by the board the name of the transferee is entered on the register and that of the transferor deleted. The company must issue a new share certificate within two months, or 14 days if the company is listed on the Stock-Exchange.

c. The procedure was introduced by the **STOCK TRANSFER ACT 1963** and it applies despite anything in the articles.

**23. Transfer of part of the shares comprised in one certificate**

a. Here a different procedure is necessary because it would be unsafe for the transferor to give the transferee the certificate in return for a consideration in respect of only part of the shares. Similarly it would be unreasonable to expect the transferee to pay for the shares whilst allowing the transferor to retain the certificate.

b. The procedure is:

i. The transferor executes the transfer and sends it with his share certificate to the company;

ii. The company secretary endorses 'certificate lodged' on the transfer and returns it to the transferor, keeping the share certificate;

iii. The transferor hands the certified transfer to the transferee who lodges it with the company for registration;

iv. The company issues two new share certificates.

c. The endorsement of 'certificate lodged' on the transfer is known as ***'certification of the transfer'***.

i. **S.184** provides that certification of the transfer by the company is a representation by the company that documents showing prima facie evidence of title have been produced. It is not a guarantee that the transferor has title.

ii. If the company fraudulently or negligently certifies the transfer when the transferor has not shown prima facie evidence of title the company is liable to anyone acting on the faith of it to his detriment.

iii. However if the company merely negligently returns the old certificate to the transferor the company is not liable to persons who deal with him. Their loss would be attributed to the transferor's fraud rather than the company's negligence.

**24. Forged transfers**

The effects of a transfer of shares under a document on which the transferor's signature has been forged are as follows:

a. A forged document has no legal effect. Therefore the transferor's name must be restored to the register of members, even if he failed to reply to a letter advising him of the transfer.

b. The company is estopped from denying the title of a subsequent transferee who takes the transfer in good faith and for value. If such a person suffers loss due to the restoration to the register of the true owner the company must pay him compensation.

c. The person who lodged the forged transfer (the original transferee) is liable to indemnify the company for any loss it suffers as a result of having to pay compensation. The original transferee must pay this indemnity even if he was not aware of the forgery. He cannot rely on estoppel.

d. The above points were illustrated in the following case.

   In **RE BAHIA AND SAN FRANCISCO RAILWAY (1868)** the holder of shares deposited the certificate with a broker. The broker forged the owner's signature and transferred them to X. When the certificate and the transfer were sent to the company for registration the secretary wrote to the owner advising of the transfer. The owner did not reply to this letter and X was registered as the new owner. X then transferred the shares to Y who was registered as owner, a new certificate being issued. When the forgery was discovered it was held:

   i. That the original owner must be restored to the register;
   ii. That the company was estopped from denying the validity of the certificate issued to Y, who was therefore entitled to damages;
   iii. X, who lodged the forged transfer, had to indemnify the company for the loss it had incurred by compensating Y. The loss therefore fell on X, the original victim of the fraud.

e. If there is a purported transfer of ***non-existing shares*** for which the company issues a certificate, the transferee will not be estopped from bringing an action against the company.

   In **BALKIS CONSOLIDATED v TOMKINSON (1893)** A transferred his shares to B who was registered as a member. A then fraudulently transferred the same shares to C, who was unaware of the previous sale. The company issued C with a share certificate. C then contracted to sell to D. When C discovered that they could not perform this contract without purchasing other shares he bought an action against the company to recover the price paid for those other shares. The action was successful. It was relevant that he had changed his position in reliance on the certificate. Also he had not lodged a forged transfer.

## 25. Restrictions on transfer

a. To retain control of private companies the articles usually contain either

   i. A pre-emption clause ie that no shares shall be transferred to an outsider as long as a member can be found to purchase them at a fair price, determined in accordance with the articles, or
   ii. A power vested in the directors to refuse to register a transfer.

b. ***Pre-emption clauses***

i. A member cannot exercise a pre-emption right in order to purchase the amount of shares that give voting control.

In OCEAN COAL CO v POWELL DUFFRYN STEAM COAL CO (1932) the plaintiff and defendant each held half of the shares of the Taff Merthyr Steam Co. The articles of this company stated that if a member wished to sell his shares to an outsider he must first offer them to other shareholders at the price at which it is proposed to sell to the outsider. The defendant wished to sell 135,000 shares, but the plaintiff only wished to buy 5,000 at the proposed price. It was held that he could not do so. The plaintiff either had to accept or reject the offer to sell the full 135,000 shares.

ii. Where the pre-emption provision is disregarded the directors cannot validly register the transfer since it is breach of the articles. However, where the transfer is to a person who has paid for the shares, that person will acquire a beneficial (equitable) interest in the shares.

c. ***The power to refuse to register transfers***

i. The directors must act bona fide in what they consider to be the best interests of the company.

ii. The directors must act on grounds personal to the transferee. They cannot for example refuse to register transfers merely because small numbers of shares are involved.

iii. The power to refuse must be exercised within a reasonable time. ***S.183*** provides that the company must give notice of refusal within two months. This statutory period now effectively determines what is a reasonable time.

## SHARES AS SECURITY FOR A LOAN

### 26. Legal mortgage

a. The shares are transferred to the mortgagee (lender) who is registered as a member. The mortgage agreement will provide for re-transfer when the loan and interest is repaid.

b. A legal mortgage is the best form of security for the lender since he obtains legal title to the shares. It is however expensive since stamp duty must be paid on each transfer, and it is unsuitable if the shares are partly paid since the mortgagee is liable to pay calls while his name is on the register.

### 27. Equitable mortgage

a. The share certificate is deposited with the mortgagee together with a ***'blank transfer'*** ie a transfer signed by the mortgagor (borrower) but with the name of the transferee left blank. The mortgagee has an implied power to fill in his name and sell the shares if the loan is not paid.

b. An equitable mortgage is not as good security as a legal mortgage because the borrower's name remains on the register. A fraudulent borrower may therefore be able to obtain another share certificate by falsely claiming that the original has been lost or stolen. The mortgagee may protect himself from this by serving a ***'stop notice'*** on the company informing it that the shares are mortgaged and compelling it to give him 8 days notice of any attempted transfer of shares. He may then apply to the court (where a copy of the notice will have been filed) to obtain an injunction to prevent the transfer.

c. This formal procedure is necessary since informal notice to the company would constitute notice of a trust, and by **S.360** no notice of a trust shall be entered on the register of members, ie the company is only concerned with the legal ownership of the shares and not with equitable interests in them. (***S.360*** is discussed in Chapter 13).

# CALLS

## 28. Payment of calls

a. A call is a demand by the company for money due on shares. If the terms of issue state that money is payable in stated instalments (for example the British Telecom share issue) strictly speaking the instalments are not calls. However Table A Article 16 deems such instalments to be calls. Thus the provisions applicable to unpaid calls will also apply to unpaid instalments.

b. The other main provisions of Table A are:

   i. Subject to the terms of allotment calls for amounts unpaid on shares may be made ***by the directors***. (Article 12)

   ii. Members must be given at least 14 days notice of time and place of payment. (Article 12)

   iii. A person on whom a call is made remains liable even if he subsequently transfers the shares. (Article 12)

   iv. A call is deemed to be made when the directors' resolution is passed. (Article 13)

   v. Joint holders are jointly and severally liable to pay calls. (Article 14)

   vi. Directors may differentiate between shareholders as to the amount and time of payment of calls. (Article 17) However directors must always use their powers in good faith and for the benefit of the company.

   In ALEXANDER v AUTOMATIC TELEPHONE CO (1900) it was held to be an abuse of power, when directors made calls on shareholders other than themselves.

c. A company may accept early payment of money not yet called if there is authority in the articles. Table A used to contain such authority, but this has been omitted from the 1985 regulations. The old Table A provided that calls paid early be treated as a loan to the company rather than as capital. Interest may therefore be paid, but not dividends.

## 29. Non-payment of calls

a. ***Late payment.*** Article 15 provides for interest to be paid from the day the call was due at a rate fixed by the terms of allotment, or in the notice of the call, but the directors may waive payment of interest wholly or in part.

b. ***Forfeiture***

i. A company may forfeit (ie take away) a member's shares for non-payment of a call or instalment provided there is authority in the articles. Shares may not be forfeited for non-payment of any other type of debt owed by the member to the company. Table A requires the directors to give at least 14 days notice of forfeiture, (Article 18). If the notice is not complied with, the shares are forfeited by a resolution of the board of directors. The forfeiture includes any dividends payable but not paid before the forfeiture. (Article 19).

ii. A person whose shares are forfeited ceases to be a member of the company, but he remains liable to the company for money which was payable in respect of the shares at the date of forfeiture (plus interest). The directors may waive payment wholly or in part or they may enforce payment in full, without any allowance for the value of the forfeited shares. (Article 21).

iii. The directors have the power to sell or re-allot forfeited shares Article 20). Any exercise of this power is subject to the provisions of the Act. Therefore the company must receive an amount, which when added to the amount received from the previous holder, is not less than the nominal value. If the amount received on re-sale brings the total amount received to more than the nominal value, the excess must be paid into the share premium account. If shares are not re-sold the capital of the company will have been reduced, even so consent of the court is not required.

c. ***Surrender.*** The voluntary surrender of shares by a member is only allowed if there is authority in the articles, (there is no authority in Table A) and then in only two circumstances:

i. Where the shares could have been forfeited, and it is desired to avoid the formalities of forfeiture; and

ii. Where the shares are surrendered in exchange for new shares of the same nominal value, but with different rights.

Surrendered shares, like forfeited shares, may be re-issued. Where either surrendered or forfeited shares are not re-issued then by **S.146** a public company must, within three years, cancel them and diminish the amount of its share capital, and if the effect of the cancellation is to bring the capital of the company below the authorised minimum, it must apply for re-registration as a private company.

d. ***Lien***

i. It is usual for the articles to give the company a lien on a member's shares for non-payment of calls (for example Table A Article 8). In addition the articles may give the company a lien for non-payment of a general debt owed to the company. However by **S.150** a lien taken by a ***public company*** is void unless it is a charge on its own partly-paid shares for an amount payable in respect of them.

ii. A lien is a form of security which gives the company an equitable interest in the member's shares. If the money owing to the company is not paid the company may enforce its security by selling the shares under a power given in the articles, (for example Table A Article 9). The balance of the money received, after deducting the amount owing to the company, must be paid to the member.

### PROGRESS TEST 8

1. What is the legal significance of a share certificate?
2. What is a 'management buyout'?
3. What is an equitable mortgage of shares? How should the lender protect himself?
4. What are the provisions in the ***FINANCIAL SERVICES ACT 1986*** that apply to share issues by private companies?
5. Describe the rights of preference shareholders in connection with dividends.
6. What is the standard procedure for obtaining the consent of holders of a class of shares to a variation of their class rights?

# 13 Membership

## METHODS OF BECOMING A MEMBER

### 1. The basic rule

A person becomes a member when:

a. He indicates that he has ***agreed*** to become a member; and

b. When his name is entered on the ***Register of Members***.

It is therefore possible for a shareholder not to be a member. This will be the case when share warrants have been issued since the name of the holder on a share warrant does not appear on the register of members. However the words 'member' and 'shareholder' are usually synonymous.

### 2. Methods of indicating agreement

a. ***Subscription to the memorandum***. By ***S.22*** the subscribers are deemed to have agreed to become members, and on registration must be entered on the register.

b. ***Application and allotment***. Like subscribers, persons who have been allotted shares take them direct from the company.

c. ***Transfer***. Here the member acquires his shares from an existing member, usually by purchasing them.

d. ***Transmission***. This is a transfer which occurs when a member dies or becomes bankrupt.

e. ***Estoppel***. If a person's name is entered on the register in error, or is not deleted when he transfers his shares, the person may be estopped from denying that he is a member if he knows of the error, but fails to take steps to rectify the register, (see 13. below).

## CAPACITY

### 3. Minors

A person under the age of 18 may be a member, however:

a. If the company knows that a person is a minor it has the power to refuse to accept him as a member;

b. Where a minor is inadvertently registered as a member, the company, provided it acts promptly, can apply to the court to have the transfer set aside and the transferor restored to the register;

c. A minor who has been registered as a member may repudiate his membership before or within a reasonable time after reaching 18.

In **STEINBERG v SCALA LTD (1923)** a minor purchased some shares. When the company made a call she repudiated the contract and attempted to recover the money paid for the shares. It was held that she did not have to pay the call, but she could not recover the money paid because there had not been a total failure of consideration. She had received something for her money, ie the right to vote and receive dividends.

4. **Personal representatives**

   a. On a member's death his shares vest in his personal representative who may require registration of himself as a member. If a personal representative is registered as a member he is entitled to vote and is personally liable for calls, although he may claim an indemnity out of the deceased's assets.

   b. A personal representative is not obliged to become a member since ***S.183(3)*** provides that he may make a valid transfer of the deceased's shares without becoming a member. If a personal representative does not register he is nevertheless entitled to all the benefits attaching to shares, such as bonuses and dividends, but the articles usually provide that he may not vote at meetings, for example Table A Article 31. He is liable for calls so far as he can meet them from the deceased's estate.

   c. If the personal representative neither registers as a member nor transfers the shares the deceased remains on the register. To avoid this unsatisfactory state of affairs continuing for too long Table A used to require the personal representative either to transfer the shares or register as a member within 90 days. If he did not do so the directors could withhold dividends. However this provision has not been repeated in the current Table A.

   d. If an article attempts to provide for the automatic transfer of the shares of a deceased member the article is void since ***S.183(1)*** requires that a 'proper instrument of transfer' be delivered to the company.

5. **Trustees in bankruptcy**

   a. The position of a trustee in bankruptcy is similar to that of a personal representative in that he can transfer the shares without being registered as a member, or he can require registration. If he does not register the bankrupt must vote as the trustee directs.

   b. If the shares are onerous property (ie they have very little value and there are calls due on them) the trustee may disclaim them. The company may prove for the damage suffered as a result of the disclaimer, ie the amount of the unpaid calls.

6. **Trustees and beneficiaries**

   Shares may be held under a trust, and the trustee will be entered on the register of members. However **S.360** states that no notice of a trust shall be entered on the register of members. The purpose of **S.360** is to avoid the involvement of the company in disputes where there are several equitable interests in one piece of property, and to relieve the company from liability to beneficiaries if a fraudulent trustee transfers the shares in breach of trust.

In **SIMPSON v MOLSON'S BANK (1895)** the executors of Mr J. Molson transferred trust property (shares in Molson's Bank) in breach of the terms of J. Molson's will. The bank registered the transfer of the shares despite the fact that it had a copy of the will and that W. Molson (J. Molson's brother) was both president of the bank and executor of his brother's estate. It was held that the company were not liable to Simpson, the intended beneficiary. Although it knew that the shares were held by executors no knowledge of the breach of trust could be imputed to the company because the Act incorporating the company contained a provision similar to ***S.360***.

7. **Companies**

   a. A company may be a member of another company. By ***S.375*** it may, by resolution of its board of directors, appoint a person as its representative at meetings.

   b. By ***S.143*** no company may acquire its own shares, ie it may not be a member of itself. This is subject to several exceptions. (See Chapter 10).

   c. By ***S.144*** where a person has acquired shares in a company as nominee of that company then the shares must be treated as held by the nominee on his own account and the company is regarded as having no beneficial interest in the shares.

   d. This rule is strengthened in respect of public companies: ***S.146*** provides that where shares have been acquired by a person as nominee for a public company the shares must be disposed of. If this is not done within three years the shares must be cancelled.

8. **Holding and subsidiary companies**

   a. By ***S.23*** a company cannot be a member of its own holding company and any allotment or transfer of shares in a company to its subsidiary is void. The exceptions are:

      i. Where the subsidiary is a ***personal representative*** and the deceased person held shares in the holding company.

      ii. Where the subsidiary holds the shares as a ***trustee***, provided the holding company does not have a beneficial interest in the trust.

      iii. Where the subsidiary has shares in a company and that company subsequently becomes its holding company. ***S.129 CA 89 (S.23)***. Such shares may be added to by way of bonus shares and dividends may be paid in respect of them but no voting rights may be exercised.

iv. Where the subsidiary is concerned only as a market maker. **S.129 CA 89 (S.23).**

b. ***S.144* CA 89 *(S.736)*** provides new definitions of holding and subsidiary companies and **S.21–22 CA 89 *(S.258)*** (for accounting purposes only) introduces two new terms – parent undertaking and subsidiary undertaking. All four terms are defined in Chapter 17.18.

c. ***S.144* CA 89 *(S.736)*** defines a ***wholly-owned subsidiary***. This term appears rather misleading since every company (including wholly-owned subsidiaries) must have at least two members. A company is a wholly owned subsidiary of another if it has no members except that other and that other's wholly-owned subsidiaries and its or their nominees.

d. The purpose of **S.23** is to protect creditors. It is similar to the basic rule that a company cannot acquire its own shares. With holding and subsidiary companies the holding company must hold at least one share in S to establish the relationship. If S also holds shares in H the capital of the group will appear to be greater than it is. For example if H gives S £100 for 100 new S shares and S gives H £100 for 100 new H shares, the issued capital of the group will increase by £200 without any increase in the group's assets. All that has happened is that each company has given the other £100. Even so the law does not prohibit cross-shareholdings provided the holding/subsidiary relationship is not established. Therefore Company A may hold up to 50% of Company B shares, while B holds up to 50% of A's shares. This represents some danger to the company's creditors since the total value of the assets of the two companies will be less than their issued capital.

## THE REGISTER OF MEMBERS

### 9. Contents of the register

a. By **S.352** every company must keep a register of members which must contain the following particulars:

   i. The name and address of each member;

   ii. A statement of the shares held by each member, with distinguish ing numbers (if any). Where the company has more than one class of issued shares they must be distinguished by class;

   iii. The amount paid up on each share;

   iv. The date of entry on the register; and

   v. The date of cessation of membership.

b. By **S.361** the register is prima facie evidence of the matters it contains.

## 10. Location of the register

**S.353** requires the register to be kept at the registered office, unless it is made up at some other place in which case it can be kept at that other place. The registrar must be informed of where the register is kept and of any change in that place.

## 11. Index of members

By **S.354** every company with more than 50 members must keep an index of members showing how each member can be readily found in the register.

## 12. Inspection of the register

a. By **S.356** members may inspect the register free of charge. Non-members may inspect the register on payment of a small fee. Any person may require a copy of the register. The fee is currently 10 pence per 100 words and the copy must be supplied within 10 days.

b. By **S.358** the company may close the register for up to 30 days each year. They must give notice in a newspaper circulating in the district where the registered office is situated. The effect of closure is that share transfers are not entered in this period and the public may not inspect the register. The purpose is to keep the register static while dividend warrants are prepared. In practice very few companies close their registers, they declare a dividend payable to members on the register at a future date and then extract a list of members at that date.

## 13. Rectification of the register

a. By **S.359** if:

   i. The name of a person is without sufficient cause ***entered in*** or ***omitted from*** the register; or

   ii. Default or delay takes place in entering the cessation of a person's membership;

   then on the application of either:

   i. The aggrieved person; or

   ii. Any member; or

   iii. The company;

   the court may order rectification of the register and the payment of damages by the company to the aggrieved person.

b. The power to rectify the register is not restricted to the above circumstances, rectification may be granted whenever the register is incorrect, and the fact that the company is in liquidation does not prevent rectification.

In **RE SUSSEX BRICK CO (1904)** the company mistakenly omitted to register a transfer of shares. It then went into voluntary liquidation with a view to reconstruction. The transferee served the liquidator with notice of dissent to the scheme of reconstruction. The liquidator refused to accept the notice on the ground that the transferee was not a member. It was held that the register could be rectified and the notice of dissent was valid.

**14. Obsolete entries**

A company may remove from the register any entry that relates to a former member provided that person has not been a member for at least 20 years ***(S.352(7))***.

**15. Trusts**

a. By ***S.360*** no notice of a trust shall be entered on the register, (see 6. above).

b. The owner of a beneficial (equitable) interest in shares, for example an equitable mortgagee or the recipient of a bequest of shares, may protect his interest by serving a 'stop notice' on the company (see Chapter 12.27).

### *PROGRESS TEST 9*

1. AB Ltd has adopted Table A. John, a member of AB Ltd, has just died. Advise John's personal representative of his legal position.
2. In what form may a register of members be kept?
3. What right has a member to require the company to alter an entry in its register?
4. A call must be authorised by an ordinary resolution. True or false?
5. Dennis deposited his share certificate with a bank as security. The bank informed the company of this. Dennis then became indebted to the company, and the company claimed a lien on his shares. Whose right prevails, the bank's or the company's?

# 14 Debentures

## 1. Borrowing by companies

### a. *Power to borrow*

i. Trading companies have an implied power to borrow and give security. Although this power existed prior to the 1989 Act it has, in effect, been enacted by ***S.110 CA 89 (S.3A)*** which states that it will be sufficient for the memorandum to state that the object of the company is to carry on business as a general commercial company. The Act states that this will allow the company to do all such things as are incidental or conducive to carrying on any trade or business, clearly this will include borrowing. Non-trading companies still require an express power to borrow in the memorandum.

ii. Private companies may borrow as soon as they are incorporated, but public companies must first obtain a certificate of compliance with the capital requirements of public companies ***(S.117)***.

### b. *Ultra vires borrowing*

i. Borrowing in excess of a limit stated in the memorandum, or borrowing for an ultra vires purpose, is itself ultra vires. However ***S.108 CA 89 (S.35(1))*** has abolished the ultra vires rule in respect of outsiders by providing that the validity of an act done by the company shall not be called into question on the ground of lack of capacity by reason of anything in the company's memorandum. Consequently both the lender and the company will be able to enforce the contract, and the lender will have the full range of remedies available in the event of the company's failure to repay interest or capital.

ii. ***S.108 CA 89 (S35(2))*** preserves members' rights to restrain ultra vires acts. Therefore any member may bring proceedings to restrain borrowing which would be beyond the capacity of the company (Chapter 7.22–23).

### c. *Borrowing in excess of authority*

i. The 1989 Act has also improved the lender's position if borrowing is within the company's powers, but in excess of the authority of the person negotiating the loan on behalf of the company. ***S.108 CA 89 (S.35A)*** provides that in favour of a person dealing with a company in good faith, the power of the board of directors to bind the company or authorise others to do so, shall be deemed to be free of any limitation under the company's constitution. (Chapter 15.15).

ii. In the unlikely event of the lender not being protected by the above provision, it would still be possible for the loan to be ratified by the company passing an ordinary resolution.

**2. The nature of debentures**

a. Strictly speaking a debenture is a document by which a company acknowledges its indebtedness under a loan, although the term is also used to describe the loan itself.

b. Debentures usually give a fixed or floating charge over the company's assets (or both) as security, although debentures may be unsecured.

However, the Stock Exchange will not allow an issue of unsecured or 'naked' debentures to be listed as 'debentures'. The listing must indicate that they are unsecured, for example 'unsecured loan stock'.

c. A debenture may be an individual debenture evidencing a large sum lent by one person, or the company may create one loan fund known as 'debenture stock'. This is issued to create a class of debentureholders each of whom is given a debenture stock certificate evidencing the proportion of the total to which he is entitled. Whether the debenture is of the first or second type the basic rights of the holder against the company are contractual.

d. Not every type of company indebtedness can be described as a debenture, the loan must have some permanence although the precise extent is uncertain.

**3. Differences between shares and debentures**

a. A shareholder owns a bundle of rights in the company, for example the right to vote, attend meetings and receive a dividend (if declared). A debentureholder is a person who has lent money to the company. Debentureholders have a ***claim against*** the company rather than an ***interest in*** it. Shares (especially ordinary shares) carry a greater degree of risk than debentures, and ordinary shareholders may get a variable return on their investment. If profits are good this will probably exceed the fixed rate of interest paid to debentureholders. Debentures carry less risk, since interest is a contract debt and because debentures will be secured by a fixed and/or a floating charge on the company's assets.

b. The other main differences arise from the fact that debentures are not 'capital' in the Company Law sense. Thus:

   i. A company's purchase of its own debentures is not subject to restrictions, in contrast to a company's purchase of its own shares;

   ii. Interest on debentures may be paid out of capital, whereas dividends must be paid out of profits;

   iii. Shares cannot be issued at a discount, whereas debentures may be issued at a discount, although these debentures cannot be exchanged for fully paid shares of an equal nominal value.

In **MOSELY v KOFFYFONTEIN MINES (1904)** the company proposed to issue £1 debentures at a discount of 20%. The terms of issue provided that each debenture could be exchanged for a fully paid

£1 share. The plaintiff, who was the company's largest shareholder, was successful in obtaining an injunction to prevent the allotment of the debentures since if the debentures were exchanged the practical result would be to issue shares at a discount.

4. **Similarities between shares and debentures**

a. The typical debenture is one of a series or 'class' similar to a class of shares.

b. Debentures are transferable, the same form being used as for a transfer of shares.

c. Debentures may be quoted on the Stock Exchange, and when debentures are issued to the public the same rules must be complied with.

d. In theory it may appear that a debentureholder is only dependent on the prosperity of the company to the same extent as any other creditor. In practice this is not the case. Since the security is generally a floating charge the debentureholder will be as concerned about the success of the company as the shareholder, because if the company is unprofitable the security is placed in jeopardy.

e. Usually a debenture is regarded as a more secure form of investment than a share. In times of high inflation this is not necessarily true. When the purchasing power of money is declining a debenture giving a fixed rate of interest and right to the future return of only the nominal value of the money advanced may well be an inadequate security. In contrast an ordinary share in a 'good' company may provide a better hedge against inflation since the nominal value of the assets is likely to appreciate as the value of money falls.

f. ***Conclusion***. In practice debentures are not regarded as differing significantly from shares. Potential investors are not really concerned with the choice of whether to be a member or creditor of a company.

They will be concerned with the potential for capital appreciation, the yield and the degree of risk. They will then make their basic choice between ***'prior charges'*** (ie debentures and preference shares) and ***'equities'*** (ie ordinary shares). From the company's point of view taxation considerations may be crucial, since debenture interest appears in the profit and loss account as an expense of running the business and therefore reduces the net profit of the company upon which corporation tax is assessed. In contrast dividends on shares are appropriations of profit after tax.

5. **Forms of security**

a. A ***fixed charge*** is a mortgage of freehold or leasehold land or fixed plant and machinery, although a fixed charge may be granted over other assets, eg book debts or uncalled capital. It prevents the company selling the assets charged without the consent of the debentureholders.

The property must be sufficiently identified and any necessary formalities for the creation of the charge must be observed. A fixed charge may be legal or equitable.

b. A ***floating charge*** is an equitable charge which has the following characteristics:

   i. It is a charge on some or all of the present and future assets of the company;

   ii. That class is one which in the ordinary course of business changes from time to time;

   iii. The charge envisages that, until some future step is taken by or on behalf of the charge holder, the company may carry on its business in the ordinary way.

c. A floating charge will ***'crystallise'*** ie convert to a fixed charge when:

   i. The company defaults ***and*** the debentureholders take steps to enforce their security either by appointing a receiver or applying to the court to do so. Note that default alone will not crystallise the charge, the debentureholders must intervene to terminate the authority of the company to deal with the property charged.

   ii. If winding-up commences. In this case no action by the debentureholders is necessary. The charge crystallises because the authority of the company to deal with the assets charged is subject to an implied condition that it carries on business.

   iii. If the company ceases business. This causes automatic crystallisation of a floating charge without any action by the debentureholders. **(RE WOODROFFES (MUSICAL INSTRUMENTS) (1986))**

   iv. If an event occurs for which the charging deed provides for automatic crystallisation **(RE BRIGHTLIFE (1986))**, for example an attempt by the company to create another charge over the assets covered by the charge. If the charge holder gives notice of the event before winding-up commences the conversion of his charge to fixed will, in effect, make him a secured creditor and give him priority over the preferential creditors.

d. Advantages of floating charges, (from the company's point of view):

   i. It can charge property which is unsuitable for a fixed charge.

      This is particularly useful if it has no fixed assets, but carries a large stock-in-trade; and

   ii. It can deal with the assets charged.

e. Disadvantages of floating charges, (from the lender's point of view):

   i. Its value is uncertain since the value of the assets subject to the charge will fluctuate;

ii. Where a seller of goods 'reserves title' until payment, a floating charge will not, on crystallisation, attach to those goods (see 6 below);

iii. The charge may be avoided under **S.245 IA** (see 9 below);

iv. If a creditor has levied and completed execution the debenture-holders cannot compel him to restore the money, and prior to crystallisation he cannot be prevented from levying execution.

v. The statutory preferential creditors (see Chapter 23.38) must be paid out of assets subject to a floating charge unless there are other uncharged assets available for this purpose.

6. Reservation of title

a. ***'Simple' reservation of title clauses*****. *S.17*** Sale of Goods Act 1979 provides the basic rule that in a contract for the sale of specific goods property passes when the parties intend it to pass. Consequently the parties can agree that the property will not pass until the goods are paid for. (In the absence of such agreement property will usually pass when the contract is made – ***S.18 Rule 1 SGA 1979***).

In **ALUMINIUM INDUSTRIE VAASSEN v ROMALPA (1976)** the following clause was the main provision in a detailed reservation of title clause.

> 'The ownership of the material to be delivered by A.I.V. will only be transferred to the purchaser when he has met all that is owing to A.I.V. no matter on what grounds'

Romalpa went into liquidation and A.I.V. sought to enforce the above clause by recovering a quantity of aluminium. It was held that they could do so, ownership had not passed to Romalpa, they were merely the bailee of A.I.V.'s goods.

b. ***'Extended' clauses covering processed goods*****.** A reservation of title clause will not apply to goods which are subjected to a process under which they become a new product. The new product will be owned by the buyer, but subject to a charge created in favour of the seller by the reservation of title clause. Such a charge is not valid unless registered.

In **BORDEN v SCOTTISH TIMBER PRODUCTS (1981)** resin was sold on reservation of title terms. Both parties knew that the resin would soon be used to manufacture chipboard. It was held that the resin ceased to exist and the suppliers title was extinguished when the resin was made into chipboard, because this was a wholly new product.

In **RE PEACHDART (1984)** leather was sold under a contract which stated that in the event of the leather being used in the manufacture of other goods the property in the whole of such other goods should 'be and remain' with the seller. Following Borden's case it was held that the supplier's title was extinguished when the leather was made into handbags.

Contrast **HENDY LENNOX v GRAHAME PUTTICK (1984)** where the sellers supplied engines to be used in diesel generators. The engines could be identified by a serial number and easily detached from the finished generators. The contract provided that the property in the engine was to remain with the sellers until the full purchase price was paid and it also provided for the right of re-possession upon default. When the buyer went into receivership it was held that the seller still had title to the engines in the generators since their identity had not been destroyed by the assembly process.

c. ***'Extended' clauses covering proceeds of sub-sales.*** The situation becomes more complicated if the clause is extended to cover the proceeds of sale of goods subject to reservation of title clauses. Such an extension will be effective if it is drafted with sufficient care. The clause must make it clear that the buyer is made the agent of the seller when re-selling the goods and that he holds the proceeds as trustee for the seller. The position of the seller will be even stronger if the contract requires the buyer to store the goods in such a way as they are clearly the property of the seller and keep any sale proceeds in a separate account. Thus in **HENDY LENNOX v GRAHAME PUTTICK (1984)** although title to the engines did not pass when they were incorporated into generators, it did pass when the generators were sold by the buyer. The simple reservation of title clause used did not expressly or implicitly give the sellers a right to the proceeds of sale since it did not create a fiduiciary relationship between the seller and buyer. In contrast in **A.I.V. v ROMALPA (1976)** the clause did impose the fiduiciary obligations of an agent and A.I.V. was therefore successful in its claim to recover the proceeds of aluminium that had been sold (in addition to recovery of a quantity of unsold aluminium).

d. ***Conclusion.*** In practice reservation of title clauses are often the extended type. Such a clause was recently considered by the Court of Appeal.

   In **CLOUGH MILL v MARTIN (1985)** a contract for the sale of yarn had a reservation of title clause with four separate paragraphs:

   i. Ownership of the yarn remained with the seller until the seller had received payment in full or the yarn was sold by the buyer in a bona fide sale at full market value.

   ii. If payment was overdue the seller could recover and re-sell the yarn and enter onto the buyer's premises for that purpose.

   iii. Payment would become due immediately on commencement of proceedings for the buyer's insolvency.

   iv. If the yarn was incorporated into other goods before payment, the property in those goods passed to the seller until payment was made or until a bona fide sale of those goods.

When a receiver was appointed the seller claimed re-possession of a quantity of unused yarn, relying on paragraph i. The receiver disputed the claim on the ground that the clause was void for lack of registration, but the Court of Appeal upheld the claim because the yarn was identifiable, unused and unpaid for and title had been effectively reserved by paragraph i. The Court made the comment that paragraph iv. created a registrable charge, but (overruling the High Court) that this did not affect the validity of paragraph i.

7. Registration of charges

a. Since most companies obtain much of their finance from debentures secured by charges, it is important that people dealing with the company are able to find out which assets are subject to charges. The provisions in the 1985 Act have been substantially altered by ***S.92–107 CA 89***.

b. By ***S.95 CA 89 (S.398)*** almost all charges created by a company must be registered within 21 days of creation. By ***S.93 CA 89 (S.396)*** the following charges must be registered:

   i. A charge on land.

   ii. A charge on goods ie any tangible movable property other than money.

   iii. A charge on goodwill.

   iv. A charge on intellectual property ie patents, trademarks, registered designs and copyrights.

   v. A charge on book debts.

   vi. A charge on uncalled share capital.

   vii. A charge for securing an issue of debentures.

   viii. A floating charge on the whole or part of a company's property.

   The Act makes it clear that there is no distinction between fixed and floating charges by defining a charge as 'any form of security interest (fixed or floating) over property, other than an interest arising by operation of law' ***(S.93 CA 89 (S.395))***.

c. The particulars to be delivered will be in a prescribed form which is likely to include at least:

   i. The date of creation of the charge, or of the acquisition of the property subject to the charge.

   ii. The amount secured.

   iii. Short particulars of the property charged.

   iv. The persons entitled to the charge.

   The registrar will file the particulars in the register, noting the date of receipt. He is required to send both the company and the chargee a copy of the particulars and a note evidencing the date of receipt. This note will provide the chargee with proof that the particulars have been received for registration. It is no longer a requirement that the instrument of charge itself be delivered to the registrar, only the prescribed particulars.

d. The registrar is no longer required to issue certificates in respect of all charges registered. However, any person may require the registrar to issue a certificate. It will state the date on which the particulars of the charge were delivered to the registrar and will constitute ***conclusive evidence*** that the particulars were delivered no later than the date stated in the certificate.

e. In general the Act has abolished the doctrine of constructive notice (for example in connection with the memorandum and articles). However, one exception relates to a person taking a charge over a company's property. By ***S.103 CA 89 (S.416)*** such a person shall be taken to have notice of any matter requiring registration and disclosed on the register at the time the charge is created.

f. If a charge is not registered within 21 days, it is no longer necessary to apply to the court for late registration. By ***S.95 CA 89 (S.400)*** the charge may be delivered late, but the security provided by the charge will only take effect in relation to events occurring after the date of registration. As under the 1985 Act, the company and its officers may be fined for failure to register in time.

g. Similarly by ***S.96 CA 89 (S.401)*** further particulars of a charge, supplementing or varying the registered particulars may be delivered for registration at any time. These must be in a prescribed form and signed by both the company and the chargee. If either refuses to sign, the court may order that the further particulars be delivered without signature. The registrar will add the further particulars to the register and make a note of the date of delivery. A copy will be sent to the company and the chargee.

h. If a charge is not delivered within the 21 day period, the charge will be void as against purchasers of an interest in, or a right over, property subject to the charge. Such protection is confined to the period before the charge is belatedly registered ie once registered the charge will be valid as against persons subsequently acquiring an interest in the charged property.

   Where a charge is registered late and insolvency proceedings are commenced before the end of the ***'relevant period'***, the charge will be void as against the administrator or liquidator. A charge will also be void as against an administrator or liquidator if, when the particulars are delivered, the company is unable to pay its debts or subesequently becomes unable to pay them as a result of the transaction under which the charge was created.

The relevant period is:

i. 2 years in the case of a floating charge created in favour of a person connected with the company, or one year if the person is not so connected.

ii. Six months in the case of a fixed charge.

The relevant period begins with the date of delivery of the particulars to the registrar.

The basic effect of late registration is that the validity of the charge is subject to a condition that the company survives for a given period.

i. By ***S.97 CA 89 (S.402)*** where there are omissions or inaccuracies in the registered particulars, reliance on the charge is restricted to disclosed particulars and it is void in respect of undisclosed rights. However the court, on the application of the chargee, may order that the charge will not be void in such circumstances, as against an administrator, liquidator or person acquiring an interest in property subject to the charge.

j. By ***S.100 CA 89 (S.408–410)*** additional particulars are required to the delivered to the registrar in the following circumstances:

i. Where the charge secures an issue of debentures, particulars of the date on which any debentures are taken up.

ii. Notice of the appointment of a receiver or manager, such notice to be given within 7 days of the appointment.

iii. In addition the Secretary of State has the power to issue regulations requiring notice of the crystallisation of a floating charge to be given to the registrar.

k. It is the duty of the company to effect registration, but any person interested in the charge may register it. In practice, since the consequences of non-registration affect the lender rather than the company, it is usually the lender's solicitor who deals with registration.

8. Priority of charges

a. There are two basic reasons why the rules concerning priorities are disadvantageous to debentureholders whose security is a floating charge:

i. Since a floating charge is equitable it is postponed to a subsequent fixed (legal) charge if the fixed charge had no notice of the floating charge. In fact this is of little importance since a floating charge is invalid unless registered, and if it is registered, later charges are fixed with constructive notice ***(S.103 CA 89)***.

ii. The more serious problem is that debentureholders have implicitly authorised the company to deal with the assets charged. Thus, subject to the limitations discussed below, a floating charge will be postponed to a later created fixed charge, whether legal or equitable, even if the fixed chargeholder has notice.

The rules are as follows:

b. Legal fixed charges rank according to their order of creation.

c. If an equitable fixed charge is created first and a legal charge over the same property is created later, the legal charge ranks before the equitable charge, unless at the time when the legal charge was created, the person to whom it was given had notice of the existing equitable charge. Notice may be given by registration of the earlier charge.

   NB. An equitable fixed charge is an informal mortgage created by depositing the borrower's title deeds or share certificate with the lender.

d. If a floating charge (always equitable) is created and a fixed charge (legal or equitable) over the same property is created later, the fixed charge will rank first since it attaches to the property at the time of creation, whereas the floating charge attaches at the time of crystallisation. Once a floating charge has crystallised it becomes fixed and any subsequent fixed charge ranks after it.

   NB. A floating charge will have priority over a later created fixed charge if:

   i. The floating charge prohibits the creation of later fixed charges with priority (known as a 'negative pledge' clause); and

   ii. The holder of the fixed charge knows of this prohibition.

   Registration of the charge is constructive notice of the charge itself, but not of the fact that it contains a prohibition on the creation of later fixed charges with priority. **(WILSON v KELLAND (1910))** In practice debentureholders make sure that the registered particulars include a note of the restriction. However it is unlikely that constructive notice extends to matters which by law do not have to be inserted in the registered particulars.

   If the company has a negative pledge clause, and then creates another charge the second charge will be valid because the company's apparent authority to create the charge will override the limit on its actual authority. However the first chargeholder will be able to take some action because the terms of his charge will have been broken.

e. If two floating charges are created over the general assets of the company they rank in order of creation **(RE BENJAMIN COPE (1914))**. However, if a company creates a floating charge over a particular kind of asset, e.g. book debts, that will rank before an existing floating charge over the general assets **(RE AUTOMATIC BOTTLE MAKERS (1926))**.

f. ***Late registration***. By **S.99 CA 89** ***(S.404)*** a later created charge will rank before an earlier crated charge if:

   i. The earlier charge was registered late (ie outside the 21 day period) and the later charge was registered before the earlier charge, or

   ii. To the extent that the particulars of the earlier charge failed to disclose certain rights.

g. The Act also includes a restriction on the voidness resulting from the above rules. ***S.99 CA 89 (S.405)*** provides that a charge is not void as against a person who acquires an interest in or a right over property where the acquisition is expressly subject to the charge ie if a charge is registered late and a second charge is entered into (expressly subject to the first charge) the first chargee has priority over the second chargee despite the late registration of the first charge.

h. Also a charge is not void in relation to any property if insolvency proceedings commence (or a person acquires a right in charged property) after the company which created the charge has disposed of the whole of its interest in that property. Where a charge has become void as against an administrator, liquidator or person acquiring an interest in property subject to the charge, the chargee may sell the property free from the charge. The purchaser is not obliged to enquire whether the charge is in fact void. The proceeds of sale must be used to discharge the sums secured by the charge.

i. When a charge becomes void under the above provisions, the whole of the sum secured by the charge (including any interest) is payable on demand, ie the chargee is not bound to leave the now unsecured loan until it becomes repayable under the terms of the charge.

**9. Avoidance of floating charges *(S.245 IA)***

a. It would be unjust to allow an unsecured creditor to obtain priority over other creditors by obtaining a floating charge when he realises that liquidation is likely. This applies in particular to directors who may have attempted to keep the company alive by making unsecured loans to it. When they realise their attempt has failed they may well wish to cause the company to execute a floating charge in their favour.

b. The Insolvency Act 1985 repealed ***S.617***, replacing it with new provisions. A floating charge may be invalidated if created in certain periods before either the commencement of liquidation or the presentation of a petition for an administration order. The periods are:

   i. 2 years, if the charge is in favour of a connected person;

   ii. 1 year, if the charge is in favour of any other person (but only if the company was insolvent at the time the charge was created, or became insolvent as a result of the transaction under which the charge was created);

   iii. At any time between the presentation of a petition for an administration order and the making of that order.

c. As under the previous legislation the new rules do not invalidate charges to secure money paid to the company at the time of, or subsequent to the creation of the charge, and in consideration for the charge.

(In fact the Insolvency Act extends the definition of consideration to cover services, discharge of debts and contractual interest payments).

d. For the purposes of the Insolvency Act a person is a ***connected person*** if:

   i. He is a director or shadow director of the company or an associate of a director or shadow director; or

   ii. He is an associate of the company.

   A shadow director is a person in accordance with whose instructions the directors are accustomed to act ***(S.741)***.

   Associate is defined in ***S.435 IA***. This extremely wide definition includes, for example:

   i. Spouse, relative or spouse of a relative; (relative includes brother, sister, uncle, aunt, nephew, niece, lineal ancestor or lineal descendant);

   ii. Business partner, or spouse or relative of a partner;

   iii. An employee or employer;

   iv. A trustee, if the person in question is a beneficiary;

   v. A company, if the person in question by himself, or with his associates, controls it.

10. Transactions at an undervalue and preferences ***(S.238-241 IA)***

   a. A charge may also be avoided if it is a transaction at an undervalue or a preference. The above sections replace ***S.615*** which is repealed. Note that they refer to a preference rather than a fraudulent preference. The sections cover any type of transaction of preference, not merely the creation of charges.

   b. A transaction at an undervalue occurs when the company makes a gift, or enters into a transaction for no consideration, or for a consideration worth significantly less than the value of the benefit received by the company. However transactions made in good faith, for the purpose of the business and in the reasonable belief that the company would benefit will not be invalid.

   c. A preference is any act that has the effect of putting one of the company's creditors in a better position in the event of the company going into insolvent liquidation. However the court may not make an order unless it is satisfied that the company was influenced by a desire to put the creditor in a better position than he otherwise would have been.

   d. A transaction may only be invalidated if the company was insolvent at the time (or if it became unable to pay its debts as a result of the transaction). The transaction must also fall within the following periods either before liquidation or the presentation of a petition for an administration order:

i. 6 months, where the transaction is a preference (not at an undervalue);

ii. 2 years, where the transaction is a preference (not at an undervalue), given to a connected person;

iii. 2 years, where the transaction is at an undervalue. (If the transaction was with a connected person the company is assumed to be insolvent unless proved to the contrary);

iv. At any time between the presentation of a petition for an administration order and the making of that order.

e. The court has power to make any order it thinks fit, for example that:

i. Property transferred be returned to the company;

ii. Security given by the company be discharged;

iii. That any person pay to the liquidator or administrator such sum as the court directs in return for the benefit received.

f. The new rules are more restrictive than the old law. Before 1985 it was a requirement that the preference was a voluntary act of the company. Thus a payment made under threat of legal proceedings would not be a fraudulent preference. Now such a payment would be a preference. Cases where fraudulent preferences were held to exist under the old law are suitable examples of what would now be regarded as a preference.

In **RE KUSHLER (1943)** the two directors of an insolvent company arranged for the company to repay a bank loan which was guaranteed by one of the directors. The ordinary creditors were not paid and winding-up commenced shortly afterwards. It was held that the payment was a fraudulent preference, and repayment was ordered.

In **RE MATTHEWS (1981)** the proprietors of a small company which had got into difficulties decided that it would have to stop trading. At the time it had an overdraft of £11,000. The next day two cheques totalling £18,000 arrived and were banked. Two days later the company did stop trading. Four days after that the proprietors (Mr and Mrs Matthews) gave notice to the bank to end their personal guarantees of company borrowing. When Mr Matthews banked the cheques he knew that other creditors could not be paid, but he believed they would be paid in due course. The company later went into liquidation, the deficiency against unsecured creditors being £130,000. The Court of Appeal held that banking the cheques after a decision to stop trading was a preference in favour of the bank. Although Mr Matthews had acted honestly and believed the other creditors would be paid, he had left them at risk when settling the bank overdraft.

**11. Company's register of charges**

a. In addition to registration at the Companies Registry **S.101 CA 89 (S.411)** requires all charges given by a company to be recorded in the company's own register of charges. The register must contain:

i. A short description of the property charged;

ii. The amount of the charge; and

iii. The names of the persons entitled to the charge.

b. Failure to register does not affect the validity of the charge, but officers of the company who knew of the omission are liable to a fine.

c. Any person may ask the company to provide a copy of any charge, or of any entry in its register of charges, subject to the payment of a fee. The company must send the copy within 10 days of the request or, if later, within 10 days of the day on which payment was received. If inspection is refused, or if the copy is sent late, the company and officers are liable to a fine.

**12. Trustees for debentureholders**

a. When debentures are issued to the public the company will enter into a trust deed with trustees (usually a trust corporation). The trustees are appointed and paid by the company to act on behalf of the debenture-holders. Any charge is in favour of the trustees who hold it on trust for the debentureholders.

b. There are two main advantages of trustees:

i. It enables the security to be a legal mortgage of the company's land; (unlike an equitable mortgagee the rights of a legal mortgagee will not be defeated by a transfer of mortgaged property to a bona fide purchaser for value). This would not be possible without trustees since under the **LAW OF PROPERTY ACT 1925** a legal estate in land cannot be vested in more than 4 persons; and

ii. The trustees are available to exercise continuous supervision of the debentureholders' rights and take the necessary action if the company defaults.

c. The contents of the trust deed will depend on a number of factors. For example it will:

i. Grant to the trustees a fixed charge over land and a floating charge over the rest of the assets;

ii. Provide for the repayment of the principal sum borrowed plus interest;

iii. Contain covenants by the company to insure and repair the property charged;

iv. Specify the events in which the security becomes enforceable, and define the trustees power to take possession of the property charged or appoint a receiver;

v. Define the powers exercisable by the company only with the trustees' consent, for example leasing charged property;

vi. Provide for meetings of debentureholders; and

vii. Provide for the remuneration of the trustees.

**13. Remedies of debentureholders**

The remedies of debentureholders are generally conferred by the trust deed. For example it may grant the power to appoint a receiver to sell charged property. In addition the debentureholders may:

a. Sue as creditors for arrears of interest;

b. Petition to wind-up the company on the ground that it is unable to pay its debts; and

c. Apply to the court for the appointment of a receiver or for an order for sale if there is no power in the trust deed.

The usual first step is for the debentureholders or their trustees to secure the appointment of a receiver. Receivers are the subject of Chapter 25.

### *PROGRESS TEST 10*

1. When will a floating charge crystallise?
2. What is a 'transaction at an undervalue'?
3. Describe the powers of the Court if there has been a transaction at an undervalue or a preference.
4. What is the effect of registration of a charge?
5. What is the procedure for registration of a charge?
6. What is the position if the registered particulars omit required information?

## COURSEWORK QUESTIONS 11–15
## COMPANY SECURITIES

11. *Describe and discuss the significance of each of the following:*

(*a*) *The pre-emption rights of existing shareholders* (*8 marks*)

(*b*) *Preference shares.* (*6 marks*)

(*c*) *Redeemable shares.* (*6 marks*)

ACCA *June 1986 Question 2*

12. *Some two years ago A Limited acquired some shares in C Limited and was duly registered as a shareholder. The investment proved disappointing, no dividends at all having been paid, and A Limited has now sold the shares to B. Having paid the price and received a duly executed transfer in his favour and the share certificate, B has been told by C Limited that the transfer in favour of A Limited two years ago was forged and that D, the true owner of the shares, is seeking to have his name restored to the register of members of C Limited.*

Consider the position. *(15 marks)*

CIMA May 1977 Question 2

13. *(a) What are the differences between shares issued at a discount and shares issued at a premium? What are the legal consequences of each type of issue?* *(10 marks)*

*(b) Rakolite plc wishes to raise capital in order to finance expansion of its activities and is considering the following alternative methods of attracting capital in a highly competitive market by public issue:*

*i. A series of debentures with a nominal value of £1. The debentures will be issued at 80p. The debentures are redeemable at nominal value on 1 January 1992;*

*ii. A series of debentures with a nominal value of £1 also to be issued at 80p and redeemable at nominal value on 1 January 1992 One of the terms of issue is that debentureholders will be entitled at any time after 1 July 1991 to convert their debentures into fully paid £1 ordinary shares;*

*iii. A series of debentures with a nominal value of £1 also to be issued at 80p and redeemable at nominal value on 1 January 1992. One of the terms of issue is that debentureholders will be entitled at any time after 1 July 1991 to convert their debentures into fully paid ordinary shares with a nominal value of 75p;*

*iv. A series of £1 ordinary shares to be issued at 95p fully paid. This issue will be underwritten.*

*Advise Rakolite plc on the legal validity of the above proposals.*

*(10 marks)*

ACCA December 1987 Question 8

14. *(a) Set out the procedures to be followed when a shareholder in a company whose securities are not listed on the Stock Exchange wishes:*

*i. To transfer the whole of his fully paid shareholding in the company to a third party; and ii. To transfer only part of his fully paid shareholding in the company to a third party.*

*NB. Details of the information contained in the instrument of transfer are not required.* *(11 marks)*

*(b) TDH Ltd is a private company whose issued share capital consists of 4,000 fully paid ordinary shares. There are three directors ie Tom, Dick and Harry who each hold 1,000 shares. Alice holds 500 shares, Mary 250 shares and Maggie 250 shares. The articles of the company contain the following provisions:*

*1. The directors may at any time in their absolute and uncontrolled discretion refuse to register any transfer of shares.*

*2. Two directors shall form a quorum at a board meeting.*

*Tom dies and his son, Jack, as executor, applies for Tom's shares to be registered in his name. Dick and Harry refuse to register the holding but offer to register 500 shares if Jack sells the remaining shares to them at an agreed price.*

*Mary agrees to sell her holding to Alice. Alice presents the transfer for registration. At the board meeting Dick wishes to accept the transfer but Harry is unwilling. They fail to agree. Dick as chairman refuses to exercise his casting vote. The company secretary notifies Alice of the result of the proceedings.*

*Maggie agrees to sell her shares to Dick. Harry who is annoyed at Dick's previous behaviour refuses to attend any further board meetings to consider transfers of shares.*

*Advise Jack, Alice and Dick.* *(9 marks)*

*(20 marks)*

ACCA *June 1987 Question 4*

15. *(a) Explain the rules governing priorities of fixed and floating charges.* *(8 marks)*

*(b) Apart from such priorities consider the value of a floating charge as an effective form of security to the debentureholder.* *(7 marks)*

*(15 marks)*

ACCA *June 1981 Question 3*

# PART V COMPANY OFFICERS

# 15 Directors

## APPOINTMENTS AND REMOVAL

1. **Position of directors**

   a. Directors are the persons to whom management of a company is entrusted. Together with the managers and the secretary they are the 'officers' of the company ***(S.742)***. It is not necessary that a natural person be appointed, a director may be another company. A person who acts as a director, eg by attending board meetings and taking part in board decisions will be a director even if he is called by another name such as 'governor' or 'trustee' ***(S.741)***.

   b. The position of a director is similar to that of an agent in that he can bind his principal (ie the company) by his acts without incurring personal liability.

   c. Directors have also been compared to trustees because they owe fiduciary duties to the company. However they are not true trustees because the legal title to the company's property is vested in the company and not in the directors.

   d. Directors are not servants of the company unless they have a separate contract of service with the company.

2. **Number of directors**

   a. By **S.282** every public company must have at least two directors and every private company must have at least one. However, Table A Article 64 provides that for all companies the number of directors shall not be less than two (unless otherwise decided by ordinary resolution.)

   b. By **S.283** every company must have a secretary, but a sole director cannot also be the secretary.

3. **Methods of appointment**

   a. ***First directors***. By **S.10** a statement of the first directors and secretary must be delivered with the application to register the company. The statement must contain their signed consent to act in the relevant capacity. By ***S.13(5)*** the persons named in the statement are, on the company's incorporation, deemed to have been appointed as its first directors and secretary. If the articles also name a person as the first director such appointment is void unless the person is also named in the statement.

   b. ***Subsequent directors***

      i. The usual method of appointment is by the company in general meeting, ie by ***ordinary resolution***. Retiring directors are eligible for re-election and, if Table A Article 75 is adopted, a retiring director who offers himself for re-election will be automatically elected unless a resolution not to fill the vacancy is passed or a resolution for his re-election is lost.

ii. Article 76 provides that no person other than a director retiring by rotation shall be appointed unless:

(a) He is recommended by the directors; or

(b) At least 14 days, but not more than 35 days before the meeting written notice of the proposal was left at the registered office. The notice must include the details that are required for the register of directors and it must be executed by the proposed director to indicate his willingness to be appointed.

If either (a) or (b) apply the company must circulate such details as would appear on the register of members to the members between 7 and 28 days before the meeting (Article 77).

iii. By **S.292** two or more directors of a ***public company*** cannot be appointed by a single resolution unless a previous resolution authorising this has been passed without dissent. This means that directors must be elected on their individual merits.

c. *Casual vacancies*

i. A casual vacancy is one that occurs between general meetings, for example because of the death or resignation of a director.

ii. Table A Article 79 empowers the board to fill casual vacancies, and also to appoint additional directors up to the maximum specified in the company's articles.

iii. A person appointed by the board holds office until the next AGM. He will then be eligible for re-election. His appointment will not be taken into account for determining who shall retire by rotation (see 9 below).

## 4. Qualification shares

a. It is often thought that a director must also be a member. This is not the case, and unless the articles require the director to hold shares he need not do so.

b. Table A does not require directors to hold qualification shares. However if the articles do impose a share qualification **S.291** states that:

i. The share qualification must be obtained within two months of appointment;

ii. A share warrant is not acceptable; and

iii. If a director fails to obtain his share qualification or ceases to hold the required number of shares, he vacates office.

5. **Assignment of office**

By **S.308** where there is provision in the articles or in any agreement, that the office of director can be assigned, the assignment will be void unless it is approved by a special resolution.

6. **Alternate directors**

An alternate director is a person appointed by a director to act for him at board meetings which he is unable to attend. There is no authority in the Act to appoint an alternate director, therefore one can only be appointed if there is authority in the articles. The extent of his powers and his entitlement to remuneration will depend on the articles. Until 1985 Table A did not contain any power to appoint alternate directors. This has now been changed. The main provisions are:

a. Any director may appoint another director or any person approved by the directors and willing to act to be an alternate director and may remove such person from office. (Article 65)

b. An alternate director is entitled to receive notice of meetings of directors, attend and vote, and perform all the functions of the person appointing him, but he shall not be entitled to any remuneration from the company. (Article 66)

c. A person shall cease to be an alternate director if his appointer ceases to be a director. (Article 67)

d. Appointment or removal of an alternate director is by notice to the company, signed by the director, or in any other manner approved by the directors. (Article 68)

e. Unless otherwise provided in the articles, an alternate director is deemed responsible for his own acts and defaults, he is not the agent of the director who appointed him. (Article 69)

7. **Persons who may not be appointed**

a. ***Undischarged bankrupts***. By **S.11 COMPANY DIRECTORS DISQUALIFICATION ACT 1986** an undischarged bankrupt commits a criminal offence if he acts as a director without the permission of the court.

b. ***Persons disqualified by the court*** under ***S.2–4* COMPANY DIRECTORS DISQUALIFICATION ACT 1986**. Where a disqualification order is made the person concerned may not (without permission of the court) during the period covered by the order, act as a liquidator, director, administrator, receiver or manager, nor may he take part in the promotion, formation or management of a company. A court of summary jurisdiction may make a disqualification order of up to five years, other courts up to fifteen years. A disqualification order may be made in the following circumstances:

i. Where a person is convicted of an indictable offence in connection with the promotion, formation, management, or liquidation or receivership of a company. (The maximum period for disqualification is fifteen years);

ii. Where a person has been persistently in default in relation to filing documents with the registrar. (Maximum period five years);

iii. Where, in the course of a winding up, it appears that a person has been guilty of fraudulent trading *(S.458)* or, while an officer, liquidator, receiver or manager of a company, has been guilty of fraud or breach of duty to the company. (Maximum period fifteen years).

c. ***A person disqualified by the court*** under ***S.6–9 COMPANY DIRECTORS DISQUALIFICATION ACT 1986***, because his conduct as a director, either considered in isolation or taken together with his conduct as a director of any other company, makes him unfit to be concerned with the management of a company. These sections are considered in more detail in paragraphs 39–40 at the end of this chapter.

d. ***Over age directors***. By ***S.293*** a person over the age of 70 years may not be appointed to the board of a public company or to the board of a subsidiary of a public company. ***S.293*** is of little value because:

i. It can be excluded by the articles; and

ii. An over age director can always be appointed if special notice is given (see Chapter 19.7).

## 8. Defects in appointment

a. ***S.285*** provides that a director's acts are valid despite any defect that may afterwards be discovered in his appointment or qualification. For example

In DAWSON v AFRICAN CONSOLIDATED LAND CO (1898) a call was disputed by some members on the grounds that one of the directors had, at the time, parted with his qualification shares. The company's articles contained a clause similar to ***S.285***. It was held that the call was valid.

b. ***S.285*** only applies to technical defects in appointment and qualification. In such cases it can validate what would otherwise be a proper act. It cannot validate an improper act, therefore it will not apply when an appointment is a complete nullity.

In MORRIS v KANSSEN (1946) K and C were the first directors of a company. Following a dispute between them, C and S planned to deprive K of his directorship. With this in mind they falsely claimed that S had been appointed a director, and forged an entry in the company's minute book to this effect. Later C and S 'appointed' M a director and the three of them then allotted shares to themselves. K sued for rectification of the register. His claim succeeded. It was held that **S.143 CA 1929** (now **S.285**) could not validate either M's appointment or the allotment of shares.

c. If the appointment is a complete nullity the outsider may nevertheless be able to rely on the rules of agency to hold the company bound, (see 16 below).

9. Vacation of office

The office of director may be vacated by:

a. ***Death of the director.***

b. ***Dissolution of the company.***

c. ***Retirement by rotation.*** Table A Articles 73–74 state that at each AGM one third of the directors shall retire. Those to retire are those who have been longest in office. Retiring directors are eligible for re-election.

d. ***Retirement under an age limit.*** By **S.293** a director of a public company or the subsidiary of a public company must retire at the first AGM after reaching the age of 70, (see 7. above).

e. ***Removal***

i. By **S.303** despite anything in the articles or any agreement between the company and the director, a company can remove a director by ***ordinary resolution.***

ii. ***Special notice*** (see Chapter 19.7) must be given of any resolution to remove a director, or to appoint another director in his place.

iii. On receipt of this notice the company must send a copy to the director. He may then make written representations to the company which must be sent to the members with notice of the meeting unless they are an attempt to gain needless publicity for defamatory matter. If the company receives the representations too late to send out with notice of the meeting the director may demand that his statement be read out at the meeting. In any case he may speak on the resolution at the meeting. ***(S.304).***

iv. Removal under **S.303** does not deprive the director of his right to damages for loss of appointment as managing director should such post be automatically terminated, see **SOUTHERN FOUNDRIES v SHIRLAW (1940)** (Chapter 8.7).A director will not, or course, be entitled to damages if he was removed as a result of his own breach of duty or breach of contract.

v. **S.303** does not prevent the company from attaching weighted voting rights to a director's shares on a resolution for his removal.

In **BUSHELL v FAITH (1970)** a company had an issued capital of 300 fully paid shares divided equally between F and his two sisters. The company's articles contained a provision that if a resolution were proposed to remove a director the shares held by that director would carry three votes each. The sisters wanted to remove F from his post as director, but he invoked the above article. The sisters disputed its validity. The House of Lords held that the article was not inconsistent with the terms of the Act and was therefore valid, although Lord Morris dissented on the grounds that the article made 'a mockery' of **S.303**.

vi. An individual member has no right to compel the company to include a resolution to remove a director on the agenda of a meeting.

In **PEDLEY v INLAND WATERWAYS (1977)** the plaintiff sent special notice to the company of an ordinary resolution to remove all the directors. The company secretary refused to include the resolution in the agenda because **S.376** had not been complied with (see Chapter 19.8). The plaintiff contended that **S.376** did not apply where by **S.379** special notice was required. It was held that **S.379** did not compel inclusion of a resolution requiring special notice in the agenda, **S.376** must be complied with.

vii. The removal of a director of a 'quasi-partnership' company may be so unfair that the court will grant a petition to wind the company up on the 'just and equitable' ground – ***S.517(1)(g)***, **RE WESTBOURNE GALLERIES (1973)**. See Chapter 23.10.

f. ***Disqualification***. Table A Article 81 provides that a director shall vacate office in the following circumstances:

i. If he ceases to be a director by virtue of a provision of the Act eg **S.293** (age limits) or if he becomes prohibited by law from being a director;

ii. If he becomes bankrupt or makes a composition arrangement with his creditors;

iii. If he becomes of unsound mind;

iv. If he resigns by notice in writing; or

v. If he is absent from board meetings for more than 6 months without permission.

### 10. Directors' remuneration

Since directors are not servants of the company they are not entitled as of right to remuneration. Table A Article 82 empowers the company in general meeting to fix directors' remuneration. Directors cannot therefore vote remuneration to themselves, but if they appoint one of their number as managing director his remuneration may be fixed by the board. Once fixed remuneration is a debt and must be paid out of capital if there are no profits. If a director works for the company he may claim remuneration on a quantum meruit basis, (a claim for as much as he deserves). Concerning directors' remuneration note **RE NEW BRITISH**

IRON CO (1898) and RE RICHMOND GATE PROPERTY CO (1965) (Chapter 8.9).

## POWERS OF DIRECTORS

### 11. Relationship between the board and the company

a. The extent of directors' powers is defined by the articles. Table A Article 70 provides that 'The business of the company shall be managed by the directors who may . . . exercise all the powers of the company'. Also 'No alteration of the memorandum or articles and no such direction shall invalidate any prior act of the directors'.

b. Thus if the shareholders do not approve of the directors' acts they must either remove them under **S.303** or alter the articles to regulate their future conduct. (The alteration cannot have a retrospective effect). They cannot simply take over the functions of the directors. For example

   In **SCOTT v SCOTT (1943)** the company in general meeting resolved, firstly to pay dividends to preference shareholders, and secondly that the financial affairs of the company be investigated by a firm of accountants. It was held that the resolutions were invalid as they usurped the powers which the articles had vested in the directors.

   However new wording in Article 70, introduced in 1985, does make the directors' powers 'subject . . . to any direction given by special resolution'.

c. If directors exceed their powers, or exercise them improperly, their acts can be ratified by an ***ordinary resolution*** of the company.

   In **BAMFORD v BAMFORD (1970)** in order to prevent a takeover bid the directors allotted 5,000 shares to another company. The articles provided that all unissued shares were to be at the disposal of the directors. Two shareholders sought a declaration that the allotment was void because it was not made bona fide for the benefit of the company. Soon afterwards an ordinary resolution approving the allotment was passed at a general meeting. Proceeding on the assumption that the directors had not acted for the benefit of the company, and had therefore acted improperly, the court had to decide whether the ordinary resolution had cured the irregularity. It was held that it had, and the allotment was valid.

### 12. Board meetings

a. Subject to the provisions of the articles the powers conferred on the directors are conferred on them collectively as a board. Prima facie therefore their powers can only be exercised at a properly constituted board meeting. However Table A Article 93 provides that a resolution in writing signed by all the directors will be valid.

b. ***Notice***. A board meeting may be summoned by a director at any time and directors must be given a reasonable period of notice. This may be days, hours or even minutes, depending on the circumstances.

c. ***Quorum***. The quorum will be fixed by the articles. Table A Article 89 provides that the quorum shall be fixed by the directors, and if it is not so fixed, shall be two. If a director has an interest in a contract to be considered at the meeting he does not count towards the quorum.

d. ***Voting***. This is also governed by the articles. Usually directors have one vote each and a majority decision will prevail. If voting is equal the resolution is lost unless the chairman has a casting vote and exercises it in favour of the resolution. A decision made by the majority at a meeting of which no notice was given to the minority is invalid.

e. ***Delegation***. The board may, of course, appoint agents or servants of the company, but it must not delegate the exercise of its discretion. It is an application of the rule of agency that a person to whom power is delegated must not delegate further without the consent of his principal. This rule is usually modified in two ways:

   i. Table A Article 72 permits the directors to delegate any of their power to committees consisting of one or some of the directors; and

   ii. Article 72 also allows the board to appoint and delegate to a managing director. Today most companies are run by a managing director rather than by the board.

f. ***Minutes***. By S.382 minutes must be kept of board meetings. Directors have a right to inspect the minute book, but members do not. When the minutes are signed by the chairman they become prima facie evidence of the proceedings.

**13. The managing director**

a. Table A Article 84 provides that the directors may appoint one of their number as managing director on such terms as they think fit. He therefore has no settled functions. His powers and duties depend on his service agreement.

   In CADDIES v HOLDSWORTH (1955) the service agreement of the managing director of a holding company provided that he should perform the duties in relation to the business of the holding company and its subsidiaries as should be assigned to him by the board of the holding company. After policy disagreements the board directed him to confine his attention to the business of one of the subsidiaries. It was held that this was not a breach of his service agreement even though he had been deprived of the power the company which was employing him.

b. It is usual to provide that the managing director is not subject to retirement by rotation, but that his appointment as managing director will automatically end if he ceases for any reason to be a director

(Article 84). In **SOUTHERN FOUNDRIES v SHIRLAW (1940)** (see Chapter 8.7) it was held that a managing director's service contract contained an implied condition that the company would not make it impossible for him to act by removing him as a director. When he was removed damages for breach of contract were therefore payable.

c. However if a managing director has not been appointed for a specific term or if there is no express provision requiring a period of notice, the appointment will be regarded as made on the terms of the articles and any period of notice will be as therein stated.

   In **READ v ASTORIA GARAGE (1952)** P was appointed as managing director for an unspecified period. The articles provided that a managing director's appointment should be automatically determined if he ceased to be a director of the company or if the company in general meeting resolved to terminate his employment. The directors dismissed P, giving him one month's notice. The general meeting later confirmed their action. P claimed damages for wrongful dismissal on the ground that he was not given reasonable notice for a man in his position. It was held that there was no ground for the inclusion of a term implying the necessity for a reasonable period of notice.

   It follows from this decision that if a managing director is appointed for an unspecified period he can retire after resigning his directorship without giving the company a reasonable period of notice.

d. A managing director's service contract must now comply with ***S.319*** (see 20 below).

e. A managing director is not a 'servant' of the company for the purpose of receiving preferential payment of his salary on winding-up.

**14. Unauthorised acts by directors**

Sometimes a company may wish to avoid a contract on the ground that either:

a. It was made by a person who was not a director (but who acted as such); or

b. It was made by the board, but in excess of the directors' collective authority as a board; or

c. It was made by an individual director without the required delegated authority of the board.

In such cases the outsider will be protected if he can persuade the company to ratify the contract. If the company will not ratify the outsider may be able to rely on ***S.108 CA 89 (S.35A)*** or on the rules of agency.

**15. Power of directors to bind the company**

a. ***S.108 CA 89 (S.35A)*** extends the protection provided under the 1985 Act. It provides that in favour of a person dealing with a company in good faith, the power of the board of directors to bind the company, or authorise others to do so, shall be deemed to be free of any limitation under the company's constitution.

b. ***'Constitution'*** is defined to include any resolution of the company and any agreement between the members as well as the constitutional documents.

c. The Act also makes it clear that even a person dealing with a company with knowledge that the transaction is beyond the directors' powers will be protected. Such knowledge, by itself, does not amount to 'bad faith'. Bad faith will, however, exist if the person dealing with the company assists the directors in the abuse of their powers, or is party to fraud.

d. This new provision basically replaces the rule in **ROYAL BRITISH BANK v TURQUAND (1855)** which stated that when a person deals with a company in a transaction which is not inconsistent with the registered documents, the transaction could be enforced despite any irregularity of internal management.

e. To prevent the new provisions being used as a vehicle for fraud ***S.109 CA 89 (S.322A)*** introduces measures invalidating certain transactions where directors have exceeded limitations placed upon their powers to bind the company. These are discussed in paragraph 22 below.

**16. The rules of agency**

Under the normal rules of agency where a person without actual authority contracts on behalf of a company, the other party can hold the company bound if he can show:

a. That he was induced to make the contract by the agent being held out as occupying a certain position in the company;

b. That the representation was made by persons with actual authority to manage the company; and

c. That the contract was one which a person in the position which the agent was held out as occupying would usually have authority to make.

In **FREEMAN & LOCKYER v BUCKHURST PARK PROPERTIES (1964)** a director who had never been appointed managing director assumed powers of management with the company's approval. He entered into a contract with the plaintiffs, who were architects. The company denied liability to pay the plaintiffs' fees, but were held bound to the contract because the act of engaging architects was within the scope of the authority of a managing director of a property company and the plaintiffs were not obliged to enquire whether the person was properly appointed. It was sufficient that under the articles there was a power to appoint a managing director, and that the board of directors had allowed him to act as such.

d. **S.35A** removes the need to rely on the rules of agency in almost all cases, for example Freeman's case. since the Act refers to the 'power of the Board of Directors to bind the company, or authorise others to do so'. There may, however, still be a few situations where a valid 'holding out' is done by someone other than the directors.

e. ***S.130* CA *89* (*S.36A*)** abolishes the rule that a company must execute documents (this is different from making contracts) by affixing its common seal. It is now sufficient for a document to be signed by two directors or a director and the secretary, provided it is expressed to be executed by the company. The Act also protects a bona fide purchaser by providing that if such a document is signed by persons purporting to be directors (or a director and secretary), but who in fact are not, the document is deemed to have been properly executed.

## ENFORCEMENT OF FAIR DEALING BY DIRECTORS

### 17. Introduction

Part X of the Act deals with specific aspects of a company's relationship with its directors. It contains 30 sections of varying complexity dealing with situations where the interests of a director and his company may conflict, concerning for example service contracts, property transactions and loans. Before proceeding it is necessary to define several terms used in Part X.

a. ***Shadow directors***

  i. For the purpose of Part X the term 'director' generally includes a shadow director.

  ii. By ***S.741(2)*** a shadow director is a person in accordance with whose instructions the directors are accustomed to act unless the directors act on that person's advice only when it is given in a professional capacity.

b. ***Connected persons***. By ***S.346*** where the Act refers to 'a person connected with a director' the following are included (unless they are already directors):

  i. The director's spouse;

  ii. The director's child (whether legitimate or not) or step-child, so long as in either case the child is aged under 18;

  iii. A company where the director, either by himself or in concert with others, controls more than 20% of the voting power or equity share capital;

iv. A person acting in the capacity of trustee of any trust, (except one operating as an employees' share scheme or pension scheme), the beneficiaries of which include the director or any person in i., ii., or iii. above; and

v. A person acting in his capacity as partner of the director or of any person in i., ii., or iii. above.

c. ***Relevant company***. By ***S.331(6)*** a relevant company is either a public company or a private company in a group which contains a public company.

d. ***Quasi-loan***. By ***S.331(3)*** a quasi-loan is basically a payment or an agreement to pay a third party on behalf of a director or connected person where the company will be reimbursed in due course. For example where the company provides the director with credit card facilities, or pays for goods and services used by a director on terms that the director reimburses the company at some future date.

e. ***Credit transaction***. By ***S.331(7)*** a credit transaction may take any one of the following forms:

i. A sale of land or a supply of goods under a hire-purchase or conditional sale agreement; or

ii. A lease of land or hire of goods in return for periodical payments; or

iii. A disposal of land or the supply of goods or services where payment is deferred.

## 18. Compensation for loss of office

a. By ***S.312*** it is unlawful for a company to pay a director compensation for loss of office or in connection with his retirement, unless particulars of the proposed payment (including the amount) have been disclosed to and approved by the members. Note that:

i. If the payment is not disclosed and approved, the directors responsible for making it are liable to repay the sum misapplied. (**RE DUOMATIC (1969)**).

ii. ***S.312*** only applied to uncovenanted payments and not to those which the company is contractually bound to make.

In **TAUPO TOTARA TIMBER v ROWE (1978)** Rowe was appointed managing director for a period of five years. His contract entitled him to resign if the company was taken over. He would then receive a lump sum payment of five times his annual salary. When he resigned under this term the company contended that such a payment would be unlawful. It was held that Rowe's contract had been properly entered into in accordance with the articles, and that payments made in accordance with such contracts were not covered by ***S.312***.

iii. ***S.312*** has general application whereas ***S.313*** and ***S.314*** (below) are limited to compensation paid to directors in connection with mergers and takeovers.

b. By ***S.313*** in connection with the transfer of the whole or any part of the undertaking or property of a company, any payment of compensation for loss of office or on retirement (whether made my the company or someone else) is unlawful unless disclosed to and approved by the members. If such an illegal payment is made the director holds it on trust for the company.

c. ***S.314*** deals with the situation where the shares of the company are being transferred. It applies where transfer results from:

   i. An offer to the general body of shareholders;

   ii. An offer by one company with a view to another becoming its subsidiary;

   iii. An offer by an individual with a view to his acquiring at least one third of the voting power; or

   iv. Any other offer which is conditional on acceptance to a given extent. (Usually when a takeover bid is made the offer is conditional upon acceptance by holders of 90% of the shares of the 'target' company).

   If a payment is to be made to a director as compensation for loss of office or on his retirement it is the duty of that director to take all reasonable steps to ensure that particulars of the proposed payments are disclosed in the offer. If ***S.314*** is not complied with the director holds the amount received on trust for those persons who have sold their shares as a result of the offer. ***(S.315)***.

d. Note that:

   i. ***S.313*** and ***S.314*** only apply where the director loses office or retires. If no change is made in the directorship, but the directors are paid an increased price for their controlling shares, there could be no recovery under the sections, (although the arrangement would be contrary to the City Code on Takeovers and Mergers).

   ii. The sections only cover compensation for loss of office of director, not another office held in conjunction. In addition they do not cover payments which the company is obliged to make under a contract of service **(TAUPO TOTARA TIMBER v ROWE (1978))**.

**19. Disclosure of interests in contracts**

a. By ***S.317*** a director who is in any way interested in a contract with the company must declare the nature of his interest at a board meeting. He must disclose his interest at the first board meeting at which the contract was discussed, or if he did not have an interest at that time, at the first board meeting after his interest arose.

b. If disclosure is not made the director is liable to a fine of unlimited amount. In addition the contract is voidable by the company unless it is too late to rescind.

   In **GUINNESS v SAUNDERS (1990)** the Court of Appeal held that **S.317** would not be satisfied by disclosure to a sub-committee of directors. However on appeal to the House of Lords, Guinness dropped this argument since, if the contract were avoided, they would have had to restore the pre-contract state of affairs and pay Saunders and his associates for services rendered. Since G wished to avoid any payment, they changed their argument to lack of authorisation by the company (see 36. below).

c. For the purposes of **S.317**.

   i. 'Contract' includes any transaction or arrangement, whether or not it constitutes a contract; and

   ii. A transaction of the kind described by **S.330** (which prohibits loans and quasi-loans to directors) made by a company for a director or connected person must be treated as a 'contract' in which the director is interested.

d. Although **S.317** applies to shadow directors, they do not have to disclose their interest at a board meeting, but by written notice to the directors.

e. **S.317** is nevertheless a weak section for the following reasons:

   i. Disclosure need only be made to the board, and not to the members, and the board may well be composed of friends or 'cronies';

   ii. It is only the nature of the interest and not all the material facts which must be disclosed, although it would cover the extent of the director's profit; and

   iii. It is not clear what 'interested' means, although the interest may be direct or indirect and it may be future rather than immediate (see also (c)(ii) above).

**20. Directors' contracts of employment**

a. **S.319** provides that a company may not enter into an agreement for the employment of a director for a period exceeding five years (where the company's ability to terminate is limited) unless the agreement has been approved by the shareholders in general meeting.

b. Details of the agreement must be available for inspection by members at the company's registered office for two weeks prior to the meeting, and at the meeting itself.

c. Where the agreement concerns a director of a company's holding company, approval must also be obtained at a general meeting of the holding company as well as at a meeting of the subsidiary. No approval is otherwise required where the company is a wholly owned subsidiary.

d. There are provisions to prevent the 'stacking' of shorter contracts. For example X takes a four year service contract. At the end of the second year he enters into a new four year contract. Shareholder approval would be required for the second contract because **S.319** provides that the unexpired term of the first contract must be added to the term of the new contract, in this case making six years.

e. If the proper procedure is not followed the offending part of the contract is void. The remainder of the contract is valid, however it is deemed to contain a term entitling the company to terminate the contract at any time by giving reasonable notice.

f. The purpose of **S.319** is to prevent directors granting to themselves long-term service agreements which would result in large compensation payments in the event of dismissal, for example as a result of a takeover of the company. However **S.319** is not retrospective and will not affect long-term service contracts negotiated before 22 December 1980.

**21. Substantial property transactions**

a. By **S.320** a company cannot transfer to or acquire from a director or any person connected with him any property the value of which exceeds the lesser of either £50,000 or 10% of the company's net assets without prior approval of the shareholders in general meeting. Arrangements to transfer the property through third parties to achieve the same objectives are subject to the same requirements.

b. Where the transfer is to a director of the company's holding company, or a person connected with him, the approval of the shareholders of the holding company is required.

c. The following are exempt

i. Transfers of less than £1,000 in value.

ii. Transfers from a holding company to its wholly owned subsidiary and vice versa, and transfers between subsidiaries in the same group **(S.321)** ie where, for example the holding company is itself a director of its subsidiary a transfer from the subsidiary to the holding company is not caught by **S.320**.

iii. Transfers entered into by companies which are in liquidation, unless the winding up is a members' voluntary winding-up. **(S.321)**.

iv. A transaction by which a member of the company acquires an asset from the company, the arrangement being made with him in his ***character as member*** of the company **(S.321)**. Thus if a director acquires a non-cash asset solely by virtue of being a shareholder of the company it will not have to be approved in general meeting.

d. If the transfer is not approved by the company beforehand, or affirmed within a reasonable time afterwards it is ***voidable*** by the company unless:

i. Restitution of the subject matter is impossible; or

ii. A third party who is not aware of the contravention has acquired rights bona fide and for value.

In addition the director or connected person in question or any other directors who authorised the improper transfer, are liable to account to the company for any gain made and indemnify it against any loss resulting from the transfer, unless they took all reasonable steps to secure the company's compliance or they were not aware of the contravention.

**22. Invalidity of certain transactions involving directors**

a. The new provisions introduced by ***S.108 CA 89 (S.35A)*** could be used as a vehicle for fraud where directors exceed the limits placed upon their powers and bind the company in a transaction where the other parties include either a director of the company or its holding company or a person connected with, or a company associated with, such a director.

b. By ***S.109 CA 89 (S.322A)*** such a transaction is voidable at the option of the company, and whether or not the transaction is avoided, any director who is a party to the transaction, or any person connected with him, or any director who authorised the transaction, is liable:

i. To account to the company for any gain, and

ii. To indemnify the company for any loss or damage.

Such persons will not be liable if they can show that, at the time of the transaction, they were unaware that the directors were exceeding their powers.

c. The transaction will cease to be voidable where:

i. Restitution of any money or other asset, being the subject matter of the transaction, is no longer possible

ii. The company is indemnified for any loss resulting from the transaction

iii. The avoidance would affect a person acquiring rights in good faith who was unaware that the directors had exceeded their powers, or

iv. The transaction is ratified by the company in general meeting. An ordinary resolution will suffice unless the transaction was beyond the company's capacity in which case a special resolution is required.

d. The basic purpose of this section is to prevent dishonest directors misusing their power to bind the company in transactions from which they can benefit. Since the company can avoid the transaction it will usually be able to recover any money or property fraudulently transferred under the transaction.

### 23. Dealings by directors in options

a. By **S.323** it is a criminal offence for a director to purchase for cash or otherwise a 'put' option, a 'call' option, or a 'put or call' option in the ***listed shares or debentures*** of any company in the group.

b. A 'put' option is an option to buy. A 'call' option is an option to sell. A 'put or call' option allows the director to choose whether to buy or sell. The transactions are clearly objectionable because the director will certainly have inside information, and he may even be able to influence the future price of the securities.

c. The term director includes a shadow director. The section also applies to a director's spouse or infant child unless the latter had no reason to know he was a director. ***(S.327)***.

d. ***S.323(5)*** permits a director to buy an option to ***subscribe*** for the unissued shares or debentures of a company.

### 24. Loans to directors. Rules applicable to all companies

It would clearly be unfair to shareholders if money invested to generate business is used personally by the directors (especially if they do not re-pay the loan). The prohibition (with exceptions) of loans to directors is therefore a well established principle. However to be really effective the rules must be extended to indirect arrangements, eg guarantees. There is also a need for careful anti-avoidance legislation designed to catch any scheme contrary to the general principle.

a. ***Basic rule***

i. By ***S.330(2)*** a company may not make a loan to its directors or to a director of its holding company, nor may it enter into any guarantee or provide any security in connection with a loan made to such directors.

ii. Clearly a guarantee or provision of security on behalf of a director is not as directly harmful as a loan, since the company may never be called on to honour it, nevertheless it is an unacceptable risk for the company.

b. ***Anti-avoidance provisions***

i. By ***S.330(6)*** a company may not arrange an assignment to it or assume any rights, obligations or liabilities under a transaction which contravenes these provisions. For example if a director borrows money from a bank, with a relative acting as guarantor, and then the relative assigns the guarantee to the company ***S.330(6)*** will be contravened.

ii. By ***S.330(7)*** a company shall not take part in any arrangement whereby:

(a) Another person enters into a transaction which if it had been entered into by the company would have contravened the above provisions; and

(b) That other person, in pursuance of the arrangement obtains a benefit from the company or another company within the group. These widely drafted provisions will prevent for example:

- A loan by X Ltd to a director of Y Ltd in return for a loan by Y Ltd to a director of X Ltd.
- A loan by a company to a director of its subsidiary, the subsidiary making up the shortfall in interest by paying the holding company 'management fees'.
- A loan by an insurance company to a director of subsidiary A on the understanding that subsidiary B will place insurance business with the company.

**25. Loans to directors. Rules applicable to relevant companies**

a. The Act draws a distinction between relevant companies and other companies because, in the past, most abuses have occurred in public companies where shareholders tend to be at greater risk from the directors. There are three basic differences:

i. The prohibition on loans and guarantees is extended to quasi-loans and credit transactions;

ii. The prohibitions apply not only to transactions with directors, but with a number of persons connected with directors, for example a spouse or business partner; and

iii. Directors of relevant companies, but not directors of other companies, commit a criminal offence if any of these rules are broken.

b. By ***S.330(3)*** a relevant company may not:

i. Make a ***quasi-loan*** to a director of the company or its holding company; or

ii. Make a ***loan or quasi-loan*** to a person connected with such a director, or

iii. Enter into a ***guarantee*** or provide any security in connection with a loan or quasi-loan made by any other person for such a director or connected person.

***unless***

i. The amount of the quasi-loan does not exceed £5,000; ***and***

ii. The terms on which it is made require repayment within 2 months of its being incurred (**S.332** and **S.138 CA 89**).

c. In addition by **S.330(4)** a relevant company may not:

   i. Enter into a ***credit transaction*** as a creditor for a director of the company or its holding company or a connected person; or

   ii. Enter into any ***guarantee*** or provide any security in connection with a credit transaction made by any other person for such a director or connected person.

   ***unless***

   i. The aggregate amount does not exceed £5,000; ***or***

   ii. Without limit the company enters into the transaction in the ordinary course of its business and the value of the credit transaction, and the terms on which it is made, are not more favourable than those which it would be reasonable to offer to an independent person of similar financial standing **(S.335)**.

26. Exceptions to S.330

In addition to the two exceptions stated in 25 (b) and (c) above there are the following:

a. ***Loans not exceeding £5,000*. (S.334** and **S.138 CA 89)**. Any company may make a loan to a director of the company or of its holding company if the amount does not exceed £5,000.

b. ***Loans, etc, to holding companies*. (S.336)**.

   i. Loans or other borrowing assistance may be given by a company to its holding company. This exception is necessary because a holding company may be a director of the company making tho loan or offering borrowing assistance. Alternatively a director of a subsidiary may control more than 20% of the voting power in the holding company, making the holding company a connected person. In either case prohibition of loans could interfere with proper intergroup lending.

   ii. Credit transactions may be entered into by a company as creditor for its holding company.

c. ***Loans, etc, to directors to enable them to perform their duties*. (S.337)**.

   Funds may be provided for a director to meet expenses incurred to enable him to perform his duties. However:

   i. The transaction must have the prior authority of the company in general meeting; ***or***

   ii. The transaction must contain a provision that if it is not approved at the next general meeting the funds must be repaid within the following six months.

   iii. In the case of a ***relevant company*** the value of the transaction must not exceed £10,000.

d. ***Loans etc, by money-lending companies (other than recognised banks)*. (S.338 and S.138 CA 89).**

i. A loan may be made or other borrowing assistance may be given by a money lending company in the ordinary course of its business provided the value of the transaction is not greater, and the terms on which it is made are not more favourable, than those which it would be reasonable to offer to an independent person of similar financial standing.

ii. Where the money lending company is a relevant company but is not a recognised bank the amount lent to any one person must not exceed £100,000. However if the loan is made in connection with the purchase or improvement of a director's residence the terms may be favourable, provided similar favourable terms are available to other employees of the company, but the amount is still limited to £100,000.

e. ***Loans, etc, by recognised banks*. (S.338).**

i. A recognised bank is one granted recognition by the Bank of England under the **BANKING ACT 1979** on the grounds of its standing in the financial community.

ii. Such banks are subject to the £100,000 limit regarding residences, but in general they may lend to their directors without limit provided the terms are commercially sound.

f. ***Inter-group loans, etc, by relevant companies*. (S.333).** Where a relevant company is a member of a group it may lend to, or otherwise assist in the borrowing by, other members of the group despite the fact that a director of the relevant company is associated with the other members of the group. Like (b) above the reason for this exception is to prevent interference with legitimate inter-group business.

g. ***Loans, etc, by a holding company to directors of its subsidiary*.** This exception is not specified in the Act. However there is nothing in the Act to prevent a holding company from making loans to directors of its subsidiaries, provided of course that those persons are not directors of, or persons connected with directors of, the holding company.

When calculating the limits permitted for these exceptions the value of the proposed arrangement must be added to other outstanding amounts due to the company or its subsidiary which are also exempted.

**27. Civil remedies for breach of S.330. (S.341).**

a. The transaction is ***voidable*** at the instance of the company unless:

i. Restitution of the money or other asset involved is no longer possible; or

ii. A third party who is not aware of the contravention has acquired rights bona fide and for value.

b. In addition any director or connected person who benefited from the prohibited loan or assistance and any director who authorised the arrangement, is liable to account for any gain made directly or indirectly by the arrangement, and are liable to indemnify the company for any loss resulting from it, unless such person can show that he took all reasonable steps to secure the company's compliance or was not aware of the contravention.

c. Note that these remedies are the same as the remedies available for breach of **S.320** (substantial property transactions) ***except*** that it is not possible for a company to validate a breach of **S.330** by a subsequent ordinary resolution at a general meeting.

**28. Criminal penalties for breach of S.330. (S.342).**

a. The criminal penalties apply only to transactions involving ***relevant companies***. The following persons may be offenders:

i. Any director who authorises or permits the transaction, knowing or having reasonable cause to believe that the transaction contravened **S.330**.

ii. The company itself, unless it shows that at the time of the transaction it did not know of the relevant circumstances; and

iii. Any person who procured the transaction, knowing or having reasonable cause to believe that the transaction contravened **S.330**.

b. A person found guilty of an offence shall be liable to a term of imprisonment not exceeding two years, or a fine or both.

**29. Other statutory duties of directors**

a. The following statutory duties relating to publicity are discussed in Chapter 17.

i. The register of directors and secretaries;

ii. The rules concerning the publication of directors' names on company stationery;

iii. The register of directors' interests in shares and debentures; and

iv. The duty to prepare annual accounts.

b. Insider dealing is discussed in Chapter 20.

c. The duty in relation to employees is a statutory fiduciary duty and is discussed in paragraph 31.

## FIDUCIARY DUTIES AND DUTIES OF CARE AND SKILL

**30. Fiduciary duties. Introduction**

a. The fiduciary duties owed by directors are basically similar to those applying to any other fiduciary, for example an agent or a trustee. They are based upon the principle that since the company places its trust in the directors they must display the utmost good faith towards the company in their dealings with it or on its behalf. The duties however only apply to what the directors undertake without the concurrence of the company in general meeting. For example directors may profit from their position, but they must not make a secret profit.

b. Note that:

i. Although the authority of the directors to bind the company usually depends on them acting collectively as a board, fiduciary duties are owed by each director individually.

ii. Fiduciary duties are owed to the company, not to individual shareholders.

In **PERCIVAL v WRIGHT (1902)** the directors purchased some shares from a member without revealing that negotiations were in progress for the sale of all shares in the company at a higher price. In fact no sale ever took place. The plaintiff nevertheless sought to have his sale to the directors set aside for non-disclosure. It was held that the sale should not be set aside since the directors owed no fiduciary duties to individual members.

This decision has been much criticised, and the directors involved would today be guilty of the criminal offence of insider dealing in a similar transaction involving ***listed securities***. However since **PERCIVAL v WRIGHT** was a private transaction the decision is not affected by the insider dealing legislation.

iii. A director may be the fiduciary of an individual shareholder if, for example, he is appointed as agent of the shareholder to sell the latter's shares to a takeover bidder as in **BRIESS v WOOLLEY (1954)**.

### 31. Directors' duty in relation to employees

a. **S.309** states that the directors are, in the performance of their functions, to have regard to the interests of the company's employees as well as the interests of the members . The section specified that the duty is ***owed to the company*** and is enforceable in the same way as any other fiduciary duty owed to a company by its directors.

b. Although directors' relationships with shareholders and employees are very different they must have regard to the interests of both groups to discharge their duty to the company as a whole. Thus **S.309** allows directors to act in the interests of employees without fear of being in breach of their duty to the company. This does not mean that they can subordinate the interest of the company to that of employees by, for example, running the company at a loss to save jobs. It does however decrease the power of the members to object to an act which may not be beneficial to them, but would nevertheless be regarded as good industrial practice. For example a merger would have to be arranged to minimise loss of jobs provided this could be done without undue harm to the interests of the company as a whole.

c. The section has been criticised for the following reasons:

   i. It requires the directors to undertake an impossible 'balancing act'. They previously had to balance the often conflicting interests of members and creditors. The balancing act is made more difficult by the addition of employees.

   ii. The section does not provide any guidance as to how directors are to interpret their responsibilities, nor does it include any procedures whereby employees can check that their interests have been safeguarded. For example there is no requirement that employees be represented on the board, nor even a provision that a representative be allowed to attend as an observer.

   iii. The section is ineffective since the duty is owed to the company. Thus **S.309** cannot be enforced by employees unless they are also shareholders. Even then they may be prevented from bringing an action by the rule in **FOSS v HARBOTTLE**, (see Chapter 21). The reason for this provision in **S.309** is to avoid numerous actions by individual employees against directors.

   iv. It is an attempt at piecemeal reform. The motives of **S.309** have general acceptance, and the whole topic of industrial democracy provokes much debate. However any reform should result from a complete review of industrial democracy and should deal with all aspects of the subject.

## 32. The duty to act bona fide and for the benefit of the company as a whole

a. The problem here is to define what is for the benefit of an artificial corporate entity. It is clear that directors do not have to maximise economic benefit to the company whilst disregarding the interests of members, since this would mean ploughing back all the profits to the exclusion of payment of dividends . The phrase 'benefit of the company' basically means that the directors must have regard to the interests of the present and future members of the company, ie they must view the company as a going concern and balance this long-term view against the interests of the present members. In addition, by virtue of **S.309**, they must have regard to the interests of employees in discharging their duty to the company. Acting for the 'benefit of the company' does not, in a narrow legal sense, oblige the directors to consider the interests of the consumers of the company's products, or the community as a whole, although they probably have to have some regard to the interests of creditors.

b. It is not for the benefit of the company if they act in their own interest or the interest of a third party, without also considering the interest of the company.

In RE ROITH (1967) the controlling shareholder and director of a company wished to provide for his widow without leaving her his shares. Acting on legal advice he entered into a service agreement with the company whereby on his death she would be entitled to a pension for life. Since the sole object of the transaction was to benefit the widow the agreement was not held to be binding on the company.

c. Charitable and political donations of moderate value may be for the benefit of the company whilst it is a going concern, but if the company is about to cease then no commercial advantage can be gained by keeping outside interests happy. In such a case benefit of the company would be restricted to the economic interests of the present members.

d. When considering the benefit of the company the question of ultra vires may also arise. In Re Roith the transaction was ultra vires the company as well as in breach of the directors' fiduciary duty, but the ultra vires rule will not necessarily invalidate this type of transaction. (RE HORSLEY AND WEIGHT (1982)) (Chapter 7.25).

e. If the breach of duty is a misapplication of company property, a person who receives such property and who knows of the breach holds the property as constructive trustee and must therefore return it to the company. (INTERNATIONAL SALES AND AGENCIES v MARCUS (1982))

**33. The duty to use their powers for the purpose for which they were conferred**

a. If directors dishonestly use their powers for an improper purpose, for example to make a personal profit at the company's expense, they will not have acted bona fide and will therefore have broken the duty described in 32. above.

b. If however the directors act honestly in what they believe to be the best interests of the company they may still be liable if they do not use their powers for the purposes for which they were conferred.

In HOGG v CRAMPHORN (1967) in order to prevent a takeover bid which they believed would be bad for the company, the directors issued shares, carrying 10 votes each, to trustees of an employee pension fund. The shares were paid for by the trustees out of an interest free loan from the company. It was held that since the proper purpose of issuing shares is to raise capital, an issue made to forestall a takeover bid was a breach of the directors' fiduciary duties. However the issue was within the power of the company and could therefore be ratified at a general meeting.

c. It is an improper purpose if shares are issued solely for the purpose of destroying the existing majority block of shares. (HOWARD SMITH v AMPOL (1974)). Shares need not however be issued solely to raise capital. It may be proper to issue shares:

i. To a larger company to ensure the stability of the issuing company; or

ii. As part of an agreement relating to the exploitation of mineral rights owned by the company, as in **TECK v MILLER (1972)**.

d. Following **S.80** the company's authority is now required for the allotment of shares by directors, and this would have a bearing on many of the decided cases, for example **HOGG v CRAMPHORN**. The principles are nevertheless equally applicable to other powers vested in directors which do not require the company's authority. For example the power to make calls, forfeit shares, or register transfers.

**34. The duty to observe limitations on their powers**

a. This clearly existed prior to 1989. However, ***S.108 CA 89 (S.35(3))*** specifically states that it remains the duty of the directors to observe any limitations on their powers flowing from the company's memorandum and that action by the directors which, but for ***S.35(1)***, would be beyond the company's capacity may only be ratified by ***special resolution***.

b. The resolution ratifying such action will not affect the directors' liability. Relief from such liability must be separately agreed by another ***special resolution***.

c. ***S.35(1)*** is an important new section stating that the validity of an act done by a company shall not be called into question on the ground of lack of capacity by reason of anything in the company's memorandum.

**35. The duty to retain freedom of action**

a. Directors cannot validly contract with each other or with third parties on the way which they will vote at future board meetings.

b. Sometimes a lender will insist that, as a condition of granting a loan, his representative sits on the board of the borrowing company. In theory the duty of such directors is owed to the company and not to the person responsible for their nomination.

**36. The duty to avoid a conflict of duty and interest**

a. A director must not misuse corporate information or opportunity.

In **INDUSTRIAL DEVELOPMENT CONSULTANTS v COOLEY(1972)** the defendant was an architect who was employed as managing director of IDC. Whilst negotiating a contract with the Gas Board on behalf of IDC, Cooley realised that the contract probably would not be offered to IDC, but that if he left IDC he could obtain the contract himself. He therefore represented to IDC that he was ill and was allowed to terminate his contract. He then successfully obtained the contract with the Gas Board. IDC claimed the profit he made. It was held that Cooley was in breach of his duty as a director and must account to IDC with the profit made. It was immaterial that

IDC might never have obtained the profit itself. What mattered was whether Cooley made a profit, not whether the company suffered a loss.

b. In some cases liability arises not from a breach of trust, but merely because of the fiduciary position of directors.

In **REGAL (HASTINGS) v GULLIVER (1942)** a company which owned one cinema decided to acquire two more cinemas with a view to selling the whole undertaking as a going concern. A subsidiary company was formed to buy the lease of the two cinemas, but the owner of the freehold insisted that the paid-up capital of the subsidiary be at least £5,000. The company could not provide this amount of capital so the directors themselves subscribed for 3,000 £1 shares in the subsidiary. Later the shares in both companies were sold, the directors making a profit of nearly £3 on each of the shares in the subsidiary. The new controllers then brought an action to recover this profit from the former directors. This claim was clearly unjust since, if successful, it would mean that they would obtain a 75% reduction in the price that they had freely agreed to pay for their shares. Nevertheless it was held that the former directors had to pay over their profit to the company because:

'i. What the directors did was so related to the affairs of the company that it can properly be said to have been done in the course of their management and in utilisation of their opportunities and special knowledge as directors; and

ii. What they did resulted in a profit to themselves.'

Note that the former directors acted in good faith. In fact they were so sure of the legality of their action that it did not occur to them to go through the formality of obtaining ratification of their action at a general meeting.

c. Thus a director must account for a profit even if it is not made at the company's expense. This is so even if the other party refused to contract with the company and even if the company is legally unable to acquire the benefit in question.

In **BOSTON DEEP SEA FISHING CO v ANSELL (1888)** directors of Boston had to pay to the company bonuses received as a result of placing contracts to purchase ice. These bonuses were only payable to shareholders who purchased ice. Boston's directors held shares in the ice-selling company, but Boston did not. The company therefore would not have been entitled to the bonus if the ice had been ordered direct.

d. There is Commonwealth authority for the proposition that a director does not misuse corporate opportunity if he enters into a transaction on his own account which the company has considered and rejected.

In **PESO SILVER MINES v CROPPER (1966)** (a Canadian case) the board of Peso considered and rejected the chance to purchase a number of prospecting claims near to the company's property. Peso's geologist then formed a company and it purchased the claims. Cropper, who was a director of Peso and a party to the original decision, was also a shareholder in the new company. The action was brought by Peso to claim from Cropper the profit he made on his shares in the new company. It was held that he did not have to account, he had acted in good faith and no information had been concealed from Peso's board when it made the decision not to purchase. There had not therefore been a misuse of corporate opportunity.

e. If there is no ***binding agreement*** between a company and its directors, any payments to directors will be secret profits, received in breach of their fiduciary duties.

In **GUINNESS v SAUNDERS (1990)** a sub-committee of the board of G, consisting of S, R and W, agreed to pay (and subsequently paid) £5.2 million to W for services rendered in connection with the merger with Distillers. The company later brought proceedings to recover this sum. Their main argument in the House of Lords, was that the company had not authorised the payment. It was held that (despite lack of clarity in the articles) the sub-committee did not have the power to authorise the payment, that power was vested in the full board. Nor could W argue that he had apparent authority, this could only be argued in respect of outsiders, not against his own company. Thus since the payment had not been expressly agreed by authorised representatives of the company, W was a constructive trustee of the money and had to repay it to the company.

f. Although there is little case law on the subject it is clear that a director must not compete with the company. If he were to do so there would be an obvious conflict of personal interest and company interest.

**37. The equitable nature of fiduciary duties**

Since fiduciary duties are equitable duties the principles of equity apply, for example 'He who comes to equity must come with clean hands', ie the plaintiff must have acted properly in past dealings with the defendant.

In **NURCOMBE v NURCOMBE (1985)** a husband and wife were the only directors and shareholders of a small company. In breach of fiduciary duty H diverted company contracts to another company in which he had an interest. Later in divorce proceedings W was awarded a lump sum which took account of H's improper profit. W then commenced a derivative action on behalf of the company to recover the lost profit for the company. The Court of Appeal rejected her claim since she had, in effect, already recovered the profit as part of the divorce settlement.

It is interesting that the judge in the divorce proceedings ignored the corporate veil when he ordered H to make a personal payment based on the improper profit of a company in which he had an interest. The Court of Appeal also lifted the veil when they refused to allow H and W's original company to recover because W personally had already been compensated.

## 38. Duties of care and skill

In contrast to their duties of utmost good faith and loyalty there is very little obligation on directors to display any skill and diligence.

Such duties as do exist were laid down by Romer J. in **RE CITY EQUITABLE FIRE INSURANCE CO (1925)**. His statement can be analysed into propositions concerning skill, diligence and liability for others:

a. ***Skill***. A director must exhibit the degree of skill which may reasonably be expected from a person of his knowledge and experience. This standard is objective in that the director must act as a reasonable man, but it is subjective in that the reasonable man is only regarded as possessing the knowledge and experience of the individual concerned. Thus in financial matters more would be expected of a director who is a qualified accountant than a director who has no accountancy training. A director's service contract may impose a objective standard by providing that a director must show reasonable skill, but whatever the standard directors will not be liable for mere errors of judgement. This is quite reasonable since although judges may be well qualified to pronounce on matters of good faith and loyalty, their training does not equip them to pass judgement on the merits of complex business decisions. it was said in **HOWARD SMITH v AMPOL (1974)**:

> 'There is no appeal on merits from management decisions to courts of law; nor will courts of law assume to act as a kind of supervisory board over decisions within the powers of management honestly arrived at.'

b. ***Diligence***. A director is not bound to give continuous attention to the company's affairs, his duties are of 'an intermittent nature'. Directors are not bound to attend all board meetings, but must attend when they are reasonably able to do so. The degree of diligence may however vary depending on the facts of the case, more would be expected from a director on whom the company relies than from one director among many, or from one who is given little effective power. If a director also has a service contract he may be expected to work for the company full time, but this obligation is undertaken as an employee and not as a director.

c. ***Liability for others***. In the absence of suspicious circumstances directors are entitled to trust the company's officers to perform their duties properly. A director will not be liable for the acts of co-directors or other officers unless he participates in the wrong. 'Participation' includes:

i. Signing minutes approving misapplication of property.
ii. Signing a cheque for an unauthorised payment.
iii. Unreasonable failure to supervise the activity, or unreasonable failure to realise that the activity was wrong.

39. Relief from liability

a. Under ***S.727*** the court has power in an action against an officer for breach of duty to grant relief where, although the officer is in breach, it appears that he has acted honestly and reasonably. The reasonableness of a director's conduct may depend on whether he has taken legal advice. For example

   In **RE CLARIDGE'S PATENT ASPHALTE CO (1921)** relief was granted even though the director had applied the company's money for an ultra vires purpose. The director honestly believed that he was acting intra vires, having taken legal advice.

   In **RE DUOMATIC (1969)** a director who arranged a payment of compensation for loss of office to another director without seeking legal advice as to what was required by the Act did not act reasonably.

b. By ***S.310*** neither the articles nor any contract may exempt or indemnify any officer for the consequences of negligence, default, breach of duty or breach of trust. This probably invalidated insurance paid for by the company on behalf of such persons. However, ***S.137 CA 89*** (amending ***S.310***) now enables companies to purchase for any of their officers or auditors, insurance against such liability. If a company does this the fact must be disclosed in the directors' report.

## DISQUALIFICATION OF DIRECTORS

40. Introduction

a. Paragraph 7 describes various situations when, under the ***COMPANY DIRECTORS DISQUALIFICATION ACT 1986***, a person may be disqualified from acting as a director.

b. These provisions, first introduced in the ***INSOLVENCY ACT 1985***, increased the chance of disqualification of irresponsible directors . The rules have now been consolidated in the CDDA 1986. The original Insolvency Bill provided for automatic disqualification of directors of companies that went into insolvent liquidation. This was highly controversial and the government was eventually persuaded to abandon it. This was partly due to pressure from insolvency practitioners who felt that there were very few directors who were intentionally fraudulent, the majority being honest people who had done their best, but failed. In such cases it was finally decided that automatic disqualification was too harsh.

c. The result is legislation which imposes a duty on the court to make a disqualification order in certain circumstances, whilst in other cases the court's power is discretionary. It also introduces 'wrongful trading' to supplement existing rules on fraudulent trading, it creates a new offence with regard to company names, and it imposes personal liability on directors who act while disqualified and on 'delinquent directors'.

**41. Mandatory disqualification *(S.6 CDDA 1986)***

a. A person may be subject to this procedure if he is, or has been, a director or a shadow director of a company which has gone into insolvent liquidation (whether voluntary or compulsory).

b. If an interested party wishes to initiate an application to disqualify a director he must inform the liquidator or official receiver in charge of the winding-up (or the receiver or administrator if the company is in receivership or subject to an administration order). Such office holders have a duty to report immediately to the Secretary of State if they become aware of prima facie evidence as to a director's unsuitability to be concerned with the management of a company. If the office holder does not take appropriate action despite reasonable evidence the informant could make a direct application to the Secretary of State linked with a complaint against the office holder.

c. The court is required to make a disqualification order if the person's conduct as a director, either considered in isolation or taken with his conduct as a director of another company, makes him unfit to be concerned with the management of a company.

d. In deciding whether the above test has been satisfied the court must consider the matters specified in Schedule 1 CDDA 1986 and any other relevant circumstances. Matters covered by Schedule I include, for example:

i. Any misfeasance, breach of fiduciary duty, or misapplication of company assets;

ii. Failure to comply with statutory requirements concerning accounting records, company registers and the annual return;

iii. Responsibility for causing the insolvency, or for causing customers to lose money;

iv. Involvement in a transaction which is liable to be set aside as a preference.

Since the Act came into force a number of disqualification orders have been made.

In **RE STANFORD SERVICES LTD (1987)** a director was held to be unfit to hold office because the company owed considerable amount of PAYE, National Insurance and VAT. The director had used available funds to finance the company's business rather than arrange for the money to be set aside to meet the above liabilities. Although commercial morality may not have been infringed it was held that there had been a serious breach of the director's duties to the company's creditors and the public interest required that the misconduct should be recognised by two years' disqualification.

e. An application for a disqualification order may not be made more than two years after the day on which the insolvency commenced, except by consent of the court.

f. Although these new rules do improve the sanctions against fraudulent and irresponsible directors a significant constraint is that applications to court are generally confined to the Secretary of State.

**42. Non-mandatory disqualification**

This may arise in two situations:

a. By ***S.8 CDDA 1986*** an application for disqualification order may be made by the Secretary of State following a Department of Trade investigation under ***S.437*** **CA** or if information or documents have been obtained under ***S.447*** or ***S.448*** **CA** (Chapter 21.12, 13 and 16). The Secretary of State must be satisfied that it is in the public interest that a disqualification order be made. As with mandatory disqualification the court must consider the matters in Schedule 1.

b. By ***S.10 CDDA 1986*** the court may make a disqualification order on its own initiative when it makes a declaration that a person is liable to make a contribution to the company's assets. This may arise under ***S.213–215*** **IA** which deal with wrongful trading and fraudulent trading.

**43. Wrongful trading *(S.214–215 IA)***

This section imposes additional personal liability on directors of companies that have gone into insolvent liquidation. It is covered in detail in Chapter 23.23.

**44. Acting while disqualified *(S.217 IA, S.15 CDDA 1986)***

A person who concerns himself with the management of a company while disqualified, or a person who acts in the management of a company on instructions given by a disqualified person, is personally liable for all debts incurred by the company during the period in which he acts. The liability is joint and several with that of the company.

**45. Other provisions**

Two other new sections relevant to directors apply only when the company goes into liquidation. They concern restrictions on the use of company names ***(S.216 IA)*** and summary remedies against delinquent directors ***(S.212 IA)***. They are dealt with in Chapter 23.

## *PROGRESS TEST 11*

1. Define the terms:
   (a) Director
   (b) Shadow director.
2. State the statutory provisions which govern directors' service contracts.
3. Who normally appoints the managing director?
4. Which of the following are 'connected persons' for the purpose of *S.320 CA 1985* (substantial property transactions).
   (a) Brother
   (b) Husband
   (c) Mother
   (d) Partner
   (e) Accountant
   (f) Infant child?
5. Bing is a director of Zanzibar PLC, which has a subsidiary called Morocco Ltd. Bing holds 25% of Morocco Ltd's shares. Fred and Ginger, the directors of Morocco want your advice on the legality of the following arrangements:
   (a) An arrangement that Morocco Ltd should pay Bing's private health insurance premiums. Bing has agreed to re-imburse the company in one year's time.
   (b) The provision of $6,000 for a trip to America for Ginger to obtain new business for the company.
   (c) A loan by Zanzibar PLC to Fred at a low rate of interest. Morocco Ltd makes up Zanzibar's shortfall by the payment of 'management fees'.

# 16 The Secretary

## APPOINTMENT AND QUALIFICATIONS

1. Appointment

   a. **S.283** states that every company must have a secretary, but a sole director cannot also be the secretary.

   b. It is usual for the secretary to be appointed by the directors on such terms as they think fit. The directors may also remove the secretary. See for example Table A Article 99.

2. Qualifications

   **S.286** introduced for the first time minimum qualifications for secretaries of ***public companies***. The directors must take all reasonable steps to ensure that the secretary is a person who appears to them to have the requisite knowledge and experience and who:

   a. Already holds office as secretary, assistant secretary or deputy secretary of the company; ***or***

   b. For at least three out of the five years immediately preceding his appointment held office as secretary of a public company; or

   c. Is a barrister, advocate or solicitor; ***or***

   d. Is a member of any of the following bodies:

      i. The Institute of Chartered Accountants;

      ii. The Association of Certified Accountants;

      iii. The Institute of Chartered Secretaries and Administrators;

      iv. The Institute of Cost and Management Accountants;

      v. The Chartered Institute of Public Finance and Accountancy; or

   e. Is a person who, by virtue of having held any other position or being a member of any other body, appears to the directors to be capable of discharging the functions of secretary. This provision renders **S.286** rather pointless, since it allows the directors to appoint an unqualified person if they think that he can do the job.

## POWERS AND DUTIES

3. Powers

   The secretary is the chief administrative officer of the company and on matters of administration he has ostensible authority to make contracts on behalf of the company. Such contracts include:

a. Hiring office staff;

b. Contracts for the purchase of office equipment; and

c. Hiring cars for business purposes.

In **PANORAMA DEVELOPMENTS v FIDELIS FURNISHING FABRICS (1971)** the secretary of the defendant company entered into a number of contracts for the hire of cars. The cars were ostensibly to be used to collect important customers from Heathrow Airport, but in fact the secretary used them for his own private purposes. Counsel for the defendants cited a passage of Lord Esher M.R. in **BARNETT HOARES v SOUTH LONDON TRAMWAYS (1877)** – 'A secretary is a mere servant; his position is to do what he is told, and no person can assume that he has any authority to represent anything at all'. The Court of Appeal however held that the defendant company was liable. Lord Denning M.R. said:

> 'Times have changed. A company secretary is a much more important person nowadays than he was in 1887. He is an officer of the company with extensive duties and responsibilities . . . He is no longer a mere clerk . . . He is certainly entitled to sign contracts connected with the administrative side of a company's affairs, such as employing staff, and ordering cars and so forth'.

d. Although a secretary has 'extensive duties and responsibilities' there are a number of decisions where it has been held that he does not have authority for particular acts. Thus he may not:

   i. Bind the company on a trading contract;

   ii. Borrow money on behalf of the company;

   iii. Issue a writ or lodge a defence in the company's name;

   iv. Register a transfer of shares;

   v. Strike a name off the register of members;

   vi. Summon a general meeting on his own authority.

**4. Duties**

The secretary's duties include:

a. Ensuring that the company's documentation is in order, that the requisite returns are made to the Companies Registry, and that the company's registers are maintained;

b. Taking minutes of meetings;

c. Sending notices to members; and

d. Countersigning documents to which the company seal is affixed.

However, note that it is no longer essential for a company to execute documents by affixing its seal *S.130 CA 89 (S.36A)*.

### *PROGRESS TEST 12*

1. What period of notice is required for a board meeting?
2. Is it acceptable for a director to also hold the post of company secretary?
3. What are the main duties of the company secretary?
4. At a board meeting it is proposed to appoint Cecil as Managing Director. Cecil has 40% of the ordinary shares. The other 3 directors each hold 20% of the shares. Can Cecil vote for himself at the board meeting? If so, what percentage of board votes does he hold?
5. What is the extent of a company secretary's authority to make contracts on behalf of the company?

## COURSEWORK QUESTIONS 16-20 COMPANY OFFICERS

16. *You are required to write short one paragraph answers to the following:*

   a. *Identify three situations under the Companies Act when a company may make a lawful loan to a director.* *(3 Marks)*

   b. *Explain the meaning of 'substantial property transaction' and when a director might be involved in such a transaction with his company.* *(3 Marks)*

   c. *What was the effect of the decision in Bushell v Faith (1970) upon the directors of a company?* *(3 Marks)*

   d. *Explain the following terms used in connection with issues of company shares; underwriting commission; return of allotment; share premium.* *(3 Marks)*

   e. *Identify three ways in which the class rights of preference shareholders might differ from those of ordinary shareholders.* *(3 Marks)*

*(Total: 15 Marks)*
CIMA May 1985 Question 4

17. *The members of a company have decided that they wish to remove one of the directors of the company before the expiration of her 10-year service contract.*

*You are required to advise the members how removal might be achieved and on the means by which the director could oppose her removal.*

*(20 Marks)*

CIMA *November* 1989 *Question* 5

18. *In* 1965 A, B *and* C *incorporated the Smokease Co Ltd ('the Company') to develop and manufacture a cigarette-substitute with a minimal nicotine content.* A, B *and* C *were directors and each held 33% of the Company's shares. Advise* C *whether he has any cause of action either in his own right, or on behalf of the Company, in respect of each of the following complaints:*

    i. A, *who was appointed managing director, has managed the business so inefficiently that the Company may now well be insolvent.*

    *(6 Marks)*

    ii. B, *who was also the Company's analytical chemist and who carried out research in the Company's laboratories on cigarette substitutes, incidentally discovered a new product which he claimed was of use as a petrol additive and capable of improving the petrol consumption of cars. He tried, unsuccessfully, to persuade the Company's Board to market this product, but the Board formally rejected it, being unconvinced of its merits. Thereafter,* B *formed a new company, in which he and his wife were the only shareholders, to market this product. It has proved highly successful, and the value of the shares in this new company has appreciated significantly.* *(7 Marks)*

    iii. C *has just received a letter signed by* A *and* B, *advising him that he has been removed as a director of the Company; yet no meeting has been held for the purpose of considering* C*'s removal from office, nor has* C *been given any opportunity to make representations on the matter.* *(7 Marks)*

*(20 Marks)*

ACCA *June* 1980 *Question* 8

19. *Directors owe their company a duty to exercise their powers only for a 'proper purpose'. Explain what is meant by a 'proper purpose' and discuss the nature and scope of this duty. Illustrate your answer by reference to decided cases, particularly those dealing with the power to issue shares.*

ACCA *June* 1986 *Question* 6

20. *Daniel was a director of Prospect Ltd, a mining company. The company was interested in acquiring two adjoining plots of land. One plot was owned by Gold Ltd in which, unknown to Prospect Ltd, Daniel is the beneficial owner of all the shares. A board meeting of Prospect Ltd, acting on a report from independent surveyors, decided that Prospect Ltd*

*would buy the plot owned by* Gold Ltd *but would reject the other plot. Daniel was present at the board meeting but never disclosed his interest in* Gold Ltd. *Prospect* Ltd *purchased the plot from* Gold Ltd *and Daniel purchased the other plot which Prospect* Ltd *rejected. The plot purchased by Prospect* Ltd *now turns out to be worthless but the plot rejected by the company has just been sold by Daniel at a great profit.*

*Advise Prospect* Ltd *of its rights against Daniel and* Gold Ltd *in respect of:*

*(a) the plot purchased from* Gold Ltd, *and* (10 Marks)

*(b) the plot rejected by the* Company (10 Marks)

(20 Marks)
ACCA *June* 1982 *Question 5*

# PART VI PROTECTION OF INVESTORS AND CREDITORS

# 17 Publicity and Accounts

## 1. Introduction

Protection by disclosure is one of the underlying principles of the Companies Act. The theory is that if members, creditors and the public can find out relevant information about a company they will do so and then conduct their affairs with it accordingly. It has however always been clear that disclosure alone is not sufficient protection and recently extensive new protective measures have been passed, for example **S.103** (which requires an independent valuation of non-cash assets received by a public company in consideration for an allotment of shares), and **S.459** (which enables any member to apply for a court order if the affairs of the company are being conducted in an unfairly prejudicial manner). Publicity nevertheless remains important and is achieved in four main ways:

a. The requirement of official notification of certain matters in the Gazette;

b. The registration of certain information at the Companies Registry;

c. The compulsory maintenance of certain registers by the company; and

d. The requirement to make an annual return and disclose the company's financial position in its published accounts and directors' report.

Although b. and c. above ensure that information is publicly available, ***S.142 CA 89 (S.711A)*** provides that a person shall not be taken to have notice of the matter merely because it is disclosed in any document kept by the registrar or made available by the company for inspection, ie it abolishes, for most purposes, the doctrine of constructive notice. One exception is that a person taking a charge over a company's property is deemed to have notice of any matter requiring registration and disclosed on the register of charges at the time the charge was created. Note also that by ***S.116 CA 89 (S.379A)*** a private company may pass an elective resolution to dispense with the requirement to lay accounts and reports before the company in general meeting and/or dispense with the requirement to hold an AGM (Chapter 19.19).

## OFFICIAL NOTIFICATION IN THE GAZETTE

## 2. The requirement of notification

When various documents are issued by, or filed at, the Companies Registry the registrar must give notice to the public of the issue or receipt of such documents by means of a notice in the ***London Gazette***. The notice merely records the name of the company, the nature of the document and the date of its receipt. The document itself is not reproduced. If a person wishes to see the document he must apply to the Registry or the company's registered office.

**3. Matters requiring notification**

By ***S.711*** the following must be officially notified:

a. The ***issue*** by the registrar of:
   i. A certificate of incorporation; and
   ii. A certificate of compliance by a public company with the minimum capital requirements.

b. The receipt by the registrar of:
   i. A resolution altering either the memorandum or articles;
   ii. A notice of any change among the directors;
   iii. Any documents required to be comprised in the accounts;
   iv. Any notice of a change in the situation of the registered office;
   v. Any order for the winding-up or dissolution of the company;
   vi. The liquidator's return of the final meeting;
   vii. A report as to the value of non cash assets made under ***S.103*** or ***S.104***.
   viii. A resolution relating to an authority to allot securities;
   ix. A resolution for the disapplication of pre-emption rights;
   x. Particulars of special rights attached to shares;
   xi. A resolution which gives details of the rights attached to shares of a public company;
   xii. A resolution which varies rights attached to any shares in a public company;
   xiii. A resolution assigning a new name or designation to any class of shares in a public company;
   xiv. Any return of allotments of a public company; and
   xv. A notice of redemption of shares by a public company.

**4. The effect of official notification *(S.42)***

Clearly the ***Gazette*** is not widely read although it is carefully scanned by, for example, credit reference agencies. The effect of notification is that the company cannot rely, as against third parties, on the happening of certain events unless their occurrence had been officially notified or the company can show that their occurrence was actually known to the third party. The events are:

a. The making of a winding-up order;
b. An alteration of the memorandum or articles;
c. A change of directors; and
d. A change of the address of the registered office.

## MATTERS REQUIRING REGISTRATION AT THE COMPANIES REGISTRY

**5. Information on record at the Companies Registry**

The following information is recorded on each company's file at the Companies Registry. Any member of the public may inspect the file. The fee is £1.

a. The company's memorandum and articles;

b. A statement containing the names and relevant particulars of the directors and the secretary;

c. Any notice of the appointment of a liquidator or receiver;

d. A statement of the address of the registered office;

e. Details of the company's nominal, issued and paid-up capital;

f. Details of charges over the company's property;

g. The annual balance sheet, profit and loss account, directors' report and auditors' report. (This requirement is modified in the case of certain small and medium-sized companies); and

h. The annual return.

**6. Resolutions requiring registration**

a. All special, extraordinary and elective resolutions must be registered within 15 days of passing the resolution.

b. In general the fact that an ordinary resolution has been passed need not be registered. However the registrar must be informed if the company passes an ordinary resolution to:

i. Appoint or remove directors, (the period for notification is 14 days);

ii. Remove auditors (notification period 14 days);

iii. Change the address of the registered office, (notification period 14 days);

iv. Increase the authorised capital, (notification period 15 days);

v. Consolidate or sub-divide shares, or convert shares to stock or vice versa, (notification period one month);

vi. Wind-up the company voluntarily because the period fixed for its duration has expired, or because an event has occurred on which the articles provide for the dissolution of the company, (notification period 15 days);

vii. Confer, vary, revoke or renew the authority of directors to allot shares, (notification period 15 days);

viii. Confer, vary, revoke or renew the authority for a company to make a market purchase of its own shares, (notification period 15 days);

ix. Authorise the acquisition by a public company of non-cash assets from its subscribers, (notification period 15 days); and

x. Revoke an elective resolution.

## REGISTERS WHICH MUST BE MAINTAINED BY THE COMPANY

**7. The registered office**

a. The documents and registers which must be kept by a company and the rights of inspection relating to them were set out in Chapter 7. 16–17. In most cases no further explanation of their contents is necessary. However the register of directors and secretaries, the register of directors' interests in shares and debentures and the register of substantial shareholdings merit further comment.

b. Note that the register of members was discussed in Chapter 13.9 and the register of charges in Chapter 14.11. The accounting records are discussed later in this chapter.

**8. The register of directors and secretaries**

a. By *S.288* every company must keep a register of its directors and its secretary at its registered office.

b. The register must contain the following particulars of each director:

i. Name and former name, (if any);

ii. Address;

iii. Nationality;

iv. Business occupation, (if any);

v. Particulars of other directorships held, or which have been held, by him in the past five years, except for directorships of companies within the same group and directorships of dormant companies, (see 37. below); and

vi. Date of birth, where the company is subject to *S.293* (see Chapter 15.7).

c. The company must notify the registrar within 14 days of any change in the particulars on the register. When a person becomes a director the notification must be accompanied by his signed consent to act.

**9. Directors' names on company stationery *(S.305)***

Prior to 1981 the names of all the directors used to be required on business stationery. It is now provided that a company may not state the name of any of its directors on its business letters (other than in the text or as a signatory) unless it states the christian name, or initials thereof, and the surname of every director who is an individual and the corporate name of every corporate director.

**10. The register of directors' interests in shares or debentures**

a. By **S.324** a director must notify the company in writing of any transaction involving his interest in the shares or debentures of the company.

   The notification period is five working days (Sch 13, paragraph 14).

b. By **S.328** the interest of a director's spouse or infant child must be treated as if it were the director's interest.

c. Schedule 13, paragraphs 1–13 contain very detailed rules for determining when a director has an 'interest' in shares or debentures. Thus, for example a person holding a beneficial interest under a trust does have an interest in shares comprised in the trust, but the trustee (although on the register of members) does not have an interest. Also a person has an interest if shares or debentures are held by a company and

   i. That company or its directors are accustomed to act in accordance with his instructions; or if

   ii. He controls one-third or more of the votes at a general meeting of that company.

d. By **S.325** every company must keep a register of directors' interests in shares or debentures. Information must be entered in the register within three working days of its receipt. (Sch 13, paragraph 22).

e. By **S.329** when a ***listed company*** receives notification from a director under **S.324**, it must, before the end of the following day, notify the Stock Exchange, which may publish the information.

**11. The register of substantial shareholdings**

a. The rules are contained in ***S.198–211*** and ***S.134 CA 89***. They only apply to ***public companies***.

b. A notifiable interest arises when a person knows that he has an interest in 3% or more of the company's voting shares. Notification must be in writing and must be made within two working days from when the obligation to notify arose. The 1985 Act specified 5% and 5 days. The change will make it more difficult for purchasers of shares to build up a secret stake in the company.

c. The 1989 Act also introduced a requirement that the notification must differentiate between the number of shares and the number of rights to acquire shares, for example interests in options to purchase shares.

d. Notification is necessary on cessation or acquisition of an interest and also when ***any change*** in a notifiable interest takes place. For example a company may issue new shares for the purpose of an acquisition. This could dilute a shareholder's interest from, say 6% to 2% without altering the total number of shares held. He would nevertheless be under an obligation to notify the company. When calculating notifiable interests fractions are rounded down, (ie a holding of 2.9% of a company's shares is regarded as 2%) and changes of less than 1% are exempt from notification.

e. The rules for defining the extent of an 'interest' are very detailed.

For example a person is deemed to have an interest if:

i. His spouse or infant child has an interest;

ii. Shares are held by a company and that company or its directors are accustomed to act in accordance with his instructions, or he controls one-third or more of the votes in general meeting of that company; or

iii. Another person is interested in the company's shares and he is ***acting together*** with that other person. This is discussed below.

f. ***Persons acting together***

i. When persons act in concert the Act attributes to each member of such a group (known as a 'concert party') the interests of the other members and places an obligation to notify on ***all*** members of the concert party, ie a person has an obligation to notify even if he does not have any shares himself but he is acting in concert with someone who has a notifiable interest.

ii. A concert party exists when there is an agreement (whether legally binding or not) under which at least one of the parties is to acquire an interest in the shares of a company. In addition there must be some understanding as to the way in which the interest acquired under the contract is to be used.

iii. The purpose of these rules is to give the company early warning of persons acting together to acquire a company's shares with a view to a takeover bid.

g. A public company must keep a register to record within three days the information notified. The register must be kept at the same place as the register of directors and secretaries. The register will also contain (in a separate part) the results of any investigations carried out under ***S.212*** (see below).

12. Investigation by a company of interests in its shares ***(S.212–216)***

a. If a ***public company*** knows, or has reasonable cause to believe, a person to be or have been interested in its voting shares within the past three years, it may make a written request of that person to indicate whether he holds or has held an interest in the shares. The request may require a written response within a specified time limit.

b. When a company receives such information if must record it in the register of substantial shareholdings.

c. Members holding not less than one tenth of the paid-up voting shares may require the company to make an investigation by depositing a requisition at the registered office. The company must prepare a report on its investigation. The report must be available for inspection at the registered office within a reasonable period (not more than 15 days) after the conclusion of the investigation. The company must notify the requisitionists within three days of making the report available. It must remain available for inspection together with the register of substantial shareholdings.

d. If a person fails to give information when requested to do so, the company may apply to the court for an order that the shares be sold or for an order imposing restrictions on the shares in question, for example:

   i. That any transfer of the shares is void;

   ii. That no voting rights are exercisable is respect of the shares;

   iii. That (except in a liquidation) no payment shall be made in respect of sums due from the company on those shares.

   The person is also liable to a maximum of two years imprisonment and an unlimited fine.

## The annual return

**13. Making the annual return *(S.139 CA 89 (S.363–365))***

a. The 1989 Act modified the requirement to deliver annual returns and simplifies requirements as to their content.

b. ***The return date.*** The annual return will have to be made up to a date not later than the company's return date and filed within 28 days of the date to which it is made up. The return date will be either:

   i. The anniversary of the company's incorporation date or

   ii. If the company's previous return was made up to a different date, the anniversary of that date.

c. The return must be signed either by a director or the secretary (not by both of them as under the 1985 Act).

d. If a company does not deliver its annual return within 28 days after the return date, or delivers a return which does not contain the required information, it is liable to a fine. Every director or secretary will also be liable unless they can show tht they took all reasonable steps to avoid the offence.

### 14. The contents of the annual return

The annual return must state the date to which it is made up and contain the following information:

a. The address of the registered office and, if the register of members is not kept at that office, the address at which it is kept.

b. A summary of share capital specifying for each class of share the total number of issued shares and the aggregate nominal value of those shares.

c. The type of company and its principal business activities.

d. A list of members on the date to which the return is made up showing individual shareholdings and changes that have taken place during the year. To avoid annual preparation of a lengthy list the company need only submit a full list of members every three years. In the intervening years only details of changes need be given.

e. Particulars of directors and the secretary taken from the register, including the date of birth of each individual director.

f. Where a private company has by elective resolution dispensed with the laying of accounts and reports before the general meeting, or with holding an AGM, a statement to that effect.

## THE ACCOUNTING RECORDS AND THE ACCOUNTS

### 15. Accounting records

a. It is important to distinguish between the accounting records and the accounts.

   i. The ***accounting records*** are the ledgers, cash book, order forms, receipts and other records maintained by the company to enable the accounts to be prepared.

   ii. The ***accounts*** (or financial statements) in the narrow sense consist of the balance sheet, the profit and loss account and the notes to the accounts, although other documents are comprised in the 'accounts' which are filed with the registrar, (see 17. below).

b. By ***S.2 CA 89 (S.221–222)*** every company must keep accounting records which must:

   i. Show with reasonable accuracy, at any time during the financial year, the financial position of the company at that time; and

   ii. Enable the directors to ensure that any balance sheet prepared by them gives a true and fair view of the company's state of affairs and any profit and loss account gives a true and fair view of the company's profit or loss.

c. In particular the records must contain:
   i. A day to day record of money received by and spent by the company;
   ii. A record of the assets and liabilities of the company;
   iii. Statements of the stock held by the company at the end of each financial year; and
   iv. A record of goods sold and purchased, with details of the goods, buyers and sellers sufficient to enable them to be identified.

d. The accounting records must be kept at the registered office or such other place as the directors think fit. They must be open for inspection by officers at any time.

e. A private company must keep its accounting records for three years. Any other company must keep the records for six years from the date when they are made.

f. Failure to keep accounting records is an offence for which officers may be fined or imprisoned for a maximum of two years.

**16. The accounting reference period and accounting reference date**

a. By ***S.4 CA 89 (S.226)*** the directors must prepare accounts based on an accounting reference period. This will commence on the day after the date to which the last annual accounts were prepared and will end on the last day of the company's financial year, known as the accounting reference date. The directors are however given a discretion to move the accounting reference date to up to seven days before or after the end of the financial year.

b. By ***S.3 CA 89 (S.224)*** a company may if it wishes give notice to the registrar specifying its accounting reference date. If no notice is given the accounting reference date is
   i. 31st March (for companies incorporated before the commencement of the 1989 Act)
   ii. The last day of the month in which the anniversary of its incorporation falls (for companies incorporated after the commencement of the 1989 Act).

c. By ***S.3 CA 89 (S.225)*** a company may change its current and all subsequent accounting reference periods by giving notice to the registrar specifying a new accounting reference date.

**17. Laying and delivering accounts**

a. By ***S.11 CA 89 (S.241)*** the directors, in respect of each accounting reference period, must lay before the company in general meeting every document required to be comprised in the accounts.

b. In respect of each accounting reference period the directors must deliver to the registrar a copy of every document required to be comprised in the accounts. In the case of a public company the time allowed for laying and delivering the accounts is a period of seven months after the accounting reference date. In the case of a private company the time allowed is ten months ***(S.11 CA 89 ((S.244))***.

c. By ***S.16 CA 89 (S.252)*** a ***private company*** may decide, by ***elective resolution***, to dispense with the laying of accounts before the company in general meeting. The accounts must still be sent to members and others entitled to receive notice of general meetings and filing requirements are not affected. While the election is in force any member, or the auditor, can require the accounts to be laid for a particular financial year.

d. The documents required to be comprised in the accounts are:
   i. The profit and loss account;
   ii. The balance sheet. By ***S.7 CA 1989 (S.233)*** this must be signed by one director;
   iii. The auditors' report. By ***S.9 CA 1989 (S.236)*** the copy sent to the registrar must state the names of the auditors and be signed by them.
   iv. The directors' report.
   v. If the company has subsidiaries, group accounts.

e. Note that:
   i. An unlimited company is exempt from delivering accounts provided it is not in the same group as a limited company.
   ii. By ***S.13 CA 89 (S.246)*** the requirements are relaxed for small and medium sized companies. In particular a small company need not deliver a profit and loss account and a directors' report. Small and medium sized companies are discussed below (32–36).
   iii. The annual return is not annexed to the accounts, it is delivered to the registrar separately.

**18. Holding and subsidiary companies *(S.144 CA 89 (S.736))*, parent undertakings and subsidiary undertakings *(S.21–22 CA 89 (S.258))***

a. The 1989 Act introduces new definitions for holding and subsidiary companies and introduces the terms ***parent undertaking*** and ***subsidiary undertaking***. The two latter terms are used for almost all accounting purposes, whilst the former are used for other purposes, for example the rule that a company cannot be a member of its own holding company.

b. The accounting definitions of parent and subsidiary undertakings include not only ***companies***, but also ***partnerships*** and ***unincorporated associations*** carrying on a business.

c. A business will be a ***subsidiary undertaking*** if it satisfies any of the six requirements listed below. A company will be a ***subsidiary*** if it satisfies any of the first four requirements:

   i. Where the 'parent' holds the majority of voting rights at general meetings of the undertaking;

   ii. Where the 'parent' is a member of the undertaking and has the right to appoint or remove a majority of its directors;

   iii. Where the 'parent' is a member of the undertaking and controls alone, pursuant to an agreement with other members, the majority of voting rights at general meetings of the undertaking;

   iv. Where the subsidiary undertaking is a subsidiary of another company (X) and X is a subsidiary of the parent;

   v. Where the 'parent' has the right to exercise a ***dominant influence*** over the undertaking:

      (a) by virtue of provisions in the undertaking's memorandum or articles, or

      (b) by virtue of a 'control contract' authorised by the undertaking's memorandum or articles;

   vi. Where the 'parent' has a ***participating interest*** in the undertaking and:

      (a) actually exercises a dominant influence over it, or

      (b) the parent and subsidiary undertaking are managed on a unified basis.

d. An undertaking is ***not*** regarded as having the right to exercise a ***dominant influence*** over another undertaking ***unless*** it has a right to give directions with respect to the operating and financial policies of that other undertaking, with which its directors are obliged to comply (even if they are not for the benefit of the undertaking). The right to give directions must be a legal right. It would not, for example, require a large retailer to consolidate the accounts of a supplier who depended entirely on that retailer.

e. A ***participating interest*** is an interest held in the shares of another undertaking on a long term basis, for the purpose of securing a contribution to its activities by the exercise of control or influence arising from or related to that interest. A holding of 20% or more of the allotted shares on an undertaking is presumed to be a participating interest unless the contrary is shown. A holding of less than 20% may constitute a participating interest.

f. The new definitions were required by the ***EC Seventh Directive***. The basic result is that certain businesses, that are not subsidiaries for general purposes, will need to be consolidated, although in one respect the new definitions are narrower in that majority equity share ownership no longer creates a holding/subsidiary nor a parent/subsidiary undertaking relationship. Consequently companies in which a majority of equity is owned, but where voting control is absent, will no longer have to be consolidated.

**19. Group accounts**

a. If a parent company has subsidiary undertakings, group accounts showing the state of affairs of the parent company and subsidiary undertakings must be laid before the AGM together with the company's own accounts.

b. By *S.5 CA 89 (S.227)* subsidiary undertakings may be excluded from consolidation in the following circumstances.

   i. If inclusion is not material for the purpose of giving a true and fair view.

   ii. Where severe long term restrictions substantially hinder the exercise of the rights of the parent over the assets of management of the subsidiary undertaking.

   iii. Where the information necessary for the preparation of consolidated accounts cannot be obtained without disproportionate expense or undue delay.

   iv. Where the interest of the parent is held exclusively with a view to subsequent resale and the subsidiary undertaking has not previously been included in consolidated group accounts prepared by the parent company.

c. *S.5 CA 89* also provides that subsidiary undertakings *must* be excluded from consolidation where their activities are so different from those of other undertakings to be included in consolidation, that their inclusion would be incompatible with the obligation to give a true and fair view. The exclusion will not apply merely because subsidiary undertakings carry on diverse activities, for example a manufacturing company and a service company.

d. *S.5 CA 89* also introduces new general exceptions from the requirement to prepare group accounts. (Previously the only general exception was where the parent company itself was a wholly-owned subsidiary of another British company). Briefly the general exceptions are:

   i. *Intermediate holding company*. This replaces the previous exception and is available when intermediate parent holds more than 50% of the shares in a company. The exception does not apply to companies having shares or debentures listed on a Stock Exchange in any EC country. It is subject to various disclosure requirements and there is a procedure by which minority shareholders have the right to request the preparation of consolidated accounts.

   ii. *Small and medium sized groups*. A parent company is exempt from the requirement to prepare group accounts, if in respect of that financial year, the group headed by the parent qualifies as a small or medium sized group, and is not a member of an ineligible group (ie a group containing a public company). To qualify the group headed by the parent must satisfy, for the financial year in question and the preceding year, at least two of the following conditions:

| | **Small** | **Medium-sized** |
|---|---|---|
| Turnover | £2.4m gross or £2.0m net | £9.6m gross or £8.0m net |
| Balance sheet total | £1.2m gross or £1.0m net | £4.7m gross or £3.9m net |
| Average number of employees | 50 | 250 |

NB. *'Net'* means with the set-offs and adjustments required by the Act in the case of group accounts, eg the elimination of intra-group transactions. *'Gross'* means without those set-offs and adjustments, ie straight aggregation.

e. Under the 1989 Act group accounts must be in consolidated form. Another form of group accounts may only be used if that is the only way to give a true and fair view. Previously other forms of group accounts could be used where the directors considered an alternative method of presentation would be more readily appreciated by the members.

f. ***S.5 CA 89*** also introduced a number of detailed new rules regarding the methods of consolidation. These are contained in a new schedule, ***Schedule 2 CA 89 (Schedule 4A CA 85)***. This contains rules on the preparation of consolidated accounts and certain disclosure requirements. Although new in law it basically formalises existing practice.

g. Prior to the 1989 Act a parent company which produced consolidated accounts did not have to prepare and publish its own profit and loss account. It is now required to prepare that account and have it approved by the board of directors, however, the accounts do not have to be audited, sent members, laid before the members at the AGM or delivered to the registrar.

h. In general a parent company must ensure that its subsidiary undertakings have the same financial year end ***(S.3 CA 89 (S.223))***.

**20. Form and content of accounts. Introduction**

a. The 1981 Act implemented the fourth EC directive which was designed to harmonise accounting practice and the form and content of accounts in member states.

b. Prior to 1981 the law did not lay down the form in which financial statements had to be presented. The methods of presentation traditionally used were evolved by the accountancy profession.

c. The 1981 Act broke from this tradition and provided that companies must present their accounts in one of the specified formats and must ensure that the notes to the accounts comply with new disclosure requirements.

d. The 1981 Act also incorporated matters which had not previously been the subject of legislation, for example there were new rules concerning accounting principles, the valuation of assets and liabilities, and for the recognition of profit.

e. The 1989 Act implemented some of the recommendations of the Dearing Report on Accounting Standards (1988). It was decided that statutory backing for accounting standards was too legalistic and difficult to change, but statutory support was recommended for:

   i. A requirement that the notes to accounts state whether or not they have been prepared in accordance with applicable accounting standards (21 below), and

   ii. A new statutory power for certain authorised bodies or the Secretary of State to apply to the courts for an order requiring the revision of accounts which do not give a true and fair view (40 below).

**21. Accounting principles and standards**

a. *S.4 CA 89 (S.226)* provides that:

   i. Every balance sheet must give a true and fair view of the company's state of affairs at the end of its financial year; and

   ii. Every profit and loss account must give a true and fair view of the company's profit or loss for that year.

b. It also requires that the accounts comply with the provisions of *SCHEDULE 4* (as amended by *Sch 1* and *2 CA 89*).

c. One of these amendments requires companies to state whether accounts have been prepared in accordance with applicable accounting standards and give details of, and the reasons for, any material departures. This disclosure requirement does not apply to small and medium sized companies.

**22. Asset valuation. Introduction**

*PART II SCHEDULE 4* deals with asset valuation. It is very detailed and the following paragraphs (23.–25.) are only an outline summary. Part II is divided into three sections:

a. ***Accounting principles***, ie the basic accounting concepts;

b. ***Historical cost accounting rules***, for example relating to the valuation of fixed and current assets; and

c. ***Alternative accounting rules***, where it is necessary to take account of inflation or of other fluctuations in value.

**23. Asset valuation. Accounting concepts**

Since the overriding consideration is to give a true and fair view the directors may depart from the accounting concepts where there are special reasons for doing so. Full details of the departure must be disclosed in notes to the accounts. The concepts are:

a. The company is presumed to be carrying on business as a ***going*** concern;

b. Accounting policies must be applied ***consistently*** from one year to the next;

c. Items must be determined on a ***prudent*** basis. In particular:

   i. The profit and loss account may include only those profits that have been realised at the balance sheet date; and

   ii. Account must be taken of all liabilities and losses that either have already arisen, or are likely to arise, in respect of the financial year in question or in respect of a previous financial year.

d. All income and expenditure relating to the financial year must be taken into account regardless of the date of receipt or payment. (The ***accruals*** concept).

e. When determining the aggregate amount of any item, each individual asset or liability falling under that item must be ***separately valued***.

**24. Asset valuation. Historical cost accounting rules**

The basic rule is that accounts should be drawn up in accordance with the historical cost convention. Thus fixed assets must be shown at either purchase price or production cost and, where such an asset has a limited life its purchase price or production cost must be written off systematically over that life. In addition this section of ***Part II Schedule 4***:

a. Contains further detailed rules relating to the depreciation of fixed assets;

b. Deals with the treatment of development costs;

c. Deals with the treatment of goodwill. The basic rule is that goodwill must be written-off over a maximum period of five years;

d. Requires that, in general, current assets are to be shown at the lower of purchase price or production cost and net realisable value;

e. Defines fixed and current assets:

   i. A ***fixed asset*** is any asset intended for use on a continuing basis in the company's activities;

   ii. A ***current asset*** is any asset not intended for use on a continuing basis in the company's activities;

f. Gives detailed definitions of purchase price and production cost; and

g. Contains rules for the valuation of stock and fungible assets, (assets which are substantially indistinguishable from one another, for example identical shares in a particular company).

**25. Asset valuation. Alternative accounting rules**

a. Instead of being valued according to the historical cost accounting rules certain assets may be valued as follows:

   i. Intangible fixed assets, other than goodwill, – at current cost;

   ii. Tangible fixed assets, – at market valuation at the date of their last valuation or at current cost;

   iii. Fixed asset investments, – ***either*** at market value at the date of their last valuation or at a value determined by the directors;

   iv. Current asset investments, – at current cost;

   v. Stocks, – at current cost.

b. The effect of these provisions is that financial statements may be prepared:

   i. According to the historical cost convention;

   ii. According to the historical cost convention, modified to take account of selective revaluations; or

   iii. According to current cost principles.

c. The ***revaluation reserve***. Where an asset has been revalued in accordance with the above rules the amount of the change on revaluation must be credited or debited (as appropriate) to the revaluation reserve. An amount may be transferred from the revaluation reserve:

   i. To the profit and loss account, if the amount was previously charged to that account or represents realised profit; or

   ii. On capitalisation ie if it is applied wholly or partly to pay up unissued share to be allotted to members as fully paid or partly paid bonus shares.

   The revaluation reserve must also be reduced to the extent that the amounts transferred to it are no longer necessary for the purposes of the valuation method used.

**26. Format of accounts. General provisions**

a. Companies may choose between two balance sheet formats and four profit and loss account formats. The system is rigid in that once a format has been chosen, the items listed must appear in the order and under the headings and sub-headings given in the format.

b. The same format must be used each year unless, in the opinion of the directors, there are special reasons to change. Where there is a change the reasons for it must be disclosed in a note to the accounts.

c. Items may be shown in greater detail than required by the format, and headings and sub-headings may be deleted if there is no amount to be shown in respect of the financial year and the previous year.

d. Items to which Arabic numbers (ie 1.2.3. etc as opposed to I.II.III. etc) are assigned may be combined if either:

   i. Individually they are not material to assessing the state of affairs or profit or loss of the company; or

   ii. The combination helps the assessment, in which case the individual amounts should be disclosed in a note to the accounts.

**27. Balance sheet formats**

a. Although the Act sets out two alternative formats (leaving the choice to the directors) most British companies choose format I, which is a vertical presentation of the balance sheet. Only format 1 is reproduced here.

b. *Balance sheet format I (PART I SCHEDULE 4)*

A Called up share capital not paid (1)

B Fixed assets

I *Intangible assets*
1 Development costs
2 Concessions, patents, licences, trade marks and similar rights and assets (2)
3 Goodwill (3)
4 Payments on account

II *Tangible assets*
1 Land and buildings
2 Plant and machinery
3 Fixtures, fittings, tools and equipment
4 Payments on account and assets in course of construction

III *Investments*
1 Shares in group undertakings
2 Loans to group undertakings
3 (a) Interests in associated undertakings
(b) Other participating interests
4 Loans to undertakings in which the company has a participating interest
5 Other investments other than loans
6 Other loans
7 Own shares (4)

**C Current assets**

I *Stocks*

1 Raw material and consumables
2 Work in progress
3 Finished goods and goods for resale
4 Payments on account

II *Debtors (5)*

1 Trade debtors
2 Amounts owed by group undertakings
3 Amounts owed by undertakings in which the company has a participating interest
4 Other debtors
5 Called up share capital not paid (1)
6 Prepayments and accrued income (6)

III *Investments*

1 Shares in group undertakings
2 Own shares (4)
3 Other investments

IV *Cash at bank and in hand*

**D Prepayments and accrued income (6)**

**E Creditors: amounts falling due within one year**

1 Debenture loans (7)
2 Bank loans and overdrafts
3 Payments received on account (8)
4 Trade creditors
5 Bills of exchange payable
6 Amounts owed to group undertakings
7 Amounts owed to undertakings in which the company has a participating interest
8 Other creditors including taxation and social security (9)
9 Accruals and deferred income (10)

**F Net current assets (liabilities) (11)**

**G Total assets less current liabilities**

**H Creditors: amounts falling due after more than one year**

1 Debenture loans (7)
2 Bank loans and overdrafts
3 Payments received on account (8)
4 Trade creditors
5 Bills of exchange payable
6 Amounts owed to group undertakings

7 Amounts owed to undertakings in which the company has a participating interest
8 Other creditors including taxation and social security (9)
9 Accruals and deferred income (10)

**I Provisions for liabilities and charges**

1 Pensions and similar obligations
2 Taxation, including deferred taxation
3 Other provisions

**J Accruals and deferred income (10)**

**Minority interests (13)**

**K Capital and reserves**

I *Called up share capital (12)*

II *Share premium account*

III *Revaluation reserve*

IV *Other reserves*

1 Capital redemption reserve
2 Reserve for own shares
3 Reserves provided for by the articles of association
4 Other reserves

V *Profit and loss account*

**Minority interests (13)**

c. The Act also attaches notes and comments to the balance sheet formats. These relate to an item followed by a number in brackets. The notes and comments are:

(1) ***Called up share capital not paid,*** (items A and C.II.5). This item may be shown in either of the two positions given.

(2) ***Concessions, patents, licences trade marks and similar rights and assets,*** (item B.I.2). Amounts in respect of assets shall only be included in a company's balance sheet under this item if either:

(a) the assets were acquired for valuable consideration and are not required to be shown under goodwill; or

(b) the assets in question were created by the company itself

(3) ***Goodwill,*** (item B.I.3). Amounts representing goodwill shall only be included to the extent that the goodwill was acquired for valuable consideration.

(4) ***Own Shares,*** (items B.III.7 and C.III.2). The nominal value of the shares held shall be shown separately.

(5) ***Debtors***, (items C.II. 1 to 6). The amount falling due after more than one year shall be shown separately for each item included under debtors.

(6) ***Prepayments and accrued income***, (items C.II.6 and D). This item may be shown in either of the two positions given.

(7) ***Debenture loans***, (items E.l and H.l). The amount of any convertible loans shall be shown separately.

(8) ***Payments received on account***, (items E.3 and H.3). Payments received on account of orders shall be shown for each of these items in so far as they are not shown as deductions from stocks.

(9) ***Other creditors including taxation and social security***, (items E.8 and H.8). The amount for creditors in respect of taxation and social security shall be shown separately from the amount for other creditors.

(10) ***Accruals and deferred income***, (items E.9, H.9 and J). The two positions given for this item at E.9 and H.9 are an alternative to the position at J, but if the item is not shown in a position corresponding to that at J it may be shown in either or both of the other two positions (as the case may require).

(11) ***Net current assets (liabilities)***, (item F). In determining the amount to be shown for this item any amounts shown under 'prepayments and accrued income' shall be taken into account wherever shown.

(12) ***Called up share capital***, (item K.I). The amount of allotted share capital and the amount of called up share capital which has been paid up shall be shown separately.

(13) ***'Minority interests'*** has been added by **CA 89**, but it has not been allocated a reference. It is to be treated as an item with an Alphabet or Roman reference. There are two alternative balance sheet positions, either as a deduction from net assets or as an addition to shareholders' funds.

**28. Profit and loss account formats**

a. There are four profit and loss account formats. The choice of format is left to the directors. Most British companies choose format 1 or 2, which are vertical presentations. Only these two formats are reproduced here.

b. ***Profit and loss account format 1 (PART 1 SCHEDULE 4)***

Format 1 *(see note (17) below)*

1 Turnover
2 Cost of sales (14)

3 Gross profit or loss
4 Distribution costs (14)
5 Administrative expenses (14)
6 Other operating income
7 Income from shares in group undertakings
8 *(a)* Income from interests in associated undertakings
*(b)* Income from other participating interests
9 Income from other fixed asset investments (15)
10 Other interest receivable and similar income (15)
11 Amounts written off investments
12 Interest payable and similar charges (16)
13 Tax on profit or loss on ordinary activities
14 Profit or loss on ordinary activities after taxation
Minority interests (18)
15 Extraordinary income
16 Extraordinary charges
17 Extraordinary profit or loss
18 Tax on extraordinary profit or loss
Minority interests (18)
19 Other taxes not shown under the above items
20 Profit or loss for the financial year

c. ***Profit and loss account format 2. (PART 1 SCHEDULE 4)***

**Format 2**

1 Turnover
2 Change in stocks of finished goods and in work in progress
3 Own work capitalised
4 Other operating income
5 *(a)* Raw materials and consumables
*(b)* Other external charges
6 Staff costs:
*(a)* Wages and salaries
*(b)* Social security costs
*(c)* Other pension costs
7 *(a)* Depreciation and other amounts written off tangible and intangible fixed assets
*(b)* Exceptional amounts written off current assets
8 Other operating charges
9 Income from shares in group undertakings
10 *(a)* Income from interests in associated undertakings
*(b)* Income from other participating interests
11 Income from other fixed asset investments (15)
12 Other interest receivable and similar income (15)
13 Amounts written off investments

14 Interest payable and similar charges (16)
15 Tax on profit or loss on ordinary activities
16 Profit or loss on ordinary activities after taxation
Minority interests (18)
17 Extraordinary income
18 Extraordinary charges
19 Extraordinary profit or loss
20 Tax on extraordinary profit or loss
Minority interests (18)
21 Other taxes not shown under the above items
22 Profit or loss for the financial year

d. There are also notes on the profit and loss account formats. The formats have been reproduced exactly as they appear in the Act. The notes have not therefore been re-numbered. The notes are:

(14) ***Cost of sales: distribution costs: administrative expenses,*** (Format 1, items 2,4 and 5). These items shall be stated after taking into account any necessary provisions for depreciation or diminution in value of assets.

(15) ***Income from other fixed asset investments: other interest receivable and similar income,*** (Format 1, items 9 and 10: Format 2 items 11 and 12). Income and interest derived from group companies shall be shown separately from income and interest derived from other sources.

(16) ***Interest payable and similar charges,*** (Format 1, item 12: Format 2, item 14). The amount payable to group companies shall be shown separately.

(17) ***Format 1.*** The amount of any provisions for depreciation and diminution in value of tangible and intangible fixed assets falling to be shown under item 7(a) in Format 2 shall be disclosed in a note to the account in any case where the profit and loss account is prepared by reference to Format 1.

(18) Minority interests is treated as an item with an Arabic reference.

**29. Information required in financial statements. General provisions**

The financial statements are the balance sheet, the profit and loss account and the notes to the accounts. The following paragraphs (29.–31.) are only an outline summary of the detailed requirements of the Act. It must be emphasised that the best way to learn the new rules for the form and content of accounts is by practice in the preparation of such accounts. The general requirements relate to:

a. ***Accounting policies.*** These must be disclosed, in particular the policy in respect of depreciation and for the translation of foreign currency.

b. *Comparatives*. Corresponding amounts for the immediately preceding financial period must be shown (subject to several exceptions).

c. *Accounting principles*. Where the directors consider that there is a special reason to depart from the accounting principles (going concern; consistency; prudence; accruals; and separate valuation) particulars of, the reasons for, and the effect of, the departure must be shown.

d. *True and fair view*. Any information supplementary to the requirements of the Act which is necessary for the accounts to give a true and fair view must be disclosed.

**30. Information required in the profit and loss account**

a. *Turnover*. The amount attributable to each geographical market supplied by the company and in respect of each class of business carried on by the company:

   i. The turnover attributable to that class; and

   ii. The pre-tax profit or loss attributable to it.

b. *Employees*. The average number of employees and the aggregate of each of the following:

   i. Wages paid or payable;

   ii. Social security costs; and

   iii. Pension costs.

c. *Directors' emoluments*, distinguishing between fees, pensions and compensation for loss of office. Where a director receives a benefit in kind, for example a car as part of a compensation package, the value of the benefit must be shown. In all cases amounts disclosed must include amounts paid to or receivable by a person connected with a director, including a corporate body controlled by a director. The following must be disclosed:

   i. Any amount paid to obtain the services of a director, ie a 'golden hello';

   ii. The aggregate amount paid to third parties for making available the services of a director.

   iii. The chairman's emoluments;

   iv. The emoluments of the highest paid director if this exceeds the chairman's emoluments;

   v. The number of directors in each rising band of £5,000; and

   vi. The number of directors who have waived emoluments and the amount waived.

e. *Depreciation*.

f. *Other income and expenditure items*:

   i. Hire charges for plant and machinery;

ii. Auditors' remuneration, including amounts payable in respect of non-audit services;

iii. Revenue from rents (after deducting outgoings, for example rates);

iv. Income from listed investments;

v. Interest charges on overdrafts, bank loans and other loans; and

vi. Amounts set aside for the redemption of share capital and repayment of loans.

g. ***Profit or loss before taxation***.

h. ***Taxation***.

i. ***Dividends***. The aggregate amount of any dividends paid and proposed.

j. ***Reserves***. The amounts to be transferred to or withdrawn from reserves.

k. ***Preceding years***. Any amounts charged or credited which relate to any preceding year.

l. ***Exceptional items***. Details of any extraordinary or exceptional income or charges arising during the year.

**31. Information required in the balance sheet**

a. ***Fixed assets***. The main requirements are:

i. For fixed assets in general to show:

(a) Cost and accumulated depreciation at the beginning and end of the year,

(b) Movements of assets during the year (ie revaluations; additions; disposals; and transfers to or from the category in question); and

(c) Movements of accumulated depreciation during the year as a result of disposals or any other adjustments.

ii. For fixed assets (other than listed investments) shown at valuation:

(a) The years and amounts of the valuations; and

(b) For assets valued during the year the names and qualifications of the valuers and the bases of valuation used.

iii. For land and buildings, that freehold, long leasehold and short leasehold be distinguished.

b. ***Goodwill***. Where goodwill is shown as an asset the balance sheet must disclose the period over which it is being written off and the reason for choosing this period.

c. ***Listed investments***. The aggregate market value must be shown and the investments must be analysed into:

i. Investments listed on a recognised stock exchange; and

ii. Other listed investments.

d. ***Own shares***. The nominal value of own shares held must be shown.

e. ***Shares of other companies***. If, at the end of the year, the company holds in another company (including a subsidiary) either:

   i. More than 10% of the issued shares of any class of equity share capital;

   ii. More than 10% of the allotted shares of that company; or

   iii. Shares with a total value exceeding 10% of its own assets:

   then the company must disclose:

   i. The name of the other company;

   ii. Its country of registration (if different from the investing company); and

   iii. The identity of, and the proportion of, the nominal value of the allotted shares of each class held.

   Additional details are required where the company holds more than 20% of the allotted shares in another company. There are also exceptional cases where the above details are not required.

f. ***Debtors***. Any amount falling due after more than one year must be shown separately for each item included under debtors.

g. ***Creditors***. In particular the balance sheet must show:

   i. In respect of each item included under creditors that fall due after more than one year, the aggregate amount of debts (repayable by instalments or otherwise) which fall due after more than five years. The repayment terms and rate of interest for each such debt must be disclosed;

   ii. In respect of each item included under creditors:

      (a) The aggregate amount of secured liabilities; and
      (b) An indication of the nature of the securities given;

   iii. Arrears of fixed cumulative dividends;

   iv. Proposed dividends; and

   v. Creditors in respect of taxation and social security, shown separately from 'other creditors'.

h. ***Stocks***. In respect of each balance sheet item, the difference (if material) between the balance sheet value and replacement cost.

i. ***Transactions with directors***. The main requirements relate to disclosure of:

   i. Details of loans, quasi-loans and credit transactions to directors of the company or to persons connected with such directors; and

   ii. Details of other transactions with the company in which a director has (or had) a material interest (either directly or through a connected person).

j. ***Transactions with officers***. The number of officers (other than directors) liable to the company and the aggregate amount outstanding in respect of loans, quasi-loans and credit transactions.

k. ***Guarantees and financial commitments***. These include:

   i. Particulars of any charge on the assets to secure the liabilities of any other person;

   ii. The estimated amount of any contingent liability, its legal nature, and details of any security provided;

   iii. The amount of future capital expenditure either contracted but not provided for, or authorised but not contracted for;

   iv. Particulars of pension commitments;

   v. Any other financial commitments not provided for and relevant to assessing the company's state of affairs; and

   vi. Separate details of commitments undertaken on behalf of other companies in the group.

l. ***Share capital and debentures***

   i. The authorised share capital.

   ii. The number and aggregate nominal value of allotted shares of each class.

   iii. Allotted, called-up and paid-up share capital.

   iv. For redeemable shares:

      (a) The earliest and latest dates on which the company has power to redeem them;
      (b) Whether redemption is compulsory or at the option of the company; and
      (c) The premium, if any, payable on redemption.

   v. For shares allotted during the year:

      (a) The reason for the allotment;
      (b) The classes of shares allotted; and
      (c) For each class – the number allotted, their aggregate nominal value, and the consideration received.

   vi. For any option to subscribe for shares, or for any other contingent right to the allotment of shares:

      (a) The number, description and amount of shares involved;
      (b) The period during which the right is exercisable; and
      (c) The price to be paid for the shares.

   vii. For debentures issued during the year

      (a) The reason for the issue;
      (b) The classes of debentures issued; and
      (c) For each class – the amount issued and the consideration received.

viii. Details of redeemed debentures which the company has power to re-issue.

ix. Details of the company's shares or debentures held by its subsidiaries or their nominees.

x. Where the company's debentures are held by a nominee of, or trustee for the company, the nominal value and the book value of the debentures must be shown.

m. ***Reserves and provisions***. In respect of each heading shown in the balance sheet the accounts must show:

i. The balance at the beginning and the end of the year;

ii. The amounts transferred to or from reserves or provisions during the year; and

iii. The source and application of the transfers.

**32. Small and medium sized companies. Definition**

a. Small and medium-sized companies are permitted to file with the registrar modified financial statements. It must be emphasised that all companies must prepare full financial statements for the members. These provisions do not therefore allow a company to do less work, in fact the opposite is true since if a company chooses to take advantage of these exemptions it will have to prepare two sets of financial statements.

b. By ***S.13 CA 89 (S.247)*** a ***small company*** is a private company which in respect of a particular financial year satisfies for that year and the preceding year at least two of the following conditions:

i. A turnover not exceeding £2,000,000;

ii. A balance sheet total not exceeding £975,000; and

iii. An average number of persons employed per week not exceeding 50.

c. By ***S.13 CA 89 (S.247)*** a ***medium-sized company*** is a private company which in respect of a particular financial year satisfies for that year and the preceding year at least two of the following conditions:

i. A turnover not exceeding £8,000,000;

ii. A balance sheet total not exceeding £3,900,000; and

iii. An average number of persons employed per week not exceeding 250.

d. ***Change of status***. If a company qualifies to be treated as either a small or medium-sized company in one year (Year X) it may file modified financial statements in the following year (Year X + 1) even if it does not satisfy the conditions in that year. However if it does not satisfy the conditions in the year after (Year X + 2) it must file financial statements appropriate to its size in that year (Year X + 2). On the other hand if the company reverts to satisfying the conditions in year X + 2 then it may continue to file modified financial statements. In other words a company's classification will only change if it fails to qualify for two consecutive years.

### 33. Small company exemptions *S.13* CA 89 *(S.246)* and *Sch 6* CA 89 *(Sch 8)*

The following modifications are allowed:

a. The ***balance sheet*** only need show those items to which a letter or Roman number is assigned. This is known as an ***'abbreviated balance sheet'***.

b. A ***profit and loss account*** is not required.

c. The ***notes to the accounts*** only need show:

   i. Accounting policies;

   ii. Share capital;

   iii. Substantial investments in other companies;

   iv. Aggregate creditors falling due after more than five years;

   v. Secured creditors;

   vi. Aggregate debtors falling due after more than one year;

   vii. The ultimate holding company;

   viii. Loans to directors and officers; and

   ix. Movements on fixed assets under the categories 'intangible assets'. 'tangible assets' and 'investments'.

d. A ***directors' report*** is not required.

e. A ***special auditors' report*** is required, (see 36. below).

### 34. Small companies. Directors' emoluments and profit or loss

It can be seen that the modified accounts of small companies are not required to disclose directors' emoluments or the amount of the company's profits.

a. The disclosure of directors' emoluments is a politically sensitive issue and was the subject of some discussion in the House. The Opposition argued that non disclosure of directors' emoluments would make it difficult to know how to interpret a company's profit in that a substantial trading profit may be significantly reduced by directors' emoluments. The Government however felt that the emoluments of directors of small private companies were of no concern to outsiders but were a private matter of interest only to the shareholders.

b. Since no profit and loss account need be disclosed it may be thought that the company's profit or loss could nevertheless be calculated by comparing the 'profit and loss' account in the balance sheet at the beginning and end of the year. This would however be very misleading since such figures are arrived at after deducting directors' emoluments and dividends, neither of which need be disclosed. The absence of a requirement to disclose the profit or loss amounts to a failure to comply with the EC fourth directive.

35. Medium-sized company exemptions *S.13* CA 89 *(S.246)* and *Sch* 6 CA 89 *(Sch* 8*)*

The only modifications permitted are:

a. Several items in the profit and loss account may be combined to give one heading – 'gross profit or loss'. For formats 1 and 2 the items which may be combined are:

   i. Items 1, 2, 3 and 6 in format 1; and

   ii. Items 1, 2, 3, 4 and 5 in format 2.

b. Neither disclosure nor analysis of turnover is required.

36. Additional requirements where modified accounts are filed *Sch* 6 CA 89 *(Sch* 8*)*

a. The ***balance sheet*** must be signed by one director. Above the signature there must be a statement by the directors that:

   i. They have relied on the exemptions for individual accounts; and

   ii. They have done so on the grounds that the company is entitled to the appropriate exemptions.

b. A ***special auditors' report*** must be delivered to the registrar with modified accounts. It must:

   i. State that, in the opinion of the auditors, the requirements for the exemption have been satisfied. This statement implies that the auditors are satisfied that the accounts have been properly prepared; and

   ii. Reproduce the full text of the auditors' report on the accounts laid before the members.

37. Dormant companies *S.14* CA 89 *(S.250)*

a. A ***dormant company*** is one in which no significant accounting transaction occurred during the period in question.

b. A ***significant accounting transaction*** is any transaction required under *S.2* CA 89 *(S.221)* to be entered in the company's accounting records (other than a subscriber taking shares in pursuance of an undertaking in the memorandum).

c. A dormant company may pass a ***special resolution*** exempting itself from the obligation to appoint auditors provided:

   i. The resolution is passed at an AGM at which the accounts are laid before shareholders; *and*

(a) The company is not required to prepare group accounts; ***and***

(b) The company is entitled to the small company exemptions for the immediately preceding period; ***and***

(c) The company has been dormant since the end of the immediately preceding period; ***or***

ii. The company has been dormant since its formation and the resolution is passed before the first AGM at which accounts are laid before shareholders.

d. A dormant company is not exempt from the obligation to prepare financial statements. The exemption only relates to the auditors' report.

e. A director must sign the balance sheet of a dormant company immediately below a statement to the effect that the company was dormant throughout the year in question.

**38. Publication of accounts**

a. By *S.742(5)* a company is regarded as publishing a balance sheet or other account if it publishes, issues or circulates it in a manner which invites the public to read it. This is a wide definition which includes preliminary announcements by listed companies, employee reports and press releases, as well as the publication of statutory accounts.

b. For the purpose of publication of accounts there are two types of accounts:

i. ***Statutory accounts***, which include the full accounts presented to shareholders and modified accounts filed with the registrar; and

ii. ***Non-statutory accounts***, which are any accounts other than the statutory accounts.

c. By *S.10 CA 89 (S.240(1))* when a company publishes statutory accounts it must publish with them the relevant auditors' report.

d. By *S.10 CA 89 (S.240(3))* when a company publishes non-statutory accounts it must not publish the auditors' report with them. It must however publish a statement indicating:

i. That the accounts are not statutory accounts;

ii. Whether statutory accounts have been delivered to the registrar;

iii. Whether the auditors have reported on the accounts laid before the shareholders, with which the non-statutory accounts purport to deal; and

iv. Whether the auditors' report was qualified.

e. Contravention of the publication requirements renders the company and any officer in default liable to a fine.

**39. Summary financial statements *(S.15 CA 89 (S.251))***

***Listed companies*** may send summary financial statements to shareholders who do not wish to receive full statutory accounts. If companies take advantage of this provision they will send summary statements to all shareholders, together with a reply paid card which can be used to request the full accounts. The detailed content of summary statements is provided by statutory instrument, however the 1989 Act provides that the summary statements must:

a. State that it is a summary of information in the accounts and directors' report;

b. Include a statement by the auditors of their opinion as to whether:

    i. It is consistent with the full accounts and directors' report, and

    ii. It complies with the requirements of the Act and any statutory instrument in relation to summary financial statements;

c. State whether the audit report on the full accounts was qualified. If it was the report must be reproduced in full.

**40. Revision of defective accounts**

a. The ***Dearing Report***, published in November 1988, recommended that the Secretary of State or other authorised persons (to be defined by statutory instrument) should be able to apply to the court for an order requiring revision of defective accounts. This has been enacted in ***S.12 CA 89 (S.245)***. If the court orders revised accounts to be prepared, it may give directions on such matters as it thinks fit, for example auditing the revised accounts, revising the directors' report and the position of dividends already paid. The court may order directors to bear the expenses of the court order and the company's costs of preparing revised accounts. ***S.7 CA 89 (S.223)*** complements the above procedure by creating a new criminal offence of approving accounts that do not comply with the Act or being reckless as to whether they comply.

b. ***S.12 CA 89 (S.245)*** also provides a procedure for the voluntary revision of accounts, without the need for court action. If the accounts have already been laid before members or delivered to the registrar, the revisions are confined to ensuring compliance with the Act plus consequential revisions. Certain points remain to be clarified by statutory instrument, for example

    i. The auditors' role in relation to voluntarily revised accounts.

    ii. The effect of the revision on dividends paid and profit-related pay.

    iii. Publication of the fact that the accounts have been revised.

## The directors' report

### 41. Introduction

a. Consideration of the directors' report is one of the items of ***ordinary business*** at the AGM, (see Chapter 19.1).

b. By ***S.10 CA 89*** *(S.238)* the balance sheet and every document which is required to be attached to it (the directors' report; the auditors' report; the profit and loss account; and group accounts, if any) must be sent to each member not less that 21 days before the AGM. They will therefore be sent to the members with notice of the AGM.

### 42. Contents of the Directors' Report (*SCHEDULE 7* as amended by *Sch 5* CA 89)

a. *General provisions*

i. A review of the development of the business of the company and its subsidiary undertakings during the financial year and of their position at the end of it;

ii. A statement of the principal activities of the company and its subsidiary undertakings in the course of the financial year and any significant changes in those activities during the year;

iii. Particulars of any important events affecting the company or any of its subsidiary undertakings which have occurred since the end of the year;

iv. An indication of likely future developments in the business of the company and its subsidiary undertakings; and

v. An indication of the activities (if any) of the company and its subsidiary undertakings in the field of research and development.

b. *Dividends and reserves*

i. The amount, if any, recommended for dividend; and

ii. The amount, if any, proposed to be carried to reserves.

c. *Fixed assets*

i. Any significant changes in the fixed assets of the company or its subsidiary undertakings during the year; and

ii. An estimate of any substantial difference between the book value and the market value of the company's interests in land and buildings (if the directors consider this to be of significance to the members or debentureholders).

d. ***Political and charitable donations***. If such donations together total more than £200 the report must show:

i. Separate totals for each; and

ii. The amount of each political contribution over £200, naming the recipient.

Wholly-owned subsidiaries are exempt from the above requirement since the holding company will make disclosure for itself and its subsidiaries.

e. *Directors*

  i. The names of persons who were directors of the company at any time during the year; and

  ii. For persons who were directors at the end of the year, the interests of each (and the interests of any spouse or infant child) in the shares or debentures of the company and other companies in the group both:

    (a) At the beginning of the year or, if later, at the date of appointment; and

    (b) At the end of the year.

    Note that:

    (a) ***Sch 5 CA 1989*** also requires details of options granted or exercised to be given;

    (b) If a director had no interest in shares or debentures at either date that fact must be stated;

    (c) The above information may be given in notes to the accounts instead of in the directors' report.

  iii. By ***S.137 CA 1989 (S.310)*** if the company has paid for professional indemnity insurance for an officer or auditor this must be stated.

f. *Employees*. Except where the company has less than 250 employees the report must state the company's policy:

  i. For giving consideration to applications for employment from disabled persons, having regard to their particular aptitude and abilities;

  ii. For continuing to employ, and for arranging appropriate training for, persons who have become disabled whilst employed by the company; and

  iii. Otherwise for the training, career development and promotion of disabled employees.

g. *Shares purchased*. Where the shares of the company are purchased by the company during the year the report must disclose:

  i. The number and nominal value of shares purchased;

  ii. The aggregate consideration paid;

  iii. The reasons for the purchase; and

  iv. The percentage of the called up share capital represented by the shares purchased.

h. *Shares otherwise acquired*. Where a company's shares are acquired by its nominee or with its financial assistance or where its shares are made subject to a lien or charge as permitted by **S.150** the report must disclose:

i. The number and nominal value of shares:
   (a) Acquired by the company;
   (b) Acquired by another person; and
   (c) Charged;

ii. The maximum number and nominal value of shares acquired or charged (whether or not during the financial year) which were held during the year by the company or other person who acquired them;

iii. The number and nominal value of such shares disposed of by the company or other person who acquired them or cancelled by the company;

iv. For each disclosure under (i.)(ii.) or (iii.) above, the percentage of called up share capital represented by the shares in question;

v. Where the shares have been charged, the amount of the charge;

vi. For each disclosure under (iii.) above, where the shares have been disposed of during the year for money or money's worth, the amount or value of the consideration.

### PROGRESS TEST 13

1. What types of resolution are needed to:
   (a) Remove the company secretary
   (b) Authorise an off-market purchase of own shares
   (c) Create reserve capital?
2. Explain the rules concerning the printing of directors' names on company stationery.
3. Define a small company.
4. For the purpose of the rules concerning substantial shareholdings, when is a person deemed to have an interest in the voting shares of a public company?
5. Summarise briefly the contents of the Annual Return. By what date must it be submitted?

# 18 Auditors

## SUPERVISORY BODIES AND PROFESSIONAL QUALIFICATIONS

### 1. Supervisory bodies

The 1989 Act introduces new rules to ensure that only persons who are properly supervised and appropriately qualified are appointed company auditors, and that audits are carried out properly and with integrity and independence.

### 2. Types of supervisory body

Two types of supervisory body will be established under the Act.

a. ***Recognised Supervisory Bodies*** (RSBs) of which all company auditors must be members.

b. ***Recognised Qualifying Bodies*** (RQBs) which will offer the professional qualifications required to become a member of an RSB.

The same body can be both a RSB and a RQB. The existing professional bodies, for example the Chartered Association of Certified Accountants and the Institute of Chartered Accountants are likely to fulfil both functions.

### 3. Recognition of RSBs

By **S.30 CA 89** each RSB must be a body established in the UK (this now includes a corporate body or an unincorporated association) which maintains and enforces rules as to

a. The eligibility of persons seeking appointment as company auditors, and

b. The conduct of company audit work.

Bodies wishing to be RSBs must apply to the Secretary of State, submitting their rules, any other written guidance, and any other information that the Secretary of State may reasonably require. The Secretary of State may refuse to recognise a body if he considers recognition unnecessary bearing in mind that there are other bodies controlling the profession which have been, or are likely to be authorised. The conditions for the grant and verification of recognition are given in ***Schedule 11* CA 89**.

### 4. Rules of RSBs *(Schedule 11 CA 89)*

a. ***Eligibility***. RSBs must ensure that only the following persons are eligible for appointment as auditors:

   i. Individuals who hold appropriate qualifications;

   ii. Firms controlled by qualified persons.

The RSB must ensure that such persons are 'fit and proper', taking into account the person's professional conduct, including the conduct of employees and close business associates.

b. *Professional integrity*. The RSBs rules must ensure that audit work is carried out properly and with integrity. A DTI consultative document on the implementation of the EC Eighth Directive considers that two areas must be addressed:

   i. The standards of performance of the audit, including compliance with approved auditing standards and guidelines, and

   ii. General ethical standards, such as rules to cover independence, objectivity and client confidentiality.

c. *Technical standards*. The technical standards to be applied in company audits must be the subject of RSB rules. This is likely to be a reference to the need for auditing standards and guidelines rather than statements of standard accounting practice (SSAPs).

d. *Maintenance of competence*. The rules of the RSB must ensure that eligible persons continue to maintain an appropriate level of competence.

e. *Investigation and enforcement*. The RSBs rules must include provisions in respect of:

   i. Monitoring and enforcement of compliance with its rules. The extent of monitoring is not yet clear and appropriate rules will be made after consultation between RSBs and the DTI. It may imply a regular examination of the activities of thousands of audit firms and individuals;

   ii. Admission and expulsion of members;

   iii. Grant and withdrawal of eligibility for appointment as an auditor;

   iv. Disciplinary procedures.

   NB. The rules relating to ii.–iv. above must be 'fair and reasonable' and there must be adequate appeals procedures.

   v. The investigation of complaints against members and against the RSB itself.

f. *Liability of RSBs*. RSBs and their officers, employees and governors are exempt from damages in respect of the exercise of their statutory duties, unless it can be shown that they have acted in bad faith. This prevents them from being joined in any action taken against auditors for negligence.

5. Appropriate qualifications

a. The 1989 Act makes it a requirement that auditors hold an 'appropriate qualification'. By *S.31 CA 89* a person will hold an appropriate qualification in the following cases:

i. He satisfied the existing criteria for appointment as an auditor under the 1985 Act by being a member of one of the bodies recognised under that Act immediately before January 1st 1990.

ii. He holds a recognised professional qualification obtained in the UK (see 6 below). In future this will be the 'appropriate qualification' for all new auditors.

iii. He holds an approved overseas qualification and satisfies any additional requirements set down by the Secretary of State.

b. Persons who have existing individual authorisation on the basis of qualifications obtained outside the UK have twelve months in which to notify the Secretary of State that they wish to continue to be treated as qualified. In order to continue in practice they will have to become members of a RSB.

c. Students who have commenced their training before January 1st 1990 and who qualify before January 1st 1996 will be treated as holding an appropriate qualification as long as their training is approved for this purpose by the Secretary of State.

6. **Recognised qualifying bodies *(S.32 and Schedule 12 CA 89)***

a. ***Recognition***. To offer a recognised professional qualifications bodies must be approved by the Secretary of State. The procedure for recognition is similar to that for recognition as a RSB. A RQB must have rules to ensure compliance with various entry, examination and training requirements.

b. ***Qualifications***

i. The RQB's qualification must only be open to persons who have attained university entrance level (without necessarily having gone to university) or have a sufficient period of professional experience. 'Sufficient period of professional experience' means at least seven years in a professional capacity in finance, law or accountancy. Periods of theoretical instruction, up to a maximum of four years, count towards necessary experience so long as the instruction lasts for at least one year and is attested by an examination recognised for this purpose by the Secretary of State.

ii. The qualification must be restricted to persons passing an examination which tests theoretical knowledge and the ability to apply it in practice, although persons may be exempted from examination in subjects in which they already hold a recognised qualification, for example a university examination of equivalent standard.

iii. It is also a requirement that persons must have completed at least three years practical training, although exemption from this requirement may be possible if the person has an approved diploma evidencing practical training. The practical training must be given by persons approved by the RQB as being suitable and at least two thirds of it must be with a fully qualified auditor. A substantial part of the training must be in company audit work.

c. *Approval of oversea qualifications*. By **S.33 CA 89** the Secretary of State is empowered to consider professional qualifications obtained outside the UK as 'approved'. This will happen if he is satisfied that it gives a level of professional competence equivalent to a recognised professional qualification. Persons with overseas qualifications may be required to obtain additional educational qualifications to demonstrate that they have a sufficient knowledge of UK law and practice.

7. **Register of auditors**

By **S.35** and **36 CA 89** RSBs are required to maintain up to date lists of approved auditors. This list must be available to the public. The details of the register will be introduced by statutory instrument following consultation between professional bodies and the DTI, however, it is clear that the register must identify the qualified individuals responsible for audit work on behalf of firms. If the approved auditor is a corporate body it is likely to include a list of its directors and shareholders.

8. **Eligibility of firms and individuals**

a. Prior to the 1989 Act it was not possible for a corporate body to be an auditor. **S.25 CA 89** now provides that an individual or firm (defined to mean either a partnership or corporate body) may be appointed. Firms may only perform audits if they are controlled by qualified persons ie a majority of those empowered to make the decisions are qualified persons.

b. *Appointment of partnerships*. Where a partnership is appointed **S.26 CA 89** makes it clear that it is the firm and not the partners that has been appointed (previously appointments were, strictly speaking, of individuals). The Act also provides that the appointment will continue despite any technical dissolution of the partnership when members join and leave. When a partnership ceases the appointment may go to any eligible partnership that succeeds the practice or any individual partner who has taken over the practice. 'Succession' applies only if substantially all of the members of the successor partnership are the same as before or, in the case of an individual, that individual has taken over substantially all of the business. If there is no 'succession' for example where two accountancy firms merge, the appointment may extend, with the consent of the company being audited, to the partnership of individual who takes over all, or an agreed part, of the partnership business.

c. *Appointment of corporate bodies*. The Act provides that the majority of decision makers in such bodies must be qualified persons, but it leaves many of the detailed rules to be laid down by the RSBs. For example the Act does not address the issue of entitlement to own voting shares in audit firms or the ownership by audit firms of shares in other companies. It is probable that separate limits will be set for the shareholding rights of non auditors (ie unqualified employees or directors of audit firms) and outsiders, with the total of such holdings amounting to less than 50%. Outsiders may also be prohibited from holding voting shares. Regulations may also be made limiting the proportion of non-auditors and outsiders on the board of directors. There may also be a prohibition against a corporate body auditing another company in which it holds shares or which holds shares in it.

d. ***Ineligibility of auditors***

i. By **S.27 CA 89** a person is ineligible to be a company's auditor if he is an officer or employee of the company, or a partner or employee of such a person. **S.27** also provides that a person will be ineligible if he is not sufficiently independent of the company, although it leaves lack of independence to be defined by regulations.

ii. If an auditor ceases to be eligible under the rules of the RSB of which he is a member, he must immediately vacate office and give written notice to the company. If such a person continues to act, or fails to give written notice, he is guilty of an offence.

iii. By **S.29 CA 89** if an auditor acts when ineligible the Secretary of State may direct the company to appoint another auditor to carry out a second audit or to review the first audit, stating (with reasons) whether a second audit is required. If a direction is given by the Secretary of State, the company has 21 days to comply. The Secretary of State must send a copy of the direction to the registrar and the company must, within 21 days of receiving any report on the first audit, send a copy of that report to the registrar. The costs of the review and the second audit may be recovered from an auditor who continues to act while knowing himself to be ineligible.

## APPOINTMENT, REMOVAL AND RESIGNATION

### 9. Appointment

a. ***First auditors***. By **S.119 CA 89 (S.385)** the first auditors may be appointed by the directors at any time before the first general meeting at which the accounts are laid. They then hold office until the end of that meeting. If the company has passed an elective resolution to dispense with the laying of accounts, the first auditors may be appointed within 28 days after the company's first annual accounts being sent to members. If the directors fail to make an appointment the general meeting may appoint.

b. ***Subsequent auditors***

i. At each general meeting at which accounts are laid the company may appoint one or more auditors. They then hold office from the end of the meeting until the end of the next meeting at which accounts are laid.

ii. However if the company chooses, by elective resolution, to dispense with the annual appointment of auditors, the auditors shall be deemed to be re-appointed annually for so long as the election remains in force. ***S.119 CA 89 (S.386)***. During this time, any member may give written notice to the company proposing that the auditors' appointment be terminated. The directors must then convene a general meeting, which must be held within 28 days of the notice being given, ***S.122 CA 89 (S.393)***.

iii. If the company passes an elective resolution not to lay accounts before the general meeting, but does not elect to dispense with the annual appointment of auditors, it must still hold a general meeting each year for the purpose of re-appointing the auditors. This meeting must be held within 28 days of the dispatch to the members of the accounts. This 28 day period is defined as 'the time for appointing auditors'. Auditors appointed in this way hold office until the end of the time for appointing auditors in the next financial year. ***S.119 CA 89 (S.385A)***.

c. ***Casual vacancies (S.119 CA 89 (S.388))***. The directors or the company in general meeting may appoint auditors to fill casual vacancies. The surviving auditor may continue to act during any vacancy. Special notice is required for a resolution:

i. Filling a casual vacancy; or

ii. Re-appointing as auditor a retiring auditor who was appointed by the directors to fill a casual vacancy.

On receipt of such notice the company must immediately send a copy to the person proposed to be appointed and (if the casual vacancy was caused by the resignation of an auditor) to the auditor who resigned.

d. ***Appointment by the Secretary of State (S.119 CA 89 (S.387))***. If no appointment or reappointment is made at a meeting at which accounts are laid the company must inform the Department of Trade within one week. The Secretary of State may then make an appointment to fill the vacancy.

e. ***Remuneration***. The term 'remuneration' includes sums paid by the company as auditors' expenses. By ***S.121 CA 89 (S.390A)***:

i. If the directors make the appointment they fix his remuneration.

ii. If he is appointed by the Secretary of State he fixes the remuneration.

iii. If the auditor is appointed by the company then the company fixes his remuneration, or determines the way by which it will be fixed.

iv. By ***S.121 CA 89 (S.390B)*** the Secretary of State may make regulations for securing the disclosure of remuneration of auditors or their associates for non-audit work.

f. *Dormant companies*. By ***S.119** CA 89 (S.388A)* a dormant company which is exempt from provisions as to audit of accounts is also exempt from the obligation to appoint auditors.

10. Removal

a. By ***S.122** CA 89 (S.391)* the company may remove an auditor before the end of his period of office despite any agreement between it and him.

b. The registrar must be notified of the removal within 14 days.

c. An auditor who has been removed is entitled to attend the meeting at which his term of office would have expired and any general meeting at which it is proposed to fill a casual vacancy caused by his removal. He is entitled to receive all communications relating to the meeting which a member is entitled to receive, and he may speak on any matter concerning him as a former auditor.

11. Resolutions to appoint and remove auditors *S.122 CA 98 (S.391A)*

a. Auditors may be appointed and removed by ***ordinary resolution***.

b. In the following cases ***special notice*** (see Chapter 19.7) is required:

i. To appoint a person other than a retiring auditor;

ii. To fill a casual vacancy;

iii. To re-appoint as auditor a retiring auditor who was appointed by the directors to fill a casual vacancy; or

iv. To remove an auditor before the end of his term of office.

c. On receipt of the special notice the company must immediately send a copy to:

i. The person proposed to be appointed or removed;

ii. The retiring auditor where it is proposed to appoint another person; and

iii. The resigning auditor where the appointment is to fill a casual vacancy caused by his resignation.

12. Written representations by auditors *S.122 CA 89 (S.391A)*

a. Where (b) (i) or (b) (iv) above apply the auditor may make written representations to the company and require the company (unless it receives them too late) to send a copy of these representations to the members with notice of the meeting.

b. If for any reason these representations are not sent to the members the auditor can require them to be read out at the meeting. In any case he has a right to speak in his defence at the meeting.

c. The representations need not be sent out, or read at the meeting, if the court is satisfied, on the application of the company or any aggrieved person, that the auditor is using his rights to secure needless publicity for defamatory matter.

13. Resignation of auditors *S.122* CA *89* (*S.392*)

   a. An auditor may resign by giving written notice to the company at its registered office.

   b. The notice will not be effective unless it contains either:

      i. A statement that there are no circumstances connected with his resignation which he considers should be brought to the notice of the company's members or creditors; or

      ii. A statement of such circumstances.

   c. Within 14 days of receipt of an effective notice the company must send a copy to:

      i. The registrar; and

      ii. If it contains a statement of connected circumstances, to every member and debentureholder of the company.

   d. Within 14 days of receipt of a notice containing a statement of connected circumstances the company or any aggrieved person may apply to the court if it is thought that the auditor is using the statement to secure needless publicity for defamatory matter. The court may then order that copies need not be sent to members and debentureholders. Within 14 days of the court's decision the company must send to every member and debentureholder:

      i. A statement of the effect of the court order, if any; or if none

      ii. A copy of the notice containing the auditor's statement of the circumstances connected with his resignation.

14. Right of the resigning auditor *S.122* CA *89* (*S.392A*)

   a. Where the notice of resignation contains a statement of connected circumstances the auditor may require the directors to convene an EGM to receive and consider the statement. This will be useful if the auditor wishes to resign mid-term.

   b. The auditor may require the company to send to the members before such an EGM, or before the AGM at which his term of office would otherwise have expired, a written statement of the circumstances connected with his resignation. Unless the company receives this statement too late, it must send it to the members with notice of the meeting. ***S.392A*** contains provisions similar to ***S.391*** (12. (b) and (c) and 10. (c) above) relating to:

      i. Reading statement at the meeting if for any reason it is not sent with the notice;

      ii. Defamatory matter;

iii. The auditor's right to attend and receive all communications relating to the meeting.

**15. Statements to persons ceasing to hold office as auditor *S.123 CA 89 (S.394)***

Prior to 1989 the statement of circumstances connected with an auditor's resignation (or the statement that there are no circumstances that should be brought to the notice of members or creditors) only applies when an auditor resigned. This requirement has now been extended by the 1989 Act to all cases where an auditor ceases to hold office, for example if an auditor is removed from office or not re-appointed at a general meeting.

## POWERS, DUTIES AND LIABILITIES OF AUDITORS

**16. The auditors' report *S.9 CA 89 (S.235–236)***

a. It is the duty of the auditors to report to the members on the accounts laid before the company during their term of office. 'Accounts' includes the balance sheet, profit and loss account and group accounts (if any).

b. The report must be read before the company in general meeting, and must be open to inspection by any member.

c. The report must state whether, in the opinion of the auditors, the accounts have been properly prepared and whether a true and fair view is given:

   i. In the case of the balance sheet, of the state of the company's affairs at the end of its financial year;

   ii. In the case of the profit and loss account, of the company's profit and loss for its financial year; and

   iii. In the case of group accounts, of the state of affairs and profit or loss of the company and its subsidiaries so far as concerns members of the company.

d. In addition:

   i. If the accounts do not contain particulars of directors' emoluments and particulars of loan and other transactions favouring directors, the auditors must include in their report a statement giving the required particulars so far as they are reasonably able to do so.

   ii. The auditors must consider whether the information given in the directors' report relating to the financial year in question is consistent with those accounts. If they are of the opinion that it is not consistent they must say so in their report.

e. The auditors' report must state the names of the auditors and be signed by them.

**17. Auditors' duties**

a. By *S.9* CA *89 (S.237)*, the auditors must carry out such investigations as will enable them to form an opinion as to whether:

i. Proper accounting records have been kept by the company, and adequate returns received from branches not visited by them; and

ii. The balance sheet and profit and loss account agree with the accounting records and returns.

If they think that proper books or returns have not been kept or received by them they must say so in their report.

b. The auditors must also:

i. Acquaint themselves with their duties under the articles and the Companies Act

ii. Report to the members, ensuring that the report complies with *S.9* CA *89 (S.235–236)*

iii. Act honestly and with reasonable care and skill (see below).

**18. Auditors' powers** ***S.120*** **CA** ***89 (S.389A)***

a. The auditors have a right of access to the books, accounts and vouchers of the company.

b The auditors may require from the officers of the company such information and explanations as they think necessary for the performance of their duties. If they fail to obtain such information they must say so in their report.

c. The auditors may attend any general meetings, they must be sent all notices and communications relating to general meetings, and they may speak at a meeting on any matter which concerns them as auditors.

**19. Power in relation to subsidiary undertakings**

a. By *S.120* CA *89 (S.389A)* it is the duty of a subsidiary and its auditors to give to the auditors of the holding company such information and explanation as they may reasonably require for the purposes of their duties as auditors of the holding company.

b. If the subsidiary is incorporated outside Great Britain, it is the duty of the holding company, if required by its auditors, to take reasonable steps to obtain such information from the subsidiary.

**20. False statements to auditors**

By *S.120* CA *89 (S.389A)* it is a criminal offence for an officer of the company to knowingly or recklessly make, either orally or in writing, a statement to the company's auditors which is misleading, false or deceptive in a material particular.

**21. The standard of care and skill.**

a. The 1989 Act relates the legal standard of care and skill closely to the professional standards set by the RSBs, since RSB rules must:

  i. Ensure that only 'fit and proper' persons are appointed as company auditors. In determining whether someone is fit and proper the RSB has to take into account that person's professional conduct.

  ii. Ensure that audits are carried out with 'professional integrity'. One component of this will be compliance with technical standards, the other will cover independence, objectivity and confidentiality.

b. To some extent this formalises the present situation since the ICA and ACCA already require their members to act in accordance with rules enforced by disciplinary committees. However the guidelines laid down by judicial decisions are still law and, to the extent that they are not covered by new RSB rules, they will still play a part in determining the required standard of care and skill. It has been held

  i. That they must ascertain that the books show the true financial position. To do this auditors must do more than merely verify the numerical accuracy, of the accounts **(FORMENTO v SELSDON (1958))**. If entries in or omissions from the books make the auditors suspicious they must make a full investigation into the circumstances. For example:

  In **RE THOMAS GERRARD (1968)** the managing director falsified the accounts by including non existant stock and altering invoices. This caused the company's profits to be overstated. Dividends were declared that would not otherwise have been declared and too much tax was paid. The auditors became suspicious when they noticed that invoices had been altered, but they accepted the managing director's explanation and made no further investigation. The auditors were held liable to the company for the cost of recovering the excess tax paid and for dividends and tax not recovered.

  ii. Auditors must check the cash in hand and the bank balance.

  iii. Where payments have been made by the company, the auditors should see that they are authorised.

  iv. Auditors should check that company borrowing has been authorised and is in accordance with the articles.

  v. Auditors should satisfy themselves that the securities of the company exist and are in safe custody, either by making a personal inspection of the securities or checking that the securities are in the possession of a person who in the ordinary course of business keeps securities for customers, for example a bank.

  vi. Auditors are not required to value stock or work in progress. They may accept the valuation of a responsible official of the company, unless they have reason to suppose it to be inaccurate. In practice auditors exceed this legal duty with regard to stock-taking.

vii. Auditors do not have a duty to comment on whether the management is running the business efficiently or profitably.

viii. If the directors do not allow auditors the time to conduct their investigations, the auditors must either refuse to make a report or make a qualified report. They must not make a report containing a statement the truth of which they have not had an opportunity to verify.

**22. To whom are the auditors' duties owed?**

a. The auditor has a contractual relationship with the company and it is therefore the company to whom the basic duty is owed. Even so auditors must, on occasions, disclose facts which may harm the company. In cases where auditors have been held liable it has usually been when an action has been brought by the company through its liquidator under ***S.631*** (misfeasance summons) now ***S.212 IA*** (Chapter 23.23).

b. Since the decision in **HEDLEY BYRNE v HELLER (1964)** it has been clear that a person may be liable for financial loss resulting from a negligent statement even if there is no contract between the maker of the statement and the recipient (although a disclaimer of responsibility will exclude the defendant's liability).

As far as auditors are concerned, recipients of statements are likely to fall into two categories, existing shareholders (members) and potential shareholders (investors). The situation of both members and investors was recently considered by the House of Lords in the following case.

In **CAPARO INDUSTRIES v DICKMAN (1990)** the plaintiff company sued two directors of Fidelity PLC and the accountants Touche Ross and Co, the auditors of Fidelity. The plaintiff had taken over Fidelity and alleged that the profits were much lower than could shown in the audited accounts, consequently they had suffered financial loss. The House of Lords considered whether a duty of care is owed to persons who rely on the accounts to deal with the company, or buy or sell its shares. This was rejected on the grounds that the extent of the auditors' liability would be indeterminate. Furthermore the fact that Caparo was an existing shareholder was regarded as irrelevant, since it would be illogical to distinguish between existing and potential shareholders. The House also attached very little weight to the fact that Fidelity were known to be vulnerable to a takeover. The House was prepared to acknowledge that liability for negligent audit can exist, but that it is limited to liability to persons who are known by the auditors to be relying on the accounts for a specific purpose. It was unanimously held that Caparo's action failed.

c. Where the articles of a private company provide for the auditor to value shares for the purpose of their acquisition under pre-emption rights the auditor owes a duty of care to both the vendor and the purchaser. The auditor need not give reasons for his valuation, but if he does give an explanation the court can enquire into the accuracy of his valuation and set it aside.

**23. Relief from liability**

Both **S.727** and **S.310** apply to auditors. (See Chapter 15.39).

### *PROGRESS TEST 14*

1. What are the main matters that must be covered by the rules of a Recognised Supervisory Body?
2. How is the remuneration of the auditor determined?
3. Advise John who wishes to resign as auditor of X Ltd.
4. What is meant by 'Official Notification'?
5. Foggy is a director of Vino Ltd. In 1982 the board of directors were approached by Compo who offered to sell to Vino Ltd his controlling interest in a fast-pudding franchise. The board of Vino Ltd rejected his offer for good business reasons. Foggy and his friend Clegg then formed a new company NB Ltd and this company purchased the franchise from Compo. The venture was a great success and Foggy has just sold his shares in NB Ltd, making a substantial profit. Advise Vino Ltd whether it can claim this profit from Foggy.

# 19 Company Meetings

## TYPES OF MEETING

**1. The annual general meeting**

a. Except for ***private companies*** that have taken advantage of the ***elective resolution*** procedure (see 19. below) every company must hold an AGM every calendar year with not more than 15 months between each AGM. However provided the first AGM is held within 18 months of incorporation it need not be held in the calendar year of incorporation or the following year. ***(S.366)***.

b. If a company fails to hold an AGM within the prescribed time the Secretary of State may, on the application of ***any member***, order it to be held. He may give such directions as he thinks fit and may fix the quorum at one member only. ***(S.367)***.

c. Prior to 1985 Table A prescribed following as the ***ordinary business*** of the AGM:

i. Consideration of the accounts, the directors' report and the auditors' report;

ii. Declaration of a dividend;

iii. Election of directors in place of those retiring; and

iv. The appointment and remuneration of auditors.

However the new Table A merely states that the notice shall specify the general nature of the business to be transacted (Article 38).

**2. Extraordinary general meetings**

a. Any meeting which is not an AGM is an EGM. The articles usually provide that an EGM may be called by the directors for example Table A Article 37.

b. Members have a statutory right to require directors to convene an EGM. By ***S.368*** despite anything in the articles the directors must call an EGM if required to do so by holders of at least 10% of the paid-up capital with voting rights. If the directors do not convene the meeting within 21 days the requisitionists (or more than half their number) may do so, and recover their expenses from the company, which may then recover them from the directors.

c. In addition ***S.370*** states that unless the articles provide otherwise two or more members holding not less than 10% of the issued share capital (even if it has no voting rights) or if there is no share capital 5%of the members, may call a meeting.

d. By **S.371** if it is impractical to call or conduct a meeting in the manner prescribed by the Act or the articles the court may, on the application of any director or member entitled to vote, order a meeting to be called, giving such directions as it thinks fit.

In **RE EL SOMBRERO (1958)** the applicant held 90% of the shares in a private company, but was not a director. The rest of the shares were divided equally between 2 persons who were directors. The company's articles stated that the quorum for meetings was 2 persons. Wishing to remove the directors the applicant convened a meeting under **S.132 CA 1948** (now **S.368**).However since the directors did not attend no quorum was present. An application was then made to the court under **S.135 CA 48** (now **S.371**). The court directed that a meeting be held and that one member would constitute a quorum. The applicant could therefore remove the directors.

e. Note also:

i. A resigning auditor may require the directors to convene an EGM *(S.122 CA 89 (S.392A))* (Chapter 18.14.)

ii. **S.142** – Which requires the directors of a public company to call an EGM when it becomes known to a director that the net assets have fallen to half or less of the company's called up share capital (Chapter 10.13).

3. **Class meetings**

Meetings of the holders of a class of shares are usually convened to consider a variation of class rights. Holders of other classes of shares have no right to attend.

## CONVENING MEETINGS

4. **Length of notice**

a. By **S.369** 21 days written notice is required for an AGM, although a shorter period is permissible if agreed by all the members entitled to attend and vote.

b. **S.369** specifies a period of 14 days written notice for an EGM unless a special resolution is to be moved in which case 21 days notice is required. A shorter period of notice is permissible if agreed by a simple majority in number of members holding at least 95% in nominal value of shares carrying the right to attend and vote. (However note 19 a. v. below).

c. 'Days' means clear days, ie the day of service of the notice and the day of the meeting are not counted.

5. **Persons entitled to notice**

   a. *S.370* states that, unless the articles provide otherwise, notice must be served on every member in the manner required by Table A. In fact Table A Article 38 requires notice to be served on all the members, on all persons entitled to a share in the consequence of the death or bankruptcy of a member, and to the directors and auditors.

   b. At common law failure to give notice, even to one member, would invalidate the meeting. Therefore the articles usually provide that accidental failure to give or non-receipt of notice shall not invalidate proceedings. (Table A Article 39).

6. **Contents of the notice**

   a. The notice must specify the date, place, and time of the meeting. It is not necessary to give details of ordinary business, but the nature of any other business must be specified. However where a special or extraordinary resolution is to be moved, the notice must set out the full text of the resolution and any amendment proposed at the meeting will be ineffective unless all the members of the company (not merely those present) agree to waive their right to notice (RE MOORGATE MERCANTILE HOLDINGS (1980)).In practice companies set out the full text of any resolution to be moved, even though this is not required by law.

   b. The notice must state that a member entitled to attend and vote may appoint a proxy to attend and vote on his behalf. (See 13. below).

7. **Special notice *(S.379)***

   a. It is important to distinguish special notice from ***notice of a special resolution***.

   b. Special notice is required for 3 types of ***ordinary resolution***:

      i. To remove a director or to appoint somebody in his place ***(S.303)***;

      ii. To appoint a director aged 70 or over, where the age limit applies under ***S.293***; and

      iii. To remove an auditor or to appoint any auditor other than the retiring auditor ***(S.122 CA 89 (S.391A))***.

   c. Where special notice is required ***the persons proposing the motion must give the company*** 28 days notice of their intention to move the resolution. The company will then give the members notice of the resolution when it sends them notice of the meeting. If it is too late to include the resolution in the notice of the meeting it may be advertised or otherwise communicated to the members at least 21 days before the meeting.

**8. Members' resolutions and statements *(S.376–377)***

Holders of at least 5% of share capital with voting rights *or* at least 100 members (whether entitled to vote or not) who have paid up on average £100 each can compel the company:

a. By six weeks requisition to give the members notice of any resolution which the requisitionists intend to move at an AGM. Unless the company resolves otherwise the requisitionists must pay the expenses. These should be small since all that will be needed is an addition to the notice of the AGM.

b. By one weeks requisition to circulate to the members a statement of up to 1000 words with respect to any proposed resolution at any general meeting. This provision is of little use in practice since no substantial saving will be made unless the circular can be sent with notice of the meeting. Furthermore if the circular is in opposition to a proposal of the board it would be a better tactic to write direct to the members since there is then no need to limit the circular to 1000 words and the board will not obtain prior warning of the opposition's case.

c. The relationship between **S.379** and **S.376** was considered in **PEDLEY v INLAND WATERWAYS (1977)** (see Chapter 15.9) where it was held that where special notice is required by **S.379** a member must nevertheless comply with **S.376** if he wishes to have a motion included on the agenda.

## CONDUCT OF MEETINGS

**9. Introduction**

A valid meeting must, by definition, consist of more than one person, even if that person holds proxies for other members **(RE SHANLEY CONTRACTING (1980))**. Also:

a. It must be properly convened by notice;
b. A quorum must be present; and
c. The meeting must be properly presided over by a chairman.

**10. The quorum**

a. A quorum is the minimum number of persons who must be present to conduct a meeting.

b. The quorum for all company meetings is two members personally present ***(S.370(4))***. Note however **RE EL SOMBRERO (1958)**, (see 2. above).

c. Table A Article 41 states that if within half an hour a quorum is not present, the meeting will stand adjourned to the same day, time and place in the next week (or to such other day, time and place as the directors shall determine).

## 11. The chairman

There must be chairman to preside over the meeting. Table A Articles 42–43 provide that the chairman of the board, or failing him another director, or failing that, any member shall act as chairman. The chairman must:

a. Act in good faith in the interests of the company as a whole;

b. Ensure that business is conducted in an orderly manner in the order set out in the agenda. Therefore he must ensure that members relate what they say to the items on the agenda and do not make irrelevant or provocative remarks;

c. Allow all points of view to be adequately expressed and then put the motion to the vote and declare the result. He has a casting vote only if given one by the articles, eg Table A Article 50;

d. Decide whether amendments to motions are admissible. He should reject an amendment if it is outside the scope of the business stated in the notice of the meeting;

e. Adjourn any meeting at which a quorum is present if so directed by the meeting; and

f. Sign the minutes of the meeting.

## 12. Voting

a. The usual practice is to vote by a show of hands, ie each member present has one vote regardless of the number of shares held.

b. However if a poll is properly demanded (which is fairly rare) then a member's votes will depend on the number of voting shares he holds. Voting rights are specified in the articles, usually one vote for each ordinary share.

c. The articles will prescribe the rules for demanding and holding a poll. However by ***S.373*** the right to demand a poll cannot be totally excluded by the articles except on the election of a chairman or a motion to adjourn the meeting. In addition the articles may not set the minimum amount of support for a poll above either five members entitled to vote or any number of members holding at least 10% of the voting shares. This protects a minority from provisions in the articles designed to make it difficult to obtain a poll.

## 13. Proxies

a. The term proxy is used both to refer to the person appointed to act on behalf of the member and to the ***instrument*** which gives him the required authority.

b. By ***S.372*** every member has the right to appoint a proxy to attend and vote for him. The proxy does not need to be a member.

c. A proxy may be deposited with the company at any time up to 48 hours before the meeting. The articles may specify a shorter, but not a longer period.

d. When a company invites proxies by issuing proxy cards it must issue them to all members, not merely to those from whom the directors expect support.

e. A proxy may be ***general***, ie given a discretionary power to vote, or ***special***, ie required to vote on a particular resolution as instructed. The Stock Exchange requires listed companies to issue ***two-way*** proxy forms which enable the member to instruct the proxy to vote against, as well as for, the resolution.

f. The instrument appointing a proxy must be in writing under the hand of the appointer, or if the appointer is a corporation, either under seal or the hand of a duly authorised officer.

g. A proxy may speak:
   i. At a meeting of a public company only if the articles allow; and
   ii. At a meeting of a private company as of right under **S.372**.

h. A proxy may vote:
   i. On a show of hands only if allowed by the articles, (which is not usual); and
   ii. On a poll. A proxy has the same right to demand a poll as the person who appointed him.

### 14. Minutes

a. By **S.382** every company must keep minutes of both company meetings and board meetings.

b. When the minutes are signed by the chairman they become evidence of the proceedings. They would only be prima facie evidence but for Table A Article 47 which provides that signed minutes are conclusive evidence that a resolution has been carried or lost. This prevents a later argument on a point which should have been challenged at the meeting.

c. By **S.383** a minute book of general meetings must be kept at the company's registered office and must be available for inspection by members for at least two hours on each working day. Any member is entitled to a copy of the minutes within seven days on payment of a small fee.

## Resolutions

### 15. Ordinary resolutions

a. This is a simple majority of members present in person or by proxy entitled to vote and voting. For example a company has ten members holding an equal number of shares. Four do not attend the meeting (or appoint proxies), three abstain, two vote for the motion, and one votes against. The resolution is passed.

b. The period of notice depends on the type of meeting at which it is moved (21 days for an AGM and generally 14 days for an EGM).

c. An ordinary resolution is the type used whenever the law or the company's articles do not require a special or extraordinary resolution. In some cases the law specifies an ordinary resolution, for example ***S.303*** (removal of directors) and ***S.122 CA 89 (S.391)*** (removal of auditors). Where a section states that 'the powers conferred by this section must be exercised by the company in general meeting' eg ***S.121*** (alteration of capital) it means that an ordinary resolution is necessary.

d. In general copies of ordinary resolutions which have been passed need not be filed with the registrar. There are several exceptions which are listed in Chapter 17.6.

**16. Special resolutions *(S.378)***

These require a three quarter majority of members present in person or by proxy entitled to vote and voting. A period of 21 days notice is required but a shorter period is acceptable if a simple majority in number holding 95% in value of the voting shares agree. Because of this notice requirement amendments to special resolutions cannot be accepted at the meeting. A copy of every special resolution which is passed must be filed with the registrar within 15 days. Special resolutions are required for a number of important company decisions, for example:

a. To alter the objects clause of its memorandum ***(S.110 CA 89 (S.4))***.
b. To alter the articles ***(S.9)***.
c. To reduce its capital, subject to the consent of the court ***(S.135)***.
d. To commence a winding-up by the court ***(S.122 IA)***.
e. To commence a voluntary winding-up ***(S.84 IA)***.
f. To authorise a reconstruction of a company in voluntary liquidation ***(S.110 IA)***.
g. To re-register an unlimited private company as limited ***(S.51)***.
h. To re-register a private company with share capital as a public company ***(S.43)***.
i. To re-register a public company as a private company ***(S.53)***.
j. To withdraw or modify statutory pre-emption rights ***(S.95)***.
k. To change the company name, subject to approval by the Secretary of State ***(S.28)***.
l. To authorise a private company to give financial assistance for the purchase of its own shares ***(S.155)***.
m. To authorise the terms of a proposed contract by which a company will make an off-market purchase of its own shares ***(S.164)*** and

n. To authorise a private company to purchase or redeem its own shares out of capital ***(S.173)***.

o. To ratify an ultra vires act ***(S.108 CA 89 (S.35(3))***.

**17. Extraordinary resolutions**

An extraordinary resolution is similar to a special resolution with regard to the majority necessary to pass the resolution, the admissibility of amendments and the requirements of filing. The difference is that only 14 days notice is required, although a shorter period is acceptable as with a special resolution. An extraordinary resolution is required in the following circumstances:

a. To wind-up the company voluntarily on the ground that it is insolvent ***(S.84 IA)***. The reason for an extraordinary rather than a special resolution is to dispense with 21 days notice when winding-up is urgent;

b. In a voluntary winding-up to sanction the exercise, by the liquidator of some of his powers, for example to pay any class of creditors in full or to make a compromise arrangement with creditors ***(S.165 IA)***;

c. To sanction a variation of class rights at a class meeting ***(S.125)***. This is referred to as an 'extraordinary resolution' in the Act although it is a ***class*** resolution rather than a company resolution.

**18. Written resolutions *(S113–114 CA 89 (S.381A–382A)***

a. The 1989 Act has introduced new rules to simplify private company procedures. There are two main changes. ***Firstly a private company*** can substitute the unanimous written agreement of its shareholders for any resolution passed at a general meeting (written resolutions). ***Secondly a private company*** can, by elective resolution, opt out of certain company law requirements, including the holding of an AGM (see 19 below).

b. Except as stated below, anything which can be done by resolution at a general meeting of a private company may, instead of the meeting being held, be done by a written resolution signed by or on behalf of all members of the company who would be entitled to attend and vote at such a meeting. Previous notice is not required and the signatures need not be on a single document, however each must be on a document accurately stating the terms of the resolution. The date of the resolution is the date when the last member signed it.

c. ***Exceptions***. A written resolution may not be used to remove a director or auditor before their period of office has expired.

d. ***Special procedures***. In the following cases certain information must be disclosed to members before, or when, the resolution is sent to them for signature. This ensures that documents which would have been available to members at the general meeting are available to members signing the resolution.

   i. The disapplication of pre-emption rights.

ii. Financial assistance for the purchase of own shares.

iii. The authority for an off-market purchase of, or a contingent purchase contract for, own shares.

iv. The approval for a payment out of capital in connection with the purchase or redemption of own shares.

In the case of (iii) and (iv) the resolution will be effective without the signatures of members whose shares are being bought.

v. The approval of a director's service contract.

vi. The funding of a director's expenditure in the performance of duties.

e. *Rights of auditors*. To preserve the auditors' right to receive notices and other communications relating to general meetings and their right to attend and be heard on matters concerning them as auditors,the 1989 Act requires a copy of any proposed written resolution to be sent to the auditors. They have the right (to be exercised within seven days) to require the resolution to be considered by the company in general meeting if they consider that it concerns them as auditors. If the company wants the resolution to have effect before the seven day period expires, it must obtain a statement from the auditors that the resolution does not concern them as auditors, or that it does concern them, but need not be considered by the company in general meeting.

f. A written resolution may be used whatever resolution would otherwise be required ie special, extraordinary, elective, ordinary, or ordinary requiring special notice. The written resolution procedure cannot be restricted by anything in the company's memorandum or articles. Once a written resolution has been agreed it must be recorded in a book in the same way as the minutes of proceedings at general meetings. The book must also contain a record of members' signatures.

**19. Elective resolutions**

a. *S.116 CA 89 (S.379A)* has introduced a new procedure enabling private companies to dispense with or modify certain internal procedures. An elective resolution must be passed if the company wishes:

i. To extend beyond five years the duration of the directors' authority to allot shares.

ii. To dispense with the requirement to lay accounts and reports before the company in general meeting.(However any member has the right to require that the accounts be laid before the meeting).

iii. To dispense with the requirement to hold an AGM. This is a major reform, it recognises that for many companies, where the directors are also the only shareholders, it is an unnecessary formality to hold an AGM. However any member may, at least three months before the end of the year, serve a notice on the company requiring it to hold an AGM in that year. If a company revokes the elective resolution, or re-registers as a public company, an AGM need not be held in the year of revocation if less than three months of the year remain.

iv. To dispense with the obligation to appoint auditors annually ie the existing auditors shall be deemed to be re-appointed.

v. To reduce the majority required to consent to the holding of a general meeting at short notice, from members holding at least 95% in nominal value of shares carrying right to attend and vote to 90%.

b. If an elective resolution is proposed for a general meeting, at least 21 days notice of the meeting must be given in writing. The notice must give the terms of the elective resolution. At the meeting the resolution must be agreed by all members entitled to attend and vote, either in person or by proxy. Alternatively the new written resolution procedure may be used.

c. An elective resolution may be revoked at any time by passing an ordinary resolution. An elective resolution will also cease to have effect if the company re-registers as public. Elective resolutions and ordinary resolutions revoking them must be delivered to the registrar.

## *PROGRESS TEST 15*

1. What types of resolution are necessary to
   (a) Approve a 'golden handshake' payment to a director
   (b) Remove an auditor
   (c) Increase the authorised capital?
2. How can a company, which is a member of another company, express its views and vote at a meeting of that company?
3. State the rules for holding the Annual General Meeting.
4. When may the chairman adjourn a general meeting? When must he do so?
5. In 1982 a private company issued 100,000 £1 shares redeemable in 1986 at a premium of 50 pence per share. In 1986 the company distributed profits of £45,000, and it intends to issue 50,000 £1 shares at a premium of 20 pence per share in order to redeem the redeemable shares. Calculate the permissible capital payment.

# 20 Insider Dealing

## 1. Introduction

a. Insider dealing concerns the duties of directors, officers, some members, and some outsiders when dealing in the company's securities with inside information which affects their value. A good example is **PERCIVAL v WRIGHT (1902)** (see Chapter 15.30). However as previously stated this decision would not be altered by the following provisions since they do not apply to private transactions.

b. Clearly insider dealing is both immoral and likely to cause damage to the reputation and operation of the securities market. For some years there had been general consensus that some legislation was needed. The problem is that any legislation must be effective, but not so strict as to damage the efficiency of the securities market. The main problem is the definition of an insider. It has to be wide enough to include the wrongdoer, but not so wide as to discourage legitimate business activities.

c. Other problems have been:

   i. Should the sanction be criminal or civil? If it were civil there would be a problem of proving loss, especially where the transaction involved listed securities bought or sold through a stockbroker, since it would be almost impossible to match up sales and purchases. If it were criminal only, persons who could prove loss would go uncompensated.

   ii. Should the legislation only cover listed securities, or include private deals, ie non-Stock Exchange transactions?

d. The 1978 Companies Bill included criminal sanctions for transactions involving listed securities, and criminal and civil provisions in respect of private deals. The ***COMPANIES ACT 1980*** dropped all proposals regarding private deals. It only legislated against insider dealing involving securities listed on the Stock Exchange and off-market dealings in advertised securities. The Act made insider dealing a criminal offence and did not provide for civil actions. Off market dealings in advertised securities are not covered by this book.

e. The provisions of the 1980 Act have not been made part of the Companies Act 1985. They have been consolidated into a separate Act – ***THE COMPANY SECURITIES (INSIDER DEALING) ACT 1985 (CSIDA)***. This has now been amended by the ***FINANCIAL SERVICES ACT 1986***. The main change is the introduction of a power to appoint inspectors, with wide powers, to investigate suspected insider dealing offences.

2. Other methods of regulating insider dealing

In addition to the *CSIDA 1985* other rules exist to discourage insider dealings. For example:

a. ***S.323*** which prohibits directors dealing in share options.

b. ***S.324*** which requires directors to disclose their shareholding in their own company.

c. ***S.198–210*** concerning disclosure of members' interests in shares of public companies.

d. ***S.212*** by which a public company can investigate a person's interest in its shares.

e. If insider dealing amounts to a breach of a director's fiduciary duty the director may be sued. The potential for this remedy has not however been fulfilled, since companies rarely take legal action against their directors unless there is a complete change of ownership, as in REGAL (HASTINGS) v GULLIVER (1942). Also if the action were successful, the amount recovered would belong to the company, not to the victim of the insider deal.

f. Self-regulatory codes including

   i. The City Code on Takeovers and Mergers (Chapter 22); and

   ii. The Stock Exchange's model code 'Securities Transactions by Directors of Listed Companies'. This code prohibits a director from dealing in his company's shares in the two months prior to the announcement of the company's annual or half-yearly results and at any other time when he possesses price sensitive information about his company which has not been published. It also prohibits him from dealing in the shares of another company when he knows price sensitive information about that company which he has acquired because of his directorship of the first company.

3. The definition of 'insider'

a. An insider is an ***individual*** who is, or has within the past six months, been ***connected with the company*** and knows that this is so. ***(S.1 CSIDA)***.

b. By ***S.9 CSIDA*** an individual connected with the company includes:

   i. A director of the company or a related company;

   ii. An officer or employee of that company or a related company; and

   iii. A person in a professional or business relationship with the company or a related company (or his employer or a company of which he is a director) who has access to unpublished price sensitive information which it would be reasonable to expect him not to disclose except in the proper performance of his work.

c. Note that:

i. Category iii. above includes all professional advisors to a company such as its auditors, legal advisors, bankers and their respective employees;

ii. The Act refers to an individual rather than a person, therefore a company cannot be an insider. Thus an institutional investor may deal in another company's securities even if inside information is known to its directors or employees;

iii. The Act extends to persons given a 'tip' by an insider, ie a tippee. Thus an individual who has knowingly obtained information from an insider and who knows, or should know, that the information has only been disclosed for the proper performance of the insider's function is subject to the same prohibitions as an insider.

**4. The definition of 'unpublished price sensitive information'**

a. By *S.10 CSIDA* this is information which:

i. Relates to *specific* matters concerning a company, and is not just of a general nature; and

ii. Is not generally known to those accustomed or likely to deal in the securities of that company; but

iii. Which would, if it were generally known, be likely materially to affect the price of those securities.

b. Note that:

i. Parliament did not intend to prohibit ordinary transactions by directors and employees in their company's shares. Although such persons may well be more aware of the prospects of the company than other people they are unlikely to possess the *specific* information contemplated by the Act, for example knowledge of a probable takeover bid, or of an oil strike by an oil company.

ii. It will be very difficult to measure the price sensitivity of a piece of information. Share prices fluctuate for many reasons. It would therefore be a problem to assess what might have happened if a particular piece of information had been made generally known.

**5. Other definitions**

a. *'Dealing'*. A person deals in securities if he buys or sells the securities. Thus a gift or a transmission of securities by operation of law is not dealing. A decision not to deal, even if based on inside information, is not 'dealing'.

b. *'Related company'*. This means any company within the same group.

**6. Basic prohibitions**

a. By *S.1 CSIDA* an insider knowingly in possession of unpublished price sensitive information about listed securities, which he has obtained by virtue of his connection with the company, and which it would be reasonable to expect him not to disclose except for the proper performance of his functions, is prohibited from:

i. Dealing himself in the listed securities;

ii. Counselling or procuring another person to deal in those securities; or

iii. Communicating that information to another person if he has reasonable cause to believe that that or some other person will make use of the information for either purpose described above.

b. The use of ***'person'*** in ii. and iii. above prevents an individual evading the legislation by dealing through a company in which he has a controlling interest.

c. The meaning of ***'obtaining'*** was the central issue in the first contested case to be brought under the Act

In **ATTORNEY-GENERAL'S REFERENCE (No. 1 of 1988)** the accused was interested in purchasing a company. He asked the company's merchant bankers to provide him with financial information about the company. A little later one of the bank's employees informed the accused that the company was subject to an agreed take-over and that an announcement would be made shortly. The employee also told the accused that the information was sensitive and highly confidential and that as a result of what she was saying to him, he would be an 'insider'. A few minutes later the accused telephoned his stockbroker and purchased 6,000 shares. The following day when the announcement was made the price rose sharply, five weeks later he sold the shares for a £3,000 profit.

When accused of insider dealing his defence was that he had not 'obtained' price sensitive information, but had only played a passive role as recipient of the information. This was accepted by the trial judge and he was acquitted. This interpretation was rejected by the House of Lords since it would water down the effect of the legislation and require the courts to make 'almost imperceptible' factual distinctions. Although penal statutes are generally interpreted narrowly, in favour of the accused, this was felt to be inappropriate in this case. 'obtained' therefore means 'no more than received'.

d. ***S.1*** also prohibits dealing in the securities of any other company when:

i. The individual has information obtained by virtue of his connection with the first company; and

ii. Which relates to any transaction (actual or contemplated) involving both companies, or one of them and the securities of the other. A takeover bid would be a transaction of the second type, as would be a decision not to make a bid.

e. *S.1* also contains provisions relating to takeovers. Where individuals acting in one capacity are proposing to take over a company they are subject to the prohibition on insider dealing when acting in other capacities while their plans remain as unpublished price sensitive information. Individuals who obtain knowledge of the proposals directly or indirectly from those planning the bid are subject to the same restrictions.

7. **Public servants (*S.2 CSIDA*, as amended by *S.173–174 FINANCIAL SERVICES ACT 1986*)**

a. Public servants and former public servants are prohibited from dealing in the securities of a company if they obtain price sensitive information in the course of their duties which they know should not be published.

b. ***'Public servant'*** includes civil servants, officials of the Securities and Investments Board established under the Financial Services Act, officials of self regulating organisations, investment exchanges and recognised clearing houses (as defined by the Financial Services Act).

8. **Exemptions (*S.3 CSIDA*)**

The main exemptions are:

a. Where the transaction is executed otherwise than with a view to making a profit or avoiding a loss. This would cover the situation where, for example, an individual in urgent need of money sells shares in a company when in possession of unpublished information which would, if published, reduce the value of the securities. Since his main motive would be to raise money the transaction would not be made with a view to avoiding a loss. The individual would however no doubt incur serious difficulties in convincing others of his motive for the sale.

b. A transaction entered into by a liquidator, receiver or trustee in bankruptcy in good faith as part of his normal duties.

c. A transaction by a jobber or market maker in good faith and in the ordinary course of business. This prevents such persons being disqualified when they obtain information in the course of business and that information is of the usual kind acquired in the ordinary course of business.

   i. ***'Jobber'*** means any person (individual, partnership or company) dealing in securities on a recognised stock exchange and recognised as such by the Council of the Stock Exchange.

   ii. ***'Market maker'*** means any person recognised by a recognised stock exchange who holds himself out as willing to buy and sell securities at prices specified by him in compliance with the rules of that exchange. *(S.174 FSA 1986)*

d. Individuals who do anything for the purpose of stabilising the price of securities if it is done according to rules for the conduct of business made under *S.48 FSA 1986*.

e. A trustee or personal representative may deal if advised to do so by an appropriate adviser who does not appear to be in a situation to which the prohibitions apply. *(S.7 CSIDA)*

**9. Penalties and remedies *(S.8 CSIDA)***

a. Insider dealing is a criminal offence, the maximum penalty being two years imprisonment plus an unlimited fine. Prosecutions must be brought by the Secretary of State for Trade or the Director of Public Prosecutions. The Act does not provide for civil actions.

b. Contravention of the Act does not effect the validity of the transaction. This is rather unusual since criminal acts are normally void or voidable. The rule is however sensible since the chain of transactions may be complex and innocent parties could be affected if the transaction were held to be void.

**10. Investigations into insider dealing**

a. Prior to 1986 there was no mechanism for the investigation of suspected insider dealing other than investigation by the police. This was a serious drawback to the effectiveness of the legislation.

b. By *S.177 FINANCIAL SERVICES ACT 1986* the Secretary of State is empowered to appoint inspectors to investigate suspected insider dealing offences. The inspectors will have basically the same powers as inspectors appointed under *S.432 CA 1985*. Thus they can require any person that may have relevant information to:

   i. Produce documents in his possession. 'Documents' includes information recorded in any form.

   ii. Attend before them;

   iii. Give evidence under oath;

   iv. Otherwise give all reasonable help in connection with the investigation.

   They also have powers to enter and search premises for evidence (*S.199 FSA 1986*, as amended by *S.76 CA 89*).

c. By *S.74 CA 89 (S.177(5A) FINANCIAL SERVICES ACT 1986)* the Secretary of State may direct inspectors to take no further steps in an insider dealing investigation, or to take only such steps as are specified in his direction. This new provision enhances the Secretary of State's ability to ensure that a possible insider dealing offence can be dealt with quickly.

d. Anyone who refuses to co-operate with an inspector can be held in contempt of court and be punished by a fine and/or imprisonment. If the person is authorised to carry on an investment business the Secretary of State may cancel or restrict his authorisation ***(S.178 FSA 1986)***.The Secretary of State can also move for the disqualification of a director under ***S.8 COMPANY DIRECTORS DISQUALIFICATION ACT 1986*** (Chapter 15.42).

### *PROGRESS TEST 16*

1. The board of directors must include a representative of the employees. True or false?
2. What are the main exemptions from the insider dealing code?
3. Why does the ***COMPANIES SECURITIES (INSIDER DEALING) ACT 1985*** not provide a right to compensation for the party who suffers loss?
4. In what circumstances is an individual deemed to be 'connected' with a company for the purpose of insider dealing?
5. Foxtrot Ltd has issued and fully paid capital consisting of 1,000,000 £1 ordinary shares and 10,000 9% £1 cumulative preference shares. The class rights are set out in the articles and there is a provision that the rights of any class of share may be varied with the consent in writing of the holders of three-fourths of the issued shares of that class.

   Victor and Sylvestor, who hold all the ordinary shares and 8,000 of the preference shares have decided to alter the articles so that the dividends on the preference shares shall no longer be cumulative and the rate shall be reduced to 6% per annum.

   Advise Gene who holds 1,600 of the preference shares and opposes the proposals.

# 21 Minority Protection

## MAJORITY RULE

1. **The rule in Foss v Harbottle**

   a. Where a wrong is done to a company, or there is an irregularity in the management of a company, and there arises a need to enforce the rights of the company, it is for the company to decide what action to take and it is the company which is the proper plaintiff in the action.

   In **FOSS v HARBOTTLE (1843)** two members brought an action against the directors of a company to compel them to make good a loss suffered by the company as a result of the defendants selling their own land to the company at more than it was worth. It was held that the action failed. The wrong was done to the company and there was nothing to stop the company taking action if it chose to do so.

   b. A more recent example of the rule occurred in the following case:

   In **PAVLIDES v JENSEN (1956)** the directors sold an asset of the company to a third party at a gross undervaluation. A minority shareholder commenced an action. It was held that he could not do so, it was up to the company to decide whether to sue the directors for negligence. Alternatively the company could decide to exonerate them.

   c. It is interesting that if the facts of Foss v Harbottle were repeated today the case would probably be decided differently, either because it is very similar to Daniels v Daniels (1978) (para 3), or because it would be covered by **S.459** (para 5). There are nevertheless several good reasons for the rule.

      i. It is the logical consequence of the fact that a company is a separate legal person. It is the company that has suffered a wrong, therefore it is the company which seeks a remedy.

      ii. It preserves the principle of majority rule.

      iii. It prevents multiple actions. If each shareholder were permitted to sue, the company might be subjected to many lawsuits started by numerous plaintiffs.

      iv. It prevents futile actions. If the irregularity is one which can effectively be ratified by the company in general meeting, it would be futile to have litigation about it without the consent of the general meeting.

2. **Controlling members' duties**

   The position of the controlling members, (ie those possessing sufficient voting power to pass the appropriate resolutions at general meetings) is quite different from that of directors, since it is only directors who owe fiduciary duties to the company. In contrast shares are proprietary rights which members may exercise in their own self interest, even to the detriment of the company. Thus directors who hold a majority of the shares may, in some cases, be able to disregard their fiduciary duties and duties of care and skill, provided they disclose what they propose to do and then pass a resolution allowing the action. Such a resolution may, for example:

a. Ratify directors' acts in excess of the powers conferred on them, for example **BAMFORD v BAMFORD (1970)** (Chapter 15.11).

b. Resolve not to sue where a director has broken his duty of care and skill, for example **PAVLIDES v JENSEN (1956)**.

c. Allow a director to retain a secret profit provided:

   i. The profit was not made at the expense of the minority; and

   ii. The director acted in good faith and in the interest of the company.

   These conditions would have been satisfied in **REGAL (HASTINGS) v GULLIVER (1942)** (Chapter 15.36), but it did not occur to the directors to pass such a resolution.

## MINORITY PROTECTION AT COMMON LAW

### 3. Exceptions to the rule in Foss v Harbottle

The rule in Foss v Harbottle places the majority in such a strong position that minority shareholders would be at a serious disadvantage if the following exceptions were not allowed:

a. Where the company does an illegal or ultra vires act. However

   i. By ***S.108 CA 89 (S.35(2))*** if a company is required to carry out an ultra vires act in pursuance of an illegal obligation arising from a previous act of the company, the members cannot restrain the act.

   ii. By ***S.108 CA 89 (S.35(3))*** a company may ratify an ultra vires act by special resolution. (See Chapter 7.23).

b. Where the company acts on a resolution which has not been properly passed.

   In **BAILLE v ORIENTAL TELEPHONE CO (1915)** a company was successfully restrained from acting on a special resolution of which inadequate notice had been given.

   This exception has been severely curtailed by ***S.108 CA 89 (S.35A)*** which provides that in favour of a person dealing with a company in good faith, the power of the board of directors to bind the company, or authorise others to do so, shall be deemed to be free of any limitation under the company's constitution. 'Constitution' includes any resolution of the company and any agreement between the members, as well as the constitutional documents.

c. Where the individual rights of the plaintiff as a shareholder have been infringed, for example **PENDER v LUSHINGTON (1877)** (Chapter 8.9).

d. Where the majority is committing a fraud on the minority. The word 'fraud' in this context does not mean deceit in the criminal sense as the following examples show:

   i. ***Expropriation of the company's property.***

   In **MENIER v HOOPER'S TELEGRAPH WORKS (1874)** D (a rival company) held a controlling interest in the company. They used this interest to put the company into voluntary liquidation so that they were left in possession of the assets to the exclusion of the minority. It was held that this amounted to an expropriation of the company's property. This was not something which the majority had power to do and could be restrained by the minority.

   In **COOK v DEEKS (1916)** the directors, whilst negotiating a contract on behalf of the company, took the contract in their own names. Then at a general meeting they used their votes to pass a resolution declaring that the company had no interest in the contract. It was held that the resolution was a fraud on the minority and was ineffective.

   ii. ***Expropriation of other members' property.*** It was shown in Chapter 8 by comparison of **BROWN v BRITISH ABRASIVE WHEEL CO (1919)** and **SIDEBOTTOM v KERSHAW LEESE (1920)** that the expropriation of a competing member's interest by means of a compulsory acquisition of his shares is valid since it is for the benefit of the company as a whole. However a bare power of expulsion is not acceptable.

   In **DAFEN TINPLATE v LLANELLY STEEL (1920)** P was a member of D and used to purchase steel from them. When P started to purchase steel elsewhere a new article was inserted which conferred on the majority an unrestricted power to buy out any shareholders they might think proper. It was held that this was a bare power of expulsion and as such went further than was necessary to protect the company's interests.

   iii. ***An issue of shares designed to harm the minority,*** for example **CLEMENS v CLEMENS (1976)** (Chapter 8.6) where the issue reduced the plaintiff's holding from 45% to 24.5%, thus removing the power to defeat a special resolution.

   iv. ***A reduction of capital designed to harm a class of shareholders.***

   In **RE HOLDERS INVESTMENT TRUST (1971)** a capital reduction scheme was not confirmed by the court because a resolution of the preference shareholders was only passed because trustees, who held a substantial number of ordinary shares, voted in favour of the scheme because it would be advantageous to their beneficiaries due to their larger holding of ordinary shares. Megarry J. held that the resolution had not been effectively passed because the majority had not considered what was best for the class of preference shareholders as a whole.

However a reduction of capital by paying off preference shares does not require a class meeting of preference shareholders.

In **HOUSE OF FRASER v A.C.G.E. INVESTMENTS (1987)** the company passed a special resolution reducing its capital by paying off and cancelling its cumulative preference shares. No class meeting of the preference shareholders was held to approve the cancellation. The articles provided for a class meeting if the rights attached to the shares were 'modified, commuted, affected or dealt with'. Some of the preference shareholders objected that the articles had been contravened. The House of Lords held that reduction was in accordance with the articles. The articles gave a prior right to return of capital when any capital was properly returned as being surplus to the company's needs. This right was not being 'modified, commuted, affected or dealt with', it was being given effect to. Since the reduction was also not unfair to preference shareholders on any other grounds the preference shareholders lost the case.

v. ***A negligent act which benefits the majority at the expense of the company.***

In **DANIELS v DANIELS (1978)** the controlling directors and shareholders (Mr and Mrs Daniels) caused the company to sell a piece of land to Mrs Daniels at an undervalue. The plaintiff, a minority shareholder, did not allege fraud because he did not know all that had happened. His action was nevertheless successful and Mrs Daniels had to account for the profit. The strongest case against the plaintiff was Pavlides v Jensen (1956), but this case was distinguished because the directors had not there benefited from their breach of duty since the sale had been to a third party.

vi. ***An act defeating the purpose for which the company was formed.*** This case also shows that the minority need not necessarily hold voting shares.

In **ESTMANCO (KILNER HOUSE) v GREATER LONDON COUNCIL (1981)** the GLC when under Conservative control decided to sell a block of 60 flats. Estmanco was formed in accordance with an agreement with the GLC to manage the block on a non-profit making basis after all 60 flats were sold. Each of the purchasers was to have one share in the company, but until all 60 flats were sold the shares of the purchasers would not carry votes and during that period the voting shares would be vested in the

GLC. After the sale of all the flats the purchasers' shares would carry votes and the GLC would withdraw. After 12 flats had been sold, control of the GLC passed to Labour and it was decided that the flats should be let rather than sold. The GLC tried to induce the 12 purchasers to give up the flats, offering to pay them damages. One of the purchasers brought an action in the name of the company (Estmanco) asking for an injunction to prevent the GLC from carrying out its scheme. Clearly the company approved the scheme since all of the voting shares were still held by the GLC. However it was held that a voteless shareholder who had an expectancy of becoming entitled to vote at a future date was within the exception of fraud against the minority. The action was allowed to proceed and an injunction was granted in favour of the shareholder. Sir Robert Megarry VC said:

> 'No right of a shareholder to vote in his own selfish interests or to ignore the interests of the company entitles him with impunity to injure his voteless fellow shareholders by depriving the company of a cause of action and by stultifying the purpose for which the company is formed'.

4. **Personal, derivative and representative actions**

a. ***Personal actions***. Such an action can be brought when a person has been deprived of his individual rights as a shareholder, as for example in **PENDER v LUSHINGTON (1877)** (Chapter 8.9).

b. ***Derivative actions***. Where there is a dispute between the company and third parties (whether they are its directors or its controlling shareholders) and any person other than the company is allowed to appear as plaintiff on behalf of the company, then the action is called a derivative action. In such cases the right to sue is derived from the company since it is the company which has suffered as a result of the action of the majority. Where an action is successful the damages awarded belong to the company. Usually a derivative action is only appropriate where the wrongdoers have voting control and therefore prevent the company from making a claim. However in **PRUDENTIAL ASSURANCE v NEWMAN INDUSTRIES (1982)** it was held in the High Court that a derivative action could be brought against persons in actual control, regardless of the votes held by them. When the case went to appeal the company adopted the case against the defendants, so that it was no longer a derivative action. The court therefore did not need to decide whether one minority shareholder could proceed, on behalf of the company, against another despite the presence of an independent majority able to make the decision. However the Court of Appeal did not think a minority shareholder should be allowed to start proceedings on the basis of allegations which he had not yet substantiated.

c. ***Representative actions***. Where individual shareholders have suffered personal loss in addition to the injury to the company one shareholder may bring a ***representative action*** on behalf of himself and all the other shareholders who have suffered similar injury. If a representative action is successful the plaintiff will obtain a declaration that the improper conduct has been proved. Each injured party may then claim damages without further need to prove improper conduct.

d. ***Procedure***. Usually the plaintiff will combine a derivative action with a representative action, but it is also possible to combine derivative and personal actions. Although a derivative action is directed against the wrongdoers the company will be the defendant, so that any court order will be binding on it, otherwise the controlling shareholders may be able to use their control to avoid some of the consequences of a decision against them. Finally in a derivative action the court may order that the company pays the plaintiff's legal costs (even if the action is lost).

## S.459–461 UNFAIR PREJUDICE

5. Basic rule

a. By ***S.459 a member*** may petition the court for an order on the ground that the affairs of the company are being or have been conducted in a manner which is ***unfairly prejudicial*** to the interests of its members generally or some part of the members (including at least himself) or that any proposed act or omission of the company is or would be so prejudicial.

b. The defendant's conduct must be both ***unfair*** and ***prejudicial***, however the section must be construed as it stands, without reference to the section which it replaced, namely ***S.210 CA 1948***, which required it to be 'just and equitable' to grant relief. (***S.210*** was repealed in 1980).

In RE LONDON SCHOOL OF ELECTRONICS (1985) the petitioner held 25% of the shares of The London School of Electronics (the company). The remaining 75% were held by City Tutorial College (CTC), which was controlled by two other persons. A dispute arose between the petitioner and CTC because CTC appropriated for itself students who approached the company. The petitioner then set up a rival college known as the London College for Electronic Engineering (LCEE) and took with him a number of students who had enrolled with the company. The petitioner claimed that CTC's conduct was unfairly prejudicial. His action was successful. The judge rejected the defence that the petitioner did not come to the court with 'clean hands' because he had taken some of the company's students. The petitioner's conduct would only be relevant if it rendered the other sides' conduct, even if prejudicial, not unfair; or if it affected the relief that the court thought fit to grant.

The judge ordered that the majority should purchase the shares of the minority and that the price would be calculated pro rata, ie the value of the 25 % shareholding would not be discounted because it was a minority interest. The date of the petition was used to ascertain the price.

c. The reference to ***'members generally'*** was added by **CA** ***89 Sch 19.11***. This had the effect of overruling a much criticised 1987 case where it was held that failure to declare dividends would not be sufficient grounds for a petition. The judge's reasoning was that failure to declare a dividend was not directed against 'some part' of the members (as apparently previously required) since it affected all members. This narrow interpretation defeated the intention of Parliament. Shareholders with identical class rights may well have different interests as members. For example well paid shareholder directors may well be more interested in building up the capital value of their shareholding by retaining profits in the business, than adding to their taxable income by distributing profits as dividends. On the other hand shareholders who are not employed by the company, who depend upon dividends for their income, will not be so enthusiastic about a policy of deferred benefits. The addition of a reference to 'members generally' now makes it clear that failure to declare reasonable dividends may be grounds for a petition.

d. It is probably not unfair prejudice to refuse to assist a minority shareholder to realise his shareholding at the expense of capital needed to expand the company's business.

   In **RE A COMPANY (1983)** the petitioners were trustees of a trust the main asset of which was shares in the company. The trustees wished to realise the shares to maintain and educate the two beneficiaries of the trust. The other shareholders were prepared to allow an open market sale, but the trustees considered that a better price would be fetched by selling the shares within the family. None of the shareholders were willing to buy, but the company had substantial capital. The petitioner alleged unfair prejudice in that the majority would not propose either a scheme of reconstruction or a company purchase of own shares, since they planned to use the capital to start a new venture. It was held that the majority's conduct was not unfairly prejudicial.

e. Action contrary to a person's 'legitimate expectation' to take part in the long term management of a quasi-partnership company may be unfairly prejudicial.

   In **RE A COMPANY** (No. 00477 of 1986) the petitioners (directors of A Ltd) sold their shares in A Ltd to O plc, relying on promises that O plc would develop A Ltd's business and that A Ltd's managing director (S) would be a director of O plc. In fact O plc sold A Ltd's assets to support its own business. S was also replaced as managing director of A Ltd and asked to resign from the board of O plc. The petitioners were successful and obtained an order that their shares be purchased at a price equivalent to the value of their shares in A Ltd at the date of the sale.

f. If the articles lay down a procedure for dealing with a breakdown of relations and that procedure is followed, then a petition based on a breakdown of 'legitimate expectations' is unlikely to succeed.

   In **RE A COMPANY** (No. 004377 of 1986) the petitioner was the managing director of a quasi-partnership company. He held 39% of the shares, the remainder being held by T and his associates. The articles provided that if a member employee or director ceased to be an employee or a director, he must offer his shares to the other members at an agreed price, or in the absence of agreement, at a price fixed by the auditor. The petitioner was dismissed as managing director and removed from the board and the above article was invoked to obtain his shares. It was held that since there was proper machinery for dealing with the breakdown there was no reason for the court to value the shares. If the valuation is incorrect the petitioner should sue the auditor for negligence.

g. Petitions under ***S.459*** have been successful in the following situations:

   i. Where directors of a private company made incorrect statements to their shareholders regarding acceptance of an offer for their shares made by another company owned by the directors.

   ii. Where the majority made a rights issue with a view to altering the voting balance, because they knew that the minority shareholder could not afford to exercise his right to purchase.

   iii. Where the majority made a rights issue with a view to depleting the funds of a shareholder engaged in litigation with the company or with the majority shareholders.

**6.** The powers of the court

The court may make any order it thinks fit ***(S.461(1))***, although the petitioner is required to state in his petition what form of relief he seeks. Two of the cases described below (**RE HARMER (1959)** and **SCOTTISH CO-OPERATIVE WHOLESALE SOCIETY v MEYER (1959)**) were brought under ***S.210 CA 1948***. This section required a ***course of oppressive conduct*** and ***facts which would justify a winding-up*** on the 'just and equitable ground' (now ***S.122 IA***). They are included because they are both examples of what would now be classified as unfair prejudice and because they are examples of the powers of the court under ***S.461***. Without affecting the general provision in ***S.461(1)***, ***S.461(2)*** gives four examples of the types of order the court can make. It can:

a. Regulate the future conduct of the company's affairs.

   In **RE HARMER (1959)** a successful family company was controlled by Mr. H. He and his wife (who always voted with him) could control both ordinary and special resolutions at general meetings. The directors were Mr and Mrs H and their two sons. Mr H was the chairman and had a casting vote. The two sons brought the action on the ground that their father repeatedly abused his controlling power, particularly with respect to the appointment and dismissal of staff, and the opening of a branch in Australia. (This was opposed by the sons and proved to be an unsuccessful venture). Mr H was generally intolerant of views contrary to his own, whether held by his sons or other shareholders: At the time of the hearing Mr H was 89 years old.

The court granted an order under **S.210** since there had been a course of oppressive conduct and the circumstances would justify winding-up. The order removed Mr H from the board and made him 'president' of the company for life at a salary of £2,500 per year. This post gave him no rights, and imposed no duties on him. It was directed that he should not interfere with the affairs of the company except in accordance with the decisions of the board.

b. Require the company to do or refrain from doing any act. Thus the court may require the company not to make any alteration either to its memorandum or articles, or to make a specific alteration.

c. Authorise civil proceedings to be brought in the name of, and on behalf of, the company by such persons and on such terms as it directs. This is important because if the court authorise proceedings a minority shareholder can sue a director on behalf of the company even if he cannot bring his claim within one of the exceptions to the rule in Foss v Harbottle.

d. Provide for the purchase of the shares of any member by other members or by the company.

In **SCOTTISH CO-OPERATIVE WHOLESALER SOCIETY v MEYER (1959)** the petitioners were minority shareholders in a subsidiary company formed by SCWS. They held 3,900 shares and SCWS held the remaining 4,000 shares. The subsidiary had five directors, three were nominees of SCWS and the petitioners were the other two directors. Both SCWS and the subsidiary were engaged in the same type of business, the subsidiary being dependent on SCWS for its supplies. After a dispute between SCWS and the petitioners SCWS adopted a policy of deliberately ruining the subsidiary by cutting off its supplies. This was supported by the three nominee directors. At one time the subsidiary's shares were worth about £6 each, but by the time of the hearing they were almost worthless.

The action under **S.210** was successful and SCWS was ordered to buy out the two minority shareholders for £3. 15s. per share. This would have been a fair value if there had been no oppression.

In **RE BIRD PRECISION BELLOWS (1984)** the petitioners held 26% of the shares in a small 'quasi-partnership' company. They suspected that the managing director was concealing bribes paid to secure contracts. After an unsuccessful attempt to secure the appointment of DTI inspectors the petitioners were removed from the board by the votes of the managing director, his wife and one other shareholder. The petitioners alleged unfair prejudice in that they had been wrongfully excluded from the company's affairs and they sought an order that the majority purchase their shares. It was held that exclusion from participation in the affairs of a 'quasi partnership' company was unfairly prejudicial and that in such companies a fair price for the purchase of the minority's shares should be calculated on a pro rata basis, not discounted because it was a minority shareholding.

7. ***S.459* and Foss v Harbottle**

   a. The rule in Foss v Harbottle and its exceptions have created several problems, in particular

      i. The extent of the 'fraud on the minority' exception; and

      ii. The procedural problems of personal, representative and derivative actions.

   b. ***S.459–461*** has undoubtedly helped in both cases:

      i. It has the potential to supersede the concept of 'fraud on the minority' and replace it with the more flexible concept of fairness; and

      ii. It provides a simpler procedure than the common law since the court can give authority for legal proceedings in the company's name. It is likely that a dissatisfied minority shareholder would proceed in this way rather than attempt to sue under the common law rules.

   c. ***S.459–461*** provide a practical and flexible remedy. They may be used, for example, to curtail excessive directors' remuneration, or to request an order that a dividend be declared. ***S.459*** also provides a remedy for an individual member. There is no minimum percentage of shares which must be held, nor minimum number of members who must join in the action. The conduct must however be unfairly prejudicial to members in their ***capacity as members*** and not, for example in their capacity as directors, creditors or employees.

## DEPARTMENT OF TRADE INVESTIGATIONS

8. **Types of investigation**

   a. There are three basic types of investigation:

      i. Investigation of the company's affairs;

      ii. Investigation of the company's ownership; and

      iii. Investigation of share dealings.

b. In addition there are provisions for the inspection of a company's documents, and new powers under the ***FINANCIAL SERVICES ACT 1986*** to investigate suspected insider dealing offences (Chapter 20.10).

**9. Investigation on the application of the members or the company**

a. By ***S.431*** the Department of Trade may appoint inspectors:

i. Where the company has a share capital, on the application of at least 200 members, or members holding at least 10% of the issued shares;

ii. Where the company has no share capital, on the application of at least 20% of the members; and

iii. In any case, on the application of the company. (An ordinary resolution would be sufficient to authorise an application).

b. The applicants (or applicant) must produce evidence in support of their application and may be required to give up to £5,000 security for costs.

c. In the past ***S.431*** has not often been used. This is because it overlaps with ***S.432***. This section is more flexible than ***S.431*** in that anyone can ask the Department to investigate and the Department may exercise their discretion to do so if there are circumstances suggesting:

i. That the affairs of the company have been conducted with intent to defraud its creditors, or in a manner unfairly prejudicial to some part of the members, or for an unlawful or fraudulent purpose; or

ii. That the promoters or managers have been guilty of fraud or misconduct; or

iii. That proper information has not been given to the members.

Where an appointment is made under ***S.432*** there is no obligation on the Department to reveal the reasons for the appointment, nor who supplied the information leading to the appointment, nor need the Department forewarn the company.

In NORWEST HOLST v SECRETARY OF STATE FOR TRADE (1978) two inspectors were appointed under ***S.432***. In the previous two years the company had made record profits, there was no evidence to doubt its solvency and the auditor's report had not been qualified. The company sought a declaration that the appointment was invalid since it knew of none of the circumstances specified in ***S.432***. It also sought disclosure of the reasons for the appointment. The action failed because:

i. There was nothing in the Act requiring the Department to disclose its reasons; and

   ii. The investigation was not necessarily directed against the company, but against persons who might be acting wrongly towards the company and its shareholders.

d. The powers conferred by **S.432** are exercisable even if the company is in voluntary liquidation. Also the word 'member' includes persons who are not members but to whom shares have been transferred or transmitted by operation of law, for example personal representatives.

e. Application for a DTI investigation is a drastic step which dissatisfied shareholders will usually only consider after they have failed to obtain a remedy at a general meeting or through the courts. When an application is received the Department will call for the company to produce documents and records for internal examination by its staff. If the complaint is trivial or insubstantial it will go no further. An inspection will only be ordered if a strong case is made out since an appointment will attract publicity and cause damage to the company. If an inspection is ordered, two inspectors are usually appointed, normally a barrister and an accountant.

**10. Investigation by order of court**

***S.432*** also provides that the Department must appoint inspectors to investigate the company's affairs if the court order it to do so.

**11. Powers of inspectors *(S.433, 434, 436, 438* as amended by CA 89*)***

a. The 1989 Act simplified and extended inspectors' powers to obtain and require disclosure of information. The legislative changes are intended to speed up investigations and make the process more effective.

b. The inspector has extensive power to:

   i. Require production of books and documents. ***'Documents'*** is defined to include information recorded in any form ***(S.56 CA 89)***. The documents must relate to a matter which inspectors believe to be relevant to the investigation. Previously the document had to relate to the company. The change in law increases their power to obtain information since it introduces a subjective approach ie inspectors do not have to demonstrate that the information requested actually relates to the company, it is sufficient if they believe it to be relevant.

   ii. Question on oath any person, and administer the oath accordingly ***(S.36 CA 89)***.

   iii. Obtain a warrant to enter premises and search for documents (whether or not the documents had been previously requested). To obtain the warrant the inspectors must have reason to believe a serious offence has been committed and that there is a danger that the relevant documents may be removed, tampered with or destroyed unless the element of suprise is available. **S.64 CA 89 (S.448).**

iv. Take copies of any documents and require any person named in the warrant to provide an explanation of documents or state where documents may be found. **S.64 CA 89 (S.448).**

v. Investigate the affairs of related companies;

vi. Inform the Secretary of State of any matters coming to his knowledge as a result of the investigation.

c. The persons referred to under ii. above must give the inspector all assistance in the investigation that they are reasonably able to give. Refusal to comply with a request for documents or information is punishable as contempt of court. Intentional obstruction of an inspector is an offence.

## 12. The inspector's report *(S.437)*

a. The inspector presents his findings in a report to the Department. In some cases the inspector will also make interim reports. The Secretary of State has a discretionary power:

i. To send a copy of the report to the company's registered office;

ii. To provide copies to specified classes of persons, for example, members, auditors or persons referred to in the report;

iii. To publish the report, unless inspectors were appointed subject to specific terms that the report would not be published (see c. below).

b. When inspectors are appointed under a court order, the court must be sent a copy of the report.

c. By **S.55 CA 89 (S.432(2A))** inspectors may now be appointed on specific terms that the report they make will not be published ie the decision not to publish is made at the outset. This allows a full investigation to be carried out merely to decide whether grounds exist for a prosecution or some form of regulatory action.

This new provision could place the Secretary of State in a difficult position. He might for example be compelled not to publish material which, in the public interest, ought to be disclosed. Alternatively a person whose reputation has suffered as a result of the investigation may be cleared by publication of the report. Clearly such a person would feel injustice if the report could not be published.

d. By **S.57 CA 89 (S.437(1B))** the Secretary of State may curtail an investigation when it becomes clear that a criminal offence may have been committed and the matter has been referred to the appropriate prosecuting authority. In such cases inspectors need not submit a final report to the Secretary of State unless they were appointed by order of the court or unless the Secretary of State otherwise directs.

**13. Consequences of the report**

a. By *S.60 CA 89 (S.124A IA 86)* if, as a result of the report, it appears to be in the public interest that the company be wound-up the Department may present a petition that the company be wound-up because it is just and equitable to do so, ie the petition is presented under *S.517(1)(g)*. An inspector's report may also be used as evidence to support a shareholder's petition under **S.122 IA** (the 'just and equitable' ground) **RE ST PIRAN (1981)**.

b. By *S.460(1)* if it appears that there are grounds for a petition by a member under *S.459* (ie that the affairs of the company have been conducted in an unfairly prejudicial manner) the Department may, as well as or instead of petitioning to wind-up the company, present a petition for an order under *S.459*.

c. By *S.58 CA 89 (S.438)* the Secretary of State may bring civil proceedings on behalf of the company when it appears from any report made or information obtained that it is in the public interest to do so.

d. The Department may also institute criminal proceedings against persons believed to be guilty of offences.

e. It may also apply to the court for an order disqualifying a person from acting as a director *(S.8 COMPANY DIRECTORS DISQUALIFICATION ACT 1986)*.

f. By *S.61 CA 89 (S.441)* an inspector's report is admissable in legal proceedings as evidence of the opinion of the inspectors in relation to any matter contained in the report.

**14. Investigation of the ownership of a company**

a. By **S.442** (as amended by **S.62 CA 89**)

   i. The Department must investigate the ownership of shares of a company on the application of 200 shareholders or holders of 10% of the issued shares, unless it considers the application is vexatious, or unless it considers it unreasonable to investigate any matter; and

   ii. The Department may investigate share ownership if there appears to be good reason to do so.

   The Secretary of State, before appointing inspectors, may require the applicants to give up to £5,000 security for costs.

b. The inspector has the same general powers as in the investigation of the affairs of a company.

c. The provisions relating to the report are also similar, except that by *S.443(3)* if, in the opinion of the Secretary of State, there is good reason for not divulging any part of the report, he may omit that part from the inspector's report.

d. **S.68 CA 89 (S.451A)** gives the Secretary of State additional powers of disclosure. He may disclose information relating to share ownership to the following persons:

   i. The company whose ownership was subject to investigation;

   ii. Any member of that company;

   iii. Any person whose conduct was investigated;

   iv. The auditors of the company;

   v. Any person whose financial interests appear to be affected by matters covered by the investigation.

e. Powerful sanctions to support **S.442** are provided by **S.445** and **S.454–457**. In particular the Secretary of State may place restrictions on shares in any case where there is difficulty in finding out relevant facts about any shares. For example no voting rights are exercisable in respect of the shares and any agreement to transfer the shares will be void unless approved by the court or the Secretary of State, acting within defined limits. There are also provisions under which the court may order the restricted shares to be sold.

f. If the Secretary of State believes that there is good reason to investigate the ownership of a company, but that it is unnecessary to to appoint inspectors for the purpose, he may require any person whom he reasonably believes to have information to give such information to him.

**15. Investigation of share dealings**

a. By **S.323** directors are prohibited from dealing in options to buy or sell the quoted securities of their company or associated companies. By **S.324** directors of all companies are required to disclose to their companies their interest in its shares or debentures.

b. By **S.446** if the Department suspects contravention of **S.323** or **S.324** it may appoint an inspector to establish whether this is the case.

**16. Inspection of documents**

a. It has already been stated that the appointment of an inspector can attract adverse publicity for a company. In 1962 the Jenkins Committee recommended that the Department should have a further power to require the production of documents and be able to exercise this power with far less publicity. Such inspection of documents may be an end in itself or it may lead to the formal appointment of an inspector. The recommendations were implemented by the Companies Act 1967.

b. By **S.447** the Department, if it thinks there is good reason to do so, may at any time give directions to any company requiring it to produce any specified books or papers. A similar direction may be made to any person who appears to be in possession of those books or papers. Copies or extracts of them may be taken and any person in possession of them, or a past or present officer or employee of the company, may be required to provide an explanation of them. There are also:

i. Provisions enabling a search warrant to be obtained in respect of premises where the documents are believed to be **S.64 CA 89 (S.448)**.

ii. Provisions allowing the Secretary of State to authorise 'any other competent person' (probably a lawyer or an accountant) to exercise his power to require the production of documents. The competent person will then report to the Secretary of State. **S.63 CA 89 (S.447)**.

iii. Provisions preventing publication or excessive disclosure (**S.449** as amended by **S.65 CA 89**)

c. In general a person cannot be required to disclose information or produce documents if he owes an obligation of confidence by virtue of carrying on banking business. However **S.69 CA 89 (S.452)** provides three exceptions:

i. If the person to whom the obligation is owed is the company under investigation;

ii. If the person to whom the obligation is owed consents to the disclosure or production; or

iii. Disclosure is authorised by the Secretary of State.

The third exception is somwhat controversial since it provides the Secretary of State with the power to require disclosure regardless of confidentiality issues.

d. It is an offence:

i. For any officer of the company to be a party to the destruction, mutilation or falsification of any document relating to the company's property of affairs, unless he proves that he did not intend to conceal the state of affairs or defeat the law **(S.450(1))**;

ii. For any officer to fraudulently part with, alter or make an omission from any such document **(S.450(2))**; and

iii. For any person to knowingly or recklessly make a false explanation or statement in response to the directions of the Department **(S.451)**.

**17. Powers to assist overseas regulatory authorities *(S.82–87 CA 89)***

a. The increase in international transactions and corresponding increase in undesirable practices has led to the introduction of several sections designed to increase the Secretary of State's power to assist international enquiries.

b. On receipt of a request for assistance the Secretary of State may require any person:

i. To attend and answer questions (on oath if necessary) or provide relevant information;

ii. To provide specified documents;

iii. To give any other reasonable assistance in connection with the enquiries.

c. Before exercising these powers the Secretary of State must take into account the following factors:

i. Whether corresponding assistance would be given in that country to a UK regulatory authority;

ii. Whether the enquiries relate to a possible breach of law which has no parallel in the UK;

iii. The seriousness of the matter, the importance of the information sought and whether it could be obtained by any other means;

iv. Whether it is in the public interest to give such assistance;

v. Whether the overseas authority undertakes to contribute towards the cost.

d. A statement made by a person in compliance with these provisions may be used in evidence against him. The information may also be used by the Secretary of State to seek disqualification of persons who are or were directors of a company.

e. In general disclosure of information is only allowed with the consent of the person from whom the information was obtained and, if different, of the person to whom it relates. The exceptions are that information may be disclosed:

i. To any person for the purposes of criminal proceedings, civil proceedings or the disciplinary proceedings of certain professional bodies, for example solicitors and accountants;

ii. To assist certain authorities, for example the Director General of Fair Trading or the Bank of England in the exercise of their functions;

iii. To the Treasury if it is in the interests of investors or the public;

iv. If the information is available to the public from other sources;

v. In a summary of information such that the identity of the person to whom the information relates cannot be ascertained; or

vi. In pursuance of any European Community obligation.

## SUMMARY

### 18. The balance between minority rule and minority protection

The basic rule of company law is majority rule and although many functions are delegated to the directors, in theory final control rest with the majority through their control of resolutions at meetings and through 'majority rule' sections, for example **S.9** (alteration of the articles by special resolution), and **S.303** (removal of directors by ordinary resolution). The position of the majority is further strengthened by the rule in

**FOSS v HARBOTTLE**. Nevertheless a balance must be achieved between the principle of majority rule and the need for minority protection. This is particularly important in small family companies and quasi-partnerships where the directors often hold a majority of the shares. Minority shareholders are therefore protected in a number of different ways.

a. Certain company decisions require more than a simple majority.

b. There are a number of exceptions to the rule in **FOSS v HARBOTTLE**.

c. There is case law preventing a fraud on the minority, for example:-

   i. An alteration of the articles must be bona fide for the benefit of the company as a whole, (**SIDEBOTTOM v KERSHAW LEESE (1920)**), (Chapter 8.6).

   ii. An issue of shares must be for a proper corporate purpose, (**CLEMENS v CLEMENS (1976)**), (Chapter 8.6).

   iii. The majority must not expropriate the company's property, (**MENIER v HOOPER'S TELEGRAPH WORKS (1874)**), (Chapter 21.3).

d. There are a number of provisions in the Acts enabling members to initiate positive action, for example:

   i. ***S.368***, enabling members to requisition an EGM;

   ii. ***S.373***, which preserves the right of members to demand a poll;

   iii. ***S.376***, concerning members' resolutions and statements;

   iv. ***S.442***, enabling members to require the DTI to investigate the ownership of a company;

   v. ***S.122 IA***, whereby a member can petition the court to wind-up the company because it is just and equitable to do so;

   vi. ***S.459***, whereby any member can apply for a court order where the affairs of the company are being conducted in an unfairly prejudicial manner; and

   vii. ***S.27 IA***, whereby any member can apply for a court order where an administrator is managing the company in an unfairly prejudicial manner; and

   viii. ***S.214***, enabling members to require the company to investigate a person's interest in the shares of a public company.

e. There are also several provisions designed to protect individual members from action initiated by others, for example:

   i. ***S.16***, whereby a member's liability cannot be increased without his written consent;

   ii. ***S.369***, under which a member can insist on a full 21 days notice for an AGM;

iii. **S.292**, under which a member can prevent the appointment of two or more directors to the board of a public company by a single resolution;
iv. **S.49**, enabling a member to prevent the re-registration of a limited company as unlimited;
v. **S.164**, enabling any member to demand a poll when a company proposes a special resolution for an off-market purchase of its own shares;
vi. **S.176**, enabling any member to apply to the court to cancel a resolution approving a private company's purchase of its own shares out of capital. The member has five weeks to object;
vii. **S.429**, in a scheme of reconstruction or amalgamation a dissenting shareholder can in certain circumstances compel the acquisition of his shares;
viii. **S.25 IA**, which enables any member to challenge a voluntary arrangement if it is unfairly prejudicial, or if there has been an irregularity at or in relation to the meetings of the company and the creditors; and
ix. **S.16 CA 89 (S.253)** which enables any member to require the accounts of a private company to be laid before the general meeting, despite the passing of an elective resolution to dispense with the laying of accounts.

f. The Acts also provide for the protection of minority groups, for example:
i. **S.5**, concerning alteration of objects. Holders of 15% of the nominal value of the issued shares (provided they did not vote in favour of the resolution) have 21 days to object;
ii. **S.127**, 15% (calculated as in (i) above) have 21 days to object to a variation of class rights;
iii. **S.378**, which enables holders of more than 5% of the voting shares or a simple majority in number of the members to insist on a full 21 days notice for a special resolution;
iv. **S.54**, 5% (calculated as in (i) above) or not less than 50 members have 28 days to object to the re-registration of a public company as private; and
v. **S.157**, which enables holders of 10% of the voting shares to apply to the court to cancel a resolution authorising a private company to give financial assistance for the acquisition of own shares.

**PROGRESS TEST 17**

1. State **S.459 CA 1985** (Unfair prejudice).
2. State the rule in **FOSS v HARBOTTLE (1843)**.
3. What is a derivative action?
4. Summarise briefly the powers of Department of Trade inspectors.
5. Advise the minority shareholder if the controlling shareholders and directors withhold payment of all dividends with a view to reducing the personal tax liability of the controlling shareholder.

# COURSEWORK QUESTIONS 21–25
# PROTECTION OF INVESTORS AND CREDITORS

21. *Section 12 of the Companies Act 1976 (now* **S.221***) requires every company to cause accounting records to be kept.*

    *(a) What must such records show?*

    *(b) What must such records contain?*

    *(c) For what period must such records be preserved?* *(15 marks)*

    CIMA May 1980 Question 2

22. *(a) Define and describe the characteristics of a 'derivative action'. Illustrate your answer with decided cases. Is there any disadvantage to the minority shareholder in bringing a derivative action?* *(10 marks)*

    *(b) Small is a minority shareholder in Mighty PLC, a public company. He discovered that David, the managing director and majority shareholder had, in breach of his duties as a director, purchased machinery from the company at a gross undervalue. A general meeting of the company, at which David attended and voted, has just ratified the sale.*

    *Advise Small as to the possible courses of action he might take.*

    *(10 marks)*

    *(20 marks)*

    ACCA June 1983 Question 5

23. *Explain the powers of the general meeting in relation to the management of the affairs of a company, and describe the procedures which must be followed for the exercise of these powers.* *(20 marks)*

    ACCA June 1986 Question 4

24. (a) *What are the statutory qualifications necessary for holding the office of secretary to a public company? How far can a company secretary bind the company contractually?* *(10 marks)*

(b) *What procedures must be followed if the directors of a company wish to remove an auditor from office?* *(10 marks)*

*(20 marks)*

ACCA *June 1987 Question 3*

25. *What are the statutory obligations of the Department of Trade to appoint an inspector to investigate*

(a) *the affairs of a company*

(b) *the ownership of a company*

(c) *share dealings within a company?*

*What are the powers of an inspector so appointed?* *(20 marks)*

ACCA *June 1988 Question 4*

# PART VII RECONSTRUCTIONS, TAKEOVERS, LIQUIDATION, RECEIVERSHIP AND ADMINISTRATION

# 22 Reconstructions, Mergers and Takeovers

## INTRODUCTION

### 1. Large companies

The development of large companies has been assisted by the ability of individual companies to merge with and take over other companies. Therefore both the legal and self-regulatory framework for takeovers and mergers will become increasingly important in future years.

### 2. Terminology where two or more companies are involved

Several terms are used to describe the methods by which two or more companies join to form one. None of these terms have precise legal meanings. The terms are:

a. ***Merger***. This occurs when two companies join together under the name of one of them, or as a new company formed for the purpose. A merger may also be called an ***amalgamation***. Mergers generally only take place when there is agreement between the directors of both companies.

b. ***Takeover***. This term describes the acquisition by one company of sufficient shares in another company (sometimes referred to as the 'target' company) to enable the purchaser to control the target company. Sometimes takeover bids are contested by the board of the target company, and on some occasions rival bids are made for the control of the same company. A takeover differs from a merger in that both companies will remain in existence (at least for the time being). Takeovers are considered later in the chapter.

### 3. Terminology where only one company is involved

Sometimes a company will wish to reorganise in some way without involving other companies. it may wish for example:

a. To transfer its assets to a new company, the persons carrying on the business remaining substantially the same. This is usually referred to as a ***reconstruction***.

b. To make an ***arrangement*** with members and/or creditors because it is in financial difficulties, but where winding-up is not appropriate.

### 4. Methods

a. A merger, reconstruction or arrangement can be effected under ***S.425*** (schemes of arrangement).

b. A merger or reconstruction can be effected under **S.110 IA** (reconstruction by a company in voluntary liquidation). An arrangement with creditors cannot be effected under **S.110 IA**.

   In **RE TRIX (1970)** an attempt was made under the **S.110 IA** procedure to distribute the assets of a company in a way that was not strictly in accordance with creditors' rights. The attempt was unsuccessful. The court said that it was 'elementary' that in cases where it was desired to distribute the assets otherwise than in accordance with creditors' rights **S.425** must be used.

   Thus although **S.110 IA** is a much simpler and cheaper procedure than **S.425** if the rights of creditors are altered it will be necessary to use **S.425**.

c. There is no particular section under which a takeover can be effected. It will however be seen that **S.428** enables a bidder who has purchased 90% or more of the shares in the target company to 'compulsorily purchase' the remaining shares.

**5. Minority protection**

Almost all cases of merger, takeover, reconstruction and arrangement will result in a change in the position of individual members. The procedures described below therefore aim to enable the majority decision to be enforced whilst safeguarding the position of the minority.

## MERGERS AND RECONSTRUCTIONS UNDER S.110–111 IA

**6. Basic procedure**

a. The first step is to ascertain the extent of opposition to the proposal from members and creditors. If the opposition is too great the scheme may fail because the company does not have enough cash to pay dissenting members and creditors.

b. The members must then pass a ***special resolution*** giving authority to the liquidator to sell the whole or part of its business or property to another company on terms that the consideration be divided among the members of the transferor company. The consideration may be cash, but it is usually shares in the transferee company.

c. Only after the majority are sure that there will be enough cash to pay dissentients should it pass the second special resolution, ie putting the company into voluntary liquidation.

d. The effect of the scheme is that the shares in the transferee company then become the assets of the transferor company and must be distributed to its members in accordance with their rights on liquidation.

The transferor company is then dissolved, its shareholders having become shareholders in the transferee company.

7. **Dissentient shareholders**

   a. A dissentient shareholder is one who did not vote for the special resolution. He can require the liquidator to abstain from the sale or buy his shares. The right must be exercised by a written notice addressed to the liquidator and deposited at the registered office within seven days of the resolution.

   b. If the parties cannot agree on a price the matter will be referred to arbitration. The price is likely to be based on the value before reconstruction was proposed rather than after.

8. **Dissentient creditors**

   a. The creditors are not as directly affected by a reconstruction as the members. They have their usual rights on liquidation, although the funds from which they will be paid have changed. (A variation of rights as opposed to a change of funds would require the use of **S.425**). There is no legal obligation for the transfer agreement to provide for creditors, but in practice it will usually provide either:

      i. That the transferee company takes over the debts of the transferor; or

      ii. That the transferor company retains sufficient funds to pay its debts.

   b. If the creditors feel that their position is jeopardised in that the new assets received by the transferor company will not be sufficient to pay their debts they can petition for the compulsory winding-up of the transferor company on the ground that it is unable to pay its debts. If the petition is successful the winding-up is then managed by the court rather than the shareholders. If a compulsory winding-up order is made within a year after the special resolution to reconstruct, the resolution is invalid unless approved by the court.

9. **Reconstruction under a power in the memorandum**

   A company may have a power in its memorandum to do what it could do under ***S.110 IA***. The memorandum cannot however purport to give the liquidator wider powers than he would have under ***S.110 IA***, thus the provisions of the section for the protection of dissentient members and creditors still apply.

10. **Uses of *S.110 IA***

    ***S.110 IA*** may be used:

    a. ***For a reconstruction***, ie Company A transfers its assets to a new company, Company B, formed for the purpose, receiving in return shares in Company B. Companies may wish to reconstruct for several reasons, for example:

i. The reconstruction will enable the transferee company to retain and realise cash assets, paying them to its members on liquidation.

ii. It may be able to raise new capital by issuing the shares in the new company as partly paid-up.

iii. To alter the objects where there has been a successful objection by a dissentient minority.

b. ***For a merger***. There are two types of merger:

i. Company A goes into voluntary liquidation, selling its assets to Company B (an established and successful company). In return the shareholders of Company A receive shares in Company B. Company A is then dissolved and the business of both companies is carried on by Company B. This is, in effect, a takeover by agreement.

ii. Companies A and B both go into voluntary liquidation. The assets of both companies are then transferred to Company C, a new company formed for the purpose, the members of A and B receiving shares in Company C. Companies A and B are then dissolved. In order to retain their goodwill Company C may change its name to A B Ltd.

## SCHEMES OF ARRANGEMENT UNDER S.425–427

### 11. Uses of *S.425*

a. ***S.425*** can be used to effect any type of ***compromise*** or ***arrangement*** with creditors or members, for example changing their rights in or against the company, or transferring their rights to another company which then issues shares or takes over liabilities in return for cancellation of existing rights against the first company, ie it can be used for both reconstructions and mergers. There must however be a 'compromise' or an 'arrangement':

i. A ***compromise*** can only be made when there has previously been a dispute.

ii. An ***arrangement*** has a much wider meaning and does not depend on the presence of a dispute.

b. A scheme which deprives members of their rights without compensation is neither a compromise nor an arrangement.

In RE NATIONAL FARMERS' UNION DEVELOPMENT TRUST (1972) over 85% of the members voted in favour of a scheme whereby members' rights were surrendered without compensation. It was held that the scheme was neither a compromise nor an arrangement since both words implied a measure of 'give and take' from both sides.

## 12. Procedure under S.425

a. The first step is for the company, or any creditor, or any member or, if the company is being wound up, the liquidator, to ask the court to convene a meeting of creditors and meetings of each class of members. The definition of a 'class' of members may not be a simple task, since what is apparently one class of shares may contain groups with different interests. Such groups must be treated as separate 'classes'.

In **RE HELLENIC AND GENERAL TRUST (1976)** S was a wholly owned subsidiary of H (Hambros Ltd). S held over 50% of the shares in HGT. A scheme was proposed whereby H would acquire all of the shares in HGT. The proposal was put to the shareholders of HGT and over 80% of them (including the 50%+ held by S) voted for the scheme. A minority shareholder opposed the scheme because he would incur a heavy tax burden as a result of receiving cash in return for his shares. The court held that the shares in HGT held by S must be regarded as constituting a separate 'class' for the purpose of **S.425** despite the fact that the shares were in reality all of the same class. Since all 'classes' had to approve the scheme, the scheme was not sanctioned by the court, because a majority of the shareholders of HGT (excluding shares held by S) did not approve the scheme.

b. By **S.426** the company must send out with the notice of any meeting called under **S.425** a statement explaining the effect of the scheme and in particular details of material interests of directors and its effect on them.

c. The compromise or arrangement must be agreed at each meeting by a ***simple majority in number*** representing **75%** ***in value*** of those voting in person or by proxy.

d. When the necessary meetings have been held and the required majorities obtained ***the court must give its approval***.

## 13. The role of the court

a. It will ensure that the scheme is not ultra vires or an improper use of **S.425** (for example to reduce capital to which **S.135** should apply).

b. It will check that the meetings were properly convened and that the required majority approval was obtained.

c. Since the requirement is only for a majority of members voting rather than of all the members, the court will examine whether the class was fairly represented at the meeting. Probably the court will have already directed that a substantial percentage of the class constitute a quorum when the initial application was made to the court to hold the meetings.

d. The court will be very careful if the majority of one class of shares also hold the shares of another class since they may vote in favour of a scheme which harms the first class of shares but benefits the second class.

e. The court will look at situations where creditors are also shareholders since a similar conflict of interest could arise.

f. In general the court will require disclosure of all relevant information, listen to any minority objections and finally only sanction the scheme if it is one that an honest and intelligent businessman would approve. Once the court has approved the scheme it binds all parties and cannot be altered.

g. By **S.427** where the court is asked to sanction a **S.425** arrangement in connection with a reconstruction or amalgamation involving the transfer of the whole or part of the undertaking or property of a company to another company, the court, to facilitate the reconstruction or amalgamation, can order:

   i. The transfer of the whole or part of the undertaking, property or liabilities of the transferor company to the transferee company;

   ii. The allotment of shares or debentures in the transferee company to appropriate persons;

   iii. The dissolution of a transferor company without a winding-up;

   iv. A provision to be made for the protection of dissentients. (A dissentient member is usually given the rights which he would have had under **S.110–111 IA**).

## VOLUNTARY ARRANGEMENTS UNDER S.1–7 INSOLVENCY ACT

### 14. Introduction

a. The Insolvency Act 1985 introduced new procedures to provide an alternative to **S.425 CA 1985**. The procedures apply to any 'composition in satisfaction of debts' (ie all creditors agree to take a proportion of what is owed to them) or to a scheme of arrangement of the company's affairs. In this part of the book 'scheme' will be used to cover both situations. The purpose of the rules is to enable a scheme to be effected with minimal involvement by the court.

b. If a bid is not contested the transaction is called a merger. **S.110 IA** may be used if creditors' rights are not affected, but **S.425** although a more time-consuming and expensive procedure (the court being involved) is more flexible and is usually used.

c. If only one company is involved and it is transferring its assets to a new company with substantially the same members, the transaction is called a reconstruction. **S.110 IA** or **S.425** may be used, depending on whether or not creditors' rights are affected.

**15. Meetings of the company and creditors**

a. The nominee will need to summon meetings of the company and creditors to decide whether to approve the proposal.

b. If the nominee is the liquidator or administrator he may summon meetings of the company and its creditors at the time, date and place he thinks fit.

c. If the nominee is not the liquidator or administrator he must submit a report to the court, stating whether in his opinion meetings of the company and creditors need to be summoned. This report must be submitted within 28 days after he is given notice of the proposal. Notice of the creditors meeting must be sent to every creditor whose claim and address are known. To enable the nominee to prepare the report the person who proposed the scheme must give him written details of the scheme and a statement of the company's affairs.

d. The meetings may approve the scheme as it stands, or subject to slight modifications. However they cannot approve any scheme that affects the priority of any secured or preferential creditors, but the modifications may include the replacement of the nominee by another qualified insolvency practitioner.

e. The result of the meetings must be reported by the chairman to the court and to such other persons who may be specified in the delegated legislation.

f. If the scheme is approved and at the time the company is being wound-up or is subject to an administration order, the court may stay all proceedings in the winding-up or discharge the administration order, or give directions that assist the implementation of the scheme. However the court may not stay winding-up or discharge the administration order before the end of 28 days after the chairman's reports on the results of the meetings has been made to the court, nor can it do so when an application to challenge the decision has been made.

**16. Challenge of decisions**

a. Within 28 days of the chairman's reports to the court an application to challenge the decision may be made by:

   i. A person entitled to vote at either the company meeting or the creditors' meeting;

   ii. The nominee or any person who has replaced him;

   iii. The liquidator or administrator (if the company is being wound up or if it is subject to an administration order).

b. The challenge may be on the grounds that:-

   i. The scheme approved at the meetings is unfairly prejudicial to the interests of a creditor, member or contributory of the company; and/or

ii. There has been a material irregularity at or in relation to either of the meetings.

c. If the court is satisfied that there is a valid challenge on ground b.i. above it may revoke or suspend approval of the scheme, or direct any person to summon further meetings to consider a revised scheme from the original proposer. If the challenge is based on material irregularity (b.ii above) the court may revoke or suspend the approval given by the meeting and may direct that the meeting be re-convened to re-consider the original scheme.

**17. Implementation**

a. If the proposal is approved without challenge, the person who implements the scheme will be known as the supervisor. He will act under the supervision of the court and he may apply to the court for directions. He may also apply to the court to have the company wound up or made subject to an administration order.

b. If a creditor or any other person is dissatisfied with an act, omission or decision of the supervisor he can apply to the court and the court may confirm, modify or reverse the act or decision. It may also give any directions or make such other order as it thinks fit.

c. The court also has the power to appoint a supervisor, either to fill a vacancy, or in addition to an existing supervisor.

## TAKEOVERS

**18. Reasons for takeovers**

The term takeover is usually used to describe a contested bid for the shares in one company (the 'target' company) by another company. Takeovers have become very common in recent years. They have also been the subject of increasing concern, because in some cases the interests of investors in general have suffered as directors and controlling shareholders have sought to further their own personal interests. Takeovers are not however undesirable as such. It may well be that larger size brings economies of scale and better management. Takeovers often take place for one of two reasons:

a. The target company may have been badly managed so that the market price of the controlling shares has fallen to less than the potential value of the company's assets. Thus even if the offeror pays slightly more than market value for the shares it will still obtain control of the assets for less than their true value.

b. A well managed and successful company may be sufficiently attractive to a larger company that the larger company is prepared to pay the true value for its shares to secure control of its assets.

**19. Basic procedure**

The bidding company will offer to purchase all the shares in the target company either for cash or in return for its own shares. Usually the offer will be conditional on acceptance in respect of a certain percentage of the shares.

**20. Legal controls**

Apart from the above regulations there are the following legal controls relating to takeovers:

a. ***S.314–315*** which concern compensation for loss of office paid to a director of the target company, (see Chapter 15.18).

b. ***S.428–430F*** (see 21. below).

c. The ***COMPANY SECURITIES (INSIDER DEALING) ACT 1985***.

d. ***S.151–158*** which prohibit a company from giving financial assistance for the purchase of its own shares. If it could give such assistance it may well do so to assist a 'friendly' third party to out-bid the bidding company.

e. The ***fiduciary duties*** of directors are very relevant when there is a takeover bid. There may be potential to make a secret profit, or there may be a temptation to issue new shares in an attempt to defeat the bid and retain control, as for example in HOGG v CRAMFHORN (1967), (see Chapter 15.33).

**21. The position of a dissenting minority in the target company *(S.428–430F)***

a. ***S.428–430F CA 1985*** were inserted by ***S.172*** and ***SCHEDULE 12 FINANCIAL SERVICES ACT 1986***. The FSA repealed the original ***S.428–430***.

b. In some cases the dissenting minority will not wish to sell their shares even at market value. This could be inconvenient for the offeror which may wish to acquire a wholly owned subsidiary. In such a situation the Act provides for the offeror to 'buy out' the dissenting minority of the target company.

c. The sections can only be used when there is a ***'takeover offer'***. This is defined as an offer to acquire all the shares (or all of a class of shares) of a company on the same terms, except for those already held by the offeror or his associates (see e. below).

d. By ***S.428*** if within ***four months*** the offer is accepted by holders of not less than ***nine-tenths*** in value of the shares to which the offer relates, the offeror may buy the shares of any dissenting shareholder in the target company by giving him notice within ***two months*** after the end of the four month period, unless the court orders otherwise, (see h. below).

e. When calculating the ***'shares to which the offer relates'***, the following are not counted:

   i. Shares already owned by the offeror.

   ii. Shares which the offeror has contracted to buy at the date of the offer.

   iii. Shares already owned by or contracted to an associate of the offeror. 'Associate' includes nominees, members of the same group of companies and companies controlled by the offeror.

   It is therefore 90% of the remaining shares that will have to be acquired. These may be acquired either as a result of the offer or by market purchase, provided the price paid is less than the offer price, or the offer price is revised upwards to the price paid.

f. A dissenting shareholder is one who did not accept the offer, positive dissent is not required.

g. If the offeror wishes to take advantage of **S.428** it must offer the minority the same terms as the majority have already accepted.

   In **RE CARLTON HOLDINGS (1971)** an offer was made which gave the shareholders a choice between an exchange of shares and cash, (in the form of an option to sell the new shares to the offeror's merchant bank). The petitioner did not receive the offer in time to act on it. Having obtained over 90% acceptances the offeror sought to buy the petitioner's shares on the exchange basis without any cash alternative. It was held that he was entitled to the cash alternative since a dissenting shareholder should receive no less favourable treatment than an accepting shareholder.

h. Once a shareholder has received a notice to purchase his shares he may apply to the court within ***six weeks*** for an order

   i. Preventing the compulsory acquisition; or

   ii. Specifying different acquisition terms.

   Such an application freezes the acquisition process until the application has been dealt with. No order for costs may be made against an applicant unless the application was improper or vexatious.

   The court will grant an order if the acquisition is unfair, for example if *S.428* is being used as a means of expropriating the minority interest when there is no genuine takeover:

   In **RE BUGLE PRESS (1961)** persons holding 90% of the shares in a company formed a new company. The new company then made an offer for the shares of the old company. Clearly the 90% accepted the offer and the new company then served a notice on the 10% shareholder in the old company stating that they wished to purchase his shares. He opposed the scheme on the ground that it amounted to an expropriation of his interest in that the shareholders of the new company were the persons who held 90% of the shares in the old company. His claim succeeded. This is a good example of the court lifting the veil of incorporation of the companies and basing its decision on the actual identity of the members concerned.

i. **S.430** gives a right to the dissenting minority whereby they can change their minds and accept the offer when it becomes clear that the offeror has a substantial majority. It applies when the shares transferred under the scheme plus those already held by the offeror amount to 90% in value of the shares or class of shares in the target company. The offeror must then give notice of this fact to the remaining shareholders within one month, whereupon any remaining shareholder can, within three months, require the offeror to buy his shares.

**22. The City Code on Takeovers and Mergers. Introduction**

a. The first informal city guidelines on the conduct of takeovers were published in 1959. They were not very successful and 1968 the City Code on Takeovers and Mergers was published. It has since been revised, the current edition being published in 1988. The Code was suggested by the Stock Exchange and the Bank of England and was prepared by the Executive Committee of the Issuing Houses Association in co-operation with other organisations, for example the Committee of London Clearing Bankers. The Code does not have the force of law, but it must be complied with by listed companies if they are to conform to Stock Exchange regulations.

b. The operation of the Code is supervised by the ***Panel on Takeovers and Mergers***. The Panel is available for consultation at any time before or during a takeover or merger. It is not however concerned with the merits of the bid itself, this must be decided by the company and its shareholders. Occasionally the Panel has intervened in a takeover, for example by asking a party to pursue a particular course of action, or by investigating the conduct of an individual.

c. If the Panel discovers a breach of the Code and proposes to take disciplinary action an appeal may be made to an ***Appeals Committee*** chaired by a member of the House of Lords.

**23. The City Code. Contents**

a. The 1988 edition contains:

   i. An Introduction;

   ii. 10 General Principles;

   iii. 38 Rules; and

   iv. Practice Notes

b. The ***Introduction*** sets out the constitution of the Panel, the nature and purpose of the Code and the companies and transactions subject to it. In particular if makes it clear that the boards of the companies involved and their advisors have a primary duty to act in the best interests of their respective shareholders. It also requires persons engaged in takeovers to be aware of and observe the spirit as well as the precise words of the code.

c. The ***General Principles*** are mainly concerned with the provision of information to shareholders and the responsibilities of the directors of both the bidding and target companies. They cover, for example:
   i. Commitment to the interests of the shareholders, in particular the final decision shall be left to the shareholders.
   ii. Directors and controlling shareholders must sub-ordinate their own interests to the interests of all the shareholders.
   iii. All shareholders must be treated equally.
   iv. Documents addressed to shareholders, especially profit forecasts, must be prepared to the same standards as a prospectus.

d. The ***Rules*** contain detailed provisions concerning conduct during takeovers. For example:
   i. As soon as the intention to make an offer is disclosed to the board of the target company the board must make an announcement to the shareholders.
   ii. On receipt of an offer the board of the target company must seek competent independent advice.
   iii. If a person (or persons acting together) acquire more than 30% of a company's shares, that person must make an offer for the rest of the shares, the offer being in cash or having a cash alternative.
   iv. If the bidder purchases shares in the 12 months before the bid, the price at which he makes the offer must not be less than the highest price he paid for shares acquired in the previous 12 month period.
   v. Shareholders in the target company must be given at least 21 days to accept the bid. If the offer is conditional on a minimum level of acceptance (eg 90%) when that level is achieved the offer becomes unconditional and the time limit for acceptance must be extended for at least 14 days.

e. The ***Practice Notes*** are rulings on specific matters usually based on decided cases. Prior to 1985 they were contained in a separate booklet, but now they are set out immediately after the Rule to which they apply.

# Conclusions

## 24. Choice of method

The following factors will influence whether the transaction is a takeover or merger and which method is to be used.

a. If a bid for a company is contested by that company the transaction is a takeover. The usual procedure is to get 90% acceptance, and then to acquire the shares of the non-accepting minority by serving a notice under **S.428**. This section applies to all companies. In contrast the City Code can only be 'enforced' against quoted public companies, but it contains a recommendation that it be observed by other types of company.

b. If a bid is not contested the transaction is called a merger. **S.110 IA** may be used if creditors' rights are not affected, but **S.425** although a more time-consuming and expensive procedure, (the court being involved) is more flexible and is usually used.

c. If only one company is involved, and it is transferring its assets to a new company with substantially the same members the transaction is called a reconstruction. **S.110 IA** or **S.425** may be used, depending on whether or not creditors' rights are affected.

d. *Taxation*. Sometimes the choice of method will be dictated by circumstances. When a'free' choice is available the most significant factor will be tax and stamp duty considerations, the companies' professional advisors taking great care to ensure that the scheme is as advantageous as possible. Occasionally tax considerations may provide the motive for a takeover, for example if a 'tax loss' company can be taken over and its loss set off against the profit of the acquiring company, however in practice the opportunity for such savings is very restricted.

**25. Self regulation or statutory control?**

The present system is a combination of self regulation and statutory control.

a. The provisions of **S.425** and **S.110 IA** are rather unsatisfactory in that they provide different methods (with different minority safeguards) of achieving similar types of straightforward mergers. Statutory control is also exercised via the provisions referred to in 16. above, and through the Monopolies Commission and the Office of Fair Trading.

b. Until the de-regulation of the Stock Exchange in 1986 the City Code and Panel were reasonably successful. The problem they face is that self regulation needs to be sufficiently flexible and general to adapt to changing circumstances and cover the many different problems and abuses which may arise in takeovers and mergers. This generality has however made it difficult to predict whether or not a particular action is in breach of the Code. However if a person is in doubt he should obtain a ruling from the Panel executive. The new Code warns that taking legal or other professional advice on matters of interpretation is not an appropriate alternative to such a ruling.

c. Recent studies revealing rapid rises in target companies' shares in the weeks prior to takeover bids have led to increased pressure for statutory controls that would bring the UK into line with other financial markets.

### *PROGRESS TEST 18*

1. What types of resolution are needed to:
   (a) Authorise a reconstruction
   (b) Commence voluntary liquidation
   (c) Commence compulsory liquidation?
2. Explain the rights of shareholders who oppose a reconstruction.
3. Explain briefly the purpose of 'voluntary arrangements'. Briefly describe the procedure.
4. Describe the stages by which a successful takeover bidder acquires all the shares in a target company.
5. As a condition of granting a loan to a company, the lender may require that one or more of his nominees be appointed as directors of the borrowing company, in order to protect the lender's interests. To what extent (if at all) is this arrangement inconsistent with the rules governing directors' duties.

# 23 Liquidations

## INTRODUCTION

### 1. Definition

a. Liquidation is the process by which the life of a company is brought to an end and its property administered for the benefit of its members and creditors.

b. Liquidation or winding-up (the two terms mean the same) begins either by court order (compulsory liquidation) or by the members passing a resolution to wind-up (voluntary liquidation).

c. This chapter starts with a description of insolvency practitioners, but it must be emphasised that although most voluntary and compulsory liquidations occur because a company cannot pay its debts, companies may be liquidated for reasons other than insolvency, for example a dissatisfied minority shareholder may petition to wind up a company because he objects to the way in which the majority are running the company and he wants to recover his share of the assets.

d. The provisions in this chapter do not necessarily apply to the insolvency of a member. of a Recognised Investment Exchange or a Recognised Clearing House. The Companies Act 1989 has introduced major changes where the insolvent company operates in a financial market. The purpose of this is to minimise the serious disruptive effects that such insolvencies have on financial markets. Broadly speaking the Act gives the bodies controlling financial markets the primary responsibility for administering the insolvency of their members. It also seeks to safeguard the performance of market contracts. The detailed rules are beyond the scope of this book.

e. Throughout this chapter the sections referred to are sections of the *INSOLVENCY ACT 1986*.

## INSOLVENCY PRACTITIONERS

### 2. Introduction

One of the major reforms in the Insolvency Act 1985 was the introduction of minimum qualifications for insolvency practitioners. Prior to the Act neither liquidators nor receivers had to have any professional qualifications or practical experience. This no doubt contributed to some illegal and highly unethical practices by a minority of liquidators, usually to the detriment of creditors.

**3. Definition**

By *S.388 IA* an insolvency practitioner is an individual who acts as:

a. Liquidator;

b. Administrator;

c. Administrative receiver, or

d. Supervisor of a voluntary arrangement under the Act.

Although the Act refers to 'insolvency practitioners' it is clear that all liquidators must be qualified, even if the company is not insolvent.

**4. Qualifications of insolvency practitioners *(S.390 IA)***

a. An individual will only be able to act as an insolvency practitioner if he is authorised to do so by:

   i. A recognised professional body; or

   ii. The 'relevant authority', to be set up by the Secretary of State.

b. In addition there must be some security in force at the time the individual acts.

c. The official receiver can act as an insolvency practitioner without satisfying the above requirements. Official receivers are civil servants who deal with the administration of compulsory liquidation and personal bankruptcies.

d. It is an offence to act as an insolvency practitioner when not qualified.

**5. Authorisation of members of recognised professional bodies *(S.390–391 IA)***

Professional bodies have to incorporate into their rules provisions to ensure that such of their members who are permitted by its rules to act as insolvency practitioners are fit and proper persons so to act, and meet acceptable requirements as to education, practical training and experience. Professional bodies will be granted recognition by the Secretary of State and such recognition may be revoked if it appears to the Secretary of State that the body no longer satisfies the specified criteria.

**6. Authorisation by the relevant authority *(S.392–397 IA)***

An individual who is not a member of a recognised professional body may apply to the 'relevant authority' for authority to act as an insolvency practitioner. The application will be granted if the relevant authority is satisfied that he is a fit and proper person with the prescribed education, practical training and experience. The authority has the power to withdraw authorisation in certain circumstances. The authority must inform an individual of its reasons if it refuses or revokes authorisation. It must also give him a statement of his rights. These include a right to make written representations to the authority, and a right to refer his case to the newly created Insolvency Practitioners Tribunal.

**7. Disqualification *(S.390 IA)***

The following cannot act as an insolvency practitioner:

a. An undischarged bankrupt.

b. A person subject to a disqualification order either under the Insolvency Act or the Companies Act.

c. A person who is a 'patient' within the meaning of the Mental Health Act 1983.

## COMPULSORY LIQUIDATION

**8. Grounds**

By ***S.122 IA*** there are seven grounds on which a company may be wound up by the court, although only two (f. and g. below) are of any importance:

a. The company has resolved by special resolution to be wound up by the court;

b. It has been formed as a public company but has not been issued with a certificate of compliance with the minimum share capital requirements;

c. Where an old public company has failed to re-register by 22nd March 1982, or a company incorporated as a public company has failed within one year to obtain a trading certificate;

d. It has not commenced business within a year of incorporation or has suspended business for a year;

e. The number of members has fallen below the statutory minimum of two;

f. The company is unable to pay its debts; and

g. The court is of the opinion that it is just and equitable that the company should be wound up.

**9. Inability to pay its debts *(S.123 IA)***

a. A company is ***deemed*** to be unable to pay its debts if:-

   i. A creditor for more than £750 has served on the company a written demand for payment and within the next three weeks the company has neither paid the debt nor given security for its payment; ***or***

   ii. Judgement has been obtained against the company for a debt (normally in excess of £750) and execution, ie payment out of the company's assets is unsatisfied; ***or***

   iii. The court is satisfied, that the company is unable to pay its debts as they fall due.

iv. The court is satisfied that the value of the company's assets is less than the amount of its liabilities, taking into account its contingent and prospective liabilities.

b. The petition will of course be presented by a creditor. The company and creditors other than the petitioner are also entitled to be heard. If some creditors oppose the petition because they feel that the continued existence of the company is their best chance of payment, the court is likely to prefer the views of the creditors to whom in aggregate the largest amount is owing.

**10. The just and equitable ground**

a. The just and equitable ground need not be construed together with the other six grounds. The court has an unfettered discretion and can make the order whenever the circumstances of justice or equity so demand. For example:

i. When the ***substratum*** of the company has gone, ie the main purpose for which the company was formed has been fulfilled or has become incapable of achievement.

In RE BLERIOT AIRCRAFT CO (1916) a company was formed to acquire the English part of an aircraft business owned by the well known French airman M. Bleriot. M. Bleriot however refused to agree to the acquisition. It was held that the company be wound up because its main object had failed.

ii. When there is ***deadlock*** in the management of the business because the directors cannot agree on vital matters or become personally antagonistic.

In RE YENIDJE TOBACCO CO (1916) the company had two shareholders who were both directors. Although the company was successful the directors failed to agree on many important matters, for example the appointment of senior employees. They would not speak to each other and all communication was via the company secretary. It was held that winding-up was justified.

iii. Where the company is in substance a partnership and there are grounds for dissolving a partnership, for example the basis of mutual trust and confidence has been broken.

In RE WESTBOURNE GALLERIES (1973) E and N had been business partners since 1945, taking an equal share in management and profit. In 1958 a private company was formed, E and N each holding one half of the shares, (500 shares each).They were also the company's directors. Later it was agreed to admit N's son, G, to the business. E and N each transferred 100 shares to him and he was appointed a director. The company made good profits, but no dividends were paid, all the profit being distributed as directors' remuneration. Following a disagreement between E and N a general meeting was called and N and G removed E as a director and excluded him from management. E petitioned for an order that the company be wound up on the 'just and equitable' ground. It was held that the company must be wound up because when E and N formed the company it was clear that the basic nature of their personal business relationship would remain the same. Therefore N and G were not entitled, in equity, to use their statutory power to remove a director.

In **RE ZINOTTY PROPERTIES (1985)** a company was formed for the acquisition and development of a particular site. The petitioner held 25% of the shares, the respondent the other 75%. The development was completed and the company had cash available for distribution, but no distribution took place. The petitioner alleged that the majority shareholder had used the money for his own business purposes, without even consulting the petitioner. It was held, following **RE WESTBOURNE GALLERIES**, that the mutual trust that had formerly existed between the shareholders had broken down to such an extent that the court would order winding-up on the 'just and equitable' ground.

iv. Where there is justifiable lack of confidence in the management.

In **LOCH v JOHN BLACKWOOD (1924)** the directors failed to call meetings, submit accounts or recommend a dividend. The reason was to keep the petitioners ignorant as to the value of the company, so that the directors could acquire their shares at an undervaluation. Winding-up was ordered.

b. An order will not be granted merely because the directors have exceeded their powers, or because they have refused to register a transfer, where a right of refusal exists under the articles.

**11. The petition**

a. Proceedings are commenced by the presentation of a petition by a person qualified to do so on one of the above grounds.

b. The petition should be presented in the High Court, or if the paid-up capital does not exceed £120,000 in the County Court of the district where the registered office of the company is situated. ***(S.117 IA)***.

**12. Petitioners *(S.124 IA)***

A petition may be presented by:

a. ***The company or its directors***. This would be very unusual.

b. ***Any creditor or creditors***.

i. Creditors are by far the most common petitioners.

ii. If a petition of an unsecured creditor is opposed by the majority in value of the unsecured creditors the court has a discretion to refuse an order. The fact that the majority oppose is not conclusive, but if they oppose for good reason (for example because the assets exceed the liabilities and there are prospects that the business can be continued) their wishes will prevail unless special circumstances render winding up desirable.

iii. A person whose debt is disputed by the company on substantial grounds is not a 'creditor' for this purpose.

c. ***A contributory***. A contributory is any person liable to contribute to the assets of a company in the event of a winding up. This includes present and certain past members (see 37 below). The term 'contributory' is rather misleading since it implies that a member whose shares are fully paid would not be entitled to petition. However such a shareholder can petition, but the court will not grant an order if the company is insolvent since he would have nothing to gain from the liquidation. A contributory must have been a member for at least 6 out of the 18 months prior to his petition, unless he acquired his shares by allotment direct from the company, or by inheritance from a deceased member, or if the petition is because the number of members is less than two.

d. ***The Official Receiver***, where the company is already in voluntary liquidation.

e. ***The Secretary of State***, usually only as a result of an investigation under ***S.431*** or ***S.432***.

f. ***The Attorney-General***, when the company is registered as a charity.

**13. Effects of a compulsory winding-up order**

a. The Official Receiver becomes the liquidator and continues in office until another person becomes liquidator ***(S.136–137 IA)***. (He does not become 'provisional liquidator' as previously. The office of ***provisional liquidator*** still exists, but only applies to a person appointed by the court to protect the assets of a company after the petition has been presented but before the winding-up order is made ***(S.135 IA)***.)

b. The liquidation is deemed to have commenced at the date when the petition was presented. If a voluntary liquidation is already in progress the compulsory liquidation is deemed to commence on the date of the resolution for voluntary liquidation ***(S.129 IA)***.

c. Any disposition of the company's property, transfer of shares or alteration in the status of members is void unless the court orders otherwise ***(S.127 IA)***.

d. No action can be commenced or proceeded with against the company without leave of the court ***(S.130 IA)***, and any seizure of the company's assets to satisfy a debt after the start of winding-up is void ***(S.128 IA)***.

e. The directors' powers cease and are assumed by the liquidator. Most of their duties also cease, one exception is the duty not to disclose confidential information, which continues after the winding-up order.

f. The company's employees are automatically dismissed, but they may sue for damages for breach of contract. The liquidator may of course re-employ the employees for the time being.

g. Floating charges crystallise, and there is a possibility that other charges and transactions may be invalidated.

h. The assets remain the legal property of the company, unless the court makes an order vesting them in the liquidator. The business may continue but only with a view to its most beneficial realisation.

14. Proceedings after a winding-up order

a. A copy of the winding-up order must immediately be sent by the company to the registrar, who must publish notice of its receipt in the Gazette.

b. The official receiver may require a ***statement of affairs (S.131 IA)***. This would normally be submitted by the directors and/or the secretary, but may be required from, for example, company employees. Persons required to submit a statement of affairs must do so within 21 days of the date when they were asked, unless the period is extended by the official receiver. It must contain:

   i. Particulars of assets, debts and liabilities;

   ii. Names and addresses of creditors;

   iii. Details of security held by creditors and the date when given;

   iv. Any further information which may be prescribed or which the official receiver may require.

   If the official receiver refuses to exercise the power conferred by this section the court may exercise it. It is a criminal offence to fail to comply with an obligation imposed by ***S.131 IA***.

c. By ***S.132 IA*** it is the duty of the official receiver to investigate:

   i. The causes of failure (if the company has failed); and

   ii. The promotion, formation, business, dealings and affairs of the company.

   He must make such report (if any) to the court as he thinks fit. The report is prima facie evidence in any legal proceedings of the facts stated therein.

d. ***Public examination***. By ***S.133–134 IA*** the liquidator may apply to the court at any time for the public examination of any person who has been an officer of the company. He must make an application if required to do so by one half in value of the creditors or three-quarters in value of the contributories.

e. By ***S.136–137 IA*** within 12 weeks of the winding-up order the official receiver must decide whether to summon meetings of creditors and contributories. If he decides not to do so he must inform the court, the creditors and the contributories. However he must summon meetings of both creditors and contributories if required to do so by one quarter in value of the creditors.

By *S.139 IA* purpose of the meetings is to choose a liquidator. If each meeting nominates a different person, the creditors' nominee shall be the liquidator, but any creditor or contributory may, within 7 days, apply to the court for some other person (including the contributories' nominee) to be appointed, either instead of, or in addition to the creditors' nominee.

If the meetings do not appoint a liquidator the official receiver must decide whether to refer the need for an appointment to the Secretary of State, who may make an appointment, or decline to make one, in which case the official receiver will continue as liquidator. If a vacancy occurs in the office of liquidator, it is filled by the official receiver.

**15. General functions of the liquidator *(S.135, 143 IA)***

a. He must ensure that the company's assets are got in, realised and distributed to the company's creditors and, if there is a surplus, to the persons entitled to it.

b. If the liquidator is not the official receiver he must:

   i. Furnish the official receiver with such information as he may reasonably require;

   ii. Produce and permit inspection of, books papers and other records;

   iii. Give such other assistance as the official receiver reasonably requires.

**16. The committee of creditors *(S.141 IA)***

a. This was formerly known as the committee of inspection, but the sections in the Companies Act dealing with the committee of inspection in compulsory winding-up *(S.546–548)* have been repealed. The new rules are substantially different.

b. ***Appointment***. The committee may be appointed by one of two methods:

   i. The meetings of creditors and contributories summoned to choose a liquidator may also choose a committee of creditors.

   ii. The liquidator (provided he is not the official receiver) can call general meetings of the company's creditors and contributories to decide whether there should be a committee and if so, who should be its members. The liquidator must call these meetings if required to do so by one tenth in value of the company's creditors. If the meetings do not agree on whether a committee should be appointed then a committee must be established, unless the court orders otherwise.

c. ***Composition and functions***. This is similar to the old committee of inspection, ie creditors and contributories in such proportions as are agreed by the meetings of creditors and contributories, or in the absence of agreement, as decided by the court.

Its functions is to act with the liquidator, generally assisting him and acting as a link between the interests it represents and the liquidator. It also has the statutory power to sanction some of the liquidator's actions, although he may well consult the committee on matters which he has the power to decide by himself since this may minimise disputes and help the smooth running of the liquidation.

d. When the official receiver is the liquidator any committee that may have been established shall have no authority to act, instead the functions of the committee will be vested in the Secretary of State.

If the official receiver is not the liquidator and no committee has been established the functions assigned to the committee are vested in the Secretary of State.

17. Liquidator's powers *(S.165, 167, 169* and *Sch 4 IA)*

a. ***With the sanction*** of the court or the committee of creditors he can:
   i. Bring and defend actions on behalf of the company;
   ii. Carry on the company's business to enable it to be wound up beneficially;
   iii. Pay any class of creditors in full; and
   iv. Make any compromises with creditors, contributories or debtors.

b. ***Without sanction*** he can:
   i. Sell the company's property;
   ii. Draw, accept and indorse bills of exchange in the company's name;
   iii. Raise money on the security of its assets;
   iv. Appoint an agent;
   v. Appoint a solicitor to assist him;
   vi. Execute deeds, receipts and other documents, using the company seal when necessary;
   vii. Prove in the bankruptcy or insolvency of any contributory; and
   viii. Do all such other things as are necessary to wind-up the company and distribute its assets.

18. Vacation of office by the liquidator *(S.172, 174 IA)*

The above sections are rather detailed, but in general the appointment will end when:

a. He is removed by order of the court, or by a general meeting of the company's creditors;

b. He resigns by giving notice to the court;

c. He ceases to be a qualified insolvency practitioner;

d. He is released after the conclusion of the winding-up.

**19. Application for early dissolution *(S.202–203 IA)***

a. If the official receiver is the liquidator and it appears to him that the assets are insufficient to cover the expenses of the winding-up and that the company's affairs do not require further investigation, he can apply to the registrar of companies for early dissolution.

b. Before doing so he must give 28 days notice to creditors, contributories and the administrative receiver (if there is one). Any creditor, contributory or the administrative receiver then has three months from the date of the application to apply to the Secretary of State for directions on the following grounds:

   i. That the assets are sufficient to cover the expenses of the winding-up;

   ii. That the affairs of the company do require further investigation;

   iii. That for any other reason early dissolution is inappropriate.

c. Unless directions are given the company is automatically dissolved three months after the date of the official receiver's application. If directions are given they will be that the winding-up proceeds as if no notice had been given by the official receiver.

**20. The final meeting of creditors *(S.146 IA)***

a. If the liquidator is someone other than the official receiver he must call a general meeting of creditors when he is satisfied that the winding-up is complete. He reports to the meeting and it decides whether he should be released from office. The liquidator should hold back from the final distribution enough funds to pay the expenses of this meeting.

b. If the official receiver is the liquidator there is no final meeting of creditors, the official receiver merely informs the registrar that the winding-up is complete.

**21. Dissolution *(S.205 IA)***

a. When the registrar of companies receives notice from the official receiver that the winding-up is complete, or receives notice that the final meeting of creditors has been held, he notes this fact on the company's file and three months later the company is dissolved.

b. **S.205 IA** replaces **S.568 CA**, which is repealed, but **S.652** on defunct companies (see 41. below) which was commonly used as the dissolution procedure in compulsory liquidation has not been repealed. However **S.205 IA** now provides the more straightforward procedure.

# PROVISIONS APPLICABLE TO EVERY KIND OF LIQUIDATION

## 22. Fraudulent trading

a. By **S.213 IA** if in a winding-up it appears that the company has been carrying on business with intent to defraud creditors or for any fraudulent purpose, the court can, on the application of the liquidator, order that persons who were knowingly parties shall be liable to make such contributions (if any) to the company's assets as the court thinks proper.

b. By **S.458** such persons may also be imprisoned or fined. Criminal liability may be imposed even if the company is not being wound-up, but winding-up is still a condition precedent to civil liability.

## 23. Wrongful trading (*S.214 IA*)

a. If in a winding-up it appears to the liquidator that a ***director*** or ***former director*** has been guilty of wrongful trading he may apply to the court for an order that the person is liable to make a contribution to the company's assets.

b. The court must be satisfied that:

   i. The company has gone into insolvent liquidation;

   ii. At some time before the start of winding-up that person knew or ought to have concluded that there was no reasonable prospect that the company would avoid insolvent liquidation; and

   iii. That person was a director of the company at the time.

c. The director will be deemed to know that the company could not avoid insolvent liquidation if that would have been the conclusion of a reasonably diligent person having:

   i. The general knowledge, skill and experience that might reasonably be expected of a person carrying out that particular director's duties; and

   ii. The general knowledge, skill and experience actually possessed by that director.

d. The court will not make an order if it is satisfied that, after the director became aware of the condition stated in b. ii. above, he took every step with a view to minimising the potential loss to the company's creditors as he ought to have taken in the circumstances.

e. **S.214 IA** is difficult for the courts to apply:

   i. How should they ascertain the 'moment of truth'? The Act merely says 'At some time before the commencement of the winding-up'.

   ii. What are the steps that a director has to take to avoid liability, and how will the court decide whether he has taken 'every' step?

In **RE PRODUCE MARKETING CONSORTIUM (1989)** (the first case on ***S.214*** to be examined by the courts) the two directors of the company were aware of a serious drop in turnover and profits, and that insolvency was inevitable (despite the absence of accounts). They nevertheless continued to trade with the purpose of reducing secured indebtedness to their bank. They also ignored a warning by the auditor and made a number of untrue statements, indicating an unwillingness to acknowledge the serious state of the company's affairs. The company was eventually wound up and the liquidator claimed £108,000 compensation from the directors for wrongful trading. The judge held that the 'moment of truth' (b.ii. above) did not have to be determined by reference to documentary material available at the time. The date was therefore fixed approximately fourteen months before the date of the winding up. He went on to say that the directors ought to have been aware of the insolvency of the company, despite the fact that the bank had not withdrawn overdraft facilities and despite the fact that the auditor (whilst stating his reservations) nevertheless accompanied the directors to the bank to seek further overdraft facilities. Although there was no deliberate course of wrong doing, the directors had not taken every step to minimise potential loss, because they allowed the company to trade for over a year after they had become (or should have become) aware of insolvency. The court held that the provisions of ***S.214*** were basically compensatory rather than penal, so the amount of personal liability was the loss caused to the company. The judge assessed this to be £75,000.

**24. Restriction on use of company names *(S.216 IA)***

When a company goes into insolvent liquidation its name becomes a 'prohibited name'. Persons who were directors or shadow directors at any time during the year before liquidation, may not, except with leave of the court, during the five years following the liquidation:

a. Be a director of any company known by a prohibited name.

b. Be concerned with or take part in any way in the promotion, formation or management of such a company; or

c. Be concerned with or take part in any business which is conducted under a prohibited name.

**25. Summary remedy against directors, liquidators etc *(S.212 IA)***

a. If in a winding-up it appears that any person who has acted as director, liquidator, administrator, receiver, or officer, or who has taken part in the promotion, formation or management of the company, has retained or misapplied company assets, or broken a fiduciary duty, then proceedings may be taken against him.

b. Such person may be required to restore assets, repay money, or pay compensation.

c. The official receiver, the liquidator or any creditor may make the application to court. A contributory may apply only with leave of the court.

d. **S.212 IA** only provides a summary remedy, it does not create a cause of action where none previously existed.

**26. Supplies by public utilities *(S.233 IA)***

If an office holder requests supplies from public utilities (telephone, water, gas and electricity) the supply cannot be made conditional on payment of outstanding bills, although the supplier may make continued supply conditional upon a personal guarantee from the office holder.

**27. Delivery of property *(S.234 IA)***

The court may order any person, for example a member, director, administrator, banker or accountant, to hand over to the office holder any property, books, papers or records in his possession.

**28. Duty to co-operate with the office holder *(S.235 IA)***

Any person who was an officer or employee during the year before the office holder took office must give the office holder any information concerning the company that he requires and must attend on the office holder at such time as he may reasonably require. Failure to comply with this provision is a criminal offence.

**29. Inquiry into company's dealings *(S.236–237 IA)***

On the application of the office holder the court may order to appear before it any officer of the company or any other person thought to be in possession of company property, or thought to be capable of giving information about the company's property or affairs.

**30. Transactions at an undervalue and preferences *(S.238–241 IA)***

Transactions at an undervalue or preferences given by insolvent companies in certain periods before winding-up commences may be invalid. (See Chapter 14.10).

**31. Extortionate credit bargains *(S.244 IA)***

Where credit has been provided to the company on terms that are extortionate having regard to the risk accepted by the provider of the credit, the office holder may apply to the court to improve the position. The section applies to transactions entered into within the three years before the start of winding-up or before the making of an administration order. When an application is made it is presumed that the bargain was extortionate, unless the provider of credit proves otherwise.

**32. Avoidance of floating charges *(S.245 IA)***

The Act introduces new rules invalidating floating charges created within certain periods before the start of winding-up. (See Chapter 14.9).

**33. Unenforceability of liens *(S.246 IA)***

Any right to reclaim possession of any books, papers or records of the company is unenforceable against the office holder, except liens on documents which give title to property and which are held as such.

**34. Executions *(S.183 IA)***

Executions commenced but not completed before the commencement of a winding-up may be avoided by the liquidator. (Executions commenced after the commencement of a compulsory winding-up are void, see 13 above).

**35. Appointment of a special manager *(S.177 IA)***

When the company is in liquidation or a provisional liquidator has been appointed, the liquidator or provisional liquidator may apply to the court to appoint a special manager if he feels that it will be in the interests of the creditors, contributories or members that someone be appointed to manage the company's business or property. The manager has the powers entrusted to him by the court and he may be required to give security.

**36. Disclaimer of onerous property *(S.178–182 IA)***

a. These sections replace **S.618–620 CA**. The main changes are that the liquidator is no longer restricted to disclaiming within 12 months of the start of winding-up and the consent of the court is not required.

b. Onerous property means any unprofitable contract or any other property of the company which is unsaleable or not easily saleable or which might give rise to some liability on the part of the company. For example:

   In **RE NOTTINGHAM GENERAL CEMETERY CO (1955)** the liquidator was permitted to disclaim land which could not be used except in accordance with contracts between the company and the holders of grave certificates.

c. The liquidator may disclaim onerous property by giving the 'prescribed notice'. This has the effect of terminating the company's interests and liabilities in the property but it does not (except so far as is necessary to release the company from liability) affect the rights or liabilities of any other person.

d. A person interested in property which the liquidator may disclaim may apply to the liquidator in writing requiring him to decide whether to disclaim. If the liquidator does not serve notice within 28 days he will not be able to do so at a later date unless he has the consent of the court.

e. When there is a disclaimer any person who has an interest in the disclaimed property may apply to the court. The court may make such order as it thinks fit in order to compensate the person.

**37. Contributories (S.74 IA)**

a. If the liquidator needs to make calls on contributories he will settle the lists of contributories:

   i. The **A List** consists of members at the commencement of the winding-up, (the presentation of the petition for compulsory winding-up, or the passing of the resolution for voluntary winding-up). Their liability is limited to the amount unpaid on their shares.

   ii. The **B List** consists of persons who were members within the year before the commencement of the winding-up. Such a person is only liable for the amount remaining unpaid on his former shares, only in respect of unpaid debts and liabilities incurred by the company before he ceased to be a member, and only if the present members cannot satisfy their contributions.

b. A contributory cannot set off a debt due to him from the company against a call except where all the creditors have been paid or he is bankrupt.

**38. Secured creditors and proof of debts**

a. ***Secured creditors***

   i. If a creditor is fully secured he can rely on his security and need not prove his debt in the liquidation.

   ii. If a creditor is partly secured he must give credit for the realised or estimated value of his security and prove as an unsecured creditor for the balance of the debt. Alternatively he may surrender his security and prove for the whole debt.

   iii. If a secured creditor has his security valued the liquidator can redeem it or require it to be sold at valuation, but the creditor can require the liquidator to elect whether or not he will exercise these powers. If the liquidator does not elect within 6 months he loses these powers.

b. ***Proof of debts***

   i. When the company is insolvent (which is usually the case) the same rules apply to proof of debts as apply in the law of bankruptcy. Therefore all debts owing at the commencement of winding-up, except unliquidated damages in tort can be proved for. This was confirmed in **RE ISLINGTON METAL AND PLATING WORKS (1984)**. If an insolvent company is found to be solvent, tort claimants may prove, even if this makes the company insolvent again.

   ii. When the company is solvent all debts are provable, including unliquidated damages in tort, but not statute barred debts.

c. ***Set-off***. Where there have been mutual dealings between the company and one of its creditors, account must be taken of what is due from one to the other, and only the balance may be claimed or paid. Set-off applies automatically, whatever the wishes of the parties, consequently the liquidator cannot deal with cross-claims free from the right of set-off.

39. Priority of debts

a. ***Winding-up costs, charges and expenses***, for example the liquidator's remuneration.

b. ***Preferential debts***. These rank and abate equally, ie if there are insufficient funds to satisfy all the preferential creditors, each gets an equal proportion of what is owed to him.

c. ***Creditors secured by floating charges***.

d. ***Ordinary unsecured creditors***. Their debts rank and abate equally.

e. ***Sums due to members*** in their capacity as members, for example return of capital, and dividends declared but not paid before the commencement of the winding-up.

40. Preferential debts *(S.175, 176, 386 IA)*

a. The Insolvency Act 1985 introduced a new list of preferential debts, replacing *Schedule 19* CA. The main changes are that local rates and corporation tax are no longer given preference, and the preferential period for VAT has been reduced from 12 to 6 months.

b. The main preferential debts are:

    i. 12 months pay as you earn (PAYE) deductions due from the company;

    ii. 6 months value added tax (VAT) due from the company;

    iii. Social security (national insurance) contributions for the 12 months prior to the relevant date;

    iv. Any sums owed in respect of occupational or state pension schemes;

    v. Employees arrears of wages or salary (including commission and holiday remuneration) for 4 months prior to the relevant date subject to a financial limit to be set by delegated legislation. (At present the limit is £800);

    vi. Loans by a third party to enable claims under iv. and v. to be paid.

c. Preferential debts are the same in both liquidation and receiverships. The 'relevant dates' for determining the size of the preferential debts are:

    i. In a receivership – the date of appointment of the receiver;

    ii. In a voluntary liquidation – the date of the resolution to wind-up;

iii. In a compulsory liquidation – the date of the appointment of a provisional liquidator (if there was one), otherwise the date of the winding-up order;

iv. In a compulsory liquidation which follows immediately from the discharge of an administration order – the date of the administration order;

v. In a compulsory liquidation which follows a voluntary liquidation – the date of the resolution for voluntary liquidation.

**41. Defunct companies**

a. **S.652** provides that if the registrar reasonably believes that a company is not carrying on business, he may, after carrying out a specified procedure, (including letters to the company and notices in the Gazette) strike it off the register, after which it is dissolved.

b. This procedure allows a company which is clearly 'dead' to be dissolved without the need for a winding-up. It also used to be used as the final step when there is a winding-up.

c. Since **S.652** provides little protection for members and creditors **S.653** provides that the liability of every officer and member shall continue as if the company had not been dissolved. In addition the court, on the application of any member or creditor, may within 20 years order the company to be restored to the register. When a company is restored by this method it is deemed to have continued in existence and things done by the company in the intervening period are effective.

d. **S.651** also provides for the revival of dissolved companies. It states that on the application of the liquidator or any other interested person the court may make an order declaring the dissolution void. In general the application must be made within two years from the date of dissolution. However if the person applying for restoration is doing so in order to pursue a claim for damages for personal or fatal injuries, which is not time barred, then there is no time limit.

**42. Publicity**

Throughout the life of a company publicity requirements are an important means of protection for members and creditors. When a company is in liquidation the duties of disclosure increase. The main publicity provisions are:

a. In a ***compulsory winding-up***:

i. Press advertisement of the more important steps in the proceedings, for example presentation of the petition, the making of the winding-up order and the appointment of the liquidator;

ii. Members and creditors may inspect the court's file of proceedings, the statement of affairs ( if any) and the minute books which have to be kept by the liquidator. They may also attend any court hearings;

iii. The liquidator must send half-yearly accounts to the DTI, which the Department may have audited. These accounts are available for public inspection and a summary is sent to every member and creditor.

b. In a ***voluntary winding-up***:

i. The winding-up resolution must be filed at the Companies Registry, together with the declaration of solvency (if any).

ii. At the end of each year and at the end of the winding-up the liquidator must call a meeting of members (and in a creditors' voluntary winding up a meeting of creditors) and present them an account of the liquidation.

c. In ***every winding-up*** all business communications must contain a statement that the company is in liquidation. By ***S.711*** the following steps in the proceedings must be advertised in the Gazette:

i. Any copy of a winding-up order;
ii. Any order for the dissolution of a company on a winding-up; and
iii. Any return by the liquidator of the final meeting.

## 43. Applicability of provisions of the Insolvency Act

This is summarised in the following table. The provisions of the Companies Act referred to above only apply to liquidations.

| | | Administration | Administrative Receiver | Liquidation | Provisional Liquidator |
|---|---|---|---|---|---|
| **S.388–398** | Insolvency practitioners | x | x | x | x |
| **S.214** | Wrongful trading | | | x | |
| **S.216** | Company names | | | x | |
| **S.212** | Summary remedy | | | x | |
| **S.233** | Public utilities | x | x | x | x |
| **S.234** | Delivery of property | x | x | x | x |
| **S.235** | Co-operation with office holder | x | x | x | x |
| **S.236–237** | Inquiry into company dealings | x | x | x | x |
| **S.238–240** | Transactions at undervalue and preferences | x | | x | |
| **S.244** | Extortionate credit bargains | x | | x | |
| **S.245** | Avoidance of floating charges | x | | x | |
| **S.246** | Unenforceability of liens | x | | x | x |
| **S.177** | Special manager | | | x | x |
| **S.178–182** | Disclaimer | | | x | |
| **S.175–176** | Preferential debts | | x | x | |

# Voluntary liquidation

## 44. Commencement

a. By **S.84 IA** a company may be wound up voluntarily

i. When the period, if any, fixed for its duration by the articles expires or the event, if any, occurs on which the articles provide for dissolution, and the company has passed an ***ordinary resolution*** to wind up voluntarily

ii. If the company passes a ***special resolution*** to be wound up voluntarily

iii. If the company passes an ***extraordinary resolution*** that it cannot, by reason of its liabilities continue its business and that it is advisable to wind-up. The reason for allowing an extraordinary rather than a special resolution is that it reduces the period of notice which may be useful if winding up is urgent because the company is insolvent.

b. By **S.86 IA** the moment of commencement of a voluntary winding-up is the time of passing the resolution.

c. Once a resolution for voluntary winding up has been passed it cannot be revoked by a subsequent resolution to the contrary.

## 45. Types of voluntary winding-up

Voluntary liquidations are far more numerous than compulsory liquidations. There are two types, ***members' voluntary liquidations*** (the more common type), and ***creditors' voluntary liquidations***. Whether a liquidation is a members' or creditors' voluntary liquidation will depend on whether or not a declaration of solvency is filed.

## 46. Members' voluntary winding-up

a. By **S.89 IA** a voluntary winding-up is a members' voluntary winding-up if, ***within 5 weeks before*** the resolution for voluntary winding-up, (or on that date but before passing the resolution) the directors, or a majority of them made a ***declaration of solvency***.

b. It must contain the latest practicable statement of the company's assets and liabilities and must state that, after inquiry, in their opinion the company will be able to pay its debts within a stated period not more than 12 months after the resolution.

c. The declaration must be delivered to the registrar within 15 days after the resolution to wind-up has been passed.

d. If a director makes the declaration without having reasonable grounds for his opinion he commits a criminal offence and if, after the company is wound up, the debts are not paid in full within the specified period, it is presumed that the director did not have reasonable grounds for his opinion. He will therefore have to prove that his opinion was reasonable if he is to avoid liability. In addition if the declaration is not delivered to the registrar within the prescribed time the company and every officer in default are liable to be fined.

e. ***Liquidator's powers***. By **S.165 IA** with the sanction of an extraordinary resolution he can pay any class of creditors in full and make any compromise with creditors, contributories, or debtors. ***Without sanction*** he has all the other powers of a liquidator in a winding-up by the court (see 17. above).

**47. Effect of insolvency of members' voluntary winding-up *(S.95, 96, 102, 105 IA)***

a. If the liquidator forms the opinion that the company will be unable to pay its debts in accordance with the declaration of solvency he must call a creditors' meeting to be held within 28 days of his having become aware of the company's insolvency. Creditors must be given at least 7 days notice and it must be advertised in two local newspapers. The notice must also be published in the Gazette.

b. The liquidator must attend and preside at the meeting, and lay before it a statement of affairs. This must be verified by affidavit and must contain:

   i. Particulars of the company's assets, debts and liabilities;

   ii. Names and addresses of the creditors;

   iii. Securities held by creditors, with the dates when the securities were given.

c. From the date of the creditors meeting the liquidation proceeds as if the declaration of solvency had never been made, ie as a creditors' voluntary liquidation. The main effects of this are that the creditors can replace the liquidator with their nominee and they can appoint a committee of inspection.

**48. Creditors' voluntary winding-up**

a. ***Meeting of creditors***. By **S.97–99 IA** the company must call a meeting of creditors to be held within 14 days of the resolution to wind-up. Creditors must be given at least 7 days notice and the notice must give the name and address of a qualified insolvency practitioner who, during the period before the meeting, will give the creditors any information they may reasonably require concerning the affairs of the company. The directors must prepare a statement of affairs to be verified by affidavit (contents as in 47b above). One of the directors must preside over the meeting and the statement of affairs is laid before the meeting.

b. ***Appointment of liquidator***. Under **S.100 IA** if the company meeting and the creditors' meeting nominate a different person, the creditors' nominee will be the liquidator.

c. ***Committee of inspection***. At their meeting the creditors may appoint up to five persons to a committee of inspection. The members then have a right to do the same, but the creditors may by resolution exclude members' nominees unless the court orders otherwise. ***(S.101 IA)***.

d. ***Liquidator's powers***. In general, by ***S.165 IA, with the sanction*** of the court, the committee of inspection, or (if none) the creditors, he can pay any class of creditors in full and make any compromise with creditors, contributories and debtors. ***Without sanction*** he has all the other powers of a liquidator in a winding-up by the court (see 17. above). However by ***S.166 IA*** where there is a members' nominee as liquidator during the period from the resolution to wind-up and the creditors' meeting, the majority of the powers conferred by ***S.165 IA*** may only be exercised with the consent of the court. ***S.166 IA*** allows the liquidator, during this period, to take control of any property he believes the company to be entitled to, dispose of perishable goods and goods likely to fall in value and do any other thing necessary to protect the company's assets.

**49. Main differences between members' and creditors' voluntary winding-up**

| *Members' Voluntary Winding-Up* | *Creditors' Voluntary Winding-Up* |
|---|---|
| Usually commenced by special resolution | Commenced by extraordinary resolution |
| Declaration of solvency | No declaration of solvency |
| No committee of inspection | Committee of inspection |
| No meeting of creditors | A meeting of creditors must be called |
| Members appoint the liquidator | The creditors' nominee will be appointed liquidator unless the court orders otherwise. |

**50. Consequences of voluntary winding-up**

a. ***After the commencement*** of the winding-up, (the time of the resolution, even if the company is later wound-up by the court):

   i. The company must cease business except so far as is necessary for its beneficial winding-up ***(S.87 IA)***;

   ii. Any transfer of shares without the liquidator's sanction, or alteration in the status of members is void ***(S.88 IA)***;

   iii. If the company is insolvent the company's servants are automatically dismissed; and

   iv. If no liquidator has been appointed or nominated by the company the directors may not exercise any of their powers except as allowed by the court. However they may dispose of perishable goods or goods that might fall in value and they may do anything necessary to protect the company's assets ***(S.114 IA)***.

b. ***On the appointment of the liquidator*** the directors' powers cease except so far as sanctioned by the company in general meeting or the liquidator in a members' voluntary winding-up, or the committee of inspection or, if none, the creditors in a creditors' voluntary winding-up.

**51. Applications to court *(S.112 IA)***

The liquidator or any creditor or contributory may apply to the court to decide any question arising in the winding-up, or to exercise any power it would have had in a winding-up by the court. The court may make such order as it thinks just, including a stay of the winding-up proceedings.

**52. Right to apply for compulsory winding-up *(S.116 IA)***

The fact that a company is in voluntary liquidation does not bar the right of any creditor or contributory to apply to have it wound up by the court. The court will only make an order on the application of a contributory if it is satisfied that the rights of contributories would be prejudiced by a voluntary winding-up. An application by a creditor will not succeed if the other creditors wish voluntary winding-up, unless the applicant's position would be prejudiced by its continuation.

**53. Vacation of office by the liquidator *(S.171 IA)***

a. The liquidator may be removed as follows:

   i. In a members' voluntary winding-up by an ordinary resolution;

   ii. In a creditors' voluntary winding-up by a general meeting of creditors in accordance with rules specified in delegated legislation;

   iii. In any situation by the court.

b. A liquidator vacates office if he ceases to be a qualified insolvency practitioner.

c. A liquidator may resign in circumstances provided by delegated legislation.

**54. Release of the liquidator *(S.173 IA)***

a. In a members' voluntary winding-up the liquidator is released at the time of the final meeting of the company.

b. In a creditors' voluntary winding-up the liquidator is released at the final meeting of creditors, unless the meeting resolves against this, in which case he must apply to the Secretary of State for release.

c. If he has been removed by a meeting of members or creditors, he is released on giving notice to the registrar of companies, unless the meeting resolves against this, in which case he must apply to the Secretary of State for release.

**55. Final meeting and dissolution** ***(S.94, 106, 201 IA)***

a. In a members' voluntary winding-up the liquidator presents his final accounts to a meeting of members, sends to the registrar a copy of the accounts and a return of the holding of the meeting. Three months later the company is deemed to be dissolved unless the court orders otherwise.

b. The procedure is the same for a creditors' voluntary winding-up, except that the accounts must be presented to separate meetings of members and creditors.

## *PROGRESS TEST 19*

1. What is the position if other creditors oppose a creditors' petition for compulsory liquidation?
2. Describe the contents of a statutory declaration of solvency.
3. In what circumstances should a liquidator refuse to pay a debt of the company?
4. What is wrongful trading? What are its consequences?
5. PQ Ltd is in voluntary liquidation. Advise the liquidator (Bill) in the following situations:

   (a) Mary, a contributory, is claiming damages because she alleges that Bill has delayed in handing over her proportion of the surplus assets of the company.

   (b) Bill has distributed the assets of the company without paying Dennis, a creditor. The books show Dennis as a creditor, but Dennis did not reply to Bill's advertisement for creditors.

# 24 Administration Orders

**1. Introduction**

Administration is a new procedure recommended by the Cork Report (The Report of the Review Committee on Insolvency Law and Practice, 1982) as an alternative to receivership. The basic purpose of an administration order is to freeze the debts of a company in financial difficulties to assist an administrator to save the company or at least achieve the better realisation of its assets. Its not a procedure designed for creditors to enforce their security.

**2. The power to make an order *(S.8 IA)***

Before making an order the court must be satisfied that the company is, or is likely to become, unable to pay its debts (as defined by ***S.123 IA***, see Chapter 23.9) and that the order would be likely to achieve one or more of the following purposes:

a. The survival of the whole or part of the business as a going concern;

b. The approval by the creditors of a composition in satisfaction of debts, or by the members of a scheme of arrangement of the company's affairs (ie the voluntary arrangements introduced by the Insolvency Act, see Chapter 22.14–22.17);

c. The sanctioning under ***S.425*** Companies Act of a compromise or arrangement (see Chapter 22.11–22.13);

d. A more advantageous realisation of the assets than would be effected on a winding-up.

An administration order cannot be made after the company has gone into liquidation.

**3. The application *(S.9 IA)***

a. Application is by petition from the company, the directors, a creditor or creditors, or a combination of these. Once presented it cannot be withdrawn.

b. Notice of presentation of the petition must be given to any person who has appointed, or is entitled to appoint a receiver.

c. The court may dismiss the application, adjourn proceedings, make an interim order (restricting the power of the directors) or any other order it thinks fit.

d. Where there is a receiver it ***must dismiss*** the petition unless it is satisfied that:

i. The person who appointed the receiver consents to the meeting of an administration order; ***or***

ii. If an order were made any security by virtue which the receiver was appointed would be liable to be avoided under **S.238–240 IA** (transactions at an undervalue and preferences) or **S.245 IA** (avoidance of floating charges).

The success of these procedures could well be curtailed by i above. We shall see in paragraph 5 below that the appointment of an administrator will probably be regarded as unsatisfactory by debentureholders. If so they will appoint a receiver after a petition has been presented, but before the court reaches its decision, their purpose being to then veto the appointment of an administrator.

**4. The effect of an application *(S.10 IA)***

a. The company cannot be wound-up.

b. No charge, hire purchase or retention of title clause can be enforced against the company without the consent of the court.

c. No other proceedings can be commenced or proceeded with against the company without the consent of the court.

**5. The effect of the order *(S.12–13 IA)***

a. The affairs, business and property of the company are managed by the administrator *(S.8 IA)*.

b. The restrictions on winding-up and legal proceedings continue.

c. Any administrative receiver vacates office.

d. Any receiver of part of the company's property must vacate office if required to do so by the administrator.

e. All company documents must indicate that an administration order is in force and must name the administrator.

**6. Appointment of the administrator *(S.13 IA)***

An administrator may be appointed

a. By an administration order; or

b. By order of the court to fill a vacancy caused by death, resignation or any other event.

**7. Administrator's powers *(S.14–16)***

a. He has the general power to do all things necessary to manage the affairs, business and property of the company. 23 examples are given in Schedule 1 of the Act, they include:

i. To carry on the business;

ii. To deal with and dispose of assets;

iii. To borrow money and grant security;

iv. To bring and defend legal proceedings on the company's behalf;

v. To establish subsidiaries and transfer to them the whole or part of the company's business;

vi. To employ and dismiss employees.

b. Further specific powers are given by **S.14–16 IA**, for example

i. To appoint and remove directors;

ii. To call meetings of members and creditors;

iii. To deal with property subject to a floating charge as if there were no charge. When property is disposed of under this power, the sale proceeds become subject to a floating charge which has the same priority as the original security.

c. If the administrator wishes to dispose of other charged property or of goods subject to hire-purchase or retention of title agreements, he must obtain the consent of the court. This will be granted if the court is satisfied that this would be likely to promote the statutory purposes (2. above) and the amount to be realised would be that obtainable on an open market sale. The proceeds of the disposal must be used to discharge the sums secured by the security or owing under the hire-purchase agreement. Any shortfall from the open market value must be made good by the administrator.

d. In exercising his powers the administrator is deemed to be the agent of the company and any person who deals with him in good faith does not have to enquire whether he is acting within his powers.

**8. Administrator's duties**

Although it is not referred to in the Act the administrator probably owes the same fiduciary duties to the company as a receiver. His main statutory duties are:

a. To take into custody or control all the property of the company **(S.17 IA)**.

b. To send notice of his appointment:

i. To the company – immediately;

ii. To the registrar – within 14 days;

iii. To the creditors – within 28 days **(S.21 IA)**.

c. To require, within 21 days, a statement of affairs, verified by affidavit, giving details of:

i. Assets, debts and liabilities;

ii. Names and addresses of creditors;

iii. Securities held by creditors with the dates when given;

iv. Other information as may be prescribed by delegated legislation **(S.22 IA)**.

d. The statement of affairs must be made and submitted by some or all of the following:

   i. Persons who are or have been officers of the company;

   ii. Persons who took part in the company's formation within one year before the administration order;

   iii. Employees, or persons employed within the past year who are, in the administrator's opinion, capable of giving the information;

   iv. Officers or employees (within the past year) of another company which is (or was within the past year) itself an officer of the company.

e. Within 3 months of the administration order(or such longer period as the court may allow) he must send to the registrar, the creditors and the members a ***statement of his proposals*** for achieving the purpose of the administration. He must lay this statement before a ***meeting of creditors*** summoned for this-purpose on not less than 14 days notice ***(S.23 IA)***. The purpose of the meeting is to approve the proposals, with modifications if the administrator agrees ***(S.24 IA)***. If, at a later date, the administrator wishes to make substantial modifications he must notify the members and call another meeting of creditors ***(S.25 IA)***.

f. To summon a meeting of creditors if requested to do so by 10% in value of the creditors, or if ordered to do so by the court ***(S.17 IA)***.

**9. Protection of members and creditors**

a. If the creditors meeting does not approve the proposals the court may discharge the administration order, or make any other order it thinks fit ***(S,24 IA)***.

b. If the meeting approves the proposals (with or without modifications) it may appoint a ***committee of creditors***. The committee may on 7 days notice require the administrator to attend before it and give such information as it may reasonably require. ***(S.26 IA)***. This committee is much weaker than the committee of creditors in a liquidation, since it has no power to give directions to the administrator and its consent is not necessary for any of his acts.

c. ***Any creditor or member*** may apply to the court for an order on the ground that the company is or has been managed by the administrator in a manner ***unfairly prejudicial*** to the creditors or members or that any act or omission of the administrator is or would be so prejudicial. The court may make any order it thinks fit ***(S.27 IA)***. Clearly this is similar to **S.459 CA**.

**10. Discharge or variation of the administration order *(S.18 IA)***

a. The administrator may apply to the court at any time to discharge or vary the order

i. If it appears to him that the purpose of the administration order has been achieved or is incapable of achievement; or

ii. If he has been instructed to apply to the court by the meeting of creditors.

b. The court may discharge or vary the order or make any other order it thinks fit. If the order is discharged or varied the administrator must,within 14 days, send a copy of the order of discharge or variation to the registrar.

**11. Vacation of office and release of the administrator** ***(S.19–20 IA)***

a. The administrator vacates office if:

i. He is removed by the court;

ii. He resigns or dies;

iii. He ceases to be a qualified insolvency practitioner; or

iv. The administration order is discharged.

b. His release date is determined by the court. From such date he is discharged form liability for acts or omissions in relation to his conduct as administrator, but if he has broken any duty the court may order him to restore property or contribute to the company's assets, even after he has been released.

c. When an administrator is released his remuneration and expenses shall be paid in priority to secured creditors, but after liabilities incurred under contracts entered into or contracts of employment adopted while he, or any predecessor, was administrator. For this purpose the administrator is not taken to have adopted a contract of employment by reason of anything done within 14 days of his appointment.

**12. Conclusion**

The Cork Committee made its recommendations after studying procedures in France, Australia, South Africa and the USA. Whether it will work here will mainly depend on two questions:

a. Will debentureholders block the procedure by appointing a receiver and then vetoing the appointment of an administrator?

b. If an administrator has been appointed how willing will people be to trade with the company?

*PROGRESS TEST 20*

1. Who is entitled to apply for an administration order?
2. What is the legal status of the administrator?
3. What remedy is available to members and creditors if they disapprove of the administrator's conduct?
4. Which of the following are required to be qualified insolvency practitioners?
   (a) Liquidator in a compulsory liquidation
   (b) Liquidator in a members' voluntary liquidation of a solvent company
   (c) Administrator
   (d) Official receiver?
5. What is an elective resolution? How would one be passed?

# 25 Receiverships

## 1. Introduction

a. The usual remedy for debentureholders when debenture interest has not been paid, or when some other term of the trust deed has been broken, is to secure the appointment of a receiver to realise the assets subject to the charge and repay the debentureholders.

b. The law on receivers has a different basis from that of liquidations and administration, since it is based on rules developed in the Court of Chancery rather than on statute. These equitable rules have been supplemented by provisions in both the *COMPANIES ACT* and the *INSOLVENCY ACT*. The changes introduced by the Insolvency Act 1985 have two main purposes:

   i. To codify the powers and duties of administrative receivers; and

   ii. To ensure that more information is given to creditors.

## 2. Definitions

a. ***Receiver***. This is a general term and it applies to any person administering any type of receivership. The powers of a receiver may include the power to manage the business, in which case the person is called a receiver and manager.

b. ***Administrative receiver***. This term was introduced by the Insolvency Act 1985. It basically means a person appointed as a receiver or manager under a floating charge over all or most of the company's assets.

## 3. Appointment

The circumstances of the appointment will depend on the terms of the trust deed and the nature of the security.

a. ***Appointment under a fixed charge***. A fixed charge will indicate the circumstances when a power of sale will arise, for example if winding-up commences or if payment of interests is in arrears. In such cases a receiver can be appointed by the debentureholders to collect the income from the property from the time of default until sale. If there is no power of sale in the trust deed it will be necessary to apply to the court to appoint a receiver.

b. ***Appointment under a floating charge***. It will be remembered that a floating charge crystallises (ie becomes fixed) either when winding-up commences or when the company defaults and the debentureholders take steps to enforce their security by appointing a receiver. If the trust deed specifies the circumstances when a receiver may be appointed no application to the court will be necessary. In any other case the court must make the appointment, which it will do when:

i. The principal sum or interest is in arrear;

ii. An event has occurred on which, under the terms of issue of the debentures, the security becomes enforceable; or

iii. There has been no direct breach of the conditions under which the debentures were issued, but the security is nevertheless in jeopardy.

c. ***Jeopardy***. This cannot arise where there is a fixed charge because the borrower under a fixed charge may not deal with the assets charged without the lender's consent. Jeopardy will not be held to exist merely because the company's assets are insufficient to pay the debenture-holders in full. There is no statutory definition of jeopardy, but it has been held to exist in the following circumstances:

i. When the company is in liquidation (even if only for the purpose of amalgamation or reconstruction);

ii. When liquidation is probable because creditors are pressing for payment;

iii. When an unsecured creditor has obtained judgement and is in a position to levy execution on the assets comprised in the charge;

iv. When business has ceased or is about to cease;

v. When a company proposes to distribute a reserve fund which is its only asset.

d. ***Receiver and manager***. If it is necessary for a receiver to carry on the company's business until realisation of the security he must be appointed as ***receiver and manager***, since appointment merely as receiver will not confer powers of management on him.

e. In general it will be better for the debentureholders if the receiver is appointed out of court since a receiver appointed by the court is an officer of the court and will have to work under its close supervision. He will have to make many applications to court for directions, slowing down the progress of the receivership and increasing its costs. There is now no advantage in an appointment by the court since, under **S.35 IA**, a receiver appointed out of court may apply to the court for directions. The persons who appointed the receiver may also apply to the court for directions.

f. By **S.33 IA** an appointment out of court will not be effective unless accepted by the receiver by the end of the business day following the day on which he received the instrument of appointment.

g. By **S.34 IA** if an appointment is discovered to be invalid the court may order the person who made the appointment to indemnify the appointee against any liability arising from the invalid appointment.

**4. Qualification and remuneration**

a. ***Qualification***. An administrative receiver must be a qualified insolvency practitioner **(S.388 IA)**, (see Chapter 23.2–23.7). In other cases any fit person may be appointed except a corporation **(S.30 IA)**, an undischarged bankrupt **(S.31 IA)** or a person disqualified by the court under the **COMPANY DIRECTORS DISQUALIFICATION ACT 1986**. In practice the receiver will usually be an experienced accountant. If the company is being wound-up the official receiver may be appointed **(S.32 IA)**.

b. ***Remuneration***

   i. If appointed by the court his remuneration will be fixed by the court, usually at 5% of the amount of the rents, profits or other income received, but a smaller percentage of the sale proceeds of any property.

   ii. If appointed by the debentureholders they fix his remuneration.

   iii. If the company goes into liquidation the liquidator may apply to court to fix the remuneration of the receiver or manager **(S.36 IA)**.

**5. Effect of appointment**

a. Floating charges crystallise.

b. The directors' powers of control are suspended, although they remain in office and are entitled to their fees. They are able to challenge the receiver's appointment. They may petition for the compulsory winding-up of the company and they may exercise their other powers provided that in doing so they do not interfere with the receiver's task of collecting in the assets. They may therefore commence proceedings on behalf of the company for breach of contract if the receiver is not prepared to do so.

   In **NEWHART DEVELOPMENTS v CO-OPERATIVE COMMERCIAL BANK (1978)** the plaintiffs and the bank were engaged in a joint venture involving property development. The bank were to provide the finance. When the venture ran into difficulties the bank exercised their power to appoint a receiver of the plaintiff company. Although not disputing the appointment of the receiver, the directors of the company felt that the company had a claim in contract against the bank arising from a breach of the bank's obligations in the venture. The directors issued a writ in the company's name against the bank. The receiver sought to have it set aside because it was issued without his consent. The claim failed and this action was allowed to proceed to trial. It was held that the appointment of a receiver did not prevent the directors from exercising their powers as long as their acts do not threaten the assets subject to the debentureholders' charge.

   The directors' powers are automatically restored when the receivership ends.

c. If the receiver is an officer of the court (ie the appointment was made by the court) or if he was appointed by the debentureholders as their agent and not the company's agent, the company's servants are automatically dismissed, although the receiver may re-employ them. If he is an agent of the company all contracts of employment will continue.

d. A floating charge holder will be able to block the appointment of an administrator ***(S.9 IA)***.

6. **Position of receiver**

a. To protect debentureholders from liability for any wrongful act of a receiver the trust deed will provide that the receiver shall be the ***agent of the company*** and not the agent of the debentureholders.

b. Although an agent is not normally personally liable on his contracts **S.37 IA** states that a receiver appointed out of court (ie by the debentureholders) is personally liable on contracts to the same extent as if he had been appointed by the court (unless the contract provides otherwise) but with a right of indemnity out of the company's assets. ie Both receivers appointed by the court and out of court are liable on any contracts entered into in the performance of their functions, including any contract of employment adopted in order to perform those functions. For this purpose a receiver is not taken to have adopted a contract of employment by reason of anything done within 14 days of his appointment. Similar rules also apply to administrative receivers ***(S.44 IA)***.

c. The only distinction that remains between receivers appointed by the court and by the debentureholders is that the former operates under the court's supervision and the latter does not. By **S.35 IA** both can apply to the court for directions.

7. **Receivers' powers**

a. A receiver will have the power conferred on him by the trust deed under which he was appointed. By **S.42 IA** an administrative receiver is also deemed to have the powers specified in **SCHEDULE 1** of the **INSOLVENCY ACT** (see Chapter 24.7), although references in the schedule to 'property of the company' must be construed as references to that part of the property subject to the charge.

b. By **S.43 IA** an administrative receiver also has powers similar to those of an administrator to apply to the court for an order allowing him to dispose of property subject to a security as if it were uncharged, provided:

i. The security is not held by the person who appointed the administrative receiver; or

ii. The security does not rank after the security over which the administrative receiver has authority.

The court will not authorise the disposal unless it will promote a more advantageous realisation of the company's assets than would otherwise be the case. The proceeds of the disposal must be applied to pay off the sum secured by the charge. The administrative receiver must send to the registrar, within 14 days, a copy of the court order authorising the sale.

c. At common law a receiver may repudiate existing contracts. However he may not do this if it would adversely affect the subsequent realisation of the company's assets or if it would injure its goodwill if it were to trade again.

   In **RE NEWDIGATE COLLIERY (1912)** the receiver could have made a greater profit by repudiating contracts for the future sale of coal. It was held that he could not do so because the contracts involved almost the entire output of the colliery and to repudiate would have lost considerable goodwill.

   Where the receiver repudiates an existing contract the only remedy normally available to the other party is to sue as an unsecured creditor. However if the latter has reserved title he may be able to recover the actual goods.

**8. Receivers' general duties**

a. By ***S.100 CA 89 (S.409)*** the person who obtains the order for the appointment of a receiver must within seven days give notice of the fact to the registrar.

b. By ***S.39 IA*** every document issued by or on behalf of the company or the receiver, for example letterheads, order forms and invoices, must show his appointment.

c. His preliminary duty is to acquaint himself with the terms of his appointment, for example his powers of selling property and the periods for presentation of accounts. He should also ensure that charges are not invalidated by ***S.95 CA 89 (S.398–400)*** (registration of charges), ***S.238–240 IA*** (transactions at an undervalue and preferences, or ***S.245 IA*** (avoidance of floating charges), since he may be held personally liable if he acts under an invalid charge.

d. His basic duty is to collect in the assets charged to collect rents and profits, and to exercise the debentureholders powers of realisation, and to pay the net proceeds to them. However if a receiver is appointed in respect of a debenture secured by a floating charge, the preferential debts (see Chapter 23.40) must be paid as soon as the receiver has assets in his hands and before any payment is made to the debentureholders.

e. Where the receiver is also appointed as manager he should take a number of practical steps to ensure that nothing is done without his authority, for example:

   i. Contact the company's bankers and arrange for the bank account to be transferred into his name as receiver and manager;

ii. Notify managers of branch offices of his appointment and instruct them that no goods are to be ordered or payments made without his authority;
iii. Obtain a list of principal officers and employees, since it may be necessary in some cases to terminate their contracts of employment;
iv. Take an inventory of plant, machinery, fixtures, fittings, etc; and
v. Prepare a list of debts due to the company, noting the period of credit which has been allowed.

**9. Duties of an administrative receiver *(S.46–49 IA)***

a. On appointment the administrative receiver must send to the company and publish (as prescribed by delegated legislation) notice of his appointment.

b. Within 28 days he must notify all creditors.

c. He must immediately require a statement of affairs. This must be submitted within 21 days. The persons responsible and the contents are the same as when an administrator is appointed (see Chapter 24.8).

d. Within 3 months he must send a report to the registrar, secured creditors and trustees for secured creditors, containing information on the following matters:

i. The events leading up to his appointment, so far as he is aware of them.
ii. His disposal or proposed disposal of any of the company's property.
iii. His plans for carrying on the business.
iv. The amounts of principal and interest payable to the debenture-holders by whom he was appointed and the amounts payable to preferential creditors.
v. The amount, if any, likely to be available to pay other creditors.
vi. A summary of the statement of affairs and his comments, if any, on it.

The administrative receiver does not have to include any information that would seriously prejudice the carrying out of his functions.

e. He must also send a copy of the report to unsecured creditors or publish in the prescribed manner a notice giving an address to which the creditors can write for a free copy of the report. In either case he must lay a copy of the report before a meeting of unsecured creditors summoned for the purpose on not less than 14 days notice. The meeting of creditors may establish a committee. Like the committee of creditors in administration it may summon the administrative receiver on 7 days notice and require reasonable information concerning the performance of his functions, but it cannot give him any directions nor is its consent required for any of his acts.

f. If the company has gone or goes into liquidation the administrative receiver must also send a copy of the report to the liquidator. If the report is sent to the liquidator within 3 months of the administrative receiver's appointment, the receiver is released from his obligation to call a meeting of unsecured creditors and send his report to them or publish it.

**10. Vacation of office by the receiver**

a. By *S.45 IA* an administrative receiver vacates office:

   i. On order of the court;

   ii. By resignation in the prescribed manner;

   iii. If he ceases to be a qualified insolvency practitioner.

   He must inform the registrar within 14 days

b. A receiver appointed by the court may only be discharged by a court order, obtained when his duties have been completed. Normally the receiver will make the application to discharge, but any other person can do so if the receiver has been incompetent or is guilty of misconduct.

c. A receiver appointed out of court must inform the registrar of companies when his duties have been completed *(S.405)*. He should also give formal notice to the company and to the persons who appointed him.

**11. The receiver and the liquidator**

a. In most cases when a receiver is appointed with a view to sale of assets the company will be forced into liquidation. On the other hand if the company is already in liquidation the debentureholders may seek to preserve their rights by the appointment of a receiver.

b. When the two functions are not vested in the same person the liquidator occupies the premier position since he is responsible for the interests of the creditors and contributories as well as the debentureholders. He must therefore:

   i. See that the receiver confines his duties to the assets subject to the charge;

   ii. See that he does not protract the receivership;

   iii. See that he discharges the preferential debts; and

   iv. Ensure that he accounts to the liquidator for any surplus after paying the debentureholders what is due to them.

c. The company's books remain with the liquidator, but the receiver must be allowed such access as is necessary to enable him to perform his duties.

d. If a receiver fails to render proper accounts to the liquidator after being requested to do so, or fails to pay the liquidator what is due to him the court may order the receiver to make good the default within a specified time *(S.41 IA)*.

### PROGRESS TEST 21

1. An administrative receiver has been appointed under the powers contained in a debenture secured by a floating charge over the whole of the property of the company. What provisions assist him in ascertaining the financial state of the company at the date of his appointment?
2. When the court appoints a receiver and manager in a debentureholders' action and the company is not in liquidation what effect has the appointment on:
   (a) The company's contracts of service with employees
   (b) The landlord's right of distress, and
   (c) The completion of contracts entered into by the company before the receiver and manager's appointment?
3. Explain the term 'extortionate credit bargain'.
4. At what point in time is winding-up deemed to commence?
5. At the beginning of October A Ltd owed B Ltd £124. Later the same month A Ltd sold goods to B Ltd for £159 on credit. A few days later A Ltd's debentureholders appointed a receiver and a floating charge over all A Ltd's assets crystallised. Early in November the goods were delivered to B Ltd. The receiver is now claiming £159 from B Ltd. Can B Ltd set-off the £124 owed to them by A Ltd?

## COURSEWORK QUESTIONS 26–30 RECONSTRUCTIONS, TAKEOVERS, LIQUIDATIONS AND RECEIVERSHIPS

26. *(a) Who may bring a winding-up petition and upon what grounds?*

    *(b) Nemo Ltd. is in liquidation as insolvent. The following proofs have been lodged with the liquidator:*

    *i. a claim for damages from Oswald caused by the negligence of one of the company's employees;*

    *ii. a claim for two years unpaid corporation tax and VAT;*

iii. *a claim for £5,000 from Patrick who lent the money to the company two weeks prior to the liquidation. The money was used to pay the company's wage bill at the time;*

iv. *other unsecured debts of £50,000.*

*Advise the liquidator as to the validity and preference of these proofs.*
ICSA December 1986 Question 6

27. (a) *What is an administrative receiver? What are the procedural duties of an administrative receiver?* (10 marks)

(b) *A company is in the process of a members' voluntary winding-up. It wishes to effect an amalgamation by transferring all its assets to another company for a consideration to be distributed amongst its members.*

*What steps must the company take? What protection is afforded to any member who is opposed to the amalgamation?* (10 marks)
(20 marks)
ACCA June 1987 Question 7

28. (a) *Give an account of the powers and duties of a liquidator of a company.* (15 marks)

(b) *Who are 'contributories' and what is the nature and extent of their liability?* (5 marks)
(20 marks)
ACCA June 1985 Question 8

29. *Describe and explain the procedures which must be observed in a voluntary winding-up to the point immediately preceding the appointment of the liquidator and the cessation of the directors' powers.* (20 marks)
ACCA December 1987 Question 3

30. (a) *In what circumstances can a court make a disqualification order against a director of a company?* (12 marks)

(b) *What is the immediate legal effect of an order for the compulsory winding-up of a company? (Do not discuss the further procedure of the liquidation.)* (8 marks)
(20 marks)
ACCA June 1986 Question 8

# PART VIII APPENDICES

# Introduction to Appendices I and II

## 1. The purposes of suggested answers

The questions and answers in these two appendices serve three purposes:

a. They illustrate the ***style, structure and content*** necessary to answer a particular question. They should not however be regarded as the only possible correct answer. In many answers different cases will be just as acceptable as the cases quoted. The most important advice in connection with style and content is ***write in your own words***. Never try to memorise word for word sentences or paragraphs from any suggested answers. Such attempts usually fail and, even if successful, there is a temptation to use the particular sentence or paragraph where it is not appropriate.

b. They provide a valuable ***means of self assessment***. Self assessment is important to avoid falling into the 'trap' referred to in Chapter 1, ie the tendency to mistake understanding for learning. Self assessment will help you to discover whether you have ***learnt*** something rather than merely understood it. Suggested answers can also be used as a rough guide to measure progress.

c. They provide an ***incentive to practice***. Practice is just as important as self assessment. It is not possible to pass any test without practice. You would not expect to pass your driving test if all you did was read about the brakes, steering wheel and clutch in a book and then step into a car for the first time on the day of the test. A written examination is the same, practice is essential and because suggested answers are a help in self assessment, they provide an incentive to practice, particularly at times when lecturer assessment is not possible, for example shortly before the examination.

## 2. How to use the questions and answers

a. The 'Coursework Questions' should be attempted at appropriate stages during the year. They may be attempted individually or as a group of five to comprise a mock examination. The 'Revision Questions' are generally slightly more difficult and should be attempted towards the end of your course.

b. Whether you are attempting a coursework question or a revision question you should adopt the following procedure:

   i. First attempt the question. Your attempt may be a 'timed answer' ie written in about 30 minutes without the aid of notes or textbooks, or a 'model answer' ie an examination length answer prepared in as much time as is necessary, using all available resources.

ii. Then, ***and only then***, read the suggested answer. You can then critically assess your own answer, perhaps awarding yourself a mark, or even re-writing the answer if you consider your attempt very poor.

3. **Author's answers not official solutions**

The author would like to make it clear that these are his own answers and they do not represent the official solutions of the bodies concerned.

# Appendix I

## SUGGESTED ANSWERS TO COURSEWORK QUESTIONS 1–5 INCORPORATION

1. (a) James is free to choose any name for his company subject to the following restrictions:

   i. The last word of a private company's name must be 'Limited' and the last words of a public company's name must be 'Public Limited Company'. These may be abbreviated to 'Ltd' or 'Plc' respectively. The words 'limited' 'unlimited' and 'public limited company' must not appear in the name other than at the end. ***(S.25)***

   ii. The name must not be the same as a name already in the index. When determining whether one name is the same as another minor differences are disregarded. For example the presence or absence of the word 'The'. ***(S.26(1)(a))***

   iii. The name must not, in the opinion of the Secretary of State, constitute a criminal offence or be offensive. ***(S.26(1)(d)*** and ***(e))***

   iv. The approval of the Secretary of State is needed if the name suggests a link with Government or with a Local Authority, or if it includes a word or expression specified in regulations issued under the Act, for example Royal, Police, International, Trade Union and Charity. ***(S.26(2))***.

   James should also be aware that if the name is so misleading as to be likely to cause harm to the public the Secretary of State can order a change at any time ***(S.32)***. The Court may order a change if James' choice amounts to the tort of passing off ie it leads customers to believe that they are dealing with a different existing company.

   (b) A promoter has a fiduciary relationship with the company he is promoting, so he must make full disclosure of any profit he makes out of the promotion. Disclosure may be made to an independent board of directors (this is unlikely since the promoter will usually be one of the first directors) or to existing and potential members.

   If James is promoting a public company and selling his own property to the company in return for payment out of the proceeds of the issue he must disclose in the prospectus:

   i. The amount payable to him is cash, shares or debentures; and

   ii. Short particulars of any transaction relating to the property completed within the preceding two years in which James had a direct or indirect interest. Clearly if he purchased the property within these two years the price he paid must be disclosed.

In the event of non-disclosure the company may rescind the contract or keep the property and sue to recover James' profit. If James has made a profit on a related transaction this may also be claimed by the company. The company may also consider suing James for negligence or fraud.

(c) The problem arises because the company cannot contract to pay him before incorporation because it does not exist, nor can it contract to pay him after incorporation because the consideration would be past, ie James' work in promoting the company would be complete before any promise to pay.

The problem may be avoided by inserting in the articles the usual provision giving the directors the power to manage the company and exercise all the powers of the company. Provided James then becomes one of the first directors he will no doubt be able to ensure that he is paid.

James should bear in mind that a provision in the articles cannot amount to a contract between James and the company, all the articles can do is give the directors the power to pay him. A more certain method of payment would be for James to sell property to the company for more than its worth (the difference being his payment). Provided all disclosure requirements are met this is acceptable.

**Comment**

In connection with part (c) note that the latest version of table A (issued in 1985) no longer gives a specific power to directors to pay promoters' expenses. This change does not show an intention that promoters are not paid, it merely indicates that the power to pay them is part of the wider power of management.

2. A public limited company is a company limited by shares, having a share capital, whose memorandum states that it is a public company and which complies with the Act's provisions as to registration as a public company.

Registration is effected by submitting the following documents to the registrar and paying the appropriate fee (£50) and capital duty (£1 for every £100 of issued capital).

a. The Memorandum of Association. This must contain

i. ***Name*** clause, stating a name ending with the words 'public limited company' or the abbreviation plc.

ii. ***Registered Office*** clause, stating whether the registered office is in England and Wales, or in Scotland.

iii. ***Objects*** clause. By **S.110 CA 89 (S.3A)** this may merely be a statement that the object of the company is to carry on business as a general commercial company. This will allow it to carry on any trade or business whatsoever and do anything incidental or conducive to the carry on of any trade or business.

iv. ***Liability*** clause, stating that the liability of members is limited.

v. ***Capital*** clause, stating the amount of share capital and its division into shares of a fixed amount.

vi. ***Public company*** clause, stating that it will be a public company.

vii. ***Association*** clause, signed by two subscribers each indicating the number of shares that they agree to take.

b. Articles. The company may adopt Table A as the regulations for its management, or it may register specially drafted articles.

c. A statement containing the name, address, nationality, business occupation, other directorships and age of of the company. The statement must also contain the signed consent of each person to act.

d. Address of the registered office.

e. A statement of capital, to enable capital duty to be assessed.

f. A statutory declaration by a solicitor engaged in forming the company or by the persons named as directors that the registration requirements of the Act have been complied with.

If the registrar is satisfied that the documents are in order he will issue a Certificate of Incorporation. This is conclusive evidence that the Act's requirements have been met, ie registration will not be invalidated even if it is subsequently discovered that the formalities of registration were not complied with. However if it is later discovered that the company was formed for an illegal purpose it may be struck off. **(AG v LINDI ST CLAIRE (1980))**.

Following registration a public company may not necessarily immediately commence trading. By **S.117** it must first obtain a certificate of compliance with capital requirements. To do this it must make a statutory declaration that, for example, the value of the allotted share capital is not less than £50,000 and that the amount paid up is at least one quarter of the nominal value of the allotted share capital. If a public company starts business before obtaining this certificate, the company and officers in default are liable to a fine. The transaction itself will be valid, but the directors are liable to indemnify the other party if he suffers loss due to the company's failure to meet any obligations under that transaction.

***Comment***

Although the question asks for procedures, it is still necessary to define a public limited company. It is also necessary to give a brief explanation of the significance of the documents which must be submitted for registration. The words 'entitled to do business' are a clear invitation to discuss one of the differences between public and private companies, ie that a private company can start trading immediately after incorporation, but a public company must obtain a certificate of compliance with capital requirements before it is entitled to do business.

3. The effect of ***S.14*** is to contractually bind the company to the members, the members to the company, and the members to each other. The contract establishes as the rights and duties of members the provisions of the memorandum and articles. The original members expressly agree to be bound and subsequent shareholders impliedly agree to be bound.

   The contractual relationship between the shareholders and the company established by ***S.14*** only exists if the member is in dispute in his capacity as member and not in the capacity of, for example, company solicitor or director. For example in **ELEY v POSITIVE LIFE ASSURANCE CO (1876)** the articles contained a clause appointing Eley as company solicitor. He acted as such for some time, but then the company ceased to employ him. His action for breach of contract failed because it was held that the articles could not constitute a contract between the company and an outsider, (or a member in his capacity as an outsider). In **HICKMAN v KENT SHEEP BREEDERS ASSOCIATION (1915)** the articles provided for disputes between members and the company to be referred to arbitration. A dispute arose concerning Hickman's membership of the Association. It was held that a court action must be stayed because the articles contractually bound Hickman to initially attempt to resolve the dispute by arbitration. But in **BEATTIE v BEATTIE LTD (1938)**, where the dispute concerned a director's remuneration and his right to inspect the books, a similar arbitration clause was not binding because the dispute was in the capacity of director.

   The articles are also a contract between the shareholders themselves. Disputes are most likely to arise when the articles give members a right of first refusal when another member wishes to sell his shares. In such cases a direct action between shareholders is possible. For example in **RAYFIELD v HANDS (1960)** the articles stated that 'Every member who intends to transfer his shares shall inform the directors, who will take the said shares equally between them at a fair price'. The articles also provided that every director should be a shareholder. It was held that a member could enforce this obligation on the directors because the section was a contract between the members and the 'member directors' and the contract imposed an obligation rather than an option purchase.

   In two respects the effect of ***S.14*** differs from contracts in general:

   Firstly it does not provide the full range of remedies for breach of contract. A member's remedies are limited to an injunction to prevent a breach, and an action for a liquidated sum due to him as a member, for example unpaid dividends. The remedy of damages is apparently not available, because of the court's desire to maintain the capital of the company.

Secondly it does not guarantee future rights and duties. The contract in ***S.14*** is subject to the provisions of the Companies Acts, which allow alteration of both the memorandum and articles. Thus when becoming a member a person agrees to a contract which is alterable by the other party (the company) at a future date.

***Comment***

There are several cases which suggest that a member should be allowed to bring a personal action to restrain any breach of the articles even if this has the effect of enforcing rights conferred on him or any one else otherwise than as a member. For example, in **QUIN AND AXTENS LTD v SALMON (1909)** a member, suing as such, obtained an injunction to prevent a company from completing transactions entered into in breach of an article which required the consent of two managing directors, of whom he was one. Thus he indirectly enforced a veto given to him by the articles in a capacity other than that of member, and made sure that the company's affairs were conducted in accordance with the articles. This case is however very difficult to reconcile with **ELEY v POSITIVE LIFE ASSURANCE CO**, and several other leading cases. Although, the Quin and Axtens case is referred to in the Association's answer a good pass could still be obtained without delving into this difficult grey area.

**4.** (a) The most significant exceptions to the concept of separate legal personality have concerned parent companies and subsidiary undertakings. Thus for the purpose of presentation of financial statements the companies in a group must be treated as one. Also in **DHN FOOD DISTRIBUTORS v TOWER HAMLETS LBC (1976)** a group of three companies were treated as one for the purpose of awarding compensation on the compulsory purchase of the group's premises which was owned solely by one of the companies in the group.

The 'veil' may also be lifted under several statutory provisions. For example by ***S.214–215 IA*** where companies have become insolvent and have traded wrongfully, directors may be held personally liable to contribute to the assets of those companies. Also by ***S.24*** if a company carries on business without having at least two members for more than six months, any person who is a member and who knows of this irregularity shall be liable for the debts of the company contracted after the six months have expired.

There are also several relevant cases, for example in **DAIMLER v CONTINENTAL TYRE AND RUBBER CO (1916)** the respondent sued Daimler for money due in respect of goods supplied. Daimler's defence was that since Continental Tyre's members and officers were German, to pay the debt would be to trade with the enemy. Despite the fact that Continental Tyre was a company registered in England the defence succeeded, since the court based its decision on the actual identity of the members.

(b) The courts will lift the veil of incorporation if a company is being used to enable a person to evade his legal obligations. For example in **GILFORD MOTOR CO v HORNE (1933)** an employee covenanted that after the termination of his employment he would not solicit his former employer's customers. Soon after the termination of his employment he formed a company, which then sent out circulars to the customers of his former employer. The Court lifted the veil of incorporation, granting an injunction which prevented both the former employee and his company from distributing the circulars even though the company was not a party to the covenant. The first situation is clearly based on this case. Walter's fraudulent scheme would therefore fail.

In the second situation the transfer of the land to Desks Ltd is a clear breach of the contract to sell to Wilf. Normally the remedy of specific performance will not be granted if a third party has acquired rights in the subject matter. However in this case the 'third party' is Walter's company. The court would therefore lift the veil and regard Walter and Desks Ltd as the same person. Following **JONES v LIPMAN (1962)**, where the facts were similar, specific performance would be granted in Wilf's favour.

***Comment***

Probably the easiest question on the paper. Remember to give both case law and statutory examples in part (a). Other cases include **RE BUGLE PRESS (1961), GOODWIN v BIRMINGHAM CITY FOOTBALL CLUB (1980)** and several others referred to in the Association's answer. Other statutory examples include ***S.117*** (Chapter 6.8) and ***S.349*** (Chapter 7.8). Note that the terms 'parent company' and 'subsidiary undertaking' were introduced by CA 89. They are defined more widely than 'holding company' and 'subsidiary company' (see Chapter 17.18).

5. (a) A public company is one which is registered or re-registered as public and which states in its memorandum that it is a public limited company. All other companies are private companies.

There are numerous differences between public and private companies, but those relating to the company's 'legal nature' are found in the memorandum. They are as follows:

i. A public company's memorandum will contain a clause which states that the company is a public company;

ii. The name clause will be different since the name of a public company must end with the words 'public limited company' or the abbreviation 'p.l.c.'. The name of a private company must end with 'Limited' or 'Ltd';

iii. The capital clause may differ since a private company has no minimum capital, but a public company must have allotted capital with a nominal value or at least £50,000.

The other differences concern, for example, share capital, (in particular the prohibition on a private company offering shares or debentures to the public ***(S.81)***) payment for shares, dividends and directors.

The Companies Act 1980 widened the substantive differences between public and private companies, but it removed several less significant differences. Thus the minimum number of members is two and the maximum is unlimited for both public and private companies.

(b) A company limited by guarantee is one where each member's liability is limited to the amount he has agreed to contribute in the event of liquidation. The amount, usually £1 or £5, will be specified in the memorandum. A company limited by guarantee may also have a share capital in which case the member is liable to pay the amount unpaid on his shares as well as the guarantee.

Apart from the provisions regarding liability the other legal distinctions between companies limited by guarantee and by shares are found in their constitutional documents. A company limited by guarantee without a share capital must set out its memorandum and articles in the form prescribed by ***TABLE C*** of the ***COMPANIES (TABLES A TO F) REGULATIONS 1985***. If it has a share capital the form of memorandum and articles prescribed by ***TABLE D*** must be used.

Liability limited by guarantee is not appropriate for trading companies. It is used by, for example, charities, educational establishments, trade associations and museums.

c. If a company wishes to remain a separate legal entity from its members, but wishes to enjoy more privacy it may change to unlimited. Then it is not required to deliver to the registrar copies of its accounts (unless it is the subsidiary of, or the holding company of, a limited company).

Only a private company may re-register as unlimited. The procedure is governed by ***S.49–50***. An application is made to the registrar setting out the appropriate changes to the memorandum and articles. The application must be signed by a director or secretary and accompanied by:

i. An assent signed by or on behalf of all the members;

ii. A statutory declaration by the directors that the signatories constitute all the members;

iii. A printed copy of the new memorandum and articles.

These safeguards are necessary because the members are giving up the advantage of limitation of liability. If satisfied with the application the registrar will issue a new certificate of incorporation.

*Comment*

The key words in part (a) are 'legal nature'. Clearly the examiner does not expect all the differences between public and private companies to be listed. The words 'legal nature' indicate that you should confine your answer to the differences in the memoranda of public and private companies, since it is in the constitutional documents of a company that its legal nature is to be found. You should also consider including some similarities between public and private companies, for example, they must both have at least two members and they both have a legal personality separate from that of their members. The reason for this is that the question starts 'Compare and contrast'. It is safest to regard this to mean compare the similarities and contrast the differences. The alternative is to assume that the examiner has unnecessarily repeated himself.

The only other comment concerns part (c). It is just a reminder to read the question. In this type of question many students adequately cover the procedure, but fail to notice that the examiner has also asked for the reason for changing the company from limited to unlimited.

## SUGGESTED ANSWERS TO COURSEWORK QUESTIONS 6–10 THE RAISING AND MAINTENANCE OF CAPITAL

6. It is clear that A Limited is in serious financial difficulties. Its net assets are approximately £175,000, compared with paid up capital of £325,000. In addition since it has substantial accumulated losses and has been unable to pay a preference dividend for five years it appears that this is not a short term fluctuation in fortune, but a permanent loss of capital.

   The best action for the company would be to reduce its capital under ***S.135***. This section allows a company to reduce its capital in any case, but in particular it specifies three situations, one of which is the cancellation of capital which is lost and no longer represented by assets.

   To reduce its capital under ***S.135*** a company must have authority in its articles and it must pass a special resolution (a three-quarter majority of members entitled to vote and voting at a meeting of which 21 days notice has been given specifying the intention to propose the special resolution). If there is not authority in the articles the same special resolution will suffice to alter the articles and reduce the capital. Finally the company must obtain the consent of the court.

Before giving its consent the court will in general consider whether the reduction is equitable between the various classes of shareholders involved. If the reduction affects creditors (as it would if the company proposed to extinguish the ordinary shareholders' liability to pay up the remaining 50 pence per share) then the court will not consent to the reduction unless the creditors agree to it, are given security, or are paid off.

In A Limited's case the scheme for the reduction would probably include the following proposals:

Firstly that the share premium account be written off. Since the share premium account is a statutory capital reserve it cannot simply be cancelled. Apart from specified purposes for which it may be used (for example to finance an issue of fully paid bonus shares) the share premium account must be reduced in accordance with ***S.135***.

Secondly the scheme should include a proposal to call up the remaining 50 pence per ordinary share. This would raise £100,000 which could be used to pay the arrears of preference dividend (£37,500) and any creditors who are pressing for payment.

Finally the nominal value of each ordinary share should be reduced to 75 pence. The debit balance on profit and loss account would then be extinguished, having been written off against a reduction of £100,000 in the share premium account and £50,000 ordinary share capital.

The effect of the above scheme is to place the burden of the reduction on the ordinary shareholders. This is usually a condition required by the court before it gives consent. Secondly it eliminates the debit balance on profit and loss account, so that if profits are earned in future years dividends may be paid. Finally it may well have helped the company's liquidity situation.

***Comment***

This question on capital reduction is more difficult than average, since it requires not only a summary of the required procedure, but also specific recommendations as to how the reduction can be achieved. Reduction of capital has been asked in several questions since 1978. For example in May 1989 the CIMA examiner asked for a report explaining the methods which may be adopted to reduce the capital. When such general questions are asked, it must be remembered that a purchase of own shares is also a capital reduction and should therefore be given as much attention as a reduction under ***S.135***.

7. By ***S.130*** when shares are issued at a premium, whether for cash or otherwise, the premium must be paid into a share premium account. This is a statutory capital reserve which cannot be cancelled or distributed by the company. It can only be utilised for the purposes specified in ***S.130(2)***

(For example to write off preliminary expenses) and if it is to be reduced the procedure set out in ***S.135*** must be followed.

***S.130*** refers to an issue for 'cash or otherwise'. Thus where shares are issued in return for property, goods, services, or shares in another company, a share premium account is generally required if the actual value of the property or other non-cash assets exceeds the nominal value of the shares issued in return. This was always the case prior to 1981 as illustrated by **HEAD v ROPNER HOLDINGS (1952)**, where the facts were similar to the question. It was confirmed by **SHEARER v BERCAIN (1980)**.

Thus prior to 1981 AB Limited would have to create a share premium account of £100,000 since the actual value of the assets transferred is £500,000 and the nominal value of the shares issued is £400,000 (A Ltd and B Ltd each had 200,000 £1 shares and it is a one-for-one issue). This would however have the unfortunate consequence of preventing the distribution of the pre-acquisition profits of A Ltd and B Ltd since these profits are part of the ' assets' transferred. The 1981 Act dealt with this by allowing merger relief in certain circumstances. Now by ***S.131*** merger relief is available when the issuing company (AB Ltd) has acquired at least 90% of the equity share capital of another company (A Ltd and B Ltd) in consequence of the allotment of its own equity shares. In such cases ***S.130*** does not apply to the premium on the shares allotted by the issuing company. ***S.131*** appears to cover the merger of A Ltd and B Ltd since AB Ltd has acquired all their assets (not merely 90%) in return for an allotment of its own shares. A share premium account need not therefore be created.

***Comment***

Like the previous question, this is unusual since most questions on the share premium account are descriptive rather than problem questions. It would have been acceptable to refer to other uses of the share premium account, namely:

i. To finance an issue of fully paid bonus shares to members;

ii. To write off commissions paid, or discounts allowed, or the expenses of an issue of shares or debentures;

iii. To provide the premium payable on the redemption of any debentures of the company;

iv. Where redeemable shares are issued at a premium, to provide the premium payable on redemption (subject to conditions).

8. (a) By ***S.143*** no company may acquire its own shares. However, since 1981 there have been a number of exceptions to this rule.

    By ***S.162–164*** a private company may make an off market purchase of its own shares provided it has authority in its articles and the purchase is authorised by special resolution. (The company is private since the question refers to 'Dog Ltd' not 'Dog Plc'.) If the shares are purchased out of distributable profits an amount equal to the nominal value of the shares purchased must be transferred to a capital redemption reserve. If Dog Ltd complies with further stringent requirements it may purchase the shares out of capital.

Dog Ltd may purchase its own debentures without restriction. Debentures are not capital and purchase of them merely amounts to early repayment of a loan.

(b) By ***S.151*** it is unlawful for a company to give financial assistance for the purchase of its own shares or shares in its holding company. This rule is subject to many exceptions. In particular a private company may give such financial assistance provided the company's net assets are not thereby reduced, or to the extent that they are reduced the financial assistance is provided out of distributable profits. The main conditions which must be complied with are:

i. A special resolution must be passed;

ii. The directors must make a statutory declaration that the company can, and will for the next 12 months be able to pay its debts; and

iii. The auditors must report that in their opinion the statutory declaration is not unreasonable.

Holders of 10% of the issued shares of any class may within 28 days apply to the court to have the resolution set aside. The guarantee by Dog Ltd of C's loan amounts to financial assistance. It would therefore be subject to the above rules. The loan to C to enable him to purchase the debentures is not however subject to restrictions.

(c) By ***S.330*** a company may not make a loan to its director or to a director of its holding company, nor may it enter into any guarantee or provide any security in connection with a loan made to such directors. There are several exceptions to this rule. The only one which may be relevant is that by ***S.334*** a loan of not more than £5,000 is allowed. Thus unless this exception applies the whole transaction will be void. It does not matter that the loan is to be used to purchase debentures as well as shares.

(d) Since Dog Ltd owns more than half the equity share capital of Fox Ltd, Dog Ltd is a holding company and Fox Ltd is its subsidiary ***S.144 CA 89 (S.736)***.

By ***S.23*** no company can be a member of its holding company, and any allotment or transfer of shares in a company to its subsidiary shall be void. Fox Ltd may however hold debentures in Dog Ltd.

**Comment**

This is a fairly difficult question. The first thing to do is to write down the main points about the participants. This will help to avoid confusion later on, for example:

| | | | | |
|---|---|---|---|---|
| A | Director; | 40% Shareholder; | Holds debentures; | Wishes to leave. |
| B | Director; | 40% Shareholder. | | |
| C | | 20% Shareholder. | | |

You should have noticed that although part (a) only appears to be one question, the sentence refers to both shares and debentures. Thus the examiner is in fact asking two questions, since the rules for the purchase of own shares are completely different from the rules for the purchase of own debentures. Another point illustrated by the question is the difference between loans to directors and loans to members. A loan to a director is generally prohibited, although exceptions include loans to directors to enable them to perform their duties and loans of less than £5,000. Loans to members are generally not prohibited although a loan for the purchase of own shares is subject to strict controls.

9. The basic rule, contained in **S.143** is that no company may acquire its own shares. There are a number of exceptions, in particular a purchase of redeemable shares (ie specifically redeemable under the terms of their issue at a fixed date or at the option of the company or the shareholder) or a purchase of own shares (ie not issued as redeemable). Redeemable shares may be issued and redeemed subject to the following conditions:

   (a) There must be shares in issue which are not redeemable;

   (b) Shares may not be redeemed unless they are fully paid;

   (c) The terms of the redemption must provide for payment on redemption;

   (d) The terms and manner of redemption must be specified at or before the time of issue, including the date on or by which (or dates between which) the shares will be (or may be) redeemed.

   (e) The amount payable on redemption must be specified in, or determined in accordance with, the articles and in the latter case the articles cannot provide for the amount to be determined by reference to any person's discretion or opinion.

   (f) The shares may only be redeemed out of distributable profits or the proceeds of a fresh issue made for the purpose of the redemption.

   To safeguard the capital fund of the company, when shares are redeemed out of distributable profits, a sum equal to the nominal value of the shares redeemed must be transferred from profits to a capital redemption reserve.

This must be treated as capital (ie it cannot be distributed) however it can be used to finance an issue of fully paid bonus shares.

If a public company wishes to purchase its own shares it must have authority in its articles. The conditions that apply to a redemption of redeemable shares also apply to a purchase of own shares (for example the shares must be fully paid) however the procedure must comply with ***S.166***. This requires the company to obtain the prior approval of an ordinary resolution for the purchase of a number of shares within specified price limits and within a specified time, which must not exceed 18 months. The maximum and minimum prices may be specified by reference to a formula. The ***S.166*** procedure applies to a 'market purchase' of own shares, ie shares quoted on the stock exchange, the unlisted securities market, or the third market. An 'off-market' purchase would not generally apply to a public company. The procedure is different, in particular a special resolution is necessary to authorise the purchase. In each case the shares to be purchased cannot vote on the resolution for their purchase.

When a company has purchased its own shares it must, within 28 days, deliver a return to the registrar stating the number and nominal value of shares purchased and the date of purchase. The aggregate amount paid must also be stated together with the maximum and minimum price paid. The shares that have been redeemed or purchased are treated as cancelled and the amount of the issued capital is reduced accordingly, however the authorised capital remains unchanged.

***Comment***

The purpose of the question is to test whether students can identify and concisely describe the important points in a complex piece of legislation. Probably the most likely cause of confusion would arise from a failure to appreciate the distinction between a redemption of redeemable shares and a purchase of own shares, in particular the fact that a redemption of redeemable shares is not governed by S.166, but by the terms of issue and/or the articles. I would advise only a very brief mention of 'off market purchase' of shares since the question is limited to public companies and it is most unlikely (but not impossible) that a public company would make an off market purchase. Note that d. and e. were added by ***S.133 CA 89 (S.159(A))***.

**10.** (a) Neither ordinary shareholders nor preference shareholders have an automatic right to a dividend, even if profits are available. It is up to the directors to decide whether or not to recommend a dividend. The dividend is then declared by the company in general meeting. Only when it has been declared does a dividend become payable and enforceable as a debt against the company. Even then, on liquidation, it is not payable until after the debentureholders and creditors have been paid.

(b) Restrictions are placed on the payment of dividends since the capital of the company must be protected. The acceptance of limited liability has led to this need to protect the capital contributed by the members, since members cannot be required to contribute funds to enable the company to pay its debts once they have paid for their shares in full. The capital is therefore a guarantee fund for creditors. The only risk that they take is that it is lost in the ordinary course of business. There is no risk that it is given back to members as dividends.

The law seeks to control the fund from which dividends are paid through the provisions of **S.263–281**.

The basic rule is in **S.263** which states that no company, whether public or private may make a distribution ( ie pay dividends) except out of its accumulated realised profits less its accumulated realised losses. The following points are relevant to this basic rule:

i. A 'distribution' is defined as any distribution of the company's assets to its members, whether in cash or otherwise. There are a few necessary exceptions, for example a distribution in a winding-up.

ii. 'Profits' includes both capital and revenue profits and 'losses' includes both capital and revenue losses.

iii. A provision (other than one arising as a result of the revaluation of all the fixed assets) must be treated as a realised loss. A provision is an amount set aside to meet a known liability the exact amount of which cannot be determined with accuracy.

iv. A profit will be regarded as realised when accepted as such by the conventions of the accountancy profession. Thus a profit on a sale is realised when the sale is made, even if the debtor has not yet paid.

The basic rule is modified in respect of public companies. By **S.264** a public company may not make a distribution if its net assets are less than the aggregate of called up share capital plus undistributable reserves, or if the result of the distribution would be to reduce net assets below the aggregate of called up share capital plus undistributable reserves. The definition of 'undistributable reserves' includes the excess of accumulated unrealised profits over accumulated unrealised losses. This means that a public company must take into account an unrealised loss, whereas a private company need not do so.

**S.270** specifies the accounts which must be referred to when determining the legality and amount of any distribution. Basically the last, properly prepared, audited, annual accounts must be used.

*Comment*

This question is fairly straightforward provided you remember that the dividend rules differ for public and private companies. The difference is that a public company must cover its unrealised losses (in so far as they exceed unrealised profits) by its realised profits before a distribution can be made, whereas a private company need only cover its realised losses. In practice such unrealised losses will usually arise from the writing down (other than by way of depreciation) of capital assets, since other unrealised losses will usually be charged to the profit and loss account.

## SUGGESTED ANSWERS TO COURSEWORK QUESTIONS 11–15 COMPANY SECURITIES

11. (a) When a company proposes to allot equity shares ( basically this means ordinary shares) it must first offer them to existing shareholders in proportion to the shares that they already hold. It cannot make any allotment unless either the offer period has expired or the company has received a reply to every offer made. The offer must remain open for at least 21 days. These provisions do not apply to shares issued under an employees' share scheme, or where the shares are issued for a consideration other than cash. Private companies may exclude these provisions in their memorandum or articles. Also any company may by special resolution resolve that the provisions do not apply to a specific allotment, although in this case the directors must also recommend the resolution and circulate a statement setting out the reasons for their recommendation.

The significance of these provisions is that they give each shareholder the opportunity to prevent his shareholding being watered down by a subsequent issue of shares.

(b) Preference shares confer on holders preference over other classes of shareholder in respect of either dividends, repayment of capital or both. The only implied difference between preference and ordinary shares is that preference shares carry a prior right to receive a fixed annual dividend, although other express differences are usually stated. Preference shareholders do not have a right to compel the company to pay a dividend if it declines to do so. The right to receive a preference dividend is cumulative unless the contrary is stated. Thus if a 6% dividend is not paid in 1990 the priority entitlement will be 12% in 1991. Preference shareholders have no right to participate in any additional dividend above their specified rate, the entire balance of available profit may be distributed to ordinary shareholders. But this rule may be expressly over-ridden by the terms of the issue. Apart from the prior right to dividends, the basic rule is that preference shares carry the same rights as ordinary shares unless otherwise stated, for example, rights as to return of capital, distribution of surplus assets, and voting. In practice preference shares are not usually issued on this basis. Probably it will be expressly provided that

i. Preference shares carry a prior right to return of capital; and

ii. They only have voting rights in specified circumstances, for example if there is a failure to pay preference dividend, or on a resolution to wind up.

The significance of preference shares is that they enable the company to expand the range of securities available to its investors. They attract investors who want a steady return on their capital combined with some level of involvement with the company and a safer investment than ordinary shares. However in Professor Gower's opinion they share the disadvantages of ordinary shares and debentures, without obtaining their advantages. They only receive a return on money if profits are earned and dividends declared, they rank after creditors on a winding up, and they have less effective remedies for enforcing their rights. Thus they get the worst of both worlds.

(c) Company articles may authorise the issue of shares which may be redeemed either at the option of the company or the shareholder. In most cases shares may only be redeemed out of distributable profits or out of the proceeds of a fresh issue of shares made for the purpose. When distributable profits are used a sum equal to the nominal value of the shares redeemed must be transferred to a capital redemption reserve. When shares are redeemed they are treated as cancelled and the amount of the company's share capital is diminished by the nominal value of those shares.

The main reason for the change in company law in 1981 allowing the issue of redeemable shares was to increase the marketability of shares. Since the company itself now becomes a potential buyer this helps to retain 'family' control or private companies, it increases interest in employee share schemes, and it assists companies to raise venture capital, since it is easier for the venture capitalist to 'get out' by selling the shares back to the company.

*Comment*

With only ten minutes for each part of this question your problem should be deciding what to leave out rather than struggling to think of things to include. Certain matters other than those discussed above would earn marks, for example, a mention of redeemable preference shares in part (c) and the detailed rules on the issue of redeemable shares. However, the most likely error is to fail to discuss the significance of pre-emption rights, preference shares and redeemable shares, as specifically required by the question.

12. The relevant law is as follows:

A forged transfer is of no legal effect. Therefore D is still the true owner of the shares and is entitled to have his name restored to the register (**RE BAHIA AND SAN FRANCISCO RAILWAY (1868)**).

A genuine share certificate (as was issued by C Ltd to B) gives rise to an estoppel in favour of a person who lodges the certificate together with a transfer executed by the person named on the certificate. Estoppel is a rule of evidence which prevents a person (in this case C Ltd) from giving evidence that the true facts are not what his conduct represented them to be (the conduct in this case being the issue of the share certificate). The company must therefore compensate B for the loss he has suffered as a result of being removed from the register. This is based on the assumption that B did not know of the defect in A Ltd's title, since estoppel cannot help a person who has knowledge of the truth.

The ultimate loss does not however fall on C Ltd since any person who lodges a forged transfer (even if he does not know that it is a forgery) must indemnify the company for any loss it suffers. For example in **SHEFFIELD CORPORATION v BARCLAY (1905)** B attempted to register a transfer of stock belonging to T and H . The transfer was however a forgery since T had forged H's signature on it. B did not know this, nor was it recognised by the company. B was therefore registered as a member. He later transferred the stock to third parties to whom new certificates were issued. When T died H discovered the forgery. The company agreed to compensate H for his loss (rather than remove the third parties from the register and then compensate them under the estoppel rule). The company were then successful in their action to claim an indemnity from B.

The final result is that the loss will fall on A Ltd (ie the original victim of the fraud) unless it can bring a successful action against the person who committed the forgery. A Ltd's loss will be the amount it originally paid for the shares.

***Comment***

These questions can be rather confusing. It is helpful to remember that the loss will generally fall on the original victim of the fraud. The original victim's only remedy will be against the fraudulent person.

13. (a) An issue at a discount occurs when shares are issued for a consideration of less than their nominal value. By ***S.100*** shares may not be issued at a discount. If they are, they must be treated as paid up to the nominal value of the shares, less the amount of the discount and the allottee is liable to pay an amount equal to the amount of the discount plus interest at 5%. An issue of shares at a discount for cash would be most unlikely, particularly since modern practice fixes nominal values at between 5 and 25 pence per share, however shares will in effect be

issued at a discount if they are issued in exchange for an overvalued non-cash consideration. This is prevented in the case of public companies by the requirement of independent valuation, however there is no corresponding provision relating to private companies.

By **S.130** when shares are issued above their nominal value (whether for cash or for non-cash assets) the premium (ie the difference between the nominal value and the issue price) must be paid into a share premium account. This can only be used for limited specified purposes, for example to finance an issue of fully paid bonus shares or to write off preliminary expenses. This recognises that the true capital of the company is the consideration received for the shares, not the arbitrarily fixed nominal value.

(b) i. Since debentures are not 'capital' they may therefore be issued at a discount. The proposal is therefore legally acceptable, although in practice it would almost never occur.

ii. Although an issue of debentures at a discount is allowed, it is not acceptable to then exchange them for the same number of shares of an equal nominal since this would amount to an issue of shares at a discount. The facts of the question resemble **MOSELY v KOFFY FONTEIN MINES (1904)**. Racalite plc cannot therefore proceed with this issue.

iii. An issue of debentures on the terms stated is acceptable. However any debentureholder who exercises the right to convert, will be in effect purchasing ordinary shares for 5p more than their nominal value. This is therefore a share premium and must be paid into a share premium account.

iv. This is an issue of shares at a discount and the consequences stated above will follow. However when a public company issues shares it is normal for the issue to be underwritten, ie underwriters will agree to take those shares that the public does not take up. Underwriters may be paid a commission not exceeding 10% of the issue price provided there is authority in the articles and disclosure in the listing particulars. The commission is charged on the number of shares underwritten. It does not depend on the number of shares the underwriter is required to take. If shares are issued at their nominal value and underwriters are called upon to take some shares they must pay the full nominal value, but since this will be offset by their commission they do in effect,receive their shares at a discount.

***Comment***

Although it is not required for this question it is worth revising one situation where a share premium account is not required. This is the case when there is a merger and the issuing company (company A) has acquired at least 90% of the equity share capital of another company (company B) as a consequence of the allotment of its own equity shares. This merger relief provision prevents the pre-acquisition distributable profits of company B becoming the non-distributable share premium account of company A. Part b is also quite straightforward, but in part iv. it is not clear whether the examiner intends us to assume that the 5p difference between the nominal value and the issue price is in fact underwriting commission.

**14.** (a) By ***S.183*** when shares are transferred a proper instrument of transfer must be delivered to the company, ie the transfer must be in writing. The following procedure was introduced by the ***STOCK TRANSFER ACT 1963*** and it applies despite anything in the articles.

A transfer form, signed by the transferor, is sent by the transferee, with the share certificate and the registration fee, to the company. If the articles restrict the right to transfer shares the transfer must be submitted to the board to ensure that the restrictions are compiled with. After approval by the board the name of the transferee is entered on the register and that of the transferor deleted. The company must issue a new share certificate within two months.

When a person wishes to transfer part of his shareholding the procedure is:

i. The transferor executes the transfer and sends it with his share certificate to the company;

ii. The company secretary endorses 'certificate lodged' on the transfer and returns it to the transferor, keeping the share certificate;

iii. The transferor hands the certified transfer to the transferee who lodges it with the company for registration;

iv. The company issues two new share certificates.

The different procedure is necessary because it would be unsafe for the transferor to give the transferee the certificate in return for a consideration in respect of only part of the shares. Similarly it would be unreasonable to expect the transferee to pay for the shares whilst allowing the transferor to retain the certificate.

(b) In Jack's case the facts resemble **RE SMITH AND FAWCETT (1942)** where it was held that the discretion of directors to register transfers is a fiduciary power that must be exercised bona fide in what they consider (not what the court considers) to be in the interest of the company. The onus of proving to the contrary is on the person alleging bad faith and the burden of proof is difficult to discharge. In **RE SMITH AND FAWCETT** the plaintiff was unsuccessful and there is no evidence in the question to suggest that Jack would do any better.

Alice's problem resembles **MOODIE v SHEPHERD (BOOKBINDERS) (1949)** where it was held that a transferee is entitled to be registered unless the directors as a board resolve to reject (ie failure to register due to lack of agreement does not amount to refusal). Alice would therefore be entitled to have the register rectified to show her increased shareholding.

In **RE COPAL VARNISH (1917)** a director purposely refused to attend board meetings so that a quorum could not be obtained and accordingly transfers could not be passed for registration. It was held that the transferee was entitled to an order directing the company to register the transfer. Maggie will therefore be able to sell to Dick.

*Comment*

Part (a) is very straightforward. Note that the shares are fully paid. When partly paid shares are transferred the transfer form must also be signed by the transferee.

The examiner's report is critical of candidates' performance on part (b). In students' defence I would suggest that the cases on which the problems are based are not regarded as leading cases, although RE SMITH AND FAWCETT is reasonably well known. Jack and Alice's problems are difficult because if you do not know the cases you need a very good general knowledge of company law principles to reach the correct answers. In Maggie's case the answer is more clear cut. The Association's answer refers to RE HACKNEY PAVILION (1924) as the basis for Alice's situation. This was approved in the later House of Lords case referred to in the above answer.

**15.** (a) The basic rule is that a fixed charge, whether legal or equitable, will take priority over a floating charge even if the floating charge was created and registered before the fixed charge. The reason for this is that by taking as security a floating charge the debentureholders have impliedly authorised the company to deal with the assets charged and 'dealing' in this context includes the creation of further charges.

The basic rule is however modified in that a fixed charge will not have priority over a floating charge if:

i. The floating charge prohibits the creation of later fixed charges with priority; and

ii. The fixed charge holder has notice of this prohibition.

The problem is that although registration is constructive notice of the charge itself it is not notice of the fact that it contains a prohibition on the creation of later fixed charges with priority (**WILSON v KELLAND (1910)**).In practice debentureholders include a note of the restriction on the registered particulars, but it is unlikely that this is effective, since constructive notice can probably only be given of matters which must be inserted in the registered particulars.

As between themselves fixed charges rank according to their date of registration. Floating charges over the same property rank according to their date of registration, but a floating charge over a particular class of assets takes priority over a general floating charge over all the company's assets **(RE AUTOMATIC BOTTLE MAKERS (1926))**.

If a charge is registered late, a later created charge will take priority if it is registered before the earlier charge. A later created charge will also take priority over an earlier charge to the extent to which the registered particulars of the earlier charge fail to disclose certain rights ***(S.99 CA 89 (S.404))***.

(b) The value of a floating charge as an effective security is reduced by the following factors.

Firstly its value is uncertain since the value of the assets will fluctuate . Furthermore when the security is most necessary, ie when the company is unsuccessful, the value of the assets is likely to be low.

Secondly if a seller of goods has 'reserved title' until payment, a floating charge will not, on crystallisation, attach to those goods **(ALUMINIUM INDUSTRIE VAASSEN v ROMALPA (1976))**.

Thirdly debentureholders rank for priority after preferential creditors, and if a trade creditor had levied and completed execution he cannot be compelled to restore the money and prior to crystallisation he cannot be prevented from levying execution.

Finally the charge may be invalidated by ***S.245 or S.238–240 IA***. By ***S.245*** when a company is being wound-up a floating charge created within the 12 months prior to commencement of winding up (2 years if the charge is in favour of a connected person) will be invalid unless it was proved that the company was solvent immediately after the creation of the charge, or unless the charge was to secure the provision of 'new' money. By ***S.238–240*** any charge made within the 6 months prior to the commencement of winding up is void if it is a preference of any of the company's creditors. If it is a transaction at an undervalue it may be avoided if entered into up to 2 years before liquidation.

***Comment***

You should be well prepared for questions on priorities, since they are asked quite frequently. It is nevertheless a difficult topic which needs to be understood and learned thoroughly.

# SUGGESTED ANSWERS TO COURSEWORK QUESTIONS 16–20 COMPANY OFFICERS

16. (a) A company may lend to its director:

i. If the loan (or aggregate of several loans) is not more than £5,000 *(S.334)*.

ii. If the loan is to enable a director to perform his duties. However the loan must have the prior approval of the company in general meeting or contain a provision that if it is not approved at the next general meeting the funds must be repaid within six months. The maximum loan to a director of a relevant company (a public company or a private company in a public company group) is £10,000 *(S.337)*.

iii. If the company is a recognised bank and the terms are commercially sound. If the loan is to purchase a house the terms must be no more favourable than those offered to employees and the loan must not exceed £100,000 *(S.338)*.

(b) By *S.320* a property transaction is substantial if the value of the property exceeds the lesser of either £50,000 or 10% of the company's net assets. Transfers of less than £1,000 are exempt. A director will be involved in the transaction if he personally transfers or acquires the property or if the party to the transaction is a person connected with the director. Connected persons include, for example, the director's spouse, infant child and business partner *(S.346)*.

(c) By *S.303* directors can be removed by ordinary resolution (a simple majority) provided a specified procedure is followed. In **BUSHELL v FAITH (1970)** a company had three members with 100 shares each. They were also the company's directors. The articles provided that on a resolution to remove a director that director's shares would carry three votes each. The House of Lords held that this article was not inconsistent with the Act, the company thus found itself with irremovable directors. The decision has attracted much criticism, Professor Schmittoff describing it as 'defeating the clear intention of the legislation'.

(d) i. Underwriting commission is a payment made to a person who, when there is a public issue of shares, agrees to purchase the shares not taken up by the public. He is paid a commission on the number of shares underwritten. The maximum rate is 10% *(S.97)* but the usual rate is 1%–2%.

ii. By *S.88* when any company allots shares it must within one month deliver to the registrar a return stating (a) The number and nominal value of the shares allotted; (b) The names, addresses and descriptions of the allottees; (c) The amount paid and payable on each share; and (d) Details of any non-cash consideration.

iii. The share premium is the difference between the nominal value of a share and its issue price. By **S.130** when shares are issued at a premium (whether for cash or otherwise) the premium must be paid into a share premium account. This may be used for several purposes, eg to write off preliminary expenses, but it cannot be distributed to members. **S.130** thus recognises that the true capital of the company (on which the creditors depend for payment) is not the arbitrarily fixed nominal value, but the actual value received for the shares.

(e) If the articles or terms of issue are silent there is a presumption of equality among all shareholders. However the articles will usually specify the rights of preference shareholders. They normally:

i. Restrict their right to vote to matters specifically affecting them;

ii. Give them a prior right to return of capital on liquidation; and

iii. Specify that preference shares are non-participating ie preference shareholders are not entitled to share in surplus profits after payment of the ordinary share dividend.

In addition to the above ways in which the class rights of preference shareholders ***might*** differ from ordinary shareholders, there will be a difference in that their dividend must be paid before ordinary shareholders receive anything (otherwise they would not be preference shares).

*Comment*

Each of the five parts is relatively straightforward but taken together they add up to a very substantial question. Clearly the difficulty would be to include sufficient material in the limited time available.

17. By **S.303** despite anything in the articles or in any agreement between the company and the director, a company can remove a director by ordinary resolution. Special notice must be given to the company by the person proposing the resolution. By **S.379** the period of special notice is 28 days. When a company receives special notice it must give its members notice of the resolution when it gives them notice of the meeting, or if this is impractical, by notice in a newspaper, or by some other method allowed by the articles, at least 21 days before the meeting.

On receipt of special notice of a resolution to remove a director the company must send a copy to the director. She may then make written representations of reasonable length to the company. These representations must then be sent to the members with notice of the meeting unless they are an attempt to gain needless publicity for defamatory matter. If the company receives the representations too late to send them with notice of the meeting the director can require that they be read out at the meeting. In addition she may speak on the resolution at the meeting.

The director whom it is proposed to remove may defeat the resolution even if she does not have the majority of voting shares since weighted voting rights may be attached to shares for particular resolutions. In **BUSHELL v FAITH (1970)** a company had 300 voting shares divided equally between the three members. Each member was also a director. The articles provided that on a resolution to remove a director, that director's shares would carry three votes each. It was held that the article was valid. A director could not therefore be removed without her consent. The decision in **BUSHELL v FAITH** has been widely criticised, but at present it represents the law.

The fact that the director has a service contract (which, since it is for more than 5 years, must be approved by the company in general meeting, ***(S.319)***) will not prevent her removal before the end of that period, However if she has complied with her contractual obligations, she will be entitled to damages for breach of contract **(SOUTHERN FOUNDRIES v SHIRLAW (1940))**.

If the company is a small 'quasi-partnership' company the director may petition for winding up on the 'just and equitable' ground ***(S.122 IA 1986)***. She would have to show that her removal destroyed the mutual trust that provided the basis for the company. A possible alternative would be to bring an action under ***S.459*** on the ground that her removal was unfairly prejudicial. However the action must be brought (and the unfair prejudice suffered) in the capacity of member. The section was not generally intended to provide a remedy for directors who had been unfairly removed.

*Comment*
The only subtlety in the question is the reference to a 10 year service contract. However, provided this has been approved by the company in general meeting, it is just as valid as a service contract for 5 years or less made by the board. You have no reason to assume that the 10 year service contract had not been approved. However if it had not, it would be deemed to contain a term entitling the company to terminate at any time on giving reasonable notice.

**18.** i. A director's (including a managing director's) basic duty of care and skill is to exhibit the degree of skill which may reasonably be expected from a person with his knowledge and experience. **(RE CITY EQUITABLE FIRE INSURANCE CO (1925))**. If neither this duty nor any obligation under a service contract has been broken C clearly has no chance of success.

On the assumption that either the common law duty or a contractual duty has been broken the rule in **FOSS v HARBOTTLE (1843)** would appear to prevent an action by C. This rule states that where a wrong is done to a company the proper plaintiff in the action is the company.

It is however possible that the company has declined to take action because B is 'in league' with A. If this is the case C should bring an action under ***S.459*** on the grounds that the affairs of the company are being conducted in an unfairly prejudicial manner. Even so in **RE FIVE MINUTE CAR WASH (1966)** neither mismanagement, nor a refusal by the majority shareholders to remove the inefficient person were held to be oppressive conduct for the purposes of ***S.210 CA 1948*** (repealed **CA *1980***). However the requirement of unfair prejudice is more favourable to the plaintiff. C must therefore be regarded as having a reasonable chance of success provided there has been both a breach of duty plus a refusal by B to join C to cause the company to take action.

Such a wrong would be regarded as suffered by the company rather than by C. A personal action would not therefore be appropriate. The court however has the power under ***S.459*** to order the action to be brought by C on the company's behalf in the company's name.

ii. A director has a fiduciary duty not to make a secret profit from the use of corporate information or opportunity. The test is not the loss to the company, but whether the director has profited. **(INDUSTRIAL DEVELOPMENT CONSULTANTS v COOLEY (1972))**.

It was however held in **PESO SILVER MINES v CROPPER (1966)** that a director does not misuse corporate opportunity if he enters into a transaction on his own account which the company has considered and rejected. This seems reasonable in that if B cannot produce and sell his discovery, even though it has been rejected by his company's board, then the new product is unlikely ever to be made available to the public solely because of an error of judgement by the board of Smokease Ltd.

Two further points are relevant. Firstly it is unlikely that the profit would be regarded as secret since disclosure of all the facts has been made to the board, and the board appears to consist of all the members of the company. Secondly the profit is not made in his capacity as director. The discovery and profit was made in his capacity as an employed analytical chemist, and employees do not owe fiduciary duties.

It is therefore suggested that **PESO SILVER MINES v CROPPER (1966)** would be followed and B would not have to account. Thus C would not succeed in either a personal action, or an action on behalf of the company (a derivative action). Furthermore unless ***S.459*** applies (see above), or unless there has been a fraud on the minority C would be prevented from bringing either action by the rule in **FOSS v HARBOTTLE (1843)** (see above).

iii. By **S.303** despite anything in the articles or in any agreement between the company and the director a company can remove a director by ordinary resolution. Special notice must be given to the company by the person proposing the motion. On receipt of this notice a copy must be sent to the director. He may then make written representations to the company which it must send to the members with notice of the meeting. If the company receives the representations too late to send out with the notice of the meeting the director can require that his statement be read out at the meeting.

The correct procedure clearly has not been followed, but A and B have sufficient shares to remove C and provided they now follow the correct procedure C will be removed in due course.

C nevertheless has two chances of 'success'. Firstly his removal may be so inequitable as to justify the compulsory winding-up of the company under ***S.122 IA*** (the 'just and equitable' ground). The company must however be a 'quasi-partnership', ie it must be a small, well established company in which each 'partner' is entitled (as in a partnership) to share in the management of the business. A winding-up order was granted in similar circumstances in **RE WESTBOURNE GALLERIES (1973)**. Secondly **S.459** (see above), may help, although it appears that if it is to apply the unfair prejudice must be suffered in the capacity of member and in this case C has only been prejudiced in his capacity as director.

***Comment***

Part (i), although it carries the least marks, probably requires the most thought. It deals with a very common situation – how can a shareholder secure the removal of an incompetent managing director? Before tackling this point you should take the opportunity to outline the standard of care and skill expected of any director. You then proceed on the assumption that this standard has not been achieved. A useful approach to this type of problem is to place yourself in C's position and to consider exactly what you would do. Obviously you would try to persuade B to vote with you to remove A from the board, thus automatically terminating his job as managing director. Presumably C has tried this and failed. Thus it looks as if A and B are acting together to maintain A, who is inefficient, as managing director. The best course of action is to petition under S.459, and C's chance of success may well depend on the degree of A's inefficiency.

Notice that although A and B are presumed to be acting together in part (i), they clearly are not acting together in part (ii). Each part of the question must be regarded as separate and the facts of part (ii) must not affect our assumptions about part (i). Part (iii) is the easiest part and deals with the important topic of removal of directors.

**19.** In exercising their powers the directors must not only act bona fide, ie in what they honestly believe is the best interests of the company, they must also use their powers for a proper purpose, ie the purpose for which they were given. If the directors infringe this rule by exercising their powers for some other purpose, the transaction will be invalid unless the outsider is saved by ***S.108 CA 89 (S35A)*** (See Chapter 15.15) or the company is bound by the rules of agency, or the company in general meeting gives approval either prospectively or retrospectively. If the improper use of directors' powers concerns the allotment of shares, the votes attached to the new shares cannot be used when voting on a resolution to sanction it.

Most of the leading cases have concerned share issues. For example, in **HOWARD SMITH v AMPOL PETROLEUM (1974)** holders of 55% of the issued shares intended to reject a takeover bid. However the directors believed that it was in the company's interest for the bid to succeed, since the bidding company was likely to provide additional capital for the company if it obtained control. The directors therefore allotted new shares to the bidder to reduce the percentage held by opposing shareholders to less than 50%. It was held that the allotment was void since it was unconstitutional for directors to use their powers purely for the purpose of destroying an existing majority or creating a new majority. This decision does not mean that shares may only be issued to raise capital. It may be proper to issue shares to ensure the stability of the issuing company or as part of a programme of general expansion and development of future business.

Where directors use their powers for an improper purpose any shareholder may apply to the Court to declare the transaction void. However the Court's usual practice is to refer the issue to the members in general meeting. If the majority approve what has been done their decision is treated as a proper case of majority rule to which the minority must submit, unless of course there has been fraud. For example in **HOGG v CRAMPHORN (1967)** the directors issued shares, carrying ten votes each, to trustees of an employee pension fund. Their purpose was to prevent a takeover bid which they honestly thought would be bad for the company. The shares were paid for by trustees out of an interest free loan from the company. A minority shareholder brought an action to prevent the share issue. It was held that since the directors had acted honestly, and the issue was within the powers of the company, the company in general meeting could ratify the allotment, thus rendering it valid. However only one vote could be attached to each of the shares, since that was what the articles provided.

Since 1980 the company's authority (ordinary resolution) has been required for the allotment of shares by directors (**S.80**). However the principles described above apply equally to other powers vested in directors. For example the power to make calls, forfeit shares or register share transfers.

*Comment*

There are several other cases which could have been included instead of, or in addition to the two cases referred to above. For example, **BAMFORD v BAMFORD (1969)** or **TECK v MILLER (1972)**. In this case shares were issued to a company as part of a contract with that company to exploit mineral rights. The issuing company's shareholders wanted this contract for themselves, but the directors action forestalled them. It was held that this share issue, which was contrary to the wishes of the majority, showed sound judgement and was in the best interests of the company as a whole. The directors' action was confirmed by the court. In the examiner' s report on this paper it was pointed out that this question was the most poorly answered because candidates wrote about fiduciary duties in general and displayed very little knowledge of the duty referred to in the question.

20. By **S.317** a director who is in any way interested in a contract with the company must declare the nature of his interest at a board meeting. If he does not do so he may be fined and, although the section does not deal with the civil consequences of non-compliance, it is generally thought that the contract would be voidable.

    By **S.320** a company cannot transfer to or acquire from a director or any person connected with him any property the value of which exceeds the lesser of either £50,000 or 10% of the company's net assets without prior approval of the shareholders in general meeting.

    A director has a fiduciary duty not to use either corporate information or opportunity to make an undisclosed personal profit. For example in **INDUSTRIAL DEVELOPMENT CONSULTANTS v COOLEY (1972)** the managing director of IDC faked illness to secure the termination of his contract. He then took a contract in his own name which he had unsuccessfully tried to obtain for the company. It was held that he had to account to IDC with his profit. There is however Commonwealth authority for the proposition that a director may retain a profit derived from an opportunity that the company has considered and rejected. In the Canadian case of **PESO SILVER MINES v CROPPER (1966)** Peso's board considered and rejected the chance to purchase prospecting claims near the company's land. One of Peso's directors bought shares in a new company subsequently formed to purchase the claims. It was held that he did not have to account.

These rules may be applied as follows:

**S.317** has been broken and although the purchase was from Gold Ltd rather than Daniel, it is probable that the court would lift the veil of incorporation of Gold Ltd and regard it as the same 'person' as its majority shareholder so as to allow rescission of the contract.

**S.320** will have been broken if the value of the property purchased from Gold Ltd exceeds certain financial limits since Gold Ltd is a 'person connected' with Daniel. Thus for this reason also rescission would be possible.

The application of the law regarding the plot rejected by the company is much more difficult. Peso's case is similar but the decision has been widely criticised and has been described by Professor Gower as 'unsatisfactory'. In practice the outcome would be influenced by several other factors, for example the percentage of Prospect Ltd's shares held by Daniel, the part Daniel played in the board's decision to reject the plot and whether there is any link between the two transactions (perhaps Daniel could only purchase the rejected plot if he could use the sale proceeds from the other plot). The conclusion is borderline, but in view of Peso's case Daniel appears to have a reasonable chance of retaining the profit made on the resale of the plot rejected by the company.

***Comment***

By way of reminder please notice that the answer follows the usual style. It starts with statements of law and only then applies them to the facts and arrives at a conclusion.

The question requires knowledge of both statutory duties and fiduciary duties, but the main comment concerns breach of fiduciary duties, in particular the extent to which the company can decide not to take action in respect of such breaches. Suppose that you have just purchased a second-hand car and the vendor told you that it had covered 10,000 miles. Soon after completing the purchase you discover that it has done 25,000 miles. The vendor is in breach. You now have a choice, you can sue or you might decide that you would have purchased the car in any case and are not interested in legal action. If a company purchases a defective car it has the same choice. If the wrong suffered by the company is not a breach of contract but a breach of a duty by a director it still basically has that choice. Thus a general meeting can either prospectively or retrospectively permit directors to contract with the company, or permit them to profit from their office. Similarly it can ratify an act in excess of directors' powers or resolve not to sue in respect of a breach of duty of care and skill. But a resolution of the company cannot authorise the directors to act fraudulently towards the company. Therefore the company cannot authorise the expropriation either of company property or the property of other members. The courts will look most carefully at situations where the directors who have made a profit are themselves the majority shareholders.

In such cases a resolution allowing the directors to keep the profit would amount to fraud, unless the profit was not made at the expense of the minority and provided the directors acted in good faith and in the interests of the company. These two conditions would have been satisfied in **REGAL (HASTINGS) v GULLIVER**, but it did not occur to the directors to pass such a resolution.

The next point concerns the conclusion. Even if you are uncertain you must commit yourself one way or the other. It is not acceptable to say that Prospect Ltd has a 50/50 chance of success, nor should your conclusion appear totally free doubt if reasonable doubt exists. Finally I hope that you did not advise Prospect Ltd to sue its surveyors. This would be good advice in practice but it is clearly not required by the question.

## SUGGESTED ANSWERS TO COURSEWORK QUESTIONS 21–25 PROTECTION OF INVESTORS AND CREDITORS

21. (a) *S.2 CA 89 (S.221)* requires that the accounting records be sufficient to show and explain the company's transactions. The records must disclose with reasonable accuracy, at any time, the financial position of the company at that time. They must also enable the directors to ensure that any balance sheet prepared by them gives a true and fair view of the company's state of affairs and any profit and loss account gives a true and fair view of the company's profit or loss.

(b) *S.221* also states that the accounting records must in particular contain:

i. A day to day record of money received by and spent by the company;

ii. A record of the assets and liabilities of the company;

iii. Statements of the stock held by the company at the end of each financial year; and

iv. A record of goods sold and purchased, showing the goods, the buyers and the sellers in sufficient detail to enable the goods, buyers and sellers to be identified.

It is important to note that the accounting records are not the same as accounts. The accounting records are ledgers and documents that enable the accounts to be prepared. The accounts are the balance sheet and the profit and loss account. The legal requirements for the content of the accounts are now comprised in Schedule 4 (as amended by CA 89).

(c) **S.2 CA 89** ***(S.222)*** requires that a private company must keep its accounting records for three years from the date on which they are made. A public company must keep them for six years.

***Comment***
**S.221** and **S.222** were both amended by **S.2 CA 89**.

**22.** (a) The rule in **FOSS v HARBOTTLE (1843)** states that if a wrong is done to a company the company decides what action to take and the company is the proper plaintiff in the action. However sometimes the alleged wrongdoer is the majority shareholder and therefore will not allow the company to commence an action. In such cases the minority shareholder may commence a derivative action to enforce the company's rights. He is not suing on his own behalf or on behalf of other members, his right to sue is derived from the company, hence the term 'derivative action'. For example in **COOK v DEEKS (1916)** the directors/majority shareholders, while negotiating a contract on behalf of the company, took the contract in their own names. They then ensured that the company passed a resolution declaring that it had no interest in the contract. This was held to be a fraud on the minority and a derivative action was allowed. It is not always necessary that fraud be committed, an action will lie if the majority have themselves acted negligently in such a way as to benefit at the expense of the company. It used to be thought that a derivative action could only be commenced if the wrongdoer held the majority of the shares, but in **PRUDENTIAL ASSURANCE v NEWMAN INDUSTRIES (1981)** it was held that an action may be brought against persons in de facto (ie actual) control regardless of the votes held by them.

The disadvantage of a derivative action is that the minority shareholder may have to bear the costs of both sides if the action fails, although the court does have a discretion to order the company to pay the costs. If the action is successful the damages belong to the company, not the shareholder. The shareholder will also have to fit his action into one of the established exceptions to the rule in **FOSS v HARBOTTLE**, 'fraud on the minority' being the most likely category. It may therefore be preferable to commence an action under ***S.459*** since it may be easier to prove 'unfair prejudice' than 'fraud'. ***S.459*** leaves open the matter of costs, but if under ***S.461*** the court authorises civil proceedings to be brought in the company's name, it will presumably impose conditions with respect to costs such that the shareholder is likely to be at less risk than in a derivative action.

(b) David has acted either fraudulently or negligently in such a way as to benefit himself at the expense of the company. For example in **DANIELS v DANIELS (1978)** the company sold land to one of the majority shareholders at an undervalue. The plaintiff only alleged negligence rather than fraud, nevertheless his derivative action succeeded. Small may therefore commence a derivative action, but it would be better to petition the court for an order under **S.459**. This states that any member may petition the court for an order on the ground that the affairs of the company are being or have been conducted in a manner which is unfairly prejudicial to the interests of members generally or some part of the members (including at least himself) or that any proposed act or omission is or would be so prejudicial. The court may make any order it thinks fit, for example regulating the future conduct of the company's affairs or requiring the company to do or refrain from doing any act. In this case it would be most appropriate for the court to order cancellation of the resolution ratifying the sale.

*Comment*

The Association's answer to Part (a) makes reference to costs. This is most surprising and I doubt if many students would have made mention of this in their answers. There is in any case very little that can be said about costs at this level of examination, except that the court has a discretion to make such orders as it thinks fit.

Part (b) again raises the common problem of what to do when a director/majority shareholder is injuring the company. Sometimes such questions expect you to consider whether or not there has been a breach of duty. On other occasions you may be told that there has been a breach, in which case you need only advise on the available remedies. It is important to recognise that this is the latter type, since we are told that David, in breach of his duties as director, purchased machinery from the company. Despite these clear words many students probably wasted time considering whether or not David had broken his duties as a director.

As you can see **S.459** is the main part of the answer. Where you do advise a petition under **S.459** you should always suggest the particular order that you want the court to make. In this case cancellation of the resolution ratifying the sale would be the most appropriate. Some of you may have suggested Small petition the court to wind up the company on the 'just and equitable' ground. This is referred to in the Association's answer, but it appears to be an unsuitable solution both for Mighty PLC and Small. We are not dealing with a small private company where such a remedy may well be appropriate, we are dealing with a public company. Winding up is much too drastic where there has only been one wrongful act by the director and majority shareholder of a public company.

**23.** The extent of directors' powers is defined by the company's constitution, in particular its articles. Table A Article 70 provides that 'the business of the company shall be managed by the directors who may . . . exercise all the powers of the company'. It also states that 'no alteration of the memorandum or articles and no such direction shall invalidate any prior act of the directors'. The word 'direction' refers to a change introduced in 1985 whereby Table A makes directors' powers 'subject to any direction given by special resolution'. Prior to this amendment if the shareholders did not approve of the directors' acts they either had to remove them under **S.303** or alter the articles to regulate their future conduct. However this amendment, if adopted by companies, does give the meeting a limited power to take over the management of the company.

Directors' powers are also subject to provisions in the Companies Act which require certain matters to be dealt with by ordinary, special or extraordinary resolutions at company meetings, for example removal of directors (ordinary resolution), change of name or alteration or articles (special resolution) or the commencement of voluntary liquidation of an insolvent company (extraordinary resolution). A company meeting also has the power to ratify by ordinary resolution any act in excess of directors' powers provided the act was within the company's powers, for example **BAMFORD v BAMFORD (1970)** when the company ratified a share issue that directors had made in breach of their fiduciary duties. The general meeting may also act when a company has no directors. For example in **ALEXANDER WARD v SAMYANG NAVIGATION (1975)** two members, without authority, were able to commence a legal action on behalf of a company which had no directors.

The procedural rules of meetings require that they be properly convened by notice, a quorum must be present, and the meeting must be properly presided over by a chairman. The period of notice for an AGM is 21 days. For any other general meeting (an EGM) the period is 14 days unless a special resolution is on the agenda in which case 21 days notice is required. Notice must be sent to every member and must specify the date, place and time of the meeting. The quorum for all company meetings is two members personally present.

An ordinary resolution may be passed by a simple majority of members present in person or by proxy entitled to vote and voting. In general the registrar need not be informed, but there are exceptions, for example, a resolution removing a director, or altering the address of the registered office. Some ordinary resolutions require special notices for example resolutions to remove a director or to remove an auditor. This is a period of 28 days and the notice is given to the company by the person proposing the resolution. A special resolution requires a three quarter majority of members present in person or by proxy entitled to vote and voting. A period of 21 days notice must be given by the company to the members. An extraordinary resolution is the same as special resolution except that only 14 days notice is required. Copies of special and extraordinary resolutions must be filed with the registrar within 15 days of being passed. Voting is by show of hands unless a poll is properly demanded, in which case members have one vote for each voting share.

Even prior to the 1989 Act it was possible for all the members of a company, acting together to do anything that was intra vires the company. This was known as the 'assent principle'. This has been formalised in respect of private companies by ***S.113 CA 89 (S.38 IA)*** which provides that anything which may be done by resolution of a private company in general meeting may be done by a written resolution signed by or on behalf of all members. Previous notice is not required and the signatures need not be on a single document, however each signature must be on a document accurately stating the terms of the resolution. The date of the resolution is the date when the last member signed it.

***Comment***

This is quite a testing essay question which requires both an explanation of the division of powers between the general meeting and the directors as well as an outline of some of the procedures that need to be followed to exercise powers at a general meeting. Clearly there is a problem selecting which material to use. Your example could quite reasonably have also included a discussion of proxies, the role of the chairman, or more examples of matters requiring ordinary, special or extraordinary resolutions.

**24.** (a) By ***S.286*** the directors must take all reasonable steps to ensure that the secretary is a person who appears to have the requisite knowledge and experience. The person must also:

i. On 22 December 1980 have held office as secretary, assistant secretary or deputy secretary of the company; or

ii. For 3 out of 5 years preceding appointment have held office as secretary of a public company; or

iii. Be a barrister or solicitor; or

iv. Be a qualified accountant (ACCA, CIMA, ACA, CIPFA) or a chartered secretary (ACIS); or

v. By virtue of having held any other position, appear to the directors to be capable of discharging the functions of secretary.

The secretary is an agent of the company. Like any agent he will bind his principal if he acts within the scope of the express authority conferred on him by the directors. In addition he has ostensible authority to bind the company on contracts concerned with office administration. Such contracts include hiring office staff, purchasing office equipment and hiring cars to collect customers. In **PANORAMA DEVELOPMENTS v FIDELIS FURNISHING FABRICS (1971)** the secretary purportedly hired cars to collect customers. In fact the cars were for his use. It was held that such a contract was within his ostensible authority. The company was therefore liable to pay the hire charges.

The secretary cannot bind the company on a trading contract, nor can he borrow money on behalf of the company. Also he may not

i. Issue a writ in the company's name;
ii. Lodge a defence in the company's name;
iii. Instruct the company as to its legal rights;
iv. Register a transfer of shares;
v. Strike a name off the register of members; and
vi. Summon a general meeting on his own authority.

(b) By ***S.122 CA 89 (S.391)*** the company may remove an auditor before the end of his period of office despite any agreement between it and him. The registrar must be notified of the removal within 14 days. An auditor who has been removed is entitled to attend the meeting at which his term of office would have expired and any general meeting at which it is proposed to fill a casual vacancy caused by his removal. He is entitled to receive all communications relating to the meeting which a member is entitled to receive, and he may speak on any matter concerning him as a former auditor.

Auditors may be removed by ordinary resolution of which special notice has been given. Special notice is a period of 28 days, given by the person proposing the resolution to the company. On receipt of the special notice the company must immediately send a copy to the auditor, who may make written representations to the company and require the company (unless it receives them too late) to send a copy of these representations to the members with notice of the meeting. If for any reason these representations are not sent to the members the auditor can require them to be read out at the meeting. In any case he has a right to speak in his defence at the meeting. The representations need not be sent out, or read at the meeting, if the court is satisfied, on the application of the company or any aggrieved person, that the auditor is using his rights to secure needless publicity for defamatory matter.

*Comment*

You should not have found this question very difficult. Part (b) is phrased in such a way that some students will assume that the directors are entitled to remove an auditor. As you can see this is not the case. The directors may however remove the company secretary. The most common error on this type of question is to confuse special resolutions with ordinary resolutions that require special notice.

**25.** By ***S.431*** the Department of Trade may appoint inspector to investigate the affairs of the company if it receives an application from either

(a) The company

(b) At least 200 members, or

(c) Members holding at least 10% of the issued shares.

The Department may also appoint an inspector under discretionary powers conferred by **S.432**, on the application of any person, if there are circumstances suggesting

(a) That the affairs of the company have been conducted with intent to fraud creditors, or in an unfairly prejudicial manner, or for an unlawful or fraudulent purpose.

(b) That the promoters or managers have been guilty of fraud or misconduct, or

(c) That proper information has not been given to members.

By **S.442** (amended by **S.62 CA 89**) the DTI must investigate the ownership of shares on the application of 200 shareholders or holders of 10% of the issued shares, unless it considers the application to be vexatious or unless it considers it unreasonable to investigate any matter. The Department may investigate share ownership if there appears to be good reason to do so.

When there is an investigation of either the affairs of a company or its ownership the DTI may require the applicants to give up to £5,000 security for costs. By **S.446** the DTI may appoint inspectors if they suspect that prohibited persons, for example directors, have been dealing in options to buy or sell the quoted securities of their company or associated companies. They may also be appointed to investigate suspected insider dealing offences ***(S.177 FSA 1986)***.

Inspectors' powers are broadly similar whatever type of inspection. They may:

(a) Require production of books and documents (defined to include information recorded in any form);

(b) Question on oath any person and administer the oath accordingly;

(c) Obtain a warrant to enter premises and search for documents;

(d) Take copies of documents and require any person named in the warrant to provide an explanation of documents;

(e) Investigate the affairs of related companies;

(f) Inform the Secretary of State of any matters coming to his attention as a result of the investigation.

***Comment***

When there is a application to investigate the affairs of a company the Department will only order the investigation if a strong case is made out. An applicant may however have too strong a case, since if the Department thinks that the applicants already have enough information to commence legal proceedings against the director they may decide that the appointment of an inspector is not appropriate. On the other hand if the applicants' case is based on vague suspicions, an inspector will not be appointed since the resulting publicity could cause unnecessary damage to the company. The Department will usually therefore make enquiries of the directors before appointing. Such enquiries themselves may cause any oppression to end, but in other cases may act as a warning to directors who may then take the opportunity to plan suppression or falsification of evidence.

Few questions are asked on DTI investigations, this being the first for several years. However it is relatively easy to score good marks provided the answer is restricted to the appointment and powers of inspectors. It is not relevant to discuss, for example, the consequences of the inspector's report.

Finally note that CA 89 simplified and extended inspectors' powers to obtain and require disclosure of information. The intention is to speed up investigations and make the process more effective.

## SUGGESTED ANSWERS TO COURSEWORK QUESTIONS 26–30 RECONSTRUCTIONS, TAKEOVERS, LIQUIDATIONS AND RECEIVERSHIPS

26. (a) A petition for compulsory winding-up may be brought by

i. The company;
ii. The directors;
iii. A creditor or creditors;
iv. A contributory;
v. The Official Receiver (where a company is already in voluntary liquidation);
vi. The Secretary of State (as a result of a Department of Trade investigation); and
vii. The Attorney-General (when the company is registered as a charity).

If creditors petition they must show that the company is unable to pay its debts. This will be deemed to be the case if a creditor (or creditors) for more than £750 have served a written demand for payment and within the next three weeks the company has neither paid them nor given security. However the court has a discretion to refuse to order winding-up and may well do so if the majority of creditors (by value) consider that they have a better chance of payment if the company is not wound up.

The term 'contributory' includes present and certain past members. The court will not grant an order to a contributory if the company is insolvent, since the contributory would have nothing to gain from the liquidation. To petition a contributory must generally have been a member for six out of the 18 months prior to the petition.

By ***S.122 INSOLVENCY ACT*** the grounds on which a company may be wound up are:

i. The company has passed a special resolution to wind up;

ii. A public company has not complied with the minimum share capital requirements;

iii. A public company has failed to obtain a trading certificate within one year;

iv. The company has not commenced business within a year of incorporation, or it has suspended business for a year;

v. It has less than two members;

vi. It is unable to pay its debts;

vii. It is just and equitable that the company be wound up. This would be the case if for example the main purpose of the company is incapable of achievement, or if the company is in substance a partnership, and the basis of mutual trust on which the company was founded has been destroyed.

(b) i. When a company is insolvent at the start of winding up a claim for unliquidated damages for tort may not be proved (RE ISLINGTON METAL AND PLATING WORKS (1984)). Assuming Oswald's claim was not liquidated (ie settled) at the start of liquidation he cannot prove.

ii. The claim for unpaid corporation tax and VAT is provable. Corporation tax is not a preferential debt (its preference was repealed by the Insolvency Act 1985). VAT is a preferential debt if referable to the period 6 months prior to the liquidation.

iii. Patrick's claim is provable. Since the money was used to pay wages Patrick ranks as a preferential creditor. (Employees are preferential creditors up to £800 each.)

iv. The other unsecured debts of £50,000 are provable.

Summarising, the above debts rank as follows:

First preferential debts ie 6 months VAT and Patrick's claim for £5,000. These debts rank and abate equally (ie if there is not enough money to pay them both they get an equal proportion of what is owed to them).

Second ordinary unsecured debts ie corporation tax, the other 18 months VAT and the unsecured debts of £50,000. These also rank and abate equally. Third non-provable debts ie Oswald's negligence claim.

***Comment***

The main difficulty is likely to involve Oswald's claim for damages for negligence. Had the company been solvent he would have been able to prove for this debt. He would also be able to prove if an insolvent company is later found to be solvent, even if it makes the company insolvent again.

27. (a) An administrative receiver is a person appointed as a receiver or manager of the whole (or substantially the whole) of the company's property, by the holders of a floating charge. Also covered are persons who would be such a receiver, but for the appointment of some other person as receiver of part of the company's property (eg when a receiver is appointed by a fixed charge holder and subsequently one is appointed under a floating charge). Most receivers will be administrative receivers since major lenders, ie banks, usually take both a fixed and floating charge as security.

On appointment the administrative receiver must send to the company and publish notice of his appointment. Within 28 days he must notify all creditors. He must immediately require a statement of affairs from officers or employers giving details of assets, debts, liabilities, creditors and security held by creditors.

Within 3 months he must send a report to the registrar, secured creditors and trustees for secured creditors, containing information on the following matters:

i. The events leading up to his appointment, so far as he is aware of them.
ii. His disposal or proposed disposal of any of the company's property.
iii. His plans for carrying on the business.
iv. The amounts of principal and interest payable to the debenture-holders by whom he was appointed and the amounts payable to preferential creditors.
v. The amount, if any, likely to be available to pay other creditors.
vi. A summary of the statement of affairs and his comments, if any, on it.

He must also send a copy of the report to the unsecured creditors or publish, in the prescribed manner, a notice giving an address to which the creditors can write for a free copy of the report. In either case he must lay a copy of the report before a meeting of unsecured creditors summoned for the purpose on not less than 14 days notice.

If the company has gone or goes into liquidation the administrative receiver must also send a copy of the report to the liquidator. If the report is sent to the liquidator within 3 months of the administrative receiver's appointment the receiver is released from his obligation to call a meeting of unsecured creditors and send his report to them or publish it.

(b) The amalgamation will be governed by the procedures in ***S.110–111 IA 1986***.

The first step is to ascertain the extent of opposition to the proposal from members and creditors. If the opposition is too great the scheme may fail because the company does not have enough cash to pay dissenting members and creditors.

The members must then pass a special resolution giving authority to the liquidator to sell the whole or part of its business or property to another company on terms that the consideration be divided among the members of the transferor company. The consideration may be cash, but it is usually shares in the transferee company.

Only after the majority are sure that there will be enough cash to pay dissentients should it pass the second special resolution, ie putting the company into voluntary liquidation. Prior to the sale the liquidator will usually seek the court's approval since, without such approval, the special resolution for the sale will be void if a compulsory winding up order is made within one year.

The effect of the scheme is that the shares in the transferee company then become the assets of the transferor company and must be distributed to its members in accordance with their rights on liquidation. The transferor company is then dissolved, its shareholders having become shareholders in the transferee company.

A dissentient shareholder is one who did not vote for the special resolution. He can require the liquidator to abstain from the sale or buy his shares. The right must be exercised by a written notice addressed to the liquidator and deposited at the registered office within seven days of the resolution. If the parties cannot agree on a price the matter will be referred to arbitration. The price is likely to be based on the value before reconstruction was proposed rather than after, and the money must be paid before the transferor is finally dissolved.

***Comment***

Questions on amalgamations often reveal some confusion between ***S.110 IA 1986*** and ***S.425 CA***. There are a number of differences between the sections:

(a) ***S.110*** can only be used by a company that is in voluntary liquidation, whereas ***S.425*** can be used by a company that is a going concern.

(b) ***S.110*** is relatively narrow in that it only allows an amalgamation or reconstruction by which a company transfers its assets to another company for a consideration to be distributed among its members. **S.425** covers a wider variety of arrangements with members or creditors.

(c) **S.110** can be used without obtaining the consent of the court, but **S.425** always requires the court's consent.

(d) Under **S.110** a dissenting member can require the liquidator to abstain from the sale or buy his shares. Under **S.425** it is up to the court to make appropriate provision for dissentients.

**28.** (a) The general duty of a liquidator in either a compulsory or voluntary liquidation is to collect in the assets of the company for the purpose of realisation, pay the proceeds to the company's creditors, and distribute any surplus amongst the members. In a compulsory liquidation, if the liquidator is not the official receiver, he must give the official receiver such information and assistance (including access to books and company records) as he may reasonably require to carry out his functions in relation to the winding up. To properly fulfil this basic duty the liquidator will need to investigate the validity of charges to ensure that no floating charge should be avoided under **S.245 IA** and that no charge has been entered into to confer preference on a particular creditor. He should investigate company transactions to ensure that none were at an undervalue and that no extortionate credit bargains were entered into. He should also satisfy himself that the directors have not been guilty of fraudulent or wrongful trading. If he suspects that either offence has been committed he should apply to the court for an order that the director makes a contribution to the company's assets.

A liquidator in a compulsory liquidation has wide statutory powers. For example, with the approval of the court or the committee of creditors he can:

i. Bring and defend actions on behalf of the company;

ii. Carry on the company's business;

iii. Pay any class of creditors in full and;

iv. Make any compromise arrangement with creditors, contributories or debtors.

Without approval he can, for example,

i. Sell the company's property;

ii. Raise money on the security of its assets;

iii. Appoint an agent or solicitor to assist him

iv. Execute deeds, receipts and other documents using the company seal.

In a members' voluntary liquidation, with the sanction of an extraordinary resolution, he can pay any class of creditors in full and make any compromise arrangement with creditors, contributories or debtors. Without approval he has all the other powers of a liquidator in a compulsory liquidation. The situation is the same if it is a creditors' voluntary liquidation except that approval is required from the court, the committee of inspection, or the creditors, rather than by extraordinary resolution of the members.

Liquidators' other powers include:

i. The power to apply to the court to appoint a special manager if the liquidator feels that it will be in the best interests of the creditors, contributories or members that someone be appointed to manage the company's business or property.

ii. To disclaim any unprofitable contract or other property of the company which may not be saleable or which may give rise to some liability on the part of the company.

(b) Every person who was a member of the company at the start of winding up and every past member is, in principle, liable to contribute to the company's assets such sums as may be needed to enable it to pay its debts in full. Thus both past and present members are called 'contributories'. However if the company is limited by shares and the issued shares are fully paid, the contributories have no liability to contribute anything in normal circumstances .

A contributory may be liable in the following circumstances:

i. If the company is limited by guarantee;

ii. If the company is unlimited;

iii. If shares which he holds or previously held are partly paid;

iv. If he was allotted shares as fully paid, but in breach of the rules on a consideration.

***Comment***

The majority of the sections in the ***CA 1985*** concerned with powers and duties of liquidators were repealed by the ***IA 1985***. New rules are now contained in the ***IA 1986***.

The key to a good answer to Part (a) is to keep separate (as far as possible) firstly powers and duties, and secondly compulsory and voluntary liquidation. The main error on this type of question is to fail to distinguish between compulsory and voluntary liquidation and to mix the powers and duties together.

Clearly the question does require a good factual knowledge, but with this type of question, it is possible to score fairly easy marks if you know the facts.

**29.** Voluntary liquidation is generally commenced by special resolution, unless the company is insolvent in which case an extraordinary resolution is passed. The shorter period of notice for an extraordinary resolution (14 days rather than 21 days) will assist the creditors of an insolvent company. A copy of the resolution must be filed with the registrar within 15 days. When he receives notice of the liquidation the registrar must publish notice of its receipt in the Gazette.

There are two types of voluntary liquidation, members' voluntary liquidation and creditors' voluntary liquidation. It will be a members' voluntary liquidation if, within 5 weeks before the resolution to wind up, the directors or a majority of them, make a declaration of solvency. This is a statement of the company's assets and liabilities and it states that, after inquiry, in the directors' opinion, the company will be able to pay its debts within a stated period not more than 12 months after the resolution. The declaration must be delivered to the registrar within 15 days after the resolution to wind up has been passed.

If there is no declaration of solvency it will be a creditors' voluntary liquidation and the company must call a meeting of creditors within 14 days of the resolution to wind up, giving them at least 7 days notice. Notice of the meeting must be advertised once in the Gazette and once in two local newspapers circulating in the district where the registered office or principal place of business is situated. The notice must give the name and address of a qualified insolvency practitioner who, before the meeting, will give the creditors any information they reasonably require concerning the company's affairs. The directors must prepare a statement of affairs containing details of the company's assets, debts, creditors, and securities held by creditors. This must be verified by affidavit and laid before the meeting of creditors. It is possible for the company to appoint a liquidator elect for the 14 days before a creditors' meeting must be held. Prior to the **IA 1985** this left the company's assets unprotected and beyond the creditors' control. The situation has now been remedied since any liquidator must be a qualified insolvency practitioner, and until any liquidator is appointed the directors' powers are subject to the courts' control **(S.114 IA)**. If the company nominates a liquidator prior to the creditors' meeting his powers can only be exercised with the court's consent.

In a members' voluntary liquidation the members appoint the liquidator, but in a creditors' voluntary liquidation both the creditors and the company at their respective meetings may nominate a liquidator. If different persons are nominated, the person nominated by the creditors is liquidator, subject to any order made by the court.

***Comment***

The question is rather narrow in that it is confined to procedures prior to the appointment of the liquidator. Detailed knowledge is therefore required. Remember that winding up commences when the resolution is passed, ie prior to the liquidator's appointment. From the start of winding up the company must cease business (except as required for beneficial winding up) and share transfers are void. However the directors' powers do not cease until the liquidator has been appointed.

30. (a) The new rules introduced by the Insolvency Act 1985 are now contained in the Company Directors Disqualification Act 1986. The Act imposes a duty on the court to make a disqualification order in certain circumstances, but in other cases the court's power is discretionary.

A person may be subject to the ***mandatory disqualification*** procedure if he is, or has been, a director or a shadow director of a company which has gone into insolvent liquidation. Following an application by the Secretary of State the court ***must*** make a disqualification order if the person's conduct as a director, either considered in isolation or taken with his conduct as a director of another company, makes him unfit to be concerned with the management of a company. In applying the above test the court must consider, for example

i. Any misfeasance, breach of fiduciary duty, or misapplication of company assets.

ii. Failure to comply with statutory requirements concerning accounting records, company registers and the annual return.

iii. Responsibility for causing the insolvency, or for causing customers to lose money.

iv. Involvement in a transaction which may be set aside as a preference.

***Non-mandatory disqualification*** may arise in two situations

i. Following a Department of Trade investigation, provided the Secretary of State is satisfied that it is in the public interest that a disqualification order be made (bearing in mind the matters specified in i.–iv. above).

ii. The court may make a disqualification order when it makes a declaration that a person is liable to make a contribution to the company's assets as a result of either fraudulent trading or wrongful trading.

(b) When a compulsory winding up order is made the winding up is deemed to commence at the date when the petition was presented, unless voluntary liquidation was already in progress in which case the compulsory liquidation is deemed to commence on the date of the resolution for voluntary liquidation. The immediate effects of the order are

i. The Official Receiver becomes the liquidator and remains in office until another person becomes liquidator.

ii. Any disposition of the company's property, transfer of shares or alteration in the status of members is void unless the court orders otherwise.

iii. No action can be commenced or proceeded with against the company without leave of the court and any seizure of the company's assets to satisfy a debt after the start of winding up is void.

iv. The directors' powers of management are terminated. Their duties also cease, except their duty not to disclose confidential information.

v. The company's employees are automatically dismissed, although they may sue for damages for breach of contract. The liquidator may choose to re-employ them for the time being.

vi. Floating charges crystallise.

***Comment***

If you have a copy of the Association's published answer you should note that it is out of date, even though the question was from the June 1986 paper.

The 1985 legislation also introduced personal liability for directors guilty of wrongful trading. However there is no power for the court to disqualify directors guilty of wrongful trading.

Part (b) i. above refers to the Official Receiver becoming the liquidator. He does not become the provisional liquidator, which was the situation prior to the ***1985 IA***.

# Appendix II

## REVISION QUESTIONS WITH ANSWERS AND COMMENTS

## QUESTIONS

1. Tom has a small but flourishing business which he has carried on alone for several years. He now feels that the time has come for an additional input of financial resources and skills. He is, however, unsure whether to convert his business into either a partnership or a private limited company, and he seeks your advice in respect of the essential legal characteristics of these two forms of business enterprise. Advise him. (15 marks)

   ACCA *June 1980 Question 1*

2. (a) i. The directors of Crossfire Limited want to change the name of the company to Crossbow Limited. They also wish to change the address of the registered office. Advise the directors. (7 marks)

   ii. Before the change of name had been effected John sold goods to Crossfire Limited and received in payment a cheque signed by one of the directors which had printed underneath his signature the words 'for and on behalf of Crossbow Limited'. The cheque was dishonoured on presentation and John is unable to obtain payment from the company. Advise him. (3 marks)

   (b) Bob has decided to start business as a sole trader using the name 'The Surefire Recruitment Agency'. Advise him of the statutory rules applicable to business names. (10 marks)

   (20 marks)

3. Beaver, intending to go into the wholesale food business, instructed his solicitor to form a company to be named 'Beaver Foods Limited'. The solicitor prepared the necessary documents which were delivered to the Companies Registration Office on the 10th March this year. The statement delivered under S.21 CA 1976 ***(now S.10)*** provided that Beaver and his wife should be the first directors, although they are not named as such in the articles of association.

   On the 21st March Beaver agreed to purchase a quantity of sugar from Sweet in a letter which he signed, 'For and on behalf of Beaver Foods Ltd, E. Beaver, Director'. The sugar has not yet been delivered and Sweet denies any liability to Beaver or the company.

   On the 2nd April, Beaver, purporting to act on behalf of the company, agreed to supply Texo, a large supermarket chain, with all its requirements for coffee for a period of five years at very competitive prices. The certificate of incorporation of the company, dated 1st April, was received by Beaver on the 3rd April. Beaver now considers the agreement with

Texo to be disadvantageous and has repudiated it, saying that he had no authority to bind the company to the agreement. There has never been either a board meeting or a general meeting of Beaver Foods Ltd.

Advise Beaver and Beaver Foods Ltd as to their rights and liabilities with regard to:

(a) Sweet (10 marks)

(b) Texo (10 marks)

(20 marks)

ACCA *December 1982 Question 1*

4. (a) How are the first directors of a company appointed? How are subsequent appointments to the board of directors made? (10 marks)

   (b) In May 1985 Alphabet Ltd duly re-registered as a public company and became Alphabet plc. The articles of association provided that the board should consist of eight directors. The first directors were Arthur, Ben, Cyril, Daniel, Eric, Frank, George and Harold. In July 1986 at the first annual general meeting the original board was re-elected.

   There are two executive directors: Arthur who is managing director and Ben who is financial director. Cyril was the founder and principal shareholder of Alphabet Ltd. At the time of re-registration, he insisted that he should be a director for life of Alphabet plc. An agreement to that effect was completed. Daniel was born on I April 1917. The company has adopted Table A articles of association but with the differences that have been described above.

   The annual general meeting is due to be held on I August 1987. The company has had a disastrous financial year for trading. The directors believe that they may well have temporarily lost the confidence of the shareholders. While they are unwilling to resign office, they are equally unwilling this year to offer themselves for re-election.

   What is the position of the individual directors and state how this difficulty can be resolved? (10 marks)

(20 marks)

ACCA *June 1987 Question 2*

5. Shale Oil plc, an unlisted but well known public company, decided to finance a new oil extraction programme by making a direct offer to the public to purchase its shares. Accordingly, six months ago, the company published a prospectus in a national newspaper and distributed many copies of it. The prospectus, which was in due form, stated that deposits of oil bearing shale had been found on 60 acres of land owned by the company. Included in the prospectus was a report by Rockspect Ltd, a company specialising in geological surveys. This report stated that the oil bearing shale found on the 60 acre site was three times richer in oil than average shales now being worked. The issue was fully subscribed.

Ten days ago reports in the financial press indicated that only 2 acres of the oil site actually belonged to the company at the time that the prospectus was issued. It had at that time almost completed several separate negotiations to purchase the rest of the site, but some of these broke down at the last minute and only a further 10 acres was actually purchased. The reports in the financial press also cast doubts upon the accuracy of the expert's report, and it was alleged that only a very small part of the site contained the very rich shale, while the rest contained only shale of below average oil content Five days ago all of these facts were admitted by the company.

Among those who subscribed for shares in the company on the strength of copies of the prospectus sent directly to them were Alexander and Peter. As soon as the company acknowledged the true state of affairs Peter sold half of his holding of the shares to Nicholas, who had seen the prospectus in a newspaper, but knew nothing of the recent developments.

Advise Alexander, Peter and Nicholas on the courses of action open to them. (20 marks)

ACCA *December 1984 Question 5*

6. Explain the extent of the obligation and also the sanction for failure to comply in respect of each of the following disclosure requirements:

   (a) The duty to disclose substantial interest in voting share capital; (5 marks)

   (b) The duty to disclose a director's interests in shares or debentures; (5 marks)

   (c) The duty to disclose a director's interests in contracts with his company. (5 marks)

   *(15 marks)*

   ACCA *June 1980 Question 5*

7. You are consulted in respect of the three following events which have occurred in respect of the Fiddle Engineering Co Ltd which received its certificate of incorporation on April 1st 1980.

   (a) In February 1980, one of the promoters of the Company contracted in the name of the Company for the purchase of machinery, paying 50% of the purchase price on placing the order and undertaking to pay the remaining 50% on delivery. The machinery was supplied in December 1980 and has been in continuous use by the Company since that date. However, the 50% payment due on delivery has not yet been met by the Company which is denying any liability to pay the supplier, on the ground that it did not place the order. Discuss. (6 marks)

   (b) In order to avoid the Company having to pay the full amount of stamp duty due on the Company's purchase of a piece of land, the Company Secretary who carried out the conveyancing work for the company fraudulently under-stated the purchase-price involved to the Revenue authorities. The evasion has come to light and you are asked to advise whether the Company can be convicted for the false declaration made. (7 marks)

(c) A contract was negotiated by the Company's managing director, without the authority of the board, giving a London based company sole distribution rights of the Company's products in the South of England, notwithstanding that the Company's Articles provided that no contract concerning the appointment of factors, agents or concessionaires could be made by the Company without the unanimous resolution of the Board. Is the Fiddle Engineering Co Ltd bound by this agency agreement? (7 marks)

(20 marks)

ACCA *June 1981 Question 8*

8. You are required to discuss the position of a company auditor with regard to the following three matters:

(a) A company wishes to remove its auditor from office before the next annual general meeting. (5 marks)

(b) An auditor considers that he has been intentionally obstructed by company officers from carrying out a full investigation into the company's affairs. (5 marks)

(c) XYZ Limited, having purchased shares in a company on the basis of the company's audited accounts, considers that the auditor has been negligent in carrying out his audit and wishes to sue him for the loss it has incurred. (5 marks)

(15 marks)

CIMA *May 1985 Question 5*

9. (a) 'The Rule in **FOSS v HARBOTTLE** is that where a wrong is done to a company then the proper plaintiff is prima facie the company itself and not its individual members'. Explain the purpose of the Rule and outline those situations when an individual member can bring an action in respect of wrongs done to the company notwithstanding the existence of the Rule. (5 marks)

(b) Gullible is a minority shareholder in the XYZ Company Limited of which Tom, Dick and Harry are the Chairman, Managing Director and Financial Director respectively. Tom, Dick and Harry together control the Company. Gullible is aggrieved that:

i. The Company has just sold a five acre site to someone (believed to be Tom's father) at less than one quarter of the price the Company paid for it last year.

ii. No dividend has ever been declared by the Company since Gullible acquired his interest in it, yet Tom and Dick have each regularly taken approximately £7,000 pa by way of directors' remuneration.

iii. The Company has recently engaged Harry (Tom's brother) as its Financial Director at an annual salary of £5,000. His service contract includes a provision whereby in the event of his death his widow shall continue to receive his annual salary by way of a pension payment for the rest of her life. Harry was in very poor health at the date of his appointment.

iv. £4,000 compensation was paid to Harry's predecessor, Sharp, to secure his early vacation of office.

Tom, Dick and Harry do not admit that anything improper has taken place. Advise Gullible whether he is likely to succeed in legal proceedings in respect of each of his complaints. (15 marks)

(20 marks)

ACCA *June 1979 Question 7*

10. The Sludge Mining and Exploration Company Ltd ('the Company'), an English private company, was incorporated in 1972 for the purpose of oil exploration of the North Sea. Harry, a member of the company, relates to you the following three events and you are asked to advise on the correctness or otherwise as to each of Harry's contentions:

(a) In 1974 the controlling shareholder Slim sold his entire shareholding in the Company to Arthur. This sale was at only 40% of the market value of the business and this was because Arthur could not find enough capital to pay the full value outright. As a solution to his difficulty it was agreed as a condition of Arthur's purchase of Slim's shareholdings that Slim should be given a service contract with the Company as its 'Consultant' for ten years at £8,000 per annum. It was mutually accepted that Slim would never in fact be called upon by the Company to advise or perform any other services and the appointment was merely an expedient to enable Slim to be paid a price approximating to the true market value of the shares when sold in 1974. These payments are still being made by the Company but Harry contends that they are illegal.

(b) In 1976 the Company's profits had fallen drastically because of increased expenses. Harry was then anxious to sell the bulk of his own shareholding in the Company and made approaches to the directors to ascertain their willingness to purchase the same. Negotiations then ensued in this matter with Harry leading to a sale in 1978 and Harry retained only a token shareholding in the company. However, in 1977 a test hole was drilled by the Company in a new area of the North Sea and this indicated an exceptionally valuable concentration of oil, but the directors kept this fact to themselves and purchased Harry's shares at a low price which reflected the Company's poor performance hitherto. Only after the sale was complete did the directors make public the new oil strike. Harry contends that the sale of his shares must be set aside.

(c) In 1980 the Scottish Gas Board invited public tenders for the mapping and related geophysical exploration services in the North Sea. The Company tendered for this project. At this time, Smart, a highly qualified civil engineer and a member of the Company' s Board, resigned his office with the Company and formed his own surveying company which sought, and was awarded, the Scottish Gas Board's contract. Harry contends that Smart must account to the Company for the profits his company has made on this contract. (20 marks)

ACCA *December 1980 Question 8*

11. You are acting as adviser to three private companies. The following situations have arisen:

(a) Knife Ltd was incorporated on I November 1985. There are five shareholders each holding 20% of the issued share capital. Two of the shareholders, Jack and Jim, are the directors named in the articles of association. Although the company appears to be functioning satisfactorily, the shareholders who are not directors are concerned that by June 1987 no general meeting of the company has been held.

What statutory obligation have Jack and Jim failed to meet? What are the possible consequences of such failure? What action can the non-director shareholders take to ensure that such a meeting is held? (8 marks)

(b) Fork Ltd has a fully paid up share capital of £10,000 divided into 10,000 £1 shares. The two directors, Bill and Ben, each hold 150 shares. The remaining 9,700 shares are held by six other shareholders. These six shareholders requisition an extraordinary general meeting of the company to pass a vote of no confidence in the board of directors.

Say why these shareholders are in a position to make a valid requisition. What are the requirements of a valid requisition? If Bill and Ben ignore the requisition, what further action can the shareholders take? (6 marks)

(c) Spoon Ltd is a small private company whose articles are regulated by Table A. The company has ten shareholders. It is agreed that the annual general meeting shall be held on 30 May 1987. A notice of the meeting is sent out in correct form on I May 1987. There is a printer's error on the notice which the company secretary has failed to see. This states that the meeting is to be held on 20 May 1987. All ten shareholders attend on 20 May.

Are the proceedings valid? Give reasons for your decision. Suppose that one of the members had NOT attended the meeting? Would you answer be different? (6 marks)

(20 marks)

ACCA *June 1987 Question 5*

12. Company A plc is intending to make a take-over bid for company B plc. The directors of B plc have discovered A plc's intentions. They are not happy about the prospective bid and intend to oppose it. They have decided to adopt a strategy which will make the bid look unattractive or increase the value of the company's shares to such an extent that the scheme becomes too expensive for A plc. The directors seek your advice on the legality of the tactics listed below.

    (a) Make a new issue of B plc equity shares to supporters of the directors who will oppose A plc's bid. (6 marks)

    (b) Use their own personal funds to buy shares in B plc on the stock exchange to cause the price of the shares to increase. (7 marks)

    (c) Tell supporters of the directors of B plc that a take-over bid is anticipated in the near future or merely encourage supporters to buy shares in B plc.

    Advise the directors. (7 marks)

    (20 marks)

    CIMA *November 1989 Question 2*

13. Bert and Fred were for many years the only directors of and shareholders in Job Ltd which carried on the business of builders. Bert held 60 of the 100 issued shares, Fred 40. Both worked full time in the business of the company. No dividends were ever declared and the profits were taken as directors' salaries. Recently, Clarence, an employee of the company, was appointed an additional director and Bert and Fred each transferred five shares to him. Differences then arose because Fred and Clarence found that Bert was diverting building work away from Job Ltd to another company in which he was interested. Bert requisitioned a general meeting at which Fred and Clarence were dismissed as directors. Since then the business of Job Ltd has declined further but Bert has doubled the salary he receives. No dividends have been declared.

    Advise Fred and Clarence. (20 marks)

    ACCA *December 1982 Question 5*

14. (a) Describe the characteristics of a floating charge. What are the advantages and disadvantages of the floating charge as a form of security? (10 marks)

    (b) In April 1979 X Ltd issued to W Bank a debenture secured by floating charge on all of X Ltd's property and undertaking. It was duly registered at the Companies Registration Office. Six months later a fixed charge on the company's principal factory was created in favour of Z. More than 12 months after the charge in favour of Z was created X Ltd went into liquidation. Prior to taking his charge Z had made a search at the Companies Registration Office and discovered the existence of W Bank's floating charge. Which charge has priority? (10 marks)

    (20 marks)

    ACCA *June 1983 Question 6*

15. Provent plc, a listed company, is considering making a takeover bid for the equity shares in Retal plc, also a listed company, and in which Provent plc at present holds 29% of the equity shares.

    You are required to advise the directors of Provent plc on the following matters which relate specifically to the proposed takeover bid:

    (a) The proportion of the equity share capital which Provent plc must purchase in Retal plc in order for Retal plc to be classified as a subsidiary company and whether this measure of holding would ensure effective control over all matters which might arise at company general meetings.

    (b) Whether Provent plc may obtain majority control of Retal plc in secret, without that company becoming aware of the build-up of majority status in Provent plc.

    (c) Whether Provent plc may, upon obtaining control of Retal plc, appoint nominee directors who would then authorise the payment of a dividend from the ample reserves of Retal plc, to all shareholders, including Provent plc. (20 marks)

    CIMA *May 1983 Question 1*

16. Who is an 'insider' and what is 'unpublished price sensitive information' for the purposes of the law relating to insider dealing? What prohibitions are imposed on the activities of insiders? State the main exemptions to these prohibitions. (20 marks)

    ACCA *June 1988 Question 8.*

17. Excess plc is a company with substantial assets not fully utilised in the operation of the business and, given its asset worth, with a relatively low stock exchange value placed upon its ordinary shares. These factors have led the board of directors to anticipate that a takeover bid may be made by Combo plc, a competing company. The directors are considering three strategies they might adopt to protect Excess plc from the threatened bid.

    You are required to examine the rules of company law relating to the following proposals and to comment on the tactics which Combo plc might adopt to counter the three strategies:

    (a) An interest-free loan would be made by Excess plc to a trust fund established for the purpose of purchasing ordinary voting shares for the benefit of employees. The company's managing director would be appointed trustee of the fund. His use of the voting power attached to the employees' shares would be used to support the directors in maintaining majority voting power.

    (b) Surplus funds of Excess plc would be utilised to pay existing shareholders a large interim dividend. This would encourage existing members to retain their shares and could increase the stock exchange valuation of Excess plc's shares.

(c) The directors would take no action until Combo plc made a successful bid and took control of Excess plc. If it became apparent that Combo plc intended to run down the business of Excess plc for the benefit of Combo plc, the directors, as shareholders, would petition the court for relief under **S.75** Companies Act 1980 (now **S.459** CA 1985).

(20 marks)

CIMA *May 1984 Question 2*

18. The issued share capital of Alpha Ltd is 500 ordinary shares with a par value of £2. 100 of these, each carrying four votes per share, are held by the directors of Alpha Ltd and of the remainder, each carrying one vote per share, 100 are held by Exco Assurance Ltd.

A few weeks ago at an extraordinary general meeting of Alpha Ltd a special resolution was passed for voluntary liquidation of the company. Exco Assurance Ltd suspected that Alpha's directors had proposed this resolution, without fully informing shareholders, in order to facilitate a takeover of Alpha Ltd.

The liquidator of Alpha Ltd is now proposing a scheme under S.287 CA 1948 (now **S.582**) for the sale of Alpha Ltd to Beta Ltd. The terms of the transfer are that Beta Ltd will issue one £2 share, credited as paid up to £1.60, in exchange for each ordinary share in Alpha Ltd and that if any member dissents from the scheme, his shares are to be sold by the liquidator and he will receive the price thus obtained. Exco Assurance Ltd believes, on the advice of its experts, that these terms are based on a substantial undervaluation of Alpha Ltd and has circulated this information to other minority shareholders.

Advise Exco Assurance Ltd and any other dissenting shareholders what courses of action are open to them. (20 marks)

ACCA *December 1982 Question 6*

19. Thomas traded as a market gardener. In 1980 he sold his business to a newly formed company Tommos Ltd for £50,000. Thomas received £40,000 in cash. He accepted the balance of £10,000 secured by a fixed legal charge on the company's freehold lands. The charge was validity registered. Since 1980 Thomas has been content to accept the interest due on the £10,000 but no repayment of capital has been made.

In January 1986 Tommos Ltd tendered for and obtained a two year contract to supply vegetables to a local restaurant. The contract was underpriced and the company has consistently lost money on the contract.

In January 1987 Gwilims plc, the company's bankers, insisted on taking a second fixed legal charge on the company's freehold land and a first floating charge on all the other assets to secure the company's overdraft. These charges were also validly registered.

On I May 1987 Tommos Ltd passed an extraordinary resolution to wind up voluntarily because it could not carry on business by reason of its liabilities.

1. The overdraft to Gwilims plc stands at £60,000.
2. The local authority are owed rates of £1,000.
3. Value added tax of £2,000 is immediately payable.
4. There are arrears of income tax due to the Inland Revenue. £3,000 is owing for the year ended 5 April 1986 and £2,000 for the year ended 5 April 1987.
5. Ten employees of the firm are each owed £600 in wages due for the four weeks prior to the passing of the resolution to wind up.
6. Various trade creditors are owed £20,000 in total.
7. The restaurant owners are threatening to sue the liquidator for the extra cost incurred in buying vegetables elsewhere .

The freehold land will realise £80,000 and the company's remaining assets will realise £10,000. Liquidation expenses are assessed at £3,000.

State how Brian should deal with these various claims. (20 marks)

ACCA *June 1987 Question 1*

20. Richard was duly appointed receiver and manager of the assets and undertaking of Shoddy Limited under an express power contained in a debenture secured by a floating charge over such assets and undertaking. He immediately dismissed the employees of the company who have not been paid their last week's wages. He subsequently sold the remaining stock of Shoddy Limited, a quantity of cloth, in the course of his receivership and has applied the proceeds in reduction of the amount secured by the debenture.

The ex-employees are pressing Richard for their wages. The cloth which was sold has turned out to be severely defective and the purchasers claim that Richard is personally liable to them in damages. The directors of the company have commenced an action in the name of the company against the debenture holder who appointed Richard, and Richard wishes to have this action set aside.

Advise Richard. (10 marks)

How. if at all, would your advice differ if Richard were the liquidator of Shoddy Limited appointed in a creditor's voluntary winding-up?

(10 marks)

(20 marks)

ACCA *Pilot Paper for Level 2 Published 1981*

# ANSWERS

1. The legal characteristics of a partnership and a private company are very different. The fundamental distinction is that a partnership is an unincorporated association and as such has no legal personality distinct from its partners. In contrast a private company is a corporation, ie an artificial legal person with an existence separate from that of its members (SALOMON v SALOMON & CO (1897)).

   Since it is a legal person a company can own property. Consequently even the majority shareholder has no insurable interest in the company's property (MACAURA v NORTHERN ASSURANCE (1925)). Similarly the majority shareholder may not regard the company's bank account as his own (UNDERWOOD v BANK OF LIVERPOOL (1924)). A company has its own name and can sue and be sued in this name. A company also has perpetual succession, ie its existence is unaffected by the death or bankruptcy of some or all of its members. Probably the most important consequence of incorporation is that a member is not liable for the debts of the company since his liability is limited to the price he has paid, or agreed to pay, for his shares. This may not however enable Tom to raise additional finance without personal risk, since any lenders will probably require their loan to the company to be personally guaranteed by Tom.

   Since a partnership is not a legal person the property is owned by the partners and the debts of the business are enforceable against the partners, although a partnership is allowed to sue and be sued in the firm's name. The consequence of a successful action against the firm may be serious since in general the liability of partners is unlimited. If this should result in the bankruptcy of a partner(or if a partner dies) the partnership is automatically dissolved unless the partnership agreement provides otherwise.

   There are many other differences between companies and partnerships of which Tom should be informed, for example:

   i. A company will incur greater expenses on formation, throughout its life and on dissolution. It will have to comply with more formalities since several registers must be maintained and various documents have to be filed with the registrar. Its accounts must be audited annually. More publicity will have to be given to its affairs, in particular with regard to its directors and charges on its assets.

   ii. All partners are entitled to share in the management of the firm whereas the powers of management of a company are vested in the directors and cannot be usurped by the members (SCOTT v SCOTT (1943)). Also each partner is an agent of the firm, therefore it will be bound by his acts. In contrast a member of a company is not an agent of the company and he cannot bind it by his acts.

iii. Subject to several exceptions (which do not appear to apply to Tom) a partnership must not have more than 20 partners, but there is no limit on the membership of a private company.

iv. Only companies can grant a floating charge as security for a loan.

v. Finally Tom should be advised of the different methods of taxation applicable to companies and partnerships.

*Comment*

Clearly this is a very straightforward question. Other differences between companies and partnerships could also be included in the answer, for example the extensive publicity and accounting requirements applicable to companies, the requirements for the maintenance of company capital and the restrictions on the choice of company names.

2. (a) i. The directors must first arrange for the official index to be inspected on their behalf to determine whether the proposed name is the same as one already registered. In determining whether one name is the same as another certain words and their abbreviations are disregarded, for example the words 'the' and 'company'. Also 'and' and '&' will be taken to be the same. Thus, for example, if a company is already registered with the name 'The Crossbow Company Limited' then the proposed name would be unacceptable.

If the name is not the same as one already on the index then by ***S.28*** the company must pass a special resolution to change its name. This requires 21 days notice to the members and a three-quarter majority of those entitled to vote and voting. Unless the AGM is imminent it will be necessary for the directors to convene an EGM. A copy of the resolution,plus the appropriate fee (currently £50),must then be sent to the registrar. The change will be effective from the date on which the altered certificate of incorporation is issued. The change of name will not affect any of the company's rights or obligations or render defective any legal proceedings.

The address of the registered office can be changed by a resolution of the board of directors if such a power is given to them by the articles. In other cases an ordinary resolution of the company is required. The company must notify the registrar within 14 days. Both a change of name and a change of registered office must be officially notified by the registrar and published in the Gazette.

ii. As stated above a creditor will not be prejudiced by a change of name. In addition by ***S.349(4)*** a director who signs a cheque, bill of exchange or similar document which does not bear the company's full name will be personally liable to the creditor if the company fails to pay. The director is therefore liable to John.

(b) Since Bob is not going to carry on business under his own surname (or an abbreviation of it) he will have to comply with the requirements of the ***BUSINESS NAMES ACT 1985.***

**S.4 BNA** requires that he must state legibly on all business letters, order forms, demands for payment and receipts, his name and an address in Great Britain at which service of documents relating to the business will be effective. In addition, in any premises to which suppliers or customers have access, he must display prominently a notice containing his name and the above address. He must also supply in writing his name and the above address to any person with whom he does or discusses business and who asks for such details.

Failure to comply with the requirements is a criminal offence for which Bob may be fined. In addition if Bob fails to display or make available details of ownership he will be unable to enforce a contract against any person who can show that he has been unable to pursue a claim against the business, or has suffered financial loss as a result of the breach, unless the court is satisfied that it would be just and equitable to enforce the contract.

*Comment*

With about one million registered companies, it can be difficult to find an acceptable name. It is advisable to write to the registrar at an early stage, to enquire whether the proposed name is available for registration. If the reply is 'yes' it is reasonably (but not absolutely) safe to prepare documents and stationery bearing the new name. The risks are that the registrar has overlooked a similar existing name, or that somebody else registers the name in the meantime. In 1962 the Jenkins Committee recommended the introduction of a system whereby, on payment of a small fee, a name could be reserved for a short period. Although this system operates in some other countries the recommendation has never been implemented.

It is important to distinguish company names from business names. Remember that the rules on business names apply equally to companies, partnerships and sole traders.

3. (a) A private company is entitled to start trading from its date of incorporation. Therefore the contract with Sweet is a pre-incorporation contract. A pre-incorporation does not bind the company and cannot be enforced or ratified by the company after its incorporation. In **KELNER v BAXTER (1866)** promoters purchased a quantity of wine 'on behalf of' a proposed company. The company was formed and the wine was delivered and consumed, but before payment was made the company went into liquidation. The company attempted to ratify the promoters' contract, to relieve the promoters of personal liability. It was held that the purported ratification was ineffective. Thus Beaver

Foods Ltd have no contract with Sweet and accordingly no rights or liabilities.

Beaver's position is now governed by **S.130 CA 89** ***(S.360)*** which provides that where a person purports to act for, or as an agent of, a company which at the date of the contract has not yet been formed, the contract shall have effect as a contract entered into by the person purporting to act for the company. For example in **PHONOGRAM v LANE (1981)** the defendant, a pop group manager, signed a contract on behalf of a company which had not yet been formed. Under this contract he received an advance payment, repayable to Phonogram if a recording contract was not entered into. In fact Lane's company was never formed and no recording contract was made. **S.36C** enabled Phonogram to recover their advance payment from Lane. Although Beaver's situation is rather different since he is trying to enforce a contract rather than resist liability **S.36C** clearly enables him to succeed.

(b) Since the contract with Texo was made after 1 st April it is not a pre-incorporation contract. It does not matter that Beaver did not receive the certificate of incorporation until 3rd April. The parties' liability is therefore determined by the principles of agency law, as modified for companies. The following points are relevant:

i. An agent will only bind his principal if he acts within the scope of his actual or apparent authority. Thus an outsider dealing with a company through an officer who purports to exercise a power which that type of officer would usually have, is entitled to hold the company liable for that officer's acts, even if the officer is exceeding his actual authority.

ii. If an agent makes a valid contract, naming his principal, only the principal can sue or be sued on that contract.

iii. Mr. and Mrs. Beaver were directors from the date of incorporation because they were named in the statement required by **S.10** ***(S.13(5))***. The fact that they were not named as directors in the articles is irrelevant.

iv. The powers of management conferred on directors by the articles are conferred collectively on the directors as a board and, prima facie, can only be exercised at a board meeting.

v. By **S.108 CA 89** ***(S.35A)*** in favour of a person dealing with a company in good faith, the power of the board of directors to bind the company, or authorise others to do so, shall be deemed to be free of any limitation under the company's constitution.

These rules may be applied as follows:

Beaver probably does not have actual authority to make the contract because there has been no board meeting to delegate authority to him (point iv). However, Beaver, who is a director (point iii), must be regarded as having apparent authority to contract on behalf of a private company which bears his name. Also the lack of actual authority is not a fact which Texo could have known because holding a board meeting is not a matter which goes on public record. Texo may rely on point v and assume that Beaver has actual authority. Thus since Beaver has apparent authority to bind Beaver Foods Ltd the company will be bound to Texo (point i), but Beaver will not incur any personal liability (point ii).

***Comment***

i. It is important to read the question carefully since it is necessary to advise both Beaver and Beaver Foods Ltd on their legal position with both Sweet and Texo. In other words four conclusions are needed.

ii. You cannot assume that the same section, case or principle is the basis for the advice concerning both Sweet and Texo. In many questions this will be the case but here the advice regarding Sweet is based on ***S.36***, whereas the advice regarding Texo is based on the rules of agency and ***S.108 CA 89 (S.35A)***.

iii. You may have been misled by the item of irrelevant information given in the question, namely the date of receipt of certificate of incorporation. It is unusual for an examiner to give irrelevant information but it is acceptable examination practice. You will have fallen into the trap if you thought that April 3rd was the date of incorporation, and that the contract with Texo was a pre-incorporation contract. Another possible error would be to have attached some significance to the fact that, at the time of making the contract, Beaver did not know that the company had been formed.

iv. At the start of the answer to part (b) it has been stated that Beaver probably does not have actual authority to make the contract. The word 'probably' is used because it is not possible to be absolutely certain. For example, Table A Article 93 states that a written resolution signed by all the directors is as valid as if it had been passed at a board meeting. Beaver could possibly have been acting under an authority delegated in this way, but the possibility is too remote to require comment in the answer.

4. (a) The first directors may be named in the articles or appointed by the method described in the articles. By ***S.10*** their names must be delivered with the application to register the company, together with their signed consent to act. By ***S.13(5)*** the persons named in the statement are, on incorporation, deemed to have been appointed the first directors of the company.

Subsequent directors may be appointed by the company or by the board of directors. The usual method is for the company to appoint by ordinary resolution (a simple majority of votes cast). By **S.292** two or more directors of a public company cannot be appointed by a single resolution unless a prior resolution authorising this has been passed without dissent. Retiring directors are eligible for re-election and if Table A is adopted a retiring director who offers himself for re-election will be automatically elected unless a resolution not to fill the vacancy is passed, or a resolution for his re-election is lost.

The board may make an appointment if a casual vacancy occurs, for example due to the death or resignation of a director. The person appointed will hold office until the next AGM, when he must stand for re-election (Table A Art 79). The board may also appoint additional directors up to the maximum allowed by the articles.

(b) The relevant statutory provisions and company articles are as follows. By **S.293** when a director of a public company (in this case Daniel) reaches the age of 70 he must declare this at the next AGM and vacate office. He may however be re-elected by an ordinary resolution if special notice (28 days notice to the company, given by the proposer) has been given.

By Table A Art 73 at each AGM one third of the directors shall retire. Those to retire are those who have been longest in office. When several directors were appointed together and they fail to agree who shall retire, those to retire shall be determined by lot (Art 74). Retirement by rotation does not apply to the managing director, or to executive directors (Article 84), nor does it apply to life directors. A life director may nevertheless be removed in the usual way (ordinary resolution of which special notice has been given) but he could seek damages for breach of his agreement with the company.

***Comment***

The question is straightforward, but part (b) concentrates on rather obscure parts of company law, such as life directors and the procedure for determining who shall retire when several directors appointed at the same time cannot reach agreement.

It is interesting that although the Act suggests that more than half of the shares are needed to control the composition of the board, the practical reality is rather different.

The existing board will be in control of the general meeting and will almost always be able to secure a majority of votes for the following reasons:

(a) The dispersal of share ownership means that a relatively small block of voting shares, if acting in a united manner, is sufficient for control. In a large quoted company as little as 5%–10% could well be adequate. The reason is that the majority of shareholders do not exercise their vote at all, and if they do they are unlikely to act in a concerted way. If they all came to the AGM they could not be accommodated. Thus as long as the controlling group acts in a concerted way an effective challenge is very unlikely.

(b) Directors are able to utilise the proxy system. Until 1975 it was common practice for the directors to send to all shareholders cards offering themselves as proxies to vote in favour of the board's resolution. Now Stock Exchange regulations require the card to enable the shareholder to require the director to either vote for or against the resolution. Even so the directors can usually rely on a sufficient number of general proxies, ie authorising them to act at their discretion, to enable them to counteract any opposing group of shareholders.

(c) Directors can usually ensure that there is no serious dispute over the election of new directors by arranging for outgoing directors to retire between general meetings and then using their power to co-opt new directors. In this way the members at the AGM are rarely given the opportunity to do anything except confirm a director's appointment.

5. A misrepresentation is an untrue statement of fact which is one of the causes which induces the contract. The prospectus contains two misrepresentations. The first is the company's fraudulent statement concerning the acreage owned by the company. The second is the negligent (or possibly fraudulent) statement by Rockspect Ltd concerning the richness of the shale. The remedies of each investor in respect of each misrepresentation are now considered in turn.

Alexander may rescind his contract with the company. He should write to the company immediately since a delay could amount to affirmation and bar this equitable remedy. Rescission will also be barred if winding-up commences. Rescission will enable Alexander to recover the purchase price of his shares. If he has suffered additional loss he may sue the company in tort for deceit. Alexander may also sue any 'person responsible' for the prospectus under ***S.166 FINANCIAL SERVICES ACT 1986***. 'Persons responsible' include the issuer, its directors, persons named in the prospectus as having agreed to become directors and persons who have accepted responsibility for, or authorised, any part of the prospectus. ***S.167 FINANCIAL SERVICES ACT 1986*** provides various defences, for example reasonable belief that the statement was true and not misleading, but none will relieve the directors from liability for fraudulent misrepresentation.

Peter cannot rescind his contract with the company because he has affirmed the contract by selling half his shares. However by ***S.131 CA 89 (S.111A)*** lack of rescission no longer prevents an action against the company for damages for fraud. This new section overrules **HOULDS-**

**WORTH v CITY OF GLASGOW BANK (1880).** Peter also has an action for damages either for fraud or under ***S.2(1) MISREPRESENTATION ACT or S.166 FINANCIAL SERVICES ACT 1986*** against the individuals responsible for the misrepresentations in the prospectus. There is very little chance of a successful defence. Peter will therefore obtain an adequate remedy.

Prior to 1986 Nicholas would have been in a very unsatisfactory position. He would not have been able to rescind against the company because he had no contract with it, and he had no right to compensation since ***S.67 CA 1985*** (now repealed) only provided a remedy for 'subscribers'. ***S.166 FINANCIAL SERVICES ACT 1986*** now provides a remedy since it is not restricted to subscribers. Since little time has elapsed Nicholas would have the same rights under ***S.166*** as Alexander. Prior to 1986 Nicholas would have had to attempt to sue the directors for fraud or Rockspect for negligence (under the rule in **HEDLEY BYRNE v HELLER (1964)**), but his problem in each case would have been to prove that a duty is owed to persons other than subscribers who relied on the prospectus. He will be able to rescind his contract with Peter if Peter has committed a misrepresentation, but this would require a false statement by Peter about the acreage or the richness of the shale. Peter's silence as to the true state of affairs does not amount to misrepresentation since Peter did not make the original false statements.

***Comment***

This is a fairly difficult question that requires knowledge of the general principles of misrepresentation as well as specific company law rules. You should start the answer by defining misrepresentation and then identifying any conduct that falls within that definition. Good organisation is most important, in particular you should treat Alexander, Peter and Nicholas quite separately.

**6.** (a) The rules concerning the disclosure of substantial interests in voting shares are contained in ***S.198–211*** and they apply to all public companies. Every public company is required to keep a register of substantial shareholdings and when a person knows that he has an interest in 3% or more of the company' s voting shares he must notify the company in writing within two days. The company must record this information in the register within the next three days. The obligation to notify also arises on the cessation, acquisition or change of an interest, although changes of less than 1% are exempt. A person is deemed to have an interest if:

i. His spouse or infant child has an interest;

ii. Shares are held by a company and that company or its directors are accustomed to act in accordance with his instructions, or he controls one-third or more of the votes at a general meeting of that company; or if

iii. Another person is interested in the company's shares and he is acting together with that other person.

In general a person will be liable to a fine of up to £1,000 and/or up to two years imprisonment if he fails to notify within the prescribed period or if he knowingly or recklessly makes a false statement in any notification.

(b) The relevant rules are contained in ***S.324–329***. Every company must keep a register of directors' interests in shares and debentures. A director must notify the company in writing within five days of any transaction involving his interest in the shares or debentures of the company, for example:

i. The sale or purchase of the company's shares or debentures;

ii. The assignment of a right granted to him by the company to subscribe for the company's shares or debentures; or

iii. The assignment of a right to subscribe for the shares or debentures of another company in the same group.

The company must record the information in the register within three days of receipt. A person is deemed to have an interest in shares or debentures if situations (i) or (ii) described in (a) above exist.

A person's liability for failure to notify is as described in (a) above.

(c) By ***S.317(1)*** a director who is interested in a contract with the company must declare the nature of his interest at the first board meeting at which the contract was discussed or, if he did not have an interest at that time, at the first board meeting after which his interest arose. By ***S.317(5)*** the definition of 'contract' includes any transaction or arrangement, whether or not it constitutes a contract. Also a transaction within ***S.330*** (which prohibits loans to directors and connected persons) must be treated as a 'contract' in which the director is interested ***(S.317(6))***.

***S.317*** also applies to shadow directors. A shadow director is a person in accordance with whose instructions the directors are accustomed to act unless the directors act on that person's advice only when it is given in a professional capacity. Since a shadow director does not attend board meetings he must disclose his interest by written notice to the directors.

The sanction for failure to disclose an interest is that the contract becomes voidable at the option of the company.

Another relevant provision is contained in ***S.320***. This provides that a company cannot transfer to or acquire from a director or any person connected with him any property the value of which exceeds the lesser of either £50,000 or 10% of the company's net assets without prior approval of the shareholders in general meeting. There are several exceptions including transfers of less than £1,000.

If a person fails to comply with ***S.320*** he must account to the company for any gain he has made. He must also indemnify the company for any loss it has suffered.

*Comment*

Like the previous question this requires a good factual knowledge of an area that only infrequently attracts the examiner's attention. However if you have that knowledge you can score very good marks on this type of question. ***S.134 CA 89*** amended ***S.198–211***, in particular reducing a notifiable interest from 5% to 3% and the period of notification from five to two days.

**7.** (a) A contract made on behalf of a company before its incorporation does not bind the company, nor can it be enforced or ratified by the company after incorporation. For example in **KELNER v BAXTER (1866)** the promoters of a company which was about to be formed signed a contract 'on behalf of' the company. After the company had been formed it attempted to ratify the contract in order to render the company liable to pay for the wine. It was held that the ratification was ineffective. It is therefore clear that the company is not liable to the vendor of the machinery.

The liability of the promoter who made the contract is governed by **S.36C** which provides that (subject to contrary agreement) where a person purports to act for, or as an agent of, a company which at the date of the contract has not yet been incorporated he shall be personally liable on the contract.

(b) There has been some debate as to whether a corporation, being an artificial legal person, can possess the necessary mens rea (guilty mind) to commit a criminal offence. In 1944 two cases suggested that a company could be held liable. In **DPP v KENT AND SUSSEX CONTRACTORS (1944)** a company was convicted under defence regulations of making use of a document with intent to deceive. It was clear from the statute that mens rea was required thus the liability of the company must have been personal. It was not a case where the company was held vicariously liable for the crime of its servant. In **MOORE v BRESLER (1944)** the company was convicted of making false tax returns despite the fact that the acts were not those of its directors. but merely of its secretary and branch manager. However not every crime of an officer or employee is regarded as a crime by the company. In **TESCO v NATRASS (1972)** an attempt was made to make the company liable for an offence under the Trade Descriptions

Act 1968 when one of the shop managers had failed to ensure that goods advertised for sale at a price were in fact being offered for sale at that price. It was held that the shop manager could not be identified with the company, but was 'another person'. The company was therefore not guilty.

A firm conclusion is difficult, but since a secretary has been described by the courts as 'an officer with extensive duties and responsibilities' (**PANORAMA DEVELOPMENTS v FIDELIS FABRICS (1971)**) it is suggested that the company would be convicted and fined as a result of his false declaration.

(c) ***S.108 CA 89 (S.35A)*** provides that in favour of a person dealing with a company in good faith, the power of the board of directors to bind the company, or authorise others to do so, shall be deemed to be free of any limitation under the company's constitution. Even if the other person knows that the transaction is beyond the directors' powers, he will be protected.

The position of the other company is further strengthened by ***S.142 CA 89 (S.111A)*** which abolishes the doctrine of constructive notice, ie a person shall not be taken to have notice of any matter merely because it is disclosed in a registered document or made available by the company for inspection.

It is therefore absolutely clear that Fiddle Engineering will be bound by this agreement.

*Comment*

Clearly the three parts of the question are unrelated. Part (b) is the most difficult, since it deals with criminal liability of the company, rather than its officers. If you only advise on the criminal liability of the company secretary you would score few marks. Prior to 1989 Part (c) would be answered by reference to the rule in **ROYAL BRITISH BANK v TURQUAND (1855)**. The 1989 Act has not altered the conclusion, but it has enabled it to be stated with far more certainty.

8. (a) Since the company is not prepared to wait until the AGM an EGM will have to be held. Usually the articles empower the directors to call an EGM whenever they think fit. If the directors are unwilling to call the meeting, 10% of the shareholders may rely on S.368 and require the directors to convene an EGM.

By ***S.122 CA 89 (S.391A)*** a company may by ordinary resolution remove an auditor before the end of his term of office, despite anything in any agreement between it and him. Special notice of this resolution must be given to the company, ie the person proposing the resolution must give the company at least-28 days notice of the proposed resolution. On receipt of this notice the company must immediately send a copy to the auditor. He may then make written representations to the company and require the company to send these to the members with notice of the meeting. If for any reason they are not sent, the auditor can require them to be read out at the meeting. He is also entitled to speak at the meeting.

(b) The auditors' duty is to report to the members on the accounts and to state whether, in their opinion, they give a true and fair view of the company's affairs. To enable them to form their opinion they have a right of access to books, accounts and vouchers and they may require from the officers of the company such information and explanations as they think necessary. If they fail to obtain the required information they must say so in their report.

The auditor may feel that the obstruction justifies resignation. By **S.122 CA 89 (*S.392*)** an auditor may resign by depositing a written notice at the company's registered office. The notice will not be effective unless it contains either a statement of circumstances connected with his resignation which should be brought to the notice of members and creditors or a statement that there are no such circumstances.

Finally if the intentional obstruction includes false, misleading or deceptive statements the officers concerned will have committed a criminal offence.

(c) To succeed in a negligence action XYZ Ltd must show that (i) They are owed a duty of care; (ii) The duty of care has been broken; and (iii) They have suffered a loss which is not too remote.

Where the alleged negligence causes financial loss the court will regard a duty as owed if (i) The loss is foreseeable; (ii) There is close proximity of plaintiff and defendant; and (iii) It is fair and reasonable that the defendant should owe a duty to the plaintiff **(CAPARO INDUSTRIES v DICKMAN (1989)**. In Caparo's case it was held that potential investors were too remote, thus even if the auditors know that XYZ Ltd were going to base an investment decision on the audited accounts it is unlikely that the court would regard a duty as owed to them.

The duty will be broken if the auditor failed to act as a reasonable auditor. What is reasonable depends on the standards set by Recognised Supervisory Bodies established under CA 89. These bodies have rules covering professional integrity, independence, competence and confidentiality. If the auditor has achieved the standard expected in the profession he will not have been negligent, ie although the standard is required by law, the standard is set by the accountancy profession.

If XYZ Ltd can establish these first two elements they are likely to recover the difference between the purchase price and the current value of their shares.

**Comment**

The 1989 Act made major changes to the law relating to auditors, in order to introduce the EC Eighth Directive into UK legislation. The main changes concern the regulation and qualification of auditors. It also removed the prohibition on an incorporated firm being appointed auditor of a company. Part (c) is the most difficult part of this question. Prior to Caparo's case it seemed that an auditor could owe a duty to a person whom he knew would rely on the audited accounts to make an investment decision. There may still be some doubt about this issue.

9. (a) The purposes of the rule in **FOSS v HARBOTTLE (1843)** are: (i) to give recognition to the fact that it is the company which has suffered a wrong; (ii) to preserve the principle of majority rule; (iii) to prevent multiple actions; and (iv) to prevent futile actions, as would occur if the irregularity were subsequently ratified by the company in general meeting.

   The main exceptions (ie where an individual can sue) are: (i) where the company does an illegal act; (ii) where his individual rights as a shareholder have been infringed, as for example in **PENDER v LUSHINGTON (1877)** where the company chairman refused to record a member's vote; and (iii) where there is a fraud on the minority. For example in **COOK v DEEKS (1916)** directors whilst negotiating a contract on behalf of the company took the contract in their own names. They then used their majority shareholding to pass a resolution declaring that the company had no interest in the contract. A minority shareholder was successful in his action. Clearly this exception is necessary since the fraudulent majority would not cause the company to bring the action.

   (b) i. In **DANIELS v DANIELS (1978)** the controlling directors and majority shareholders (Mr and Mrs Daniels) caused the company to sell land to Mrs Daniels at less than its value. A majority shareholder, although he did not allege fraud, was successful in his action against Mr and Mrs Daniels, it being held that the majority are in breach of their duty as controlling shareholders if they act negligently in such a way that benefits themselves at the expense of the company.

   **S.459** is also relevant. Under this section a member may petition the court on the ground that the affairs of the company are being conducted in a manner which is unfairly prejudicial to the interests of members generally or some part of the members (including at least himself), or that a proposed act or omission of the company would be so prejudicial.

It is suggested that although the controlling shareholders have not themselves benefited, since the sale is to Tom's father, the principle of the above case would apply. Alternatively Gullible would have a good chance of success under **S.459**.

ii. Shareholders do not have an automatic right to a dividend. A dividend only becomes a debt once it has been recommended by the directors and declared by the company in general meeting.

Following the amendment made by CA 89 (ie the addition of 'members generally') non-payment of a dividend may however be grounds for an order under **S.459**, but on the facts given it is not possible to say whether the majorities' conduct is unfairly prejudicial, indeed £7,000 per annum is not excessive remuneration if Tom and Dick are full-time directors.

iii. Company directors have a fiduciary duty to act in the best interests of the company as a whole. They will break this duty if they make a contract to benefit a third party without considering the interests of the company. In RE ROITH (1967) the controlling shareholder and director of a company entered into a service contract with the company under which, on his death, his widow would be entitled to a pension for life. Since the sole object of the contract was to benefit his wife the contract was not binding on the company.

The facts of the problem are sufficiently similar to enable the same conclusion to be reached. Such a breach of duty could not be ratified by the majority. Gullible would therefore succeed if he were to bring an action.

iv. By **S.312** it is unlawful for a company to pay a director compensation for loss of office unless particulars of the proposed payment have been disclosed to and approved by an ordinary resolution of the members.

Such action does not appear to have been taken. Even if **S.312** has been complied with, Gullible may succeed with a claim under **S.459** if the payment is part of a 'fraud' to replace Sharp with Harry.

*Comment*

Time pressure makes this a difficult question. In part (a) you probably should not state the rule in **FOSS v HARBOTTLE**.

In part (b.i.) note that **S.320** (substantial property transactions) is not relevant since a director's father is not a 'connected person'.

You should not assume that the majority's conduct in all four situations is improper merely because it is clearly wrong in some of them. There may well be a reasonable explanation for the non-payment of dividends. The final important point is to keep the four situations quite separate. Do not jumble them together in one long paragraph which results in just one long conclusion.

10. (a) By ***S.151*** it is illegal for a company directly or indirectly to give any financial assistance for the acquisition of any of its shares. It does not matter whether the financial assistance is given before, at the same time as, or after the acquisition.

Financial assistance is widely defined by the Act. It includes, for example, a gift, a guarantee, a loan or any other financial assistance by a company whose net assets are as a result reduced to a material extent.

It is therefore clear that a sham consultancy contract whereby Slim is paid, but does not have to do any work amounts to financial assistance and contravenes ***S.151***. There are several exceptions to ***S.151*** and in certain cases the rules are relaxed in respect of private companies. The exceptions and relaxation provisions would not apply to Slim's case. Harry's contention is therefore correct.

(b) In **PERCIVAL v WRIGHT (1902)** a member approached the directors with a view to selling them his shares at £12.50p each. The directors purchased his shares without revealing that negotiations were in progress for the sale of all shares in the company at a substantially higher price. The sale never in fact took place, but the plaintiff nevertheless sought to have the directors' purchase of his shares set aside for non-disclosure. It was held that the sale should not be set aside because the directors do not owe any fiduciary duties to individual shareholders.

The facts of the question are sufficiently similar to reach the same conclusion, ie the sale of shares will not be set aside. However it should be noted that the directors have clearly made a profit by virtue of their position as directors of the company. The profit may therefore be claimed by the company. In addition if Sludge Ltd had been a public company the directors would be guilty of the criminal offence of insider dealings, although even if this were the case the sale would not be set aside.

(c) A director may not make a secret profit from the misuse of corporate information or opportunity. For example in **INDUSTRIAL DEVELOPMENT CONSULTANTS v COOLEY (1972)** the managing director of IDC, whilst negotiating a contract on their behalf, left the company and obtained the contract for himself. Although it was unlikely that IDC could ever have obtained the contract, it was held that the acquisition of the profit was so closely related to the affairs of the company that it properly belonged to the company.

It is therefore clear that Smart has broken his fiduciary duty as a director of the company. Harry's contention is therefore correct.

***Comment***
Most students soon realise that Parts (b) and (c) concern directors' duties. This seems to make it more difficult to 'spot' that Part (a) is about financial assistance for the purchase of own shares. The only way to avoid misspotting the main point of a problem question is to learn the facts as well as you possibly can.

11. (a) Except for private companies that have passed an elective resolution to dispense with the requirement to hold an AGM, every company must hold an AGM every calendar year, with not more than 15 months between each AGM. A new company need not hold its first AGM in the year of incorporation, or in the following year, but it must be held within 18 months of incorporation. Clearly Jack and Jim have failed to meet this obligation imposed by ***S.366***. This renders them, the company and any other officer, liable to be fined. In addition, by ***S.377***, the Secretary of State may, on the application of any member, order an AGM to be held. He may give such directions as he thinks fit and may fix the quorum at one member. Failure to comply with such directions is a criminal offence for which the persons responsible may be fined. A further, less direct, consequence is that the majority shareholders may consider removing Jack and Jim from their position as directors.

(b) By ***S.368*** despite anything in the articles, the directors must call an AGM if required to do so by holders of at least 10% of the paid up capital with voting rights. The requisition must be in writing, it must state the objects of the meeting, it must be signed and deposited at the company's registered office. If the directors do not convene the meeting within 21 days, the requisitionists (or a majority of them) may convene the meeting themselves. They are entitled to recover their reasonable expenses from the company, which may in turn be reimbursed by the directors. Clearly with 97% of the shares the six members will be able to use ***S.368***.

(c) By ***S.369*** 21 clear days written notice is required for an AGM. 'Clear days' means that the date of service and the date of the meeting are not counted. This rule applies despite anything in the articles, however by ***S.369(3)*** a shorter period of notice is permissible if it is agreed by all members entitled to attend and vote. Since only 19 days notice has been given the proceedings are prima facie invalid. However since all 10 shareholders attended and presumably agreed to the shorter period this would validate proceedings. If one of the members had not attended the meeting the conclusion would not necessarily be different. *S.369(3)* merely requires all members to agree to the shorter period. The absent member could well have agreed, and then decided not to attend. His agreement could not however be assumed merely because he did not make any objection. His positive prior agreement would be needed.

*Comment*

When this question was set the ability to pass an elective resolution to dispense with an AGM did not exist. This was introduced in 1989. If a similar question were asked today it would be correct to refer to elective resolutions, but it would be incorrect to assume that one had been passed.

Although the question requires fairly detailed knowledge it could not be regarded as difficult. Nevertheless the examiner's report states that it was not well done. The only difficult point arises in part (c) because we do not know whether the absent shareholder had consented to the shorter period of notice, and since the answer depends on this, a firm conclusion cannot be reached. Of course you should not assume that because the examiner changes the facts by saying 'Suppose that . . .', that you must reach a different conclusion. Far too many students fall into this trap, you must keep an open mind. Finally note that the 'shorter period' need not be days or even hours. The meeting can be held immediately if all members entitled to attend and vote agree.

**12.** (a) Directors owe fiduciary duties to the company. One of these duties requires them to use their powers for the purpose for which they were conferred. In the case of share issues this is to raise capital. It is possible for directors to break this fiduciary duty even if they act in good faith in what they believe to be the best interests of the company, for example by issuing shares solely to destroy the existing majority block of shares and create a new majority, as in **HOWARD SMITH v AMPOL (1974)**. However in **BAMFORD v BAMFORD (1970)** when shares were issued to prevent a take-over bid it was held that the directors' action could be ratified and their breach waived by an ordinary resolution of the company. If the problem of breach of duty can be resolved there is still the requirement to offer any new issue of ordinary shares for cash to existing shareholders in proportion to their shareholding before offering the shares to the public *(S.89)*. Consequently A plc will be able to maintain its percentage shareholding in B plc. However by *S.80* the company may empower the directors to authorise an issue of shares. If the company does this it may also pass a special resolution resolving that *S.89* will not apply to the issue.

b. By ***S.1 COMPANY SECURITIES (INSIDER DEALING) ACT 1985*** it is a criminal offence for an insider knowingly in possession of unpublished price sensitive information about listed securities, which he has obtained by virtue of his connection with the company, to deal in those securities. The directors of B plc are insiders and the knowledge of the intended take-over is unpublished price sensitive information. A defence is available if it can be proved that the dealing was for a motive other than profit, but it is unlikely to be available in this case. If the directors were to profit from insider dealing, then apart from committing a criminal offence, they would be in possession of a profit obtained by virtue of their office. Such profits are the property of the company although, provided it is not a fraud on the minority, the company could pass an ordinary resolution allowing the directors to retain the profit.

(c) The offence of insider dealing will also be committed by persons who counsel or procure third parties to deal in company securities, or by persons who communicate information to people who are reasonably thought to be likely to deal in the securities. The directors of B plc will therefore commit an offence in the situation described. Their supporters would also be guilty if they dealt with knowledge of the take-over bid, but not if they had responded to mere encouragement to purchase, without any indication of the take-over.

*Comment*

An interesting point is raised in part (b) by the possibility of a resolution allowing the directors to retain their profit. It is certainly contrary to common law to allow a person to benefit from a crime. In the unlikely event of such a situation arising the court may regard the majority's conduct as a fraud on the minority. Alternatively the criminal court (which is of course quite separate) may have ensured, via the imposition of a large fine, that whatever action the company took, the guilty persons could not benefit.

**13.** This question concerns the powers and duties of directors and controlling shareholders.

Directors owe fiduciary duties to the company. In particular they must act in good faith and for the benefit of the company. One aspect of this is the duty to avoid a conflict of personal interest and duty to the company.

The duties of controlling shareholders are quite different. A shareholder may exercise his right to vote as he wishes. He may vote on a matter in which he has a personal interest and in general he may even vote to the detriment of the company.

In many cases the directors who are alleged to have done wrong are themselves the controlling shareholders. In some cases the directors can use their majority shareholding to legitimately ensure that the breach of duty is waived and no action taken. In other situations the use of a majority shareholding for this purpose would amount to a fraud in the minority.

Bert has done three things which have concerned Fred and Clarence.

The first is the diversion of building work. This is a clear breach of the fiduciary duty to avoid a conflict of duty and interest. In **COOK v DEEKS (1916)** the directors/majority shareholders took a contract in their own name which was properly a company contract. They then passed a resolution that the company had no interest in the contract. This was held to be an expropriation of company property and a fraud on the minority.

The second is the removal of Fred and Clarence as directors. This may be sufficiently unjust to justify winding-up the company. In **RE WESTBOURNE GALLERIES (1973)** it was held that a quasi-partnership company, ie one founded on the basis of trust, may be wound-up under *S.122 IA* (the 'just and equitable' ground) if the basis of trust is destroyed to such an extent that, if it were a partnership, dissolution would be ordered.

The third is the doubled salary and the refusal to declare dividends. Taken separately these actions would not necessarily be improper, but when taken together they suggest unfair prejudice.

The best action for Fred and Clarence would be to petition the court under *S.459*. This states that any member may petition the court for an order on the ground that the affairs of the company are being or have been conducted in a manner which is unfairly prejudicial to the interests of members generally or some part of the members (including at least himself) or that any proposed act or omission of the company is or would be so prejudicial. Under this section the court may make any order it thinks fit.

It seems very likely that the court would regard all Bert's actions as part of the same unfair prejudice and make an appropriate order in respect of them together. The best solution for Fred and Clarence would be an order that either Fred and Clarence or the company compulsorily purchase Bert's shares at a fair price.

If the court were to regard each of Bert's acts as separate, Fred and Clarence would certainly succeed in respect of the diverted building work and they would probably succeed in respect of the salary and dividends. The removal of Fred and Clarence as directors would present the most difficulty under *S.459* since the wrong has been suffered in the capacity of directors rather than as members. However the facts are sufficiently similar to **RE WESTBOURNE GALLERIES** to conclude that a petition under *S.122 IA* would succeed.

*Comment*

The difficulty with this question is to know what to include and how best to organise your answer in the limited time available. You could have given more information on recommending and declaring dividends or on the procedure for removal of directors. It would also have been acceptable to expand the information about **S.459** by giving examples of the type of order the Court can make or by mentioning **RE HARMER (1959)**. On the other hand you would have been wrong if you had assumed that the correct procedure for the removal of a director had not been followed. You may also have noticed that either Fred, Clarence or both of them attended the meeting at which they were removed as directors, otherwise there would have been no meeting because there would have been no one for Bert to meet (in any case the quorum for company meetings is usually fixed at two). Therefore it appears that Fred and Clarence have made a tactical error by attending the meeting. However it would not have been correct to discuss this in your answer.

The best approach to a question which involves directors and minority protection is to identify the areas of complaint and quote the law on each separately. It must then be decided whether the different areas can be taken together for one conclusion, or whether they must be treated separately. Certainly if a question is divided into distinct numbered parts, then separate conclusions must be reached for each part. However this question is not split into parts and this indicates that one conclusion will probably suffice. In this case the conclusion is that the most suitable remedy is to petition under **S.459**, with the alternative of a petition to wind up the company.

Under **S.459** the Court can make any order it thinks fit. Therefore you should use your common sense to decide what you think the plaintiff really wants – what would you want if you were Fred? The Association's published answer states that 'The purchase of Fred and Clarence's shares by Bert at a fair value would be the most obvious remedy sought'. Surely this is the wrong advice. Fred is the injured party, why should he want to sell his shares in a company that he has built up for many years? Would it not be more reasonable for Fred to ask the Court to order Bert to sell his shares because Bert is obviously the wrongdoer? It does not matter that Bert holds 55% of the shares because, as already stated, the Court can make any order it thinks fit. Thus if you get a question where **S.459** is the remedy, then use your common sense and imagination to suggest the remedy that you would want if you had to face the situation in real life.

14. (a) In **RE YORKSHIRE WOOLCOMBERS ASSOCIATION (1903)** it was said that if a charge has the following three characteristics it is a floating charge, (although if it does not have all the characteristics it does not necessarily mean that it is not a floating charge):

i. It is a charge on a class of assets present and future.

ii. That class is one which in the ordinary course of business changes from time to time.

iii. The charge envisages that, until some future step is taken by or on behalf of the charge, the company may carry on its business in the ordinary way.

The main advantage of a floating charge is that the company may raise money on the security of assets which are unavailable as security for fixed charge. This is very useful if a company has small premises but a valuable stock-in-trade, for example a jewellers.

There are several disadvantages of floating charges. In particular the value of the assets subject to the charge fluctuates so that on crystallisation the value of these assets may be insufficient to discharge the company's liability. Secondly if a seller of goods uses a 'Romalpa Clause' to reserve title until payment then a floating charge will not, on crysallisation, attach to those goods. The other main disadvantage of a floating charge is that the rules concerning priorities do not favour the holders of such charges. This is because the essence of a floating charge is that the company retains the power to deal with the assets in the ordinary course of business. Thus as a general rule the holder of a floating charge will be postponed to interests in the charged property (for example a lien or other charge) which are created or arise in the ordinary course of business.

(b) The priority between fixed and floating charges is governed by the rule that a later created fixed charge will have priority over an existing floating charge unless the floating charge prohibits the creation of later fixed charges with priority and the fixed charge holder knows of this prohibition.

In order to reach a firm conclusion on this problem it is essential to know whether W Bank's charge contains a prohibition on the creation of later fixed charges with priority (known as a negative pledge clause) and whether the registered particulars contain a note of this clause (it is not a legal requirement that such a note be included). Since the normal practice is to include such a clause in the charge and a note of it in the registered details, it must be assumed that this was done. It may also be assumed that since Z carried out a search he discovered the existence of W Bank's charge. It therefore seems likely that even if Z's charge has been registered (a fact omitted from the question) he will not obtain priority over W Bank.

*Comment*

In Part (a) in addition to the points mentioned above, it would have been relevant to say that a floating charge is an equitable charge. It is equitable because only equity recognises the existence of a charge which does not fix upon any particular asset. Usually when a question asks for advantages and disadvantages, the answer need only be given from one point of view. This question is different. The advantages must be described from the company's point of view, since as far as the lender is concerned a floating charge has no advantages over a fixed charge. It merely enables him to get some security for his loan. In contrast the disadvantages must be described from the lender's point of view, since as far as the company is concerned there are no disadvantages of a floating charge.

Part (b) appears to invite a very short answer, but of course you are expected to state the priority rules. In fact the question requires good technique since it 'contains' omitted facts and thus invites assumptions to be made; There are three important things we are not told

i. Did the floating charge prohibit the creation of later fixed charges with priority?

ii. Did the registered details contain a note of any such prohibition?

iii. Did Z register his charge within 21 days?

In real life the answer in each case would certainly be 'yes'. But in the examination room it would certainly be acceptable to discuss, for example, the consequences of non-registration of the charge within the 21 day period.

15. (a) By *S.144 CA 89 (S.736)* H will be a holding company and S its subsidiary if:

i. H holds the majority of voting rights at general meeting of S;

ii. H is a member of S and has the right to appoint or remove a majority of S's directors;

iii. H is a member of S and controls alone, pursuant to an agreement with other members, the majority of voting rights at general meeting of S;

iv. S is a subsidiary of X and X is a subsidiary of H.

It can be seen that the minimum shareholding in each situation to establish the relationship of holding and subsidiary company is (i) 50% plus one; (ii) and (iii) one; (iv) zero.

Most decisions at general meetings are made by ordinary resolution ie a simple majority of members entitled to vote and voting, but some decisions require a special resolution, ie a three-quarter majority as above, eg an alteration of articles. In some cases the agreement of all the members is required, eg a change to unlimited liability.

Therefore only in situation (i) will the minimum shareholding ensure any direct control over resolutions and then only over ordinary resolutions, although in situation (iii) the holding company will clearly have indirect control of ordinary resolutions and may also have control of special resolutions. This will depend upon the terms of the agreement with other members.

(b) ***S.198–211*** require public companies to keep a register of substantial shareholdings. Under these rules a person must notify the company within two days when he knows that he has an interest in 3% or more of a company's voting shares. These rules are not easy to avoid since a person will be deemed to have an interest in Retal's shares if his spouse or infant child has an interest or if the shares are held by a company (eg X Ltd) and X Ltd, or its directors are accustomed to act in accordance with his instructions, or if he controls more than one third of the votes at a general meeting of X Ltd. Notification is also required if a group of people acting together acquire an interest in 3% or more of Retal's shares. Non compliance with these rules is a criminal offence.

If Retal suspects that Provent have not complied with the above rules, or if they want to be aware of Provent's shareholding even if it is less than 3%, then by ***S.212*** Retal may require Provent to indicate whether they hold any interest in Retal's shares. Provent must reply within a specified time and the information is recorded in the register of substantial shareholdings.

Finally the advisory rules of the Council for the Securities Industry and the City Code on Takeovers and Mergers prevent the secret acquisition of majority control of Retal by Provent.

(c) Directors are appointed by ordinary resolution, therefore if Provent obtain control they may appoint the directors. Dividends are recommended by the directors and declared by the company. They are paid out of accumulated realised profits (after deducting realised and unrealised losses). Thus there are no procedural barriers to a dividend payment.

However by ***S.151*** the payment must not amount to financial assistance by Retal for the acquisition of its own shares. (It does not matter that the assistance is given after the acquisition). There are several exceptions to this rule including the lawful payment of dividends, but if Provent planned the takeover on the basis that it would later strip Retal of its assets to obtain reimbursement of its takeover expenses the exception would not apply. Another exception concerns the situation where although the distribution does amount to financial assistance, the principal purpose of the distribution was not to give financial assistance ***(S.153)***. If this exception is to assist Provent it must be shown that the financial assistance was given in good faith and in the interests of the company. The applicability of these two exceptions will depend on the circumstances of the acquisition.

**Comment**

This was a difficult question at the time when it was set and the answer to Part (a) has been made more complicated since the 1989 Act was passed. The answer is restricted to the definition of holding and subsidiary companies, but for almost all accounting purposes the 1989 Act has introduced two new terms, 'parent undertaking' and 'subsidiary undertaking'. These two terms are more widely defined than 'holding company' and 'subsidiary company'.

When defining holding companies answers often state that a holding company is one that has 51% of the shares of another company. This is wrong, the requirement is a majority of voting shares, ie more than half. The difference is easily illustrated – 51% of 1,000 is 510, more than half of 1,000 is 501.

16. Insider dealing may be defined as the misuse of confidential information likely to affect the value of company securities. It has long been regarded as at least unfair. It is an abuse of the insider's position of trust and it is harmful to the securities market because of the damage it does to investors' confidence. The provisions of the ***1980 COMPANIES ACT*** on insider dealing were generally welcomed by the city institutions as an attempt to govern a type of malpractice that the city's self regulatory machinery had been unable to control. However many people are not very optimistic about the chance of success of the legislation because of the many detailed requirements that must be satisfied before a crime is proved. The 1980 provisions have now been consolidated into the ***COMPANY SECURITIES (INSIDER DEALING) ACT1985 (CSIDA)***.

The CSIDA 1985 only legislates against the insider dealing involving securities listed on the Stock Exchange and off-market deals in advertised securities. The Act makes insider dealing a criminal offence and does not provide for civil actions.

The basic prohibition is in ***S.1***. This section prohibits an insider who is knowingly in possession of unpublished price sensitive information about quoted securities, which he has obtained by virtue of his connection with the company from:

(a) Dealing himself in the securities;

(b) Counselling or procuring another person to deal in those securities; or

(c) Communicating that information to another person if he has reasonable cause to believe that that or some other person will make use of the information for either purpose described above.

It is necessary to define two terms in order to understand this basic prohibition:

An insider is an individual (a corporate body cannot be an insider) who is, or within the past 6 months has been connected with the company and knows that this is so. By ***S.9 CSIDA*** persons connected with the company include, for example, the directors, employees and professional advisors of the company. Persons who receive a 'tip' from an insider are subject to the same prohibitions as insiders.

Unpublished price sensitive information is information of a specific nature which is not generally known, but which would if it were generally known be likely to materially affect the price of securities.

An insider will have a defence if the transaction was executed otherwise than with a view to making a profit or avoiding a loss. Transactions entered into by jobbers, market makers, liquidators, receivers and trustees in bankruptcy in good faith are exempt.

***Comment***
The machinery for investigating suspected insider dealing offences has been strengthened by ***S.177 FINANCIAL SERVICES ACT 1986*** which empowers the Secretary of State to appoint inspectors to investigate suspected offences. The inspectors have wide powers to require any person to produce documents in their possession, attend before them, give evidence under oath, and give all other reasonable help in connection with the investigation. They also have power to enter and search premises. Any person who refuses to co-operate with them is guilty of contempt of court and may be fined or imprisoned.

In addition to the provisions in the 1985 Act the statutory requirement to maintain registers of substantial shareholdings and of directors' interests in shares and debentures discourage insider dealing.

17. (a) ***S.151*** prohibits financial assistance for the acquisition of own shares. There is an exception where the loan is to trustees of an employees' share scheme to enable them to purchase fully paid shares ***(S.153(4))***. Combo Plc could possibly challenge the scheme at common law on the ground that the purpose of this exception is to encourage employee participation rather than to enable takeover bids to be defeated. Thus the directors have broken their fiduciary duties because they have not exercised their powers for the purpose for which they were conferred. However, the challenge would probably fail since the company may ratify the loan and share issue (assuming the loan is not to purchase existing shares) at a general meeting, as occurred in **HOGG v CRAMPHORN (1967)**.

Alternatively Combo may bring an action under ***S.459***. This section provides a remedy if the majority act in an unfairly prejudicial manner. Combo's action would be supported by **CLEMENS v CLEMENS**

**(1976)** where a share issue to trustees of an employees' share scheme which diluted a minority shareholding from 45% to 24.5% was set aside by the court. However, **CLEMENS v CLEMENS** concerned a small family company rather than a public company, and the share issue was designed to reduce the minority shareholding to such an extent that the minority could not defeat a special resolution rather than to prevent a takeover bid. It therefore seems unlikely that Combo can prevent this scheme.

(b) A payment of dividends must comply with **S.263–264**. The effect of these sections is that a public company can only pay a dividend out of accumulated realised profits less realised and unrealised losses. If an interim dividend is paid interim accounts will be necessary **(S.272)**. The payment must also comply with the articles. Table A requires the company to declare the dividend by ordinary resolution, but the declaration cannot exceed the amount recommended by the directors. If the dividend payment complies with both the Act and the articles it will be difficult for Combo to mount a challenge, since even if the directors have broken their fiduciary duty to act for the benefit of the company the declaration has been made by the company, thus waiving the breach.

Combo's best tactic would be to write to the members of Excess who did not attend the meeting at which the declaration was made. Combo should point out that if surplus funds have been used to pay dividends now this may well reduce the company's ability to earn profit and pay dividends in the future. Clearly intelligent shareholders will not be influenced by a dividend payment that resembles a bribe, they will make their decisions as to whether to accept Combo's offer on the basis of the abilities of the competing management teams and their future plans for the company.

(c) If the directors take no action until Combo has control, then any action they then take will have to be in their capacity as shareholders, since presumably Combo will remove the present directors by ordinary resolution and replace them with its own representatives.

If Combo deliberately and unjustifiably run down Excess an action by Excess' minority shareholders under **S.459** would probably be successful. In **SCOTTISH CO-OPERATIVE WHOLESALE SOCIETY v MEYER (1959)** where a holding company deliberately ruined its own subsidiary it was held that the majority must purchase the minority's shares at a fair value. A similar conclusion would however be a very hollow victory since the former directors would be left without any shares at all. Their alternative would be to ask the court to order that they purchase the shares held by Combo (if they can afford them) or that the shares be purchased by the company (Excess) itself (it seems a more equitable solution if the wrongdoers rather than the victims lose their shares), or they could request an injunction to prevent the unfair conduct. Finally they could purchase a few Combo shares and publicise the unfair and unwise conduct at Combo's AGM; they could even propose a resolution to remove Combo's directors.

Combo do not really need a 'tactic' to counter this 'wait and see' strategy. They should merely ensure that if they do run down Excess it is for valid business reasons, and not for the main purpose of injuring – Excess shareholders who did not accept their offer.

*Comment*

This is a very difficult question since it deals with three different and complex areas of law. It also requires a common sense approach to the tactics that Combo should adopt, as well as analysis of the legal options available to them. For example, the suggestion in Part (b) of the answer that Combo write to members of Excess. The mobilisation of shareholder support is often relevant advice in an examination answer, but it is very rarely mentioned by students. It is also very common in practice. Recently some large companies have also placed press advertisements to contact and influence members in connection with take-over battles.

18. To effect a merger under ***S.110–111 IA*** the company (Alpha Ltd) must pass a resolution to wind-up, or must already be in voluntary liquidation. Normally the members will have already passed a special resolution giving the liquidator authority to sell the business to another company (Beta Ltd) on terms that the consideration (usually shares in B Ltd) be divided among the members of A Ltd on the final dissolution of A Ltd. If as in this case, the sale is at an undervaluation, at least some of the shareholders will suffer a loss. However they will not be able to challenge the scheme solely on the ground that it involves distribution of partly paid shares (**BISGOOD v HENDERSON'S TRANSVAAL ESTATES (1908)**). They should consider the following courses of action.

Since the scheme is still a proposal (the second special resolution giving authority for the sale by the liquidator has not been passed) Exco should continue to try to persuade the other members to vote against the scheme. They could invoke ***S.376***, and circulate a statement of up to 1,000 words, but it would be preferable to write directly to the other members, offering their representative as proxy for members who cannot attend the meeting. E Ltd need the support of just over one third of the 'other' members to defeat the special resolution.

If the special resolution is passed despite their opposition, E Ltd may within 7 days deposit a written notice at the registered office requiring the liquidator to abstain from the sale or buy their shares at a price fixed by agreement or arbitration. The price must reflect the value of the shares before the sale and the purchase money must be paid before A Ltd is finally dissolved. Even if no notice is served E Ltd cannot be compelled to accept shares in B Ltd. Those shares will be sold and the proceeds of sale passed to E Ltd.

E Ltd may also wish to consider:

(a) A petition for the compulsory liquidation of A Ltd. If a compulsory winding-up order is made within one year of the special resolution the resolution will not be valid unless sanctioned by the court.

(b) An application to the court to convene meetings of members and creditors and proceed with a **S.425** scheme of arrangement. E Ltd will have to propose their own scheme for the court to consider. However the court will not exercise its discretion to call the meetings if it is clear that, having regard to the opposition of holders of the majority of the votes, the meetings could serve no useful purpose (**RE SAVOY HOTEL (1981)**).

(c) A petition under **S.459** on the ground that the affairs of the company are being conducted in an unfairly prejudicial manner or that proposed act is, or would be, so prejudicial. Under this section the court can make any order it thinks fit. In particular E Ltd should ask that the court give them authority to bring civil proceedings in the name of and on behalf of A Ltd against the directors, since it appears that the directors are in breach of duty by selling at an undervalue and by failing to provide adequate information. It appears that the undervaluation is deliberate, presumably because the directors will gain more from unstated links with B Ltd than they will lose as directors and shareholders of A Ltd. In similar circumstances in **PRUDENTIAL ASSURANCE v NEWMAN INDUSTRIES (1980)** an action by a minority shareholder was successful. E Ltd would therefore have a good chance of success.

If it becomes a choice between the above 3 alternatives the decision should be either (a) or (c) since **S.425** is not intended as a 'defence' against alleged improper conduct. However whatever action E Ltd takes the result will probably be the same. The court is unlikely to prohibit the merger. It is likely to order the purchase of E Ltd's shares at a fair price. This is similar to the provision in the original scheme. E Ltd should therefore prepare for any dispute about the price by obtaining an independent valuation of their interest in A Ltd.

*Comment*

This question is much more difficult than most and is worthy of some detailed comments. Before starting your answer you should have considered the following points:

(a) Weighted voting rights are allowed, accordingly the directors have exactly one half of the voting power.

(b) The special resolution giving the liquidator the power to sell the business to Beta Ltd has not yet been passed. Therefore you must advise the minority about what to do about an unfair proposal rather than an unfair completed act. You must then assume that the proposal is implemented and advise accordingly. Whenever you are asked to advise a minority about how to oppose a proposed course of action you should always advise them to try to convince the other shareholders also to oppose the action. **S.376** may help, but it is usually better to advise the minority to write direct to other minority shareholders.

(c) You should ask yourself whether the sale at an undervalue is deliberate or negligent. There is no evidence to make an assumption one way or the other. We are not told, for example, whether the directors of Alpha Ltd hold any shares in Beta Ltd, but if they were to hold a large number of shares in Beta Ltd it would be correct to proceed on the basis that the undervaluation was deliberate.

It is difficult to know what best to include in the answer. The facts of **PRUDENTIAL ASSURANCE v NEWMAN** and discussion of personal or representative actions would be relevant. It would also be acceptable to give more detail about the **S.110 IA** procedure stating for example that the resolution to wind-up and the resolution authorising the sale may be passed at the same meeting, also that any interest of the directors in the transferee company must be disclosed to the members of the transferor company. However you should not say any more about **S.425**. The Association's answer suggests that **S.425** may be of help to Exco, and certainly Exco could try to invoke the **S.425** procedure. What is rather puzzling is that if the directors of Alpha had wanted to injure the minority they would have done better to use a **S.425** scheme from the start, because it is only the IA which has a specific sub-section (which cannot be excluded) designed to protect a dissenting minority. In fact in practice it is often sought to overcome the problem of dissenting shareholders by adopting a **S.425** scheme rather than using **S.110 IA**. However such attempts usually fail when the Court insists on minority protection measures similar to those offered by the IA. Thus whether **S.110 IA** or **S.425** is used the outcome for dissenting shareholders is likely to be the same. They will be given a way out. If you now refer back to the question you will realise that Alpha Ltd's scheme does give the minority a way out, so as long as they obtain the true value of their shares, they almost certainly have nothing to gain by any of the courses of action suggested. This is why the final advice is that they should get an independent valuation of their interest as a basis for negotiation.

19. When a company goes into liquidation the order for the discharge of its liabilities is as follows:

(a) Liquidator's expenses.

(b) Debts secured by fixed charges on company assets.

(c) Preferential debts, including for example, 6 months VAT, 12 months PAYE income tax and employees' wages for a period of 4 months prior to liquidation up to a maximum of £800 per employee.

(d) Debts secured by floating charges.

(e) Ordinary unsecured creditors, for example local rates and trade creditors.

The following provisions are also relevant to Tommos Ltd.

By *S.238–241 IA 1986* a preference made within 6 months before insolvent liquidation may be avoided by the liquidator. A preference is any act by an insolvent company (for example the grant of the fixed and floating charges in favour of Gwilims Bank) that has the effect of putting any of the company's creditors in a better position than the others in the event of insolvent liquidation. It is also possible that the payment of loan interest to Thomas was a preference. If so it can be re-claimed by Brian and added to the assets available for distribution.

By *S.178–182 IA 1986* a liquidator may disclaim any onerous property (ie the unprofitable contract to supply vegetables) by giving notice in the prescribed form to the other party to the contract. The other party may then apply to the court and the court may make such order as it thinks fit to compensate him.

Assuming that none of the transactions were preferences, the £90,000 would be distributed as follows:

| | |
|---|---|
| Liquidator's expenses | 3,000 |
| Thomas' fixed charge | 10,000 |
| Bank's fixed charge | 60,000 |
| Employees (preferential creditors) | 6,000 |
| VAT (preferential creditor) | 2,000 |
| Income tax (preferential creditor) | 3,000 |
| *(The Inland Revenue can choose which year's tax to claim)* | |
| Rates | |
| Trade creditors<br>Income tax<br>Restaurant owner | 6 000 |
| | £90,000 |

The ordinary debts, for which £6,000 is available, rank and abate equally, ie each person would get an equal proportion of what is owed to them. This is subject to the court's order (if any) in favour of the restaurant owner.

If the charges in favour of the bank are preferences, the liquidator, Thomas and the preferential creditors will be paid in full. The remaining £66,000 would be divided among the others in proportion to the amount owing to each of them.

*Comment*

The Association's answer refers to IA 1985. This was repealed by IA 1986. Income tax may have caused some difficulties. It is important to realise that the company owes sums deducted from employees' wages under the Pay As You Earn (PAYE) system of taxation. They do not owe tax on company profits. This is corporation tax and since 1985 the Inland Revenue has only been an ordinary creditor in respect of corporation tax due.

It would also be correct to refer to **S.245 IA** in your answer. This invalidates floating charges created by insolvent companies within one year before insolvent liquidation (unless the charge secured an advance of 'new' money). This could invalidate the bank's charge, even if its grant was not influenced by any desire to put the bank in a better position than the other creditors.

20. (a) When a person is appointed as an administrative receiver and manager by debentureholders under a power in the trust deed he becomes an agent of the debentureholders unless the trust deed provides (as is usual) that the receiver is an agent of the company.

The basic duty of a receiver is to collect in the assets charged, to collect rents and profits, to exercise the debentureholders' powers of realisation and to pay the net proceeds to them. As an administrative receiver he has the power to carry on the business if necessary until the realisation of the security ***(SCHEDULE 1 IA)***.

There are several provisions in the **COMPANIES ACT** and the **INSOVENCY ACT** which are relevant to the duties and liabilities of receivers:

By **S.196 CA** a receiver must pay the company's creditors out of the assets available to him in the same order of priority as applies in a liquidation. Thus preferential creditors take priority over debentureholders secured by floating charges. Employees are preferential creditors to the extent of four months wages up to a maximum of £800 ***(SCHEDULE 6 IA)***. It appears that Richard has broken this duty and if there are no assets available to satisfy the employees' claims Richard will be personally liable to them.

By **S.492 CA** a receiver appointed by the debentureholders will be personally liable on his contracts (unless the contract provides otherwise) but with a right of indemnity out of the company's assets. Richard may therefore be sued for breach of contract.

The effect of the appointment of a receiver on the directors is to suspend their powers of control. They do however remain in office and they are entitled to their fees. They have power to challenge the receiver's appointment, petition to wind-up the company or bring an action in the company's name provided this does not interfere with the receiver's task of getting in the assets. For example in **NEWHART DEVELOPMENTS v CO-OPERATIVE COMMERCIAL BANK (1978)** P and D had been engaged in a joint venture, D providing the finance. When the venture ran into difficulties D appointed a receiver of P. P however issued a writ against D for breach of contract. D applied to the court to have the action struck out because the writ had been issued by the directors without the receiver's consent. The application was unsuccessful since the appointment of a receiver did not prevent the directors from exercising their powers to govern the company as long as their acts do not threaten the assets subject to the debentureholders' charge. It therefore seems likely that the directors' action will be allowed to proceed.

(b) If Richard had been appointed liquidator in a creditors' voluntary winding-up he would be an agent of the company and therefore not under any personal liability in respect of his transactions. He would not therefore be liable to the purchasers of the cloth. There is no counterpart in liquidation to ***S.492***.

With regard to the employees the position is the same. As preferential creditors they are entitled to priority over the debentureholders.

With regard to the directors the position is very different. On the appointment of a liquidator the powers of the directors cease. They could not therefore use the company's name to bring proceedings against the liquidator. Richard could have an action to remove him set aside.

As a liquidator Richard is an officer of the company for the purpose of misfeasance proceedings under ***S.212 IA***. This section could therefore be used to bring proceedings in respect of his failure to pay the preferential creditors. This section also applies to administrative receivers.

***Comment***

This is another quite difficult question that requires a detailed knowledge of the powers and the liabilities of liquidators and receivers. One danger is getting the law relating to liquidators and receivers mixed up. Another common error where part (b) of a question says 'How would your advice differ if. . .' is to spend about 80% of your time on part (a) and only write one or two sentences for part (b). In this case the mark allocation is equal for each part, so clearly you must spend roughly equal time on each part.

# Appendix III

## ANSWERS TO PROGRESS TESTS

### *Progress test 1*

1. It is conclusive evidence of the fact that the formalities of registration have been complied with. 'Conclusive evidence' means that the registration cannot be challenged even if actual evidence is produced to show that the formalities were not complied with.

2. The usual method is to give the directors an absolute right to refuse to register a transfer. Another method is to give a right of 'first refusal' to existing members.

3. £50,000.

4. False.

5. The general rule is that a company is a separate legal entity from its members (**SALOMON v SALOMON & CO (1897)**). Therefore the members cannot be usually made liable for the company's debts. However, there are three exceptions which may be relevant in Z's case. Firstly, by ***S.24 CA 1985***, if a company carries on business without having at least two members for more than six months, any person who is a member and knows of this irregularity shall be liable for the debts of the company contracted after the six months have expired. Secondly, by ***S.213 IA 1986***, if it appears that business has been carried on with intent to defraud creditors the persons responsible may be made personally liable for the company's debts without limitation of liability. Thirdly, by ***S.214 IA 1986***, the liquidator of an insolvent company may apply to the Court to declare that a director be personally liable to contribute to the company's assets. Before making an order the Court will have to be satisfied that the director knew, or ought to have concluded, that there was no reasonable prospect of avoiding insolvent liquidation and that he failed to take every step to minimise the creditors' loss.

   The conclusion on ***S.24*** clearly depends on when X and Y died. If they died more than six months ago then Z may have some personal liability (it is assumed that he is aware of the irregularity). If they died less than six months ago Z cannot be liable under ***S.24***. He should nevertheless transfer a few shares to someone else to avoid the possibility of future liability.

   It is most unlikely that Z would be liable under ***S.213 IA 1986***, since intent to defraud creditors requires 'positive steps in the carrying on of the company's business in a fraudulent manner' (**RE MAIDSTONE BUILDING PROVISIONS (1971)**), and incompetence would not amount to such 'positive steps'.

When applying ***S.214 IA 1986*** the Court will consider whether the director has acted as a reasonably diligent person having:

(a) The general knowledge, skill and experience that might reasonably be expected of a person carrying out that particular director's duties; and

(b) The general knowledge, skill and experience actually possessed by that director.

Thus provided Z takes reasonable decisions, bearing in mind the knowledge that he should have, and the knowledge that he does have, he would probably avoid liability under this section. However the facts given are not adequate for a firm conclusion.

*Comments*

No comments required on questions 1–4. However question 5 raises some interesting points. Firstly the question includes a deliberate piece of vague information. You are told that X and Y were killed a ***few*** months ago. You should be alert to such statements since the conclusion may depend on how many months. In such cases it is acceptable to give alternative conclusions. For example, 'If X and Y were killed less than six months ago Z is not liable. On the other hand if they were killed more than six months ago Z may be liable under ***S.24 CA 1985***'. A second point concerns the style of the answer. You should always start the answer by stating the relevant law, never start with the conclusion. Thus the first paragraph does not even mention X, Y and Z. It only deals with the law. The third point concerns content. It could possibly be argued that ***S.213 IA 1986*** should not be referred to since it does not render Z liable. However this is not correct, a section may be sufficiently relevant for discussion in such circumstances. There is no golden rule, it is a matter for individual judgement in each case. Note also **RE PRODUCE MARKETING CONSORTIUM** (1989), the first case to be decided on wrongful trading.

### *Progress test 2*

1. (a) Add the Public Limited Company Clause to the memorandum

   (b) Change the Name Clause in the memorandum

   (c) Remove any restriction on the right to transfer shares from the articles.

   It may also be necessary to increase the company's capital.

2. The maximum for a trading partnership is twenty. However professional partnerships, for example, solicitors, accountants, auctioneers, valuers and estate agents may have more than twenty partners.

3. (a) Ordinary resolution

   (b) It is impossible to ratify a pre-incorporation contract

   (c) Special resolution.

4. The transaction will be valid, but if the company fails to comply with its obligations within 21 days of being called upon to do so, the directors are liable to indemnify the other party if he suffers loss due to the company's failure to comply. In addition the company and its officers may be fined.
5. The pre-incorporation contract should include a term that the promoters' liability will cease when the company, after incorporation, enters into an identical agreement. If possible it should also provide that if the company does not enter into such an agreement within a stated period either party may rescind.

*Comments*
All these questions were straightforward. Clearly question 4 is a good example of lifting the 'veil of incorporation'. **S.36C** (Q5) was previously **S.36(4)**, the amendment being made by **S.130 CA 89**.

## Progress test 3

1. False.
2. The validity of an act done by a company shall not be called into question on the ground of lack of capacity by reason of anything in the company's memorandum.
3. (a) Special
   (b) Ordinary
   (c) The change requires the prescribed form of assent signed by all the members.
4. Most companies limited by guarantee are educational or charitable organisations which raise their funds by subscription. The liability of members is limited to the amount that they have agreed to pay in the event of winding up.
5. The country in which the registered office is situated, not its address.
6. The facts of the case are similar to **R v McDONNELL (1966)**, where a number of charges were brought against a director including conspiracy with his own company. The court rejected the conspiracy allegation on the ground that where the sole person responsible in the company is the defendant himself, it could not be said that there were two persons or two minds as is required for a conviction of conspiracy.

*Comments*

**S.35(1)** abolishes the ultra vires rule, giving outsiders complete protection where the act of the company is complete. The outsiders position is also helped by **S.142 CA 89** abolishing the doctrine of constructive notice for most purposes.

Question 6 is an illustration of lifting the veil of incorporation. Although it is possible for a company to be guilty of a criminal conspiracy, the Courts are not prepared to allow a director to be convicted of conspiring with his own one-man company'.

## *Progress test 4*

1. (a) Special.
   (b) Special.
   (c) Special.
2. Every company must publish its name
   (a) Outside all its places of business
   (b) On all letters, orders, invoices, notices, cheques and receipts
   (c) On its seal, if it has a seal.
3. Two in each case.
4. The articles are a contract between the company and its members, but only with respect to rights and obligations which affect members in their capacity as members.
5. If there is no power to purchase in the articles (there is no provision in Table A) then the articles must be changed. John can block a change of articles if he has enough shares, since a change requires a special resolution, ie a three quarter majority of members entitled to vote and voting. If he has insufficient shares to block the alteration, he could try to argue that the change is a fraud on the minority, or unfairly prejudicial conduct ***(S.459 CA 1985)***. However in SIDEBOTTOM v KERSHAW LEESE a private company altered its articles to give the directors power to require any shareholder who competed with the company to transfer his shares to nominees of the directors at a fair price. This alteration was held to be valid since it was for the benefit of the company as a whole to be able to expel a competitor from its membership. In Sidebottom's case the member was a member of another company rather than an employee of another company, but this is probably not a significant distinction. John has very little chance of successfully opposing the proposed change unless he has enough shares.

*Comments*

There is often confusion over the right to object to either a change of articles or an alteration of the objects clause. There is no statutory right given to any percentage of minority shareholders to object to an alteration of the articles. In contrast, holders of 15% of the issued shares have 21 days to apply to the Court to have an alteration of objects set aside.

Several interesting points are raised by question 5

(a) We are not told how many shares John holds. Thus a crucial piece of information has been deliberately omitted from the question. You may therefore be forced to give alternative conclusions, allowing for the possibility of different percentage shareholdings.

(b) It is of little use for a company to be able to expel a member who has some connection with a competing company, since a member's right of access to company documents and registers is only marginally greater than that of any member of the public.

(c) Many students assume that the articles will always contain the power to do the thing specified in the question. Where such things are not standard, as in this case, it is better to assume that the articles do not contain such a power, and that they must therefore be changed.

In connection with question 2, note that it is no longer compulsory for a company to have a seal. A document may be executed by the signature of two directors or one director and the secretary, if the company so chooses.

## *Progress test 5*

1. A ***direct offer*** is an offer by a company to persons who will subscribe directly for the shares or debentures in the company, without there being any intervening contractual involvement by an issuing house (eg a merchant bank). A merchant bank may nevertheless underwrite the issue and may well be involved in the preparation of the listing particulars or prospectus.

   An ***offer for sale*** is an issue where the shares are first sold to an issuing house and then resold to the public at a slightly higher price. The expression may also be used to describe a sale by a substantial shareholder who has held shares for a period of time. Neither a direct offer nor an offer for sale is an 'offer' in the contractual sense.

   Alternatively a private company may use the new written resolution procedure. This requires the unanimous consent of all members ***(S.113–114* CA 89)**.

2. A ***rights issue*** is an issue of new shares to existing members in proportion to their shareholdings, normally at less than the current market price of existing shares. Usually the rights are renounceable.

   A ***bonus issue*** is a capitalisation of profits, ie shareholders are allotted fully paid shares in proportion to dividend entitlement. The term 'bonus' is misleading, since if profits had not been capitalised a dividend would usually have been paid.

3. Supplementary listing particulars are required when there is a significant change affecting any matter included in the original particulars, or a sig-

nificant new matter arises, ie a matter that would have justified inclusion in the original listing particulars. A change or new matter is significant if it would affect the making of an informed assessment of the issuer's assets and liabilities, financial position, results and prospects.

4. (i) The issuer

   (ii) The directors

   (iii) Persons named as having agreed to become directors

   (iv) Persons who have accepted responsibility for any part of the particulars

   (v) Persons who authorised the contents of any part of the prospectus.

   The directors are not responsible if the listing particulars were published without their knowledge and consent and persons responsible under (iv) and (v) are only liable for the part for which they have accepted responsibility or authorised.

5. A person may be entitled to rescind his contract with the company and recover his subscription money if he can show that

   (a) The listing particulars or prospectus included a false statement of a material fact; ***and***

   (b) The listing particulars or prospectus was issued by or on behalf of the company and that he was one of the persons to whom it was addressed; ***and***

   (c) The false statement induced him to subscribe.

6. The right to rescind is lost in any of the following situations

   (a) If the allottee, after discovering the true facts, by his conduct, affirms the contract. He may do this even though it was not his intention to do so. for example, by exercising membership rights such as attending a meeting or attempting to sell the shares.

   (b) If on discovering the truth he fails to rescind promptly

   (c) If it is no longer possible to restore both parties to their pre-contract position. This would be the case if the company had gone into liquidation.

7. The general duty of disclosure applies to both listing particulars and the prospectus. It requires that in addition to any matters required by the listing rules, the particulars must give the information that investors and their advisors would reasonably require to make an informed decision on whether to buy the securities, ie assets and liabilities, financial position, results and prospects, and the rights attaching to the securities.

8. ***'Subscription'*** means the acquisition for cash from the company, by application and allotment, of unissued shares or debentures in the company.

***'Purchase'*** means acquisition for cash by transfer from a person to whom the company has allotted them, of already issued shares or debentures in the company.

Subscription and purchase both require the acquisition of shares for cash. An offer by Company A to issue its shares in exchange for shares of Company B does not therefore require listing particulars or a prospectus.

*Comments*
The only comment concerns offers for sale. An offer for sale may be at a fixed price or by tender. The examiner has not yet asked a question about offers for sale by tender, but such offers were quite fashionable in the mid 1980s. You should be aware of how such offers work. This is described in the chapter.

## *Progress test 6*

1. (a) Any share issue must comply with ***S.80 CA 1985*** (unless excluded). This requires that an ordinary resolution be passed.
   (b) The articles must authorise the issue of redeemable shares.
   (c) The terms of the issue must provide for payment on redemption (not at some later date).
   (d) There must be shares in issue which are not redeemable.
   (e) The terms and manner of redemption must be specified at or before the time of issue.
2. (a) There must be authority in the articles
   (b) A special resolution must be passed
   (c) The Court must give its consent.
3. (a) Ordinary
   (b) Ordinary
   (c) Ordinary.
4. A share premium account must be created when shares are issued, whether for cash or for a consideration other than for cash, at a price above their nominal value. However, no share premium account need be opened when, to effect a merger, the issuing company acquires at least 90% of the equity shares of another company as a consequence of the allotment of its own equity shares.
5. (a) Shares may not be issued at a discount ***(S.100 CA 1985)***, but debentures can be issued at a discount, ie in return for a consideration worth less than their nominal value. A share issue in return for the liability to pay a liquidated sum is defined as an issue for cash. The cash value

is less than the total nominal value, but it exceeds the nominal value of the shares. **S.100** has not been contravened. The shares must be regarded as issued at par and the debentures at a discount of £1,500.

(b) By **S.103 CA 1985** a public company may not allot shares for a consideration other than cash unless the non-cash asset has been independently valued and a report on the valuation made to the company within the six months prior to the allotment. The report must state that the value of the consideration is not less than the nominal value of the shares, plus any premium. The valuer must be a person qualified to be the auditor of a company or some other person who appears to the auditor to have the requisite knowledge and experience to make the valuation. The validity of the issue therefore depends on whether the lease of shooting rights is worth £100,000 or more.

*Comments*

Although an ordinary resolution does not normally require delivery to the registrar, a copy of each of the resolutions mentioned in question 3 must be delivered to the registrar within 15 days.

Question 6 is rather difficult. On part (a) some students fail to realise that there is an issue for cash. Another common error is to try to apportion the total discount between shares and debentures. On part (b) it is possible to miss the point of the question by failing to realise that a 99 year exclusive right to shoot game birds is a valuable non- cash asset. If the examiner only wanted to test whether or not you have learned the facts he would have asked 'what conditions must be complied with if a public company wishes to issue shares in return for a non-cash consideration'. But if the examiner wants to test understanding as well as memory he will ask a question such as number 5(b). The only way to avoid being caught out is to keep on practising problem questions.

## *Progress test 7*

1. True. Debenture interest is a debt and must be paid whether or not there are profits.
2. These are dividends which are paid between annual general meetings. Usually the payment is made mid-way through the year and the amount will be roughly equal to the final dividend. In the case of a public company, interim accounts will be necessary to support an interim dividend.
3. (a) The company must have authority in its articles. They will probably authorise an issue provided an ordinary resolution is passed.

   (b) The nominal capital must be sufficient.

   (c) Following the issue the company must make a return of allotments to the registrar.

4. The company declares the dividend by ordinary resolution, but the declaration cannot exceed the amount recommended by the directors, although the directors can reduce the recommended amount. The dividends are paid in proportion to the amount paid up on shares, and normally a cheque will be sent by post to the registered address of the shareholder.
5. Any director who was knowingly a party to the unlawful distribution is liable to pay to the company the amount lost plus interest.
6. The company may recover an unlawful dividend from its members if at the time of receipt they knew, or had reasonable grounds for knowing, that it was unlawful. If only part of the dividend is unlawful, ie it exceeds the distributable profits by a margin, then only the excess can be recovered.

*Comments*

The liability of directors described in question 5 can arise in three ways.

(a) They recommend or declare a dividend which they know is paid out of capital.

(b) Without preparing any accounts they declare or recommend a dividend which proves to be paid out of capital, since it is their duty to ensure that profits are available.

(c) They make some mistake of law or interpretation of the memorandum or articles which leads them to declare an unlawful dividend. However in this case the directors may be entitled to relief if they acted honestly and reasonably.

Question 6 is another example of a question where an important fact has been omitted. Do the members know that the dividend was unlawfully paid?

## *Progress test 8*

1. A share certificate is not a document of title. It states that the person named is the holder of the shares and specifies the amount paid up on them. It is prima facie evidence of ownership and must be surrendered when the holder transfers all or some of his shares. If the company issues a share certificate which is incorrect it is estopped from denying that it is correct, but only against a person who has relied on it to his detriment.
2. A management buy-out is the disposal of a company to its management. It may occur when, for example, the owner/directors of a company wish to retire and the only suitable persons to take over are the senior managers immediately below them. In most cases the senior managers would not have enough money to purchase all the shares. A scheme can be devised whereby a bank lends adequate money to the managers and the loan is secured on the assets of the company. Although this amounts to financial

assistance for an acquisition of own shares, such a scheme has been possible since 1981, provided a number of conditions are satisfied.

3. For an equitable mortgage the borrower gives a lender his share certificate plus a signed transfer. The lender has an implied power to fill in his name and sell the shares if the loan is not repaid. The lender should protect himself by serving a 'stop notice' on the company.

4. There are two provisions

   (a) By ***S.143*** a private company must not apply for a Stock Exchange listing.

   (b) By ***S.170*** a private company must not issue any advertisement offering its shares for sale (subject to certain exceptional companies exempted by the Secretary of State for specific reasons, for example an advertisement aimed at a specialist market).

5. (a) The right to receive a dividend at the specified rate before any dividend is paid to ordinary shareholders. (They do not have a right to compel the company to pay the dividend if the directors decide not to do so.)

   (b) The right to a preference dividend is cumulative unless the contrary is stated. Therefore if an 8% dividend is not paid in one year the priority entitlement will be 16% in the next year.

   (c) If a company with arrears of unpaid cumulative preference dividend goes into liquidation, the preference shareholders are not entitled to the arrears unless

      i. The dividend was declared, but not yet paid, when liquidation commenced or

      ii. The articles expressly provide that on liquidation arrears are to be paid in priority to return of capital to members.

   (d) Preference shareholders have no entitlement to participate in any additional dividend over and above their specified rate, unless the articles expressly provide that they are 'participating preference shares'.

6. The standard procedure requires that an extraordinary resolution approving the variation be passed by a three quarter majority of the votes cast at a separate meeting of the class, or the written consent be obtained from the holders of three quarters of the issued shares of the class.

*Comments*

Prior to 1981 a management buy-out of the type described above was not possible. One of the main reasons for the changes introduced by the 1981 Act was to facilitate such schemes. The Act increased the marketability of a company's shares, both by allowing the company to purchase them itself, and by allowing it to give financial assistance. This helps to keep 'family' control or private companies, it increases interest in employees share schemes, and it makes it casicr for companies to raise venture capital.

When arrears of cumulative preference dividend are paid, the holders of the shares at the time when the dividend is declared are entitled to the whole of it, even if they did not hold the shares in the year to which the arrears relate.

*S.143 FINANCIAL SERVICES ACT 1986* replaces *S.81 CA 1985* which prohibited private companies from offering shares or debentures to the public. *S.81* has been repealed.

## Progress test 9

1. Upon production of evidence that he is the personal representative, John is entitled to become the holder of the shares himself, or he may have some other person nominated by him registered as the transferee. If he elects to become the holder he should give notice to the company to that effect. If he elects to have another person registered he must execute the transfer in their favour (Article 30). Once registered, the personal representative or his nominee has all the rights of a member. However before registration the personal representative may not attend or vote at any company meeting (Article 31).
2. A small private company may keep a bound book (which may also incorporate other statutory registers and records). This will be adequate if few changes are likely to be entered. Alternatively, a company may keep a loose leaf card register, with members' cards in alphabetical order. By *S.722* the company must take precautions against falsification, for example, by having a locking mechanism which prevents tampering with the cards. Large companies usually keep the register of members by computer. The company must ensure that the register can be legibly printed if required. *(S.723 CA 1985)*.
3. If the company agrees that there has been a simple error, a name may be entered or removed to correct that error. However if the company denies the need for an alteration, for example, because it refused to register a transfer of shares, or if two people claim title to the same shares, the court has the power to consider the complaint and order rectification of the register *(S.359 CA 1985)*.
4. False. A call is made by the directors.
5. The problem is concerned with the legal position when a company acquires an equitable interest in its own shares, when there already exists an earlier equitable interest in the shares. In such cases the company's equitable interest will rank after any prior equitable interest of which it knows.

The facts of the question are similar to **BRADFORD BANKING COMPANY v BRIGGS (1886).**

*Comments*

Question 1 refers to Table A. The provisions of Table A changed in 1985. However, some companies will still operate under the old Table A. This provided that a personal representative could sell the shares without becoming a member or require that he be registered as a member. If he did neither the deceased would remain on the register. To avoid this the articles provided that the personal representative either had to transfer the shares or register as a member within 90 days. If he did neither the directors could withhold dividends.

Question 5 deals with a difficult point not directly referred to in the text, namely the priority of equitable interests in shares, where one such interest is held by the company itself by virtue of lien over the shares. It might be thought that **S.360 CA 1985** (which provides that no notice of any trust shall be entered on the register) would give the company an advantage since it appears to prevent a company from having notice of the equitable interests of other persons. This is not the case since **S.360** is not intended to place the company in a better legal position than holders of other equitable interests. It merely exists for the purpose of administrative convenience.

## *Progress test 10*

1. A floating charge will crystallise when
   (a) the company defaults and the debenture holders appoint a receiver or apply to the Court to do so; or
   (b) winding-up commences;
   (c) business ceases;
   (d) an event occurs for which the charging deed provides for automatic crystallisation.
2. A transaction at an undervalue occurs when a company makes a gift, or enters into a transaction for no consideration, or for a consideration worth significantly less than the value of the benefit received by the company. However a transaction in good faith, for the purpose of the business and in the reasonable belief that the company will benefit will not be invalid. Nor will a transaction be invalidated if the company was solvent at the time it was made, and if that time fell outside certain periods before either liquidation or the presentation of a petition for an administration order.
3. The Court may make any order it thinks fit, examples include
   (a) Property transferred must be returned to the company.

(b) Security given by the company may be discharged.

(c) Any person must pay to the liquidator or administrator such sum as the Court directs in return for the benefit received.

4. Registration of a charge operates to give constructive notice of any matter requiring registration and disclosed on the register at the time the charge is created.

5. Charges created by a company must be registered within 21 days of creation. There is no requirement that the instrument of charge itself will be delivered to the registrar, only the prescribed particulars. These are still to be specified, but will include the date of creation of the charge, the amount secured, short particulars of the property charged and the persons entitled to the charge. The basic duty to register is with the company, but any person interested in the charge may register it. In practice this will usually be the lender's solicitor.

6. Where required information is omitted from the registered particulars, reliance on the charge is restricted to disclosed particulars and it is void in respect of undisclosed rights. However the court may order that the charge will not be void as against an administrator, liquidator or person acquiring an interest in charged property.

*Comments*

Compulsory winding up commences when the petition is presented, not when the winding up order is made. This is a common error. Voluntary winding up commences when the resolution is passed.

There used to be some doubt about whether cessation of business or the happening of a specified event could crystallise a floating charge. However two 1986 decisions – **RE WOODROFFES (MUSICAL INSTRUMENTS)** and **RE BRIGHTLIFE** have made it clear that crystallisation will occur in such circumstances. However crystallisation of a second floating charge to which a first charge is subject will not crystallise the first charge.

## Progress test 11

1. A director is any person occupying a position of director by whatever name called ***(S.741 CA 1985)***. A shadow director is a person in accordance with whose instructions the directors are accustomed to act, unless the directors act on that person's advice only when it is given in a professional capacity (also ***S.741***).

2. An agreement for more than five years must be approved by the shareholders in general meeting (ordinary resolution). Details of the agreement must be available for inspection by members at the registered office for two weeks prior to the meeting and at the meeting itself. Where a director has

a current contract, the unexpired term of the current contract must be added to the term of the new contract, when calculating the five years.

3. The managing director is usually appointed by the directors on such terms as they think fit.
4. Only the husband, partner and infant child are 'connected persons'.
5. (a) Morocco Ltd is a relevant company because it is a subsidiary of a public company. The agreement is a quasi-loan because it is an agreement to pay a third party on behalf of a director on terms that the company will be reimbursed in due course. The rule is that a relevant company may not make a quasi-loan to a director, unless the amount of the quasi-loan does not exceed £5,000 and the terms require the director to reimburse the company within two months. Although the size of the quasi-loan is not given it is stated that the company will be reimbursed in one year's time. The agreement is therefore illegal and void.

   (b) One exception to the rule that a company cannot lend to its own directors allows loans to enable directors to perform their duties. The conditions are

   i. The transaction must have the prior approval of the company in general meeting; or
   ii. The transaction must contain a provision that if it is not approved at the next general meeting the funds must be repaid within six months.

   In the case of a relevant company the value of the transaction must not exceed £10,000. It therefore seems likely that the loan to Ginger will be acceptable.

   (c) Widely drafted anti-avoidance provisions prevent this type of transaction. Clearly the 'management fees' are not genuine, they are merely a payment by Morocco to finance Zanzibar's loan to a director of Morocco.

*Comments*

Clearly question 5 is the most testing. Apart from detailed knowledge of the rules, it requires recognition of the fact that one company is public and the other is private. For part (c) note that the transaction would have been acceptable but for the anti-avoidance provisions, since there is no prohibition on a company lending to a director of one of its subsidiary companies. However a subsidiary cannot lend to a director of its own holding company.

## *Progress test 12*

1. A reasonable period of notice.
2. Yes, provided the secretary is not the only director.

3. Main duties

   (a) Responsibility for company documentation and returns to the registrar.

   (b) Taking minutes of meetings.

   (c) Sending notices to members.

   (d) Signing documents which bear the company seal.

4. Cecil may vote for himself at the board meeting. He has 25% of the votes at that meeting.

5. The secretary is an agent of the company. Like any agent he will bind his principal if he acts within the scope of the express authority conferred on him by the directors. In addition he has ostensible authority to bind the company on contract concerned with office administration. Such contracts include hiring office staff, purchasing office equipment and hiring cars to collect customers. In **PANORAMA DEVELOPMENTS v FIDELIS FURNISHING FABRICS (1971)** the secretary purportedly hired cars to collect customers. In fact the cars were for his use. It was held that such a contract was within his ostensible authority. The company was therefore liable to pay the hire charges.

   The secretary cannot bind the company on a trading contract nor can he borrow money on behalf of the company. In **RE CLEADON TRUST (1939)** at the request of the secretary, a director lent over £17,000 to the company. The loan was 'confirmed' by the directors but the confirmation was invalid since no quorum was present at the board meeting. The company later went into liquidation. It was held that the company was not bound by the contract since it was in excess of the secretary's authority and it had not been ratified by those with power to make such a contract. The director therefore ranked after creditors for repayment of the loan. The secretary also does not have authority to

   (a) Issue a writ in the company's name

   (b) Lodge a defence in the company's name

   (c) Instruct the company as to its legal rights

   (d) Register a transfer of shares

   (e) Strike a name off the register of members

   (f) Summon a meeting on his own authority.

   Furthermore it was stated by Lord Parker in **DAIMLER v CONTINENTAL TYRE COMPANY (1916)** that the secretary is not an official who can manage all its affairs, with or without the help of servants, in the absence of directors.

*Comments*
The Panorama Developments case is important because it illustrates the changed nature of the secretary's position. In **BARNETT HOARES v SOUTH LONDON.TRAMWAYS (1887)** it was said that a secretary is a mere servant, whose position was to do what he was told. In contrast he is now regarded as 'an officer of the company with extensive duties and responsibilities. He is no longer a mere clerk', Lord Denning.

## *Progress test 13*

1. (a) The company secretary is removed by the directors. There is no need for a company resolution.
   (b) Special resolution.
   (c) Special resolution.
2. The company must state the names of all the directors or none of them.
3. A private company which in respect of a particular financial year satisfies for that year and the preceding year at least two of the following conditions
   (a) Turnover not exceeding £2,000,000
   (b) Balance sheet total not exceeding £975,000
   (c) Average number of employees each week not exceeding fifty.
4. A person has an interest in shares if
   (a) He owns them, or
   (b) His spouse or infant child has an interest, or
   (c) The shares are held by a company and that company or its directors are accustomed to act in accordance with his instructions, or
   (d) The shares are held by a company and he controls one third or more of the votes at a general meeting of that company, or
   (e) Any other person has an interest and he is acting in concert with that person.
5. The annual return contains
   (a) The address of the registered office
   (b) Details of shares and debentures
   (c) Details of indebtedness secured by registered charges
   (d) A list of members (a full list must be included every three years, in the intervening years only changes are submitted)
   (e) Particulars of the directors and secretary.

The annual return must be delivered within 28 days after the return date, ie the anniversary of the company's incorporation or, if the company's previous return was made up to a different date, the anniversary of that date.

*Comments*

An off-market purchase of shares will almost certainly be made by a private company. In contrast a market purchase by a public company only needs the authority of an ordinary resolution. In either case the shares that are to be purchased may not vote on the resolution and despite anything in the articles any member may demand a poll on such a resolution.

Reserve capital may only be called up in the event of a winding up. It is therefore an extra guarantee fund for the creditors. The special resolution creating reserve capital is irrevocable. The only other irrevocable resolutions are those that commence liquidation.

The rules concerning substantial shareholdings only apply to public companies. A notifiable interest arises when a person knows that he has an interest in 3% or more of a company's voting shares. Notification is necessary on cessation or acquisition of an interest and when there is any change in a notifiable interest. Notification must be in writing and must be made within two working days from when the obligation to notify arises.

## Progress test 14

1. The rules of recognised supervisory bodies must ensure that only individuals with appropriate qualifications, or firms controlled by such persons are eligible for appointment as auditors. They must also ensure that audit work is carried out properly and with integrity. This will require the rules to cover both the technical standards required by auditors and general ethical standards such as independence and confidentiality. The rules will also cover continuing professional education in order to ensure that eligible persons continue to maintain an appropriate level of competence. Finally they will deal with investigation of members and enforcement of rules, for example admission of members, complaints procedures and disciplinary procedures.
2. In theory it is fixed by the company, or if the auditor was appointed by the directors to fill a casual vacancy, then they fix his remuneration. In practice the auditors submit their bill, and unless the circumstances are very exceptional it would be paid in the normal course of business.
3. John must send written notice of his resignation to the registered office. The notice must contain a statement of circumstances connected with his resignation that should be brought to the notice of the members or creditors, or a statement that there are no such circumstances. If there are such circumstances, the auditor may require the directors to convene an extraordinary general meeting to receive and consider the statement, and

he may require that members be sent a copy of the statement with notice of the meeting.

4. When various documents are issued by or filed at the company's registry, the registrar must publish notice of such issue or receipt in the London Gazette.

5. The fiduciary duties of a director include

   (a) An obligation not to place himself in a position where his personal interest and his duty to the company come into conflict.

   (b) An obligation not to misuse corporate information or opportunity.

   If a fiduciary duty is broken the company may (in some cases) be able to pass are solution waiving the breach. If they do not do this the director must account to the company for the profit he has made. The test is 'has the director profited from his position as director?', it is not 'has the company suffered a loss?' Although fiduciary duties are very strict it was held in **PESO SILVER MINES v CROPPER (1966)** that a director does not break a fiduciary duty if he enters into a transaction on his own account which the company has considered and rejected.

   In Foggy's case it does not appear that he has misused corporate information or opportunity. He has used such information but not improperly. He may however have allowed a conflict of interest to develop. This could depend on whether Vino Ltd and N B Ltd are in the same line of business. Clearly a director of Vino Ltd should not start a competing business. If the type of business is unrelated Foggy probably will not have to account for the profit.

*Comments*

The reason for requiring a statement that there were no circumstances connected with an auditor's resignation which ought to be brought to the notice of the company's members or creditors, is to dispel any fears that the auditor is resigning because he is unwilling to certify a dubious set of accounts.

Question 5 concerns the common topic of a conflict of duty and interest. In this question we are not told the nature of Vino Ltd's business, nevertheless there is sufficient possibility of conflict that the matter should bc discussed.

## *Progress test 15*

1. (a) Ordinary resolution

   (b) Ordinary resolution

   (c) Ordinary resolution.

2. Any member, including a corporate member, entitled to attend and vote at a meeting, may appoint a proxy to attend and vote in his place. The proxy need not be a member of either company. The notice appointing the proxy must generally be in the form prescribed by the company's articles, which in the case of a corporate member will require the proxy to be appointed under seal. There is a more simple procedure allowed by **S.375 CA 1985** by which a company which is a member of another company may appoint a representative by resolution. His appointment is proved by a copy of the resolution and he may exercise the same powers as an individual shareholder. The appointment of such a representative is preferable to the appointment of a proxy, since a proxy's rights are limited in that he is not entitled to vote on a show of hands (unless the articles provide otherwise), and he cannot speak at a meeting of a public company.
3. Private companies may use the elective resolution procedure to dispense with the requirement to hold an AGM. Other companies must hold an AGM every calendar year with not more than 15 months between each AGM. However provided the first AGM is held within 18 months of incorporation, it need not be held in the calendar year of incorporation or the following year. 21 days written notice is required for an AGM, although a shorter period is permissible if agreed by all the members entitled to attend and vote.
4. The chairman may adjourn the meeting if it has become disorderly or if the members present agree (for example because there is inadequate time to complete the business). He must adjourn the meeting if the majority of members present instruct him to do so. If he attempts to end a meeting before it is proper to do so, the members may elect a new chairman and continue the meeting.
5. When a company redeems or purchases its own shares out of capital, payment out of capital must not exceed the 'permissible capital payment'. This is the amount by which the price of the redemption or purchase exceeds the aggregate of the company's distributable profits and the proceeds of any new issue. The effect of this rule is to require a private company to use its available profits and any proceeds of a new issue before it makes a payment out of capital. Thus only when there is a deficiency may a payment out of capital be made. The permissible capital payment is as follows:

| | £ | £ |
|---|---|---|
| Price of redemption – 100,000 £1 shares at a premium of 50 pence per share | | 150,000 |
| Less Distributable profits | 45,000 | |
| Proceeds of issue (50,000 £1 shares at a premium of 20 pence) | 60,000 | 105,000 |
| *Permissible Capital Payment* | | 45,000 |

*Comments*

The elective resolution procedure was introduced in 1989. It recognises that for many small companies it is an unnecessary formality to hold an AGM. However members are protected by provisions allowing any member to serve a notice requiring the company to hold an AGM.

An ordinary resolution to approve a golden handshake payment (ie compensation for loss of office) is only required for uncovenanted payments, not payments agreed in the director's service contract.

Special notice (28 days) must be given to the company by the person proposing to remove an auditor. The procedure is exactly the same as for the removal of a director.

When there is an increase in the authorised capital a copy of the resolution must be filed with the registrar within 15 days.

When a private company purchases its own shares out of capital numerous conditions must be complied with (although the consent of the Court is not required)

(a) A special resolution must be passed (the shares to be purchased may not vote on the resolution).

(b) The directors must make a statutory declaration that the company will be able to carry on business throughout the following year.

(c) An auditor's report confirming the statutory declaration must be attached to it.

(d) Detailed publicity requirements must be complied with.

(e) Any member or creditor has five weeks to apply to the Court to cancel the resolution.

(f) A transfer to the capital redemption reserve may be necessary.

Since the capital of the company is the guarantee fund to which creditors look for payment both the persons whose shares were redeemed or purchased and the directors who signed the statutory declaration may be liable to contribute to the assets of the company if winding up commences within one year after payment out of capital.

## *Progress test 16*

1. False.

2. The exemptions are

   (a) An individual who deals without intending that he, or any other person, shall make a profit or avoid a loss.

   (b) A liquidator, receiver or trustee in bankruptcy who deals in good faith as part of his normal duties.

(c) A professional dealer on the stock exchange (a jobber or market maker) provided he is dealing in good faith in the normal course of business.

(d) A trustee or personal representative who is dealing on the advice of an appropriate person who is not himself in a situation to which the prohibitions apply.

(e) Persons who act in accordance with conduct of business rules to stabilise the price of securities.

3. There is no statutory right to compensation for the party who suffers loss because the parties do not know the identity of each other. Under the stock exchange procedure for share transfers shares go into a pool, and no one can say, for example, that shares purchased by Fred were in fact sold by and put into the pool by John. Thus the loss caused by the person breaking the rules cannot be traced to any particular share purchaser.

4. An individual is connected with a company if

   (a) He is a director of the company or of another company in the same group.

   (b) His position within the company (or some other company in the group) or his professional or business relationship with it, gives him access to confidential price sensitive information. This group includes the company secretary, the company's accountants, its stockbrokers, employees and employees of its accountants stockbrokers or bankers. There are also borderline situations, for example, an office cleaner who might find confidential information in a waste paper basket.

5. By ***S.125 CA 1985*** if there is a variation clause in the articles, class rights may only be varied in accordance with that clause. However by ***S.127*** holders of 15% of the issued shares of that class have 21 days to apply to the Court to cancel the variation. Gene has 16% of the preference shares, so he may use ***S.127***. He clearly has a good chance of convincing the Court that the variation is unfair and should be cancelled.

*Comments*

Probably the most significant exception to the insider dealing rules concerns personal representatives. It is intended to apply where, for example, a director is also a trustee of a trust which holds shares in the company. As trustee he must manage trust investments to gain the maximum benefit for the trust, but as a director he is automatically an insider and may well be prohibited from dealing. In such cases he should consult a suitable adviser, for example, the banker who usually advises the trustees on their investments, and act on his advice. However he should only act on this advice if it appears to him that the adviser is not himself prohibited from dealing. The exceptions for market makers and price stabilisers were added by the *FINANCIAL SERVICES ACT 1986*.

Question 5 is similar to **RE HOLDERS INVESTMENT TRUST (1971)** when a majority who voted in favour of a resolution were seeking some advantage to themselves as members of a different class, instead of considering the interests of the class in which they were then voting. The case in fact concerned a reduction of share capital rather than a variation of class rights, but the principle was similar.

## *Progress test 17*

1. Any member may petition the Court for an order on the ground that the affairs of the company are being or have been conducted in a matter which is unfairly prejudicial to the interests of its members generally or some part of the members (including at least himself) or that any proposed act or omission of the company is or would be so prejudicial.
2. Where a wrong is done to a company, or there is an irregularity in the management of a company and there arises a need to enforce the rights of the company, it is for the company to decide what action to take and it is the company which is the proper plaintiff in the action.
3. A derivative action occurs when the company has suffered an alleged wrong and any person other than the company is allowed to appear as plaintiff on behalf of the company, because the wrongdoers have control and are preventing the company from making the claim.
4. Inspectors have power to
   (a) Require production of books and documents and take copies
   (b) Question on oath any person
   (c) Obtain a warrant to enter premises and search for documents
   (d) Investigate the affairs of related companies
   (e) Inform the Department of matters tending to show the commission of an offence.
5. Although the declaration of dividends is at the discretion of the directors, there are circumstances when if the directors act fraudulently or arbitrarily in refusing to declare a dividend when a company has a surplus, a shareholder will be able to obtain relief from the Court. ***S.459 CA 1985***, concerning unfairly prejudicial conduct, now that it has been amended by ***CA 89*** to cover 'members generally', not merely a 'part of the members' would clearly cover the situation and it is most likely that the Court would declare a dividend out of the company's assets.

*Comments*

Note the following three points concerning derivative actions

(a) A derivative action is normally combined with representative action, ie the plaintiff asserts that he sues on behalf of himself and all other shareholders (except the defendants). If he is successful each injured party may claim damages without further need to prove improper conduct.

(b) In **PRUDENTIAL ASSURANCE v NEWMAN INDUSTRIES (1982)** it was held that a derivative action could be brought against persons in actual control, even if they did not have the majority of the shares.

(c) Although the plaintiff in a derivative action is suing on behalf of the company, the procedure appears rather confusing since the company is made the defendant. The reason for this is so that any order made by the Court will be binding on the company. If this were not done the controlling shareholders might continue to use their control of the company to avoid some of the consequences of a court decision against them.

## *Progress test 18*

1. The types of resolution are

   (a) Special.

   (b) Special, unless the company is insolvent in which case an extraordinary resolution is needed. An ordinary resolution is needed if a period fixed for the duration of the company has expired or if an event has occurred for which the articles provide for dissolution.

   (c) Special.

2. Any shareholder who did not vote for the special resolution can require the liquidator to abstain from the sale of the company to the new company or purchase his shares. This right must be exercised by written notice addressed to the liquidator and deposited at the registered office within 7 days of the resolution.

3. The voluntary arrangement procedure provides a means by which a company may come to terms with its creditors with the minimum of formality and court involvement. Where the appropriate majority approves, it will bind all the creditors.

   The procedure creates the new offices of ***'nominee'*** and ***'supervisor'*** both of whom must be licensed insolvency practitioners. The nominee will help the directors to put together a proposal and will summon meetings of members and creditors to consider it. If both meetings approve the proposal by the necessary majority, in its original form or with modifications, the scheme or compostion will take immediate effect. Any persons who object may appeal to the Court within 28 days. The rights of secured and preferential creditors may not be amended without their consent.

The arrangement will be administered by the nominee who, on approval of the proposal, will become the supervisor unless the meetings of members and creditors appoint another practitioner to act in his place.

Although the new system will be available to companies in administration or liquidation, it is expected to be especially attractive to small companies experiencing short-term financial difficulties which are capable of being overcome.

4. The standard procedure is to state that if 90% acceptance is obtained compulsory acquisition will follow. This procedure applies whether the acquiring company offers its own shares or cash for shares in the target company. Acceptance by holders of 90% of the shares for which the offer is made, must be obtained within four months from making the offer. The acquiring company then has two months in which to serve notice on the non-accepting shareholders of its intention to compulsorily acquire their shares on the same terms. They then have six weeks, from receiving the notice, to appeal to the Court against the proposed acquisition of their shares. If there is no objection of if it fails, the target company, as trustee for the non-accepting shareholders, transfers their shares to the acquiring company in exchange for the agreed price.

5. The situation envisaged by the question is allowed by law and is in fact quite common. However it poses problems in relation to fiduciary duties of directors. These are

   (a) To act bona fide for the benefit of the company as a whole

   (b) To use their powers for a proper purpose

   (c) To retain freedom of action, and

   (d) To avoid a conflict of duty and interest.

   The most relevant duty is (c) above. Since fiduciary duties are held in trust by the directors for the company they cannot, without the consent of the company, make a contract with an outsider as to how they will vote at board meetings. This will apply even if there is no improper motive of purpose for such a contract and even if the director receives no personal benefit under the agreement. However since such a breach of duty would not amount to an expropriation of the company's property it could either be permitted in advance by the company or waived subsequently.

   The duty to act tor the benefit of the company as a whole is also relevant. This prevents a director from acting for the benefit of a particular group of members or for the benefit of an outsider. A breach of this duty could also be waived by the company, although there is a possibility that a minority of members could succeed in an action under **S.459 CA 1985** if such a waiver were unfairly prejudicial to them, as it would be if, for example. the loan is at a low rate of interest which is detrimental to the company as a whole, but beneficial to the majority shareholders who lent money to the company. However in most cases unfair prejudice seems unlikely since the company has presumably benefited from receipt of the loan.

*Comments*

The only difference between a special resolution and an extraordinary resolution is the period of notice. For a special resolution it is 21 days for an extraordinary resolution it is 14 days.

Question 5 is part of an ACCA question from June 1977. It carried 10 marks.

## *Progress test 19*

1. The Court is likely to decide in favour of the creditors to whom the larger amount is owing. However it may also consider the reasons for the differences between the creditors.
2. A declaration of solvency contains the latest practicable statement of the company's assets and liabilities and states that, after enquiry, the directors are of the opinion that the company will be able to pay its debts within a stated period not more than twelve months after the resolution to wind up.

   The declaration must be made within five weeks before the resolution to wind up and it must be delivered to the registrar within 15 days after the resolution to wind up.
3. There are two situations
   (a) If the company is insolvent, unliquidated claims for damages in tort are not admissible if the amount due is not settled at the time the claimant come to prove
   (b) Statute barred debts
4. If a director of a company that has gone into insolvent liquidation knew or should have concluded (at some time before the start of liquidation) that there was no reasonable prospect that the company would avoid insolvent liquidation, that person may be liable to make a contribution to the company's assets, unless after concluding that liquidation could not be avoided, he took every step to minimise the creditors' potential loss.

   The Court will consider the general knowledge, skill and experience that might reasonably be expected of a person carrying out that particular director's duties and the general knowledge, skill and experience actually possessed by that director.

5. A liquidator is an agent of the company, not a trustee for individual creditors or contributories. Thus in the absence of fraud, bad faith or misconduct, an action for damages cannot be brought against the liquidator by any creditor or contributory. The best course of action for Mary would be to apply to the Court under ***S.112 IA 1986*** to control the liquidator in the exercise of his powers.

   If the liquidator breaks a statutory duty he will be liable in damages to any creditor or contributory that suffers loss. The duty of a liquidator is not merely to advertise for creditors but write to those who he knows exist but who did not send in claims. Dennis will therefore probably succeed in his claim for damages.

*Comments*

In RE SOUTHARD (1979) in a dispute between creditors, the Court chose to support the wishes of the creditors to whom smaller sums were owed. In the case a holding company arranged for its subsidiary, of which it was the largest creditor, to go into voluntary liquidation. The holding company later petitioned for the compulsory liquidation of the subsidiary in order to replace the original liquidator. The trade creditors to whom smaller sums were owed, were successful in their opposition to the petition, ensuring that the voluntary liquidation continued.

In most cases a debt becomes statute barred if it remains unpaid for six years and the creditor does not within that time commence legal proceedings to recover it. However a company becomes liable again to pay a statute barred debt (for example unpaid dividends) if it issues to the creditor a written acknowledgement of its indebtedness.

## *Progress test 20*

1. The company, the directors, a creditor or creditors, or a combination of these. Once presented an application cannot be withdrawn.
2. An administrator is the agent of the company. It will therefore be bound by all that he does.
3. Any creditor or member may apply to the Court for an order on the ground that the company is or has been managed by the administrator in a manner unfairly prejudicial to the creditors of members or that any act or omission of the administrator is or would be so prejudicial. The Court may make any order it thinks fit.
4. All of them except the Official Receiver.
5. An elective resolution is a new type of resolution introduced by the Companies Act 1989 to enable private companies to dispense with or modify certain internal procedures, for example the requirement to hold an AGM and the obligation to appoint auditors annually. If an elective

resolution is proposed for a general meeting, at least 21 days notice of the meeting must be given in writing. A notice must give the terms of the elective resolution. At the meeting the resolution must be agreed by all members entitled to attend and vote either in person or by proxy. Alternatively the company may use the new written resolution procedure. This allows anything which can be done by resolution at a general meeting of a private company to be done by a written resolution signed by or on behalf of all members of the company who would be entitled to attend and vote. No meeting need be held if the written resolution procedure is used.

*Comments*

When the directors apply for an administration order there is no need for them to first obtain the approval of a general meeting of members. However the board must act collectively, there is no provision for an individual director to make an application, although an individual may of course seek to persuade his colleagues that an order should be applied for.

When a person deals with an administrator in good faith and for value, he need not enquire whether the administrator is acting within his powers. This prevents the administrator raising the defence that his own act was ultra vires, if it turns out that he in fact had no power to enter into a particular transaction. However no presumption is expressed to apply in relation to good faith or value. It will therefore be the responsibility of the person claiming protection to establish that he acted in good faith and that the transaction was for value.

## Progress test 21

1. When an administrative receiver is appointed he must immediately require a statement of affairs. This must be submitted within 21 days from the date when he gave notice. It must be verified by affidavit and submitted by some or all of:

   (a) Persons who are or have been officers of the company.

   (b) Persons who took part in the company's formation at any time within one year before the receivership.

   (c) Employees, or persons employed within the past 12 months, who are capable of giving the required information.

   (d) Officers or employees of a company which was, within the past 12 months, itself an officer of the company.

   The statement of affairs must show, as at the date of the receiver's appointment (i) particulars of the company's assets and liabilities; (ii) the names, addresses of its creditors; (iii) the securities held by them with the dates when the securities were given; and (iv) other information as may be prescribed. At present the rules also require details of preferential creditors and debentureholders secured by floating charges, the estimated realisable value of all assets, and the estimated surplus or deficiency. Trading profits and losses for not less than three years must also be shown.

2. The effect of the appointment of a receiver and manager by the court is as follows:

   (a) Employees' contracts of service are brought to an end. A new contract may however be entered into between an employee and the receiver and manager. An employee whose contract has been terminated by the appointment can claim damages from the company for wrongful dismissal.

   (b) Since the appointment is by the court the goods are under the control of the court. The landlord cannot therefore distrain without leave of the court. The court will usually grant leave. A receiver who wishes to avoid distraint should therefore negotiate an arrangement with the landlord if possible.

   (c) The basic rule is that a receiver may repudiate existing contracts. However he may not do so if it would adversely affect the subsequent realisation of the company's assets or if it would injure the company's goodwill. **(RE NEWDIGATE COLLIERY (1912))**. When a contract is continued it is continued in the name of the company and will not be binding on the receiver personally (unless it also becomes binding by novation). Such contracts remain binding against the company so that in the event of a breach the company will be liable to damages.

3. An extortionate credit bargain is a transaction by which credit is provided on grossly unfair terms, having regard to the risk accepted by the creditor. If the transaction was entered into within the three years before liquidation, administration or receivership, the office holder may apply to the court for relief: When an application is made it is presumed that the bargain was extortionate unless the creditor proves otherwise ***(S.244 IA)***.

4. Voluntary liquidation is generally commenced by special resolution, unless the company is insolvent in which case an extraordinary resolution is passed. The shorter period of notice for an extraordinary resolution (14 days rather than 21 days) will assist the creditors of an insolvent company. When the registrar receives notice of the resolution to commence liquidation he must publish notice of its receipt in the Gazette.

   There are two types of voluntary liquidation, members' voluntary liquidation and creditors' voluntary liquidation. It will be a members' voluntary liquidation if, within 5 weeks before the resolution to wind up, the directors or a majority of them, make a declaration of solvency. This is a statement of the company's assets and liabilities and it states that, after inquiry, in the directors' opinion, the company will be able to pay its debts within a stated period not more than 12 months after the resolution.

If there is no declaration of solvency it will be a creditors' voluntary liquidation and the company must call a meeting of creditors within 14 days of the resolution to wind up, giving them at least 7 days notice. The notice must give the name and address of a qualified insolvency practitioner who, before the meeting, will give the creditors any information they reasonably require concerning the company's affairs. The directors must prepare a statement of affairs containing details of the company's assets, debts, creditors, and securities held by creditors. This must be verified by affidavit and laid before the meeting of creditors.

In a members' voluntary liquidation the members appoint the liquidator, but in a creditors' voluntary liquidation the creditors are entitled to make the appointment.

On the appointment of the liquidator the directors' powers cease, unless otherwise agreed by the general meeting or by the liquidator, or by the committee of inspection or creditors in a creditors' voluntary liquidation.

5. In general any disposition of assets after the crystallisation of a floating charge over those assets results in the purchaser of those assets taking them subject to the charge, ie the debenture holders can proceed against the assets to satisfy their debts. However, rights of set-off which have arisen before the charge crystallised are not affected. Thus the receiver would only be entitled to £35.

*Comments*

Relief from extortionate credit bargains was introduced by the *IA 1985*.

The facts of question 5 are the same as ROTHER IRONWORKS v CANTERBURY PRECISION ENGINEERS (1973).

# Appendix IV

## QUESTIONS WITHOUT ANSWERS

***Lecturers may obtain from the publishers, free of charge, summary answers to the following questions.***

1. A firm of yacht outfitters sold a steering system to Sam. The written order for the system was however made out in the name of Sam's company, Ocean Charters Ltd. The company had an issued capital of £2, divided into two £1 shares. It failed to pay. Can the vendor sue Sam?
2. Donald was the majority shareholder in a small private company. He wished to expand the business into the adjoining premises which he had let to another business. Under the Landlord and Tenant Act a landlord may claim possession of premises if they are required for his own use. Can Donald gain possession of the premises?
3. How can a company, which is a member of another company, express its views and vote at a meeting of that company?
4. Dennis deposited his share certificate with a bank as security. The bank informed the company of this. Dennis then became indebted to the company, and the company claimed a lien on his shares. Whose right prevails, the bank's or the company's?
5. A transferred some debentures to a trustee on trust for X, Y and Z. The transfer was never registered. X sold his interest to B. Some time later A deposited his debentures at a bank for security. When the bank discovered B's interest it applied for registration. Whose right prevails,the bank's or B's?
6. Private companies A, B, C and D each wish to redeem 10,000 redeemable shares at a premium of 10 pence per share. The nominal value of each share is £1. The redemptions are financed as follows:

| | A | B | C | D |
|---|---|---|---|---|
| Out of distributable profits | 11,000 | 6,000 | 7,000 | 3,500 |
| Out of the proceeds of a fresh issue | — | 5,000 | — | 5,000 |
| Out of capital | — | — | 4,000 | 2,500 |
| Cost of redemption | 11,000 | 11,000 | 11,000 | 11,000 |

How much must be transferred to the capital redemption reserve in each case?

7. In 1982 a private company issued 100,000 £1 shares redeemable in 1986 at a premium of 50 pence per share. In 1986 the company has distributable profits of £45,000, and it intends to issue 50,000 £1 shares at a premium of 20 pence per share in order to redeem the redeemable shares. Calculate the permissible capital payment.

8. a. The Articles of Association of X Limited provide that the directors may refuse to register a transfer of shares, but that they must give notice of their refusal to the transferee within two months from the lodging of the transfer for registration. Four months ago Alfred, who is the registered holder of 100 shares in X Limited, executed a transfer of his shares to Bernard and immediately lodged the transfer with the Company for registration. The directors have not registered the transfer and have not given any kind of notification to Bernard. Advise Bernard whether he has any rights in respect of the shares and if so how he should protect them.

   b. On inspecting the registered documents in respect of X Limited at the Companies Registry you find that a special resolution was passed last August altering the Articles of Association so that they now provide that before a member can dispose of his shares to a person who is not a member of the Company, he must first offer his shares for purchase by the existing members at a fair value fixed by the Company's auditors. Bernard tells you that Alfred was not given advance notice of the meeting at which the special resolution was passed, and that he did not offer his shares to the existing members before executing the transfer of his shares to Bernard. Advise Bernard.

9. Advise the minority member in the following situations:

   The controlling shareholders and directors of a corporation withheld payment of all dividends with a view to reducing the personal tax liability of the controlling shareholder.

   A trade association wished to increase its membership fees and passed a resolution approving the increase by a show of hands. A member objected because the association rules provided for a secret ballot.

10. Bill and Mary were the first directors of X Ltd, a private company incorporated in 1943. The articles appointed Bill and Mary permanent life directors and provided that "The permanent life directors shall have the power to terminate forthwith the directorship of any of the ordinary directors by notice in writing". Mary has recently died and Bill wants to know if he has the power to remove one of the ordinary directors.

11. At the beginning of October A Ltd owed B Ltd £124. Later the same month A Ltd sold goods to B Ltd for £159 on credit. A few days later A Ltd's debentureholders appointed a receiver and a floating charge over all A Ltd's assets crystallised. Early in November the goods were delivered to B Ltd. The receiver is now claiming 159 from B Ltd. Can B Ltd set-off the £124 owed to them by A Ltd?

12. PQ Ltd is a private company which is in voluntary liquidation. Advise the liquidator (Bill) in the following situations:

    Mary, a contributory, is claiming damages because she alleges that Bill has delayed in handing over her proportion of the surplus assets of the company.

    Bill has distributed the assets of the company without paying Dennis, a creditor. The books show Dennis as a creditor, but Dennis did not reply to Bill's advertisement for creditors.

13. a. Explain how a company may alter its articles and enumerate some of the restrictions applicable to alteration of articles.

    b. The shares of the Xlap Co Ltd ('the Company'), a private company, are held by the members of four families, the Jones, the Smiths, the Browns and the Clarks. The Jones and the Smiths, who together hold 90% of the Company's shares, are concerned about two matters. First, the Company is in need of further capital, but by reason of family differences, neither the Jones nor the Smiths are willing to inject additional funds so long as the Browns hold any shares in the Company. Secondly, the Jones and the Smiths have good reason to believe that one of the Clarks is running a business of his own which competes with that of the Company. It is known that he is obtaining information as a member of the Company which he is using to the benefit of this competing business. To resolve both matters of difficulty, the Jones and the Smiths propose to pass two resolutions. The first will enable the majority to acquire compulsorily, at full value the shares of the minority. The second will require any shareholder who competes with the Company's business, to transfer his shares, at full value, to nominees of the directors. Discuss the validity of these resolutions.

14. a. At what point in time is winding-up deemed to commence?

    b. Explain the difference between the committee of creditors in a liquidation and the committee of creditors in administration proceedings.

    c. What is meant by an application for early dissolution and when is it available?

15. Your client, Happy, has been offered the managing directorship of Grumpy Ltd, with a 40% shareholding in the company. The rest of the shares will be divided between Dopey and Sleepy, who at present hold all the shares and who will remain as directors of the company. Dopey and Sleepy are anxious to bring Happy into the company, and are prepared to consider any conditions Happy may seek to impose, save that they are not willing to increase his shareholding.

    Advise Happy on any TWO methods by which he might seek to secure himself against dismissal from the managing directorship of Grumpy Ltd, and comment on the effectiveness of these methods.

16. You are approached by Jerry and Tom who carry on the business of building contractors under the name "Jerry Builders". In view of a recession in the building trade they wish to obtain the benefits of limited liability. They instruct you to incorporate their business, which is presently worth £30,000 and which is owned equally by Jerry and Tom.

 Describe the steps which would be necessary in order to carry out these instructions.

17. TLC Limited is a private company engaged in the development of specialist scientific instruments. It was founded in 1972 by Lee and 20% of the shares are still held by the Lee family; 18% are held by Mighty Bank and the remainder by several small shareholders.

 The articles of TLC Limited incorporate Table A, with the following exceptions:

 - that Lee is to be managing director of the company for a term of 30 years at an annual salary of £18,000 (Art. 75);
 - that during this period Lee has sole power to appoint to the posts of Finance Director and Research Director (Art. 76);
 - that each Director has ten votes in respect of each share held by him on any resolution for his dismissal (Art. 77).

 Lee has appointed his nephew Alan as Finance Director and his son Ben as Research Director. In 1983 Mighty Bank refused loan finance for a new research project planned by the company, and since that time Lee and Ben have carried out that research in the company's laboratories in their spare time and have patented in their own names the new technique developed.

 Now the bank, with the support of other shareholders, proposes the following alterations to the company's articles:

 - that articles 75, 76 and 77 be deleted;
 - that directors be elected annually by the company in general meeting;
 - that any patent rights in respect of work carried out on the company's premises should belong to the company.

 Advise the directors generally.

18. Sandra is employed as a secretary in the taxation department of a large firm of accountants who are the auditors of Mammoth Plc, a public, quoted company. Sandra's husband, Herbert, owned a large number of shares in Mammoth Plc. Last week, whilst Sandra was having lunch with Arthur, an accountant who works in the audit department of the same firm, he told her that the unpublished accounts of Mammoth Plc showed a considerably lower trading profit than would have been expected from current market trends. Arthur knew Herbert owned shares in Mammoth Plc. Sandra passed on the information to Herbert. Herbert had recently incurred large gambling debts and was being pressed for payment. After

receiving the information from Sandra, Herbert sold his shares in Mammoth Plc and applied the proceeds in paying his gambling debts.

Discuss the criminal liabilities (if any) of the parties.

19. Discuss the legal methods of:

    a. Amalgamation of companies, and

    b. Takeover of companies,

    with particular regard, in each case, to the rights of dissenting shareholders and the rights of creditors.

20. a. As a condition of granting a loan to a company, the lender may require that one or more of his nominees be appointed as directors of the borrowing company, in order to protect the lender's interests. To what extent (if at all) is this arrangement inconsistent with the rules governing directors' duties?

    b. Alfred promoted GBH Ltd in January 1983 to acquire and develop a coastal site as a harbour for pleasure craft. The articles required each director to hold 1,000 £1 shares as his shareholding qualification. Alfred wished to have Joshua, a well known yachtsman, on the board of directors but Joshua was reluctant to risk the investment in his qualification shares . Alfred accordingly wrote to Joshua undertaking to purchase, at the price which Joshua had paid for them, any shares which Joshua might acquire in GBH Ltd. Joshua allowed himself to be appointed a director of GBH Ltd and purchased his 1,000 qualification shares, at par, for cash. The other directors and members of GBH Ltd were not informed of Alfred's undertaking to Joshua.

    By late 1985 GBH Ltd was in difficulties and its shares were valued at about 20 pence each. Joshua resigned from the board of directors and sold his shares to Alfred at £1 each in accordance with Alfred's 1983 undertaking. In June 1986 the other directors of GBH learned the price at which Joshua had sold his shares to Alfred. They now claim that Joshua must pay over to GBH Ltd the profit of 80 pence per share which he made from his sale of shares to Alfred.

    Advise Joshua on the merits of the directors' claim.

# Index


Accounting Concepts 227
Accounting Principles 226
Accounting Records 220
Accounting Reference Date 221
Accounting Reference Period 221
Accounts
- asset valuation rules 227
- content
  - *balance sheet* 236
  - *general provisions* 234
  - *profit and loss account* 235
- documents comprised in 222
- dormant companies 241
- form of
  - *balance sheet format 1* 229
  - *general provisions* 228
  - *profit and loss account formats 1 and 2* 232
- group accounts 224
- laying and delivering 221
- medium-sized company exemptions 241
- modified accounts 240
- publication of 242
- small company exemptions 240
- statutory accounts 242
- unlimited company exemption 222

Acquisition Accounting 110
Action by Company 277
Action by Shareholders 281
Administration Order 338
Administrative Receiver 344
Administration
- appointment 339
- duties 340
- powers 339
- vacation of office 342

Agency, Rules of 182
Allotment of Shares
- restrictions on allotment
  - *company authority required* 138
  - *minimum payment* 105
  - *non-cash consideration* 105
- return of allotments

Amalgamation. See Merger
Annual Return 219
Approved Exchange 94
Arrangement, Schemes of 304
Articles of Association
- alteration
  - *basic rule* 77
  - *effect on outsiders* 79
  - *limitations on freedom to alter* 78
- effect of 80
- requirements as to form 77
- Table A 77

Asset Valuation
- alternative rules 228
- historical cost basis 227

Association Clause 76
Auditors
- appointment 251
- duty of care and skill 257
- false statements to 256
- persons who may not be appointed 251
- power in relation to subsidiaries 256
- qualifications 248
- register of 250
- removal 253
- report of 255
- resignation 254
- supervisory bodies 247

Balance Sheet
- format of 229
- information required 236

Board Meetings 179
Bonus Shares 127
Borrowing by Companies 154
Brokerage 104
Bubble Act 16
Business Names 64

Calls 145
Capital. See Share Capital
Capital Clause 75
Capital Redemption Reserve
 examples of transfers to 122
 rules 120
 uses of 127
Capitalisation Issues 127
Capitalist System 21
Certificate of Compliance With Capital Requirements 59
Certificate of Incorporation 53
Chairman 264
Charges
 avoidance of 164
 fixed 156
 floating 157
 priority of 162
 register of 167
 registration of 160
Chartered Companies 20
City Code on Takeovers and Mergers 311
Class Rights
 definition 135
 in memorandum 76
 variation of 135
Committee of Creditors
 in administration 341
 in liquidation 322
Committee of Inspection 335
Community Institutions 29
Community Legislation 30
Companies
 chartered 20
 compared with partnerships 39
 domestic 16
 investment 128
 joint stock 15
 limited by guarantee 74
 limited by shares 74
 oversea 50
 partnership 41
 private (see also Private Companies) 44
 public (see also Public Companies) 44
 registration procedure 49
 re-registration
  *limited as unlimited* 75
  *private as public* 51
  *public as private* 52
  *unlimited as limited* 75
 statutory 20
 unlimited 74
Companies Registry 215
Competent Authority 91
Compromise, Schemes of, 304
Contingent Purchase Contract
Contributories 118
Corporate Personality 329
Counterveiling Powers 37
Crime by Company 421
Current Assets Definition 227

Dearing Report 243
Debentures
 compared with shares 155
 forms of security 156
 priority of charges 162
 remedies of debentureholders 168
 trustees for debentureholders 167
Declaration of Compliance 49
Declaration of Solvency 333
Defunct Companies 331
Department of Trade Investigations. See Investigations
Derivative Actions 281
Direct Offers 90
Directors
 alternate 175
 appointment
  *defects in* 176
  *methods of* 173
 assignment of office 175
 board meetings 179
 common law duties 199
 disqualification of 201
 fiduciary duties 193
 liability for co-directors 200

managing director 180
motives of 26
names on stationary 217
number of 173
persons who cannot be appointed 175
powers 179
register of directors 216
register of directors interests in shares, etc 217
relief from liability 200
removal of 177
remuneration 178
report 244
self perpetuating 25
shadow 183
share qualification 174
statutory duties relating to
*compensation for loss of office* 184
*disclosure of interests in shares, etc* 185
*employees* 194
*loans* 189
*option contracts* 189
*property transactions* 187
*service contracts* 186
vacation of office 177
Directors Report 244
Distribution, Definition of 124
Dividends
articles 127
capitalisation issue 127
definition 124
interim 126
investment companies 128
payment of 124
relevant accounts 126
unlawful payment 127
Domestic Companies 16
Dormant Companies 241

East India Company 15
Elective Resolution 268
Employees
as directors 32
provision for on the cessation, etc of business 72
European Community 28
European Company
Execution of Documents 59
Extraordinary Resolutions
definition 267
when required 267

Financial Assistance for Acquisition of Shares 112
Fixed Assets Definition 227
Fixed Charge 156
Floating Charge 157
Forfeiture of Shares 146
Formation of Companies 49
Foss v Harbottle, Rule In 277
Fraud on the Minority 279
Fraudulent Trading 325

Gazette, The London 213
Gift by Companies 70
Group Accounts 224
Guarantee, Liability Limited by 74

History of Company Law
early 15
recent 17
Holding and Subsidiary Companies 222

Incorporation
certificate of 50
consequences of 37
veil of 41
Index of Members 152
Insider Dealing 270
Insolvency Practicioners 315
Investigation
by company of interests in its own shares 218
by Department of Trade
*by order or the court* 288
*inspection of documents* 291
*inspector's report* 289

*of insider dealing* 275
*of ownership* 290
*of share dealings* 291
*on application of members* 287
*powers of inspectors* 288

Jobber 274
Joint Stock Companies 15

Lien on Shares 147
Limitation of Liability
by guarantee 74
by shares 74
unlimited liability 74
Liquidation
compulsory
*committee of creditors* 322
*consequences of* 320
*dissolution* 324
*grounds for* 317
*liquidator's powers* 323
*petition for* 319
*petitioners* 319
*proceedings* 321
contributories 320
defunct companies 331
disclaimer 328
misfeasance summons 326
priority of debts 330
proof of debts 329
publicity 331
secured creditors 329
voluntary
*applications for compulsory liquidation* 336
*applications to court* 336
*commencement of* 333
*consequences of* 335
*creditors' voluntary liquidation* 334
*dissolution* 337
*liquidator's powers* 335
*members' voluntary liquidation* 333
Listed Companies 48
Listing Particulars 92
Listing Rules 91
Loss of Capital 107

Managing Director 180
Market Maker 274
Market Purchase of Own Shares 118
Medium-Sized Companies' Accounts 241
Meetings
annual general 260
chairman 264
class 261
extraordinary general 260
minutes 265
notice 261
proxies 264
quorum 263
voting 264
Members
actions by 281
capacity
*bankrupts* 149
*companies* 150
*minors* 148
*personal representatives* 149
*trustees* 149
controlling members duties 277
methods of becoming a member 148
motives of 26
number of 44
reduction in number 42
resolutions and statements 263
Memorandum of Association
alteration generally 76
clauses
*association* 76
*capital* 75
*liability* 73
*name* 60
*objects* 68
*public company* 60
*registered office* 66
effect of 80
Merger Accounting 110

Merger Relief 110
Mergers
  definition 301
  methods 301
Mixed Economy 21
Mortgage of Shares
  equitable 144
  legal 144

Name
  business names 64
  company names
    *change of* 62
    *forbidden* 61
    *index of* 62
    *passing off* 63
    *power to dispense with 'limited'* 60
    *publication of* 63
Negligent Statements
  by auditors 257
  in prospectus 97

Objects Clause
  alteration of 73
  purposes of 68
  statement of 69
  ultra vires rule 69
Off Market Purchase of Own Shares 117
Offers for Sale 90
Officers of the Company 173
Official Listing 91
Official Notification
  effect of 214
  when required 213
Official receiver 320
Ordinary resolutions
  definition 265
  requiring registration 215
  requiring special notice 262
Ordinary shares 135
Oversea Companies 50

Parent Undertaking 222
Partnership Companies 41
Partnerships 39
Passing-Off Action 63
Personal Action 281
Placings 90
Pre-emption Rights
  on allotment of shares 138
  on sale of shares 144
Preference 165
Preference Shares 133
Pre-incorporation Contracts 57
Primary Offer 94
Priority of Charges 162
Private Companies
  advertisements for shares 89
  definition 44
  distinguished from public companies 44
  re-registration as public 51
  restrictions on transfer of shares 144
Profit and Loss Account
  format of 232
  information required 235
Promoters
  definition 55
  duties 55
  remedies for breach of duty 56
Prospectus
  civil remedies for misrepresentation
    *compensation* 97
    *damages* 98
    *rescission* 99
  definition 94
Public Companies
  definition 44
  distinguished from private companies 44
  re-registration as private 52
Purchase of Own Shares
  contingent purchase 118
  failure to purchase 123
  general rule 111
  market purchase 118
  off market purchase 117
  out of capital 119

Qualification Shares 174
Quasi-partnerships 318

Receivers
- and liquidator 350
- and manager 345
- appointment
  - *effect of* 346
  - *method of* 344
- duties 348
- position 347
- powers 347
- publicity requirements 349
- qualification 345
- remuneration 346
- vacation of office 350

Reconstructions
- definitions 301
- methods 301

Redeemable Shares 116
Reduction of Capital 108
Register of Auditors 250
Register of Charges 167
Register of Directors and Secretaries 216
Register of Directors Interests in Shares and Debentures 217
Register of Members
- contents 151
- index 152
- inspection of 152
- location 152
- notice of trusts 153
- obsolete entries 153
- rectification 152

Register of Substantial Shareholdings 217
Registered Office
- change of address 67
- clause in memorandum 66
- documents kept at 66
- purpose of 66

Registrar of Companies 48
Registration of Charges 160
Registration of Resolutions 215
Representative Actions 281
Re-registration of Companies. See Companies
Reservation of Title 158
Reserve Capital 102
Resolutions
- elective 268
- extraordinary 267
- ordinary 265
- ordinary requiring registration 215
- ordinary requiring special notice 262
- special 266
- written 267

Return of Allotments 140
Revaluation Reserve 228
Rights Issues 91
Royal British Bank v Turquand, Rule in 182

Schemes of Arrangement 304
Scrip Issue 128
Secondary Offer 94
Secretary
- appointment 205
- duties 206
- powers 205
- qualifications 205

Share Capital (see also Shares)
- alteration 102
- clause in memorandum 75
- reduction 108
- serious loss 107
- types 101

Share Certificates
- forged 140
- genuine 140

Share Premium Account
- merger relief 110
- uses 109
- when created 109

Share Transfers 141

Share Warrants 141
Shares (see also Share Capital)
acquisition and purchase of own shares
*financial assistance* 112
*general rule* 111
*market purchase* 118
*off market purchase* 117
*out of capital* 119
compared with debentures 115
definition 133
forfeiture of 146
issue at a discount 105
issue at a premium
*basic rule* 109
*merger relief* 110
issue methods of
*direct offer* 90
*offer for sale* 90
*placing* 90
*rights issue* 91
lien 147
mortgage 144
ordinary 135
payment
*general rule* 104
*minimum payment* 105
*of non-cash consideration* 105
preference 133
redeemable 116
surrender 146
transfer 141
transmission 148
Small Company Accounts 240
South Sea Company 16
Special Notice 262
Special Resolutions
definition 266
when required 266
Stagging 90
Statutory Companies 20
Stock Exchange
and City Code 311
model code 'Securities Transactions by Directors etc' 271
Stop Notice 145
Subsidiary Companies Definition 222
Summary Financial Statements 243
Supplementary Listing Particulars 93
Supplementary Prospectus 96
Surrender of Shares 146

Table A 77
Takeovers
City Code
*general principles* 312
*rules* 312
legal controls 309
Third Market 48
Transfer of Shares
certification of transfer 142
definition 148
forged transfers 142
form of 141
Transmission of Shares 148
Trustees for Debentureholders 167

Ultra Vires Rule 69
Undervalue, Transaction at 165
Underwriting Commission 103
Undistributable Reserves 125
Unfair Prejudice 282
Unlimited Liability 74
Unlisted Securities Market 48

Veil of Incorporation 41
Voluntary Arrangement 306

Winding-up. See Liquidation
Worker Directors 32
Written Resolutions 267
Wrongful Trading 325

**The English Legal System**
The Main Sources of English Law
The subsidiary Sources of Law
English Legal History
The Courts
Tribunals and Arbitration
The Personnel of the Law
Procedure and Evidence
The Law of Persons
Property Law
Trusts

**The Law of Contract**
The Concept of a Contract
The Formation of a Contract
Capacity of Contract
Form of Contracts
The Contents of Contracts
Vitiating Factors
Discharge of Contracts
Remedies for Breach of Contract
Privity of Contract

**The Law of Tort**
The Nature of a Tort
General Defences
Capacity
Negligence
Strict Liability
Consumer Protection Act 1987
Nuisance
Trespass and Conversion
Defamation
Remedies and Limitation Periods

**Commercial Law**
Agency
sale of Goods
Supply of Goods and Services
Consumer Credit
Negotiable Instruments
Insurance
Carriage of Goods
Lien and Bailment
Bankruptcy
Patents, Copyright, Trade Marks and Passing Off

**Labour Law**
The Contract of Employment
The Common Law Duties of an Employer
Wages
Maternity Rights
Discrimination
Termination of Contracts of Employment
redundancy
Social Security
Industrial Injuries – Employers' Liability
The Factories Act 1961
The Health and Safety at Work Act 1974
Institutions and Tribunals
Trade Unions